DEVOTIONAL LITERATURE IN SOUTH ASIA
CURRENT RESEARCH 1997-2000

DEVOTIONAL LITERATURE IN SOUTH ASIA
CURRENT RESEARCH 1997-2000

Proceedings of the Eighth International Conference on
Early Literature in New Indo-Aryan Languages,
Leuven, 23-26 August 2000

Edited by
WINAND M. CALLEWAERT
DIETER TAILLIEU

MANOHAR
2002

First published 2002

ISBN 81-7304-444-9

Published by
Ajay Kumar Jain for
Manohar Publishers & Distributors
4753/23 Ansari Road, Daryaganj
New Delhi 110002

Printed at
Rajkamal Electric Press
Delhi 110033

PROCEEDINGS OF THE BHAKTI CONFERENCES

Winand M. Callewaert (ed.)
Early Hindī Devotional Literature in Current Research. Proceedings of the International Middle Hindī Bhakti Conference (April 1979) Organized by the Katholieke Universiteit Leuven (*Orientalia Lovaniensia Analecta*, 8), Leuven: Departement Oriëntalistiek KUL, [1979] 1980.

Monika Thiel-Horstmann (ed.)
Bhakti in Current Research, 1979-1982. Proceedings of the Second International Conference on Early Devotional Literature in New Indo-Aryan Languages, St. Augustin, 19-21 March 1982 (*Collectanea Instituti Anthropos*, 30), Berlin: Dietrich Reimer Verlag, 1983.

M.K. Gautam & G.H. Schokker (eds.)
Bhakti in Current Research, 1982-85, Proceedings of the Third International Conference on Devotional Literature in the New Indo-Aryan Languages, Noordwijkerhout, 1985. Lucknow-Ghaziabad-Delhi: Indo-European Publishers. [Kern Institute Miscellanea. 10].

R. S. McGregor (ed.)
Devotional Literature in South Asia. Current Research, 1985-1988. Papers of the Fourth Conference on Devotional Literature in New Indo-Aryan Languages, held at Wolfson College, Cambridge, 1-4 September 1988 (*University of Cambridge Oriental Publications*, 46), Cambridge: Cambridge UP, 1992.

Alan W. Entwistle & Françoise Mallison (eds.)
Studies in South Asian Devotional Literature. Research Papers, 1988-1991, presented at the Fifth Conference on Devotional Literature in New Indo-Aryan Languages, held at Paris – Ecole Française d'Extrême Orient, 9-12 July 1991, New Delhi: Manohar & Paris: EFEO, 1994.

Alan W. Entwistle & Carol Salomon, with Heidi Pauwels and Michael Shapiro (eds.)

Studies in Early Modern Indo-Aryan Languages, Literature and Culture. Research Papers, 1992-1994, presented at the Sixth Conference on Devotional Literature in New Indo-Aryan Languages, held at Seattle, University of Washington, 7-9 July 1994, New Delhi: Manohar, 1999.

Mariola Offredi (ed.)

The Banyan Tree. Essays on Early Literature in New Indo-Aryan Languages (Proceedings of the Seventh International Conference on Early Literature in New Indo-Aryan Languages, Venice, 1997), 2 vols., New Delhi: Manohar & Venezia: Università degli Studi di Venezia. Dipartemento di Studi Eurasiatici, 2000.

NOTE ON TRANSCRIPTION

In view of the difficulties involved in using a single system of transcription for all the articles in the book, individual authors' decision as to the method of transcription has been respected. We have tried to maintain consistency within each paper.

CONTENTS

LIST OF ADDRESSES

AHLUWALIA, M.S.
Dept. of History, Himachal Pradesh University
Summer Hill, Shimla 171 005, India
tel. 91/ 177-230778, -230266 (res.) sp_singh@satyam.net.in

ASANI, Ali
Study of Religion, Harvard University
Barker Center Rm 305, 12 Quincy St.
Cambridge, Ma 02138, USA
fax 1/ 617-496-5798 aliasani@fas.harvard.edu

BANGHA, Imre
The Oriental Institute, University of Oxford
Pusey Lane,
Oxford, OX1 2LE, UK
and
Faculty of Humanities and Social Sciences,
De Montfort University, Clephan Building,
Leicester, LE1 9BH, UK
imre.bangha@oriental-institute.oxford.ac.uk

BHATTACHARYA, France
Langues 'O,
2, rue de Lille
75343 Paris, France
tel. 33/ 1 4926 -4200; fax -4299 france.bhattacharya@inalco.fr

BOSE, Mandakranta
Centre for India and South Asia Research
Institute of Asian Research, University of British Columbia
Vancouver B.C. V6T 1Z2, Canada
mbose@interchange.ubc.ca

BURTON, Adrian
Faculty of Asian Studies, ANU
Canberra 0200 ACT, Australia
tel. 61/ 2 6279 -8240; fax -8326 e960852@pophost.anu.edu.au

CALLEWAERT, Winand
Dept. Asian Studies
Blijde Inkomststraat 21
3000 Leuven, Belgium
tel. 32/ 16 -324945, -489843 (res.); fax -324932
winand.callewaert@arts.kuleuven.ac.be

CARACCHI, Pinuccia
Via Cap. Gatti 27/B
10075 Mathi (Torino), Italy
tel. 39/ 11 9269 063

de BRUIJN, Thomas
IIAS, P.O. Box 9515
2300 RA Leiden, The Netherlands
tel. 31/ 71 527 -2227; fax -4162 th.de.bruijn@let.leidenuniv.nl
IIAS@Rullet.LeidenUniv.nl

DEOL, Jeevan Singh
St John's College,
Cambridge CB2 1TP, UK jsd25@cam.ac.uk

DHILLON, Balwant Singh
res. T.F. 24, Guru Nanak Dev University,
143005 Amritsar, India
tel. 91/ 183 257624 balwantdhillon@yahoo.com

du PERRON, Lalita
Royal Asiatic Society
60 Queen's Gardens
London W2 3AF, UK lalitad@onetel.net.uk

FELDHAUS, Anne
Dept. of Religious Studies, Arizona State University,
AZ 85287-0402 Tempe, USA
tel. 1/ 602 965 4749, 1/ 480 –756 2909 (res.); fax. –965 5139
Anne.Feldhaus@asu.edu

FENECH, Louis E.
2126 Hickory Lane,
Cedar Falls, Iowa, 50613 USA
tel. 1/ 319 268 1473 Lou.Fenech@uni.edu

GOLD, Daniel
Department of Asian Studies, Cornell University
College of Arts & Sciences
388 Rockefeller Hall
Ithaca, NY 14853, USA
tel. 1/ 607 255 -5095; fax -1686 drg4@cornell.edu

HAWLEY, J.S.
Barnard College, Columbia University
3009 Broadway
New York, NY 10027-6598, USA
tel. 1/ 212 854 -2597; fax –7491 jsh3@columbia.edu

HESS, Linda
1520 Blake Street
Berkeley CA94703, USA lionda@lionda.pobox.stanford.edu
lionda@stanford.edu

HINES, Naseem A.
Dept. of Asian & Near Eastern Lgs. and Lits.
Washington University, Campus Box 1111
One Brookings Drive
St. Louis, MO 63130, USA nhines@artsci.wustl.edu

HORSTMANN, Monika
Abteilung Moderne Indologie, Südasien-Institut,
Im Neuenheimer Feld 330
D-69170 Heidelberg, Germany
tel. 49/ 6221 548 -926; fax. -841 an9@ix.urz.uni-heidelberg.de

JANI, B.
Vice-Chancellor North Gujarat University
University Road
384 265 Patan, India
tel. 91/ 2766 32851 ngu_vc@wilnetonline.net

JASH, P.
Visva-Bharati University
Prabapalli (North), Santiniketan 731 235, India
vcjha@vbharat.ernet.in

KAMPHORST, Janet
Research School CNWS, Leiden University
Nonnensteeg 1-3, P.O. Box 9515,
2300RA, Leiden, The Netherlands jankam65@hotmail.com

KIEHNLE, Catharina
Institut für Indologie und Zentralasienwissenschaften,
Universität Leipzig, Schillerstrasse 6,
04109 Leipzig, Germany
tel. 49/ 341 9737 -120; fax -148
tel./fax 49/ 34291 88545 (res.) 106674.372@compuserve.com

LORENZEN, David
El Colegio de México
Camino al Ajusco 20
México, D.F. 01000, Mexico lorenzen@colmex.mx

LUTGENDORF, Philip
Dept. of Asian Languages & Literatures, University of Iowa
314 Gilmore Hall,
Iowa City, 52242 IA, USA
tel. 1/ 319 -335 2156, -354 6234 (res.)
plutgend@blue.weeg.uiowa.edu

MALLISON, Françoise
Ecole Pratique des Hautes Etudes,
Section des sciences Historiques et Philologiques à la Sorbonne,
45-47 rue des Ecoles, 75005 Paris, France
tel. 33/ 1 4046 -3125; fax -3139
[Les Montèzes, Monoblet 30170, France
tel. 33/ 466 852606] fmallison@hotmail.com

MANN, Gurinder Singh
Department of Religious Studies
3051 HSSB, University of California
Santa Barbara, CA 93106, USA mann@humanitas.ucsb.edu

MANRING, Rebecca J.
Dept. of Religous Studies, Indiana University
Sycamore Hall 230
Bloomington, Indiana 47405-2601, USA
tel. 1/ 812 855 -6757; fax -4687 rmanring@indiana.edu

MARTIN, Nancy M.
Dept. of Religious Studies, Chapman University
1 University Drive,
Orange, CA 92866, USA
tel. 1/ 714 633-3556 (res.); fax -5504 nancy2martin@earthlink.net

McLEOD, Hew
Department of History, University of Otago
PO Box 56
Dunedin, New Zealand hew.mcleod@stonebow.otago.ac.nz

MIZOKAMI, Tomio
Osaka University of Foreign Studies
8-1-1, Aomatani-higashi, Mino-shi
Osaka 562, Japan mizokami@post01.osaka-gaidai.ac.jp

OFFREDI, Mariola
Department of Eurasiatic Studies, University of Venice
San Polo 2035
30125 Venezia, Italy
tel. 39/ 041 52 -87220, fax -41847,
tel./fax 39/ 035 -960175 (res.) offred21@helios.unive.it

PANDEY, Shyam Manohar
24 Midnoor Rd
Wimbledon, London SW 19, UK
tel. 44/ 181 946 3326
[Via Virniche 68, Casalnuovo
Napoli, Italy, tel. 39/ 181 522 4424]

PAUWELS, Heidi
Dept. of Asian Lgs and Lits
Box 353 521, University of Washington
Seattle WA 98195-3521, USA
fax 1/ 206 685-4268 hpauwels@u.washington.edu

PINCH, William R.
Department of History, Wesleyan University
Middletown, CT 06459, USA
wpinch@wpinch.mail.wesleyan.edu

RINEHART, Robin
Dept. of Religion, Lafayette College
Easton, PA 18042, USA
tel.1/ 610 330 -5179; fax -5585 rineharr@lafayette.edu

ROSENSTEIN, Lucy
Asian Studies, SOAS
Thornhaugh Street, Russell Square
London WC1H 0XG, UK
tel. 44/ 20 -7637 2388; fax -7436 3844 lr1@SOAS.ac.uk

ROUSSEVA-SOKOLOVA, Galina
Centre for Eastern Languages and Cultures, Sofia University
Naycho Tsanov Str. 79
1303 Sofia, Bulgaria sokol@techno-link.com

SAKATA, Teiji
Takushoku University
Bunkyo Campus, 4-14, kohinata 3-chome
Bunkyo-ku, Tokyo, 112-8585, Japan
tel. 81/ 3 3947 -2261; fax -5333
[124-34 Aoyagi, Sayama City, 350-1301, Japan]
tsakata@ner.takushoku-u.ac.jp

SALOMON, Carol
Dept. of Asian Lgs & Lits,
University of Washington, Box 353521
Seattle, WA 98195-3521, USA
fax 1/ 206 685 4268 rsalomon@u.washington.edu

SANFORD, Whitney A.
Philosophy and Religious Studies
423 Catt Hall, Iowa State University
Ames, IA 50011, USA
tel. 1/ 515 294 -6018; fax –0780 wsanford@pop-1.iastate.edu

SAWANT, Surekha R.
L.J.N.J, Mahila Mahavidyalaya,
Vile-Parle(e), Mumbai 400 057, India
fax: 91/ 22-8205565.
[Manish-Nagar, Bldg #28/D/315, Four-Bungalows
Andheri (w), Mumbai 400 053, India] surekha_agw@usa.net

SHAPIRO, Michael
Dept. of Asian Languages and Literature
University of Washington, Box 353521
Seattle, WA 98195-3521, USA
tel. 1/ 206 –543 4958; fax –685 4268 hindimcs@u.washington.edu

SHARMA, Swapna
Dept. Asian Studies, KULeuven
Blijde Inkomststraat 21
3000 Leuven, Belgium
tel. 32/ 16 324942 swapna.sharma@arts.kuleuven.ac.be

SHELKE, Christopher
Pontificia Università Gregoriana
Piazza della Pilotta, 4
00187 Rome, Italy
tel. 39/ 6 670 15244 shelke@unigre.urbe.it

SHIMA, Iwao
Faculty of Letters, Kanazawa University
Kakuma-cho, Kanazawa
920-1192 Japan
tel. 81/ 76 -264 5312; fax -234 4062 sima@kenroku.kanazawa-u.ac.jp

SINGH, Bahadur
Institut für Kultur und Geschichte Indiens und Tibets
Neue Rabenstr. 3
20354 Hamburg, Germany
tel. 49/ 42838 –3385; fax -6267
[Prahlsdorfer Weg 3B, 21465 Reinbek, Germany] bsingh@nikocity.de

SINGH, Pashaura
Department of Asian Languages and Cultures
3070 Frieze Building, University of Michigan
Ann Arbor, MI 48109-1285, USA
tel. 1/ 734 -763 7889; fax -647 0157 psingh@umich.edu
psingh@breakout.gpcc.itd.umich.edu

SMITH, William L.
Department of Indology, Stockholm University
S – 106 91 Stockholm, Sweden
tel. 46/ 8 -55464; fax -163619 William.Smith@orient.su.se

STASIK, Danuta
Instytut Orientalistyczny UW
ul. Krak. Przedmiescie 26/28
00-927 Warszawa, Poland STASIKD@PLEARN.EDU.PL

STEWART, Tony K.
Dept. of Philosophy and Religion
Box 8103, North Carolina State University
Raleigh, NC 27695-8101, USA
tel. 1/ 919 -515 6335; fax –513 4351 tony_stewart@ncsu.edu

THIELEMANN, Selina
Vraja Kalā evaṃ Saṃskṛti Samsthāna
288 121 Vrindaban, India

VASISHTA, Om Parkash
School of Punjabi Studies, Panjab University,
H.N. 289 Sector 15-A
160 014 Chandigarh, India
tel. 91/ 172 -541 980; -771 589 (res.) vasishta@chandigarhx.com

WULFF, Donna M.
Steiger House, Brown University,
59 George Street/Box 1927
Providence, Rhode Island 02912, USA
tel. 1/ 401 863 -3104; fax -3109

YAJNIK, Hasu
3, Sheetal Plaza Row House, Nr. Lad Soc.
Vastrapur, Amdabad 380 054, India
tel. 91/ 79 675 3624 purvayan@yahoo.com

ZELLIOT, Eleanor
Carleton College, Dept. of History
One North College Street
Northfield, Minnesota 55057, USA
[30240 Cannon River Blvd.
Randolph, MN 55065-7502, USA] ezelliot@carleton.edu

PREFACE

The First International Conference on Early Literature in New Indo-Aryan Languages was organized in Leuven in 1979 and "was attended by fourteen scholars (from all over Europe, one from the USA and one from Canada), who gave a short survey of the research done during the last five years, a description of their current research and a communication about plans for the future. The meeting became a very lively and informal exchange and it was unanimously suggested that we should meet again" (Proceedings, 1980, Preface).

We did meet again — in Bonn, Leiden, Cambridge, Paris, Seattle and Venice — and the Eighth "Bhakti Conference" was held in Leuven in August 2000.

Much has changed in 20 years. The Proceedings then were printed by lead letter setting and sold for Rs. 60; now we send CD- roms to the printer. Fourteen participants came to Leuven; at the Seattle Conference there were more then one hundred. And the research on Bhakti has gained immensely in both quantity and quality. The list of publications in part 2 of these Proceedings have 1162 entries.

Forty scholars came to Leuven, hailing from fourteen different countries — from Japan to the west coast of the United States (not via the Pacific!) — each one bringing his or her expertise and experience. Nearly all the Reports are published here. In addition, another twenty scholars sent a Report or a List of Publications. The result is a fascinating overview of the very wide field that Bhakti studies have become.

The hosting of the "Leuven 2000 Bhakti Conference" would not have been possible without the assistance of many persons and organizations. Financial support was given by the Flemish Research Foundation (FWO), the KULeuven 575 Anniversary Foundation, the Faculty of Arts, and the Department of Asian Studies. For the practical assistance that made the stay of the participants so pleasant in Leuven, I thank Gracienne Lauwers, Frans Goossens, Anand Singh and our son Lieven Callewaert.

I should like to conclude with the words of the Vice-Rector, Prof. Marc Vervenne, at the opening of the Conference:

'The pen is mightier than the sword, and it is my earnest desire that this Academic Session too may contribute to a better global understanding, and to a better world'.

WINAND M. CALLEWAERT

Photograph of the participants in Leuven, courtesy Frans Goossens.

The Early Sikh Scriptural Tradition

M.S. AHLUWALIA

In recent years some scholars interested in Sikh studies, have examined the different manuscripts notably the *Gurū Har Sahāi Pothī*, the *Goindwāl Pothī*-s and manuscript no. 1245 (in the Guru Nanak Dev University, Amritsar) in order to find out whether the holy *Gurū Granth Sāhib* was based on documents prepared during the pontificate of Gurū Amar Dās (the third Gurū) or, whether these documents were scribed after Gurū Arjan Dev (the fifth Gurū) had codified the *Bāṇī*-compositions of the earlier Gurūs and Bhagats together with his own hymns in A.D. 1604. The most recent study of these manuscripts has been made by Dr. Balwant Singh Dhillon, published in his book entitled: *Early Sikh Scriptural Tradition: Myth and Reality*. Singh Brothers, Bazar Mai Sewan, Amritsar, December, 1999. [See also below, Dhillon]. In this book the author has painstakingly analysed the early Sikh scriptural sources from a textual point of view, so that their role in the formation of the Sikh canon could be understood in its proper perspective.

The first chapter of the book, besides giving attention to the musical or oral tradition of *Gurbāṇī*, traces the scribal tradition that had developed in the hands of Gurū Nānak and his immediate successors. The second chapter deals with the Gurū Har Sahāi Pothī, said to be the core of the Sikh scriptural corpus. However, the Pothī is no more available for examination and Dr. Dhillon has made an attempt to find out its internal as well as external features on the basis of earlier studies of it. The third chapter investigates the origin, history and contents of the extant *Goindwāl Pothī*-s. It explores their genuineness and evaluates their role in the formation of the Sikh scripture. The fourth chapter studies in detail the various features of the recently found manuscript no. 1245 and addresses the question whether it qualifies to be an earlier draft of the *Ādi Granth*. In the last chapter Dr. Dhillon has discussed the various rules which may be applied to evaluate a manuscript of *Gurbāṇī* and he gives the parameters to ascertain the authenticity of a document and its possible connection with the Sikh scriptural tradition. The study helps to understand the scenario in which various scribes worked to produce the Pothī-s of *Gurbāṇī* for different uses and purposes.

There is no doubt that while compiling the *Ādi Granth*, Gurū Arjan Dev had some other sources of the *Bāṇī* at hand, besides the Pothī he had inherited from the fourth Gurū. Unfortunately none of the early sources or original writings of the early Sikh Gurūs, has survived to come down to us. The oldest manuscripts of the *Bāṇī* in our possession are copies which in turn were copied from yet other copies and so on. The scholars interested in textual studies have thus found it difficult to undertake textual criticism.

The available sources are either silent or reveal very little about the criteria of selection adopted in respect of sacred writings which were included in or excluded from the Sikh scripture. This prompted certain scholars (notably W. H. McLeod) to remark that the final version established by Gurū Arjan Dev in 1604 continued to be tampered with under the influence of socio-religious developments taking place in the history of the Sikh community.

Since the 1970s western scholars have shown a renewed interest in the textual studies of the Sikh scripture so that a sure and certain text of the *Ādi Granth* could be established. Resultantly, two Ph.D. dissertations — one at Toronto University and the other at Columbia University — were completed under the guidance of western scholars of North American universities. The first Study was confined to reconstructing the history of the text of the *Ādi Granth* whereas the second study tries to clarify the process of scriptural evolution.

The inquiries of both scholars about old manuscripts and versions (such as Gurū Har Sahāi Pothī, the *Goindwāl Pothī*-s and manuscript no. 1245) which are said to antedate AD 1604, resulted in the hypothesis that there may have been a source or a document available to Gurū Arjan Dev that may have provided a basis for the *Ādi Granth*. Both the scholars claim that the above manuscripts represented the pre-canonical position of the Sikh scripture. Apart from these two scholars who worked under the guidance of western scholars, in India Prof. Piar Singh also used the above manuscripts and produced a controversial book in 1992. With some minor differences here and there, all the three above-mentioned scholars conclude that:

1. The history of the text of the *Ādi Granth* as it stands today is quite obscure.

2. The hymns of the Sikh Gurūs, before taking the scribal form, have been in circulation through oral or musical tradition.
3. The text of the *Ādi Granth*, that we have in its present form lacks in originality.
4. The *Bāṇī* of Gurū Nānak Dev and his immediate successors have been revised in the final version.
5. Gurū Arjan Dev had frequently modified his own hymns.
6. The Mūl Mantra found in its present form has also undergone a series of changes.
7. A considerable number of genuine hymns of the Sikh Gurūs have been left out in the *Ādi Granth*.
8. Several writings of the Bhagats have been in and out of the Sikh scriptures due to secular motives and so on.

Dr. Dhillon who has reflected upon the above issues genuinely feels that scholars of Sikh studies have either very little information or they could not have access to the manuscripts in question. The issues therefore, led Dr. Dhillon to examine the available manuscripts thoroughly and rigorously in his book under review. The textual analysis of the *Ādi Granth* faces a problem that neither an authentic version of its text coming from the earlier Gurūs is available nor do we have irrefutable historical sources. In their attempts to establish the actual text of *Gurū Granth Sāhib*, the scholars have identified three sources, namely the Gurū Har Sahāi Pothī, the two extant *Goindwāl Pothī*-s, and manuscript no. 1245.

The Gurū Har Sahāi Pothī is said to be the original Pothī of *Gurbāṇī* compiled by Gurū Nānak. The Pothī was in the possession of the Sodhī family of Gurū Har Sahāi, a village near Ferozepur in Punjab. It is said Gurū Arjan inherited it through his predecessors and subsequently it remained in the possession of Prithī Chand and his descendants. Recently it has been argued that even though *Gurū Har Sahāi Pothī* was not the original manuscript attributed to Gurū Nānak, it may have been a copy of the manuscript that represented the core of the Sikh scriptural corpus.

However, on the basis of evidence at hand the author of the book under review concludes that neither the text of the Pothī belonged to the main tradition nor it was remotely concerned with the sources of *Ādi Granth*. Contrary to the claim of the family, the

Pothī's movement from Gurū Arjan Dev to Prithī Chand or his son Miharbān, is highly debatable. Internal evidence suggests that it had its origin in the post-*Ādi Granth* period and that it had originated at the rival camp to Gurū Arjan Dev. Its production in no way can be attributed to Gurū Nānak and his early successors. Instead of representing the main Sikh tradition it is closely related to the schism caused by the rivals of the Sikh Gurūs, especially the Mīnā-s. To call it a document of pre-scriptural Sikh tradition originating from the time of Gurū Nānak seems to be unwarranted and uncalled for.

The *Goindwāl Pothī*-s were claimed to be the Pothī-s that were compiled by Gurū Amar Dās which were once with his elder son Mohan. These Pothī-s are in the possession of two Bhallā families who claim them as inherited ones from the days of Bābā Mohan through successive generations. The common feature of these Pothī-s was that a large number of Sikhs had traditionally believed in their veracity and paid obeisance to them whenever their custodians displayed them ceremoniously. However, their custodians had always avoided their academic and scientific study. It has always been claimed that these Pothī-s have been the chief sources for the compilation of the *Ādi Granth* by Gurū Arjan Dev.

Some scholars consider them important documents, which help us to understand the formation of early Sikh canon. On the other hand there are a few critics who believe that the *Goindwāl Pothī*-s do not belong to the main Sikh scriptural tradition and have been of no use for Gurū Arjan Dev in codifying the *Ādi Granth.* Even the much-publicised story of Gurū Arjan's visit to Bābā Mohan at Goindwāl to procure them, has been proved to be an apocryphal and later concoction. The same scholars feel that the extant Pothī-s had been prepared by Gurū Amar Dās to serve the purpose of Sikh scripture. If it was so, then the Japujī, the most significant *Bāṇī* of the Sikhs, should have been recorded on the initial folios. Even the *Bāṇī* of Gurū Amar Dās, has not been preserved in its totality. Omissions are so important that they do not help us to believe that Gurū Amar Dās had got them prepared to serve the Sikh scripture.

The sequence of *rāga*-s, their distinct modes and tunes are radically different than that of the *Ādi Granth* tradition. Therefore, the text of the *Goindwāl Pothī*-s, instead of coming down from the scribal tradition, belongs to a musicological tradition. The inclusion of *Kachī-bāṇī* of the Pothī-s has not found favour with Gurū Arjan Dev to preserve them in the *Ādi Granth.* The fact of the existence of *Kachī-Bāṇī* in the *Goindwāl Pothī*-s severely undermines the extant Pothī's claim to be the original product belonging to Gurū Amar Dās. The textual variants and some other features of the *Goindwāl Pothī*-s certainly point out their origin to a schismatic trend in Sikhism and bear close resemblance to the sectarian literature produced by Miharbān and his descendants. These Pothī-s were scribed under the strong influence of the rivals of Gurū Rām Dās, especially the Bhallā-s.

Why do the two traditions have so much in common? Which tradition has borrowed from the other or which one is thriving on the other is an important issue that requires further investigations. Instead of representing the pre-scriptural tradition of the main Sikh stream, the *Goindwāl Pothī*-s represent the sectarian developments in Sikhism during the period under review.

The recently surfaced manuscript no. 1245 has generated a lot of controversy in the field of Sikh studies. While a scholar remarks it be an anterior and unique manuscript, another finds it to be an early draft on which Gurū Arjan seems to have worked to finally produce the text of the *Ādi Granth*. It has also been concluded in the above mentioned studies that the Sikh Gurūs had often manipulated and revised their own as well as their predecessor's *Bāṇī* including the Mūl Mantra.

Amazingly the features of the manuscript no. 1245, such as various omissions, incomplete text, irregularities between the index and text, scribal and musical variants, violation of structural pattern, confusion about authorship, inclusion of *Kachī-Bāṇī* etc., certainly jeopardise its credentials as a genuine product of the main stream. Internal evidence too proves that its scribe has depended heavily on another source to prepare it. This voluminous and neatly written document, without any cutting and erasures, seems to be impossible unless its scribe had the patronage of a group or an institution which, however, still remains to be identified.

The studies undertaken by scholars in India and abroad, intentionally or unintentionally, sought to undermine the preaching of the Sikh Gurūs enshrined in the *Ādi Granth* which otherwise is *dhur-kī-bāṇī* or Divine Word revealed to the followers of the Sikh faith. For the reaction by Sikh scholars the lead was taken by the Chandigarh based Institute of Sikh Studies; these scholars forcefully challenged these unfortunate conclusions. The two scholars Dr. Pashaura Singh and Dr. Piar Singh were charged with blasphemy and had to apologise before the Akāl Takht and undergo traditional cleansing penance. It may be noted here that the highest religious authority of the Sikh Panth was kind, charitable and forgiving as per the Sikh tradition. The Christian Church in the Middle Ages had gone to the extent of burning people on the charges of blasphemy. Again, had these offending scholars been Muslims, they would have now been facing terminal *fatwas* like Sulman Rushdie.

The book under review exhaustively traces the ways, means and traditions for the transmission of the *Bāṇī* that were prevalent in the Panth as well as rival traditions that had come up to compete with the Sikh Gurūs. The role of the Udāsī-s, the Bhallā-s, the Mīnā-s and the Handālīā-s, that had got prepared their own Pothī-s simply to usurp the guru-ship of the Sikhs and to add a *Bāṇī* faked by them to the Sikh scripture, has been dealt with in detail by Dr. Dhillon. It has been successfully established by the author that all the Pothī-s of the *Gurbāṇī* produced in the pre-*Ādi Granth* period could not be authentic mainstream Sikh texts, as many features of the rival traditions could be seen in some of them. This type of treatment is totally missing in the earlier studies on the *Ādi Granth*.

Dr. Dhillon has rightly relied upon the internal evidence to find out the truth about the three controversial sources in question. He has systematically demolished the aura of authenticity woven around the so called earlier sources of the *Ādi Granth* which he rightly claims as representing different traditions/lineage and were not of the antiquity claimed and thus could never have been the source for the compilation of the *Ādi Granth*. The author has proved his point by going through the whole rigmarole of applying the Biblical or western methods of textual criticism by analysing all possible aspects of the physiognomy, orthography, poetic genres, dating, scribing habits, textual as well as musicological variants and what not of the relevant texts lest his methods be found lacking by the western scholars, or he be branded as partisan and sectarian. He has been overconscious of the Biblical canons of critical studies such as employed by the scholar at Toronto, Canada. He has gone for overkill, but he has amply achieved his aim.

It is well known that it was only through the machinations of the Mīnā-s that Gurū Arjan Dev had suffered martyrdom. The collusion of the Mīnā-s led by Prithī Chand and his son Miharbān with the Mughal rulers had eventually forced the succeeding Sikh

Gurūs to withdraw to the Shiwalik foothills. For the next almost a century the Mīnā-s ruled the roost, enjoying the Gurū status in central Punjab. They did not even permit the ninth Gurū, Tegh Bahādur to pay obeisance at Harimandir soon after his investiture. It should be remembered that after preparing a compilation, Miharbān had made copies to distribute and install them in various establishments. In these circumstances most of the religious establishments in Punjab would enshrine the Mīnā version of the Sikh scripture and production of such Pothī-s would abound. The common features of the manuscript No. 1245 too suggest that most probably this manuscript had originated in the above environment and sequence.

The facts prove that it is not only an incorrect, but also incomplete document. It can not be regarded as an earlier draft on the basis of orthography too, because besides the dot, we also find the usage of half *kannā* in it. Examples of text filled in later on in a different hand are clearly visible. To associate it with Bhāī Gurdās and Bhāī Buddha, is illogical because no internal or external evidence validates it. Its scribe has brought various modifications into the text, probably to suit musical requirements. The evidence at hand confirms that its scribe instead of depending on a single document has taken into account a number of sources. Whether it was the result of cross-fertilisation between different recessions? Or was it a cautious blend of various text families? These pertinent issues have yet to be explored satisfactorily.

The scribe of manuscript no. 1245 on the one hand has tried to put together all the *Kachī-Bāṇī* writings attributed to the Sikh gurus and on the other he has omitted from record the compositions that were in his full knowledge. It can be safely assumed that the manuscript in question was a deliberate act of editing on the part of its scribe or the patrons, who were weary of some writings that had been made part of the *Ādi Granth.* Thus even after the establishment of canon in AD 1604, some sections within the Panth continued to compile collections of the *Bāṇī* that were not strictly canonical in nature. In which part of the Sikh world and among whom this type of collections were popular, are the issues which need further research. The problem of authenticity of the basis of a scripture is not unique with the *Ādi Granth.* The various religious traditions have faced such a problem. Fortunately the Sikh scripture has one redeeming factor: its history is not more than 400 years old. The age of some of the ancient holy books can scarcely be pinpointed. The scholars, as in the case of the Bible face the difficulty of naming the original versus translated sources.

The *Ādi Granth* as compiled and edited by Gurū Arjan Dev is an organised scripture, precisely dated. Its order of contents leave no room for doubt or interpolation. The only problem that arises with the holy Granth relates to the basic documents that have gone into the compilation of the scripture. During the pontificate of the first three Gurūs, the rival camps had started composing songs on the lines of *Gurbāṇī*, most often making use of the pen-name 'Nānak'. These compositions were designated *Kachī-bāṇī* in contrast with the *Sachī-bāṇī* of the Gurūs. Gurū Arjan Dev, therefore, decided to codify the Sikh scripture once and for all into a volume which is today known as the *Ādi Granth*.

Dr. Dhillon carefully examined all the three documents and rightly concludes that a number of textual variants have crept into their text. The variety of textual variants present in them prove that neither of them is a direct copy of the other, nor have they been a basis of the *Ādi Granth*. It can be safely stated that neither of the above mentioned three sources have descended one from the other. They in fact represent three different recensions. These manuscripts are the products of a group or people who were interested in preserving and propagating a particular recension of the *Bāṇī* other than the one we have in the form of *Ādi Granth*. It is hoped that Dr. Balwant Singh Dhillon's attempt at sifting reality from myth and laying at rest some of the contentious issues relating to early Sikh scriptural tradition, will bear fruit. The book written by Dr. Dhillon would not only be of interest to the common reader, but to the scholars also who may like to go ahead and further clear the cobwebs.

DISCUSSION

Callewaert:

The persons I know who had access to the *Mohan Pothī*-s are Prof. Pritam Singh, Patiala [see below, Dhillon] and Gurinder Singh Mann, Santa Barbara, California. How do you relate Pritam Singh's findings with regard to the Mohan Pothī to Dhillon's work?

Ahluwalia:
Dhillon has tried to compare and contrast each and every word in the Bāṇī.

Callewaert:
Do you see an agreement between Pritam Singh's work and the results of Dhillon's research? Or is there a difference?

Ahluwalia:
I have focused mainly on Dhillon's work which set straight some of the controversies regarding the *Ādi-Granth*.

Hawley:
I would like to refer to your words "undermining intentionally or un-intentionally" [see above, p. 5] which I want to flag as something I regret, because I do not believe it is true on the part of either Pashaura Singh or Gurinder Singh Mann. I should just like to say that there are two positions in regard to the set of issues that you have raised, and they are significantly different. Just to put them together, in a single basket, may be a little misleading. There is no time here to talk about the actual textual evidence, so I do not want to raise that issue.

Ahluwalia:
We are sure that there were certain Pothī-s, or religious books of the Sikhs which were written right from the time of Gurū Nānak up to the time of the final compilation in 1604, by the fifth Gurū, Gurū Arjan Dev. Unfortunately, we do not have access to either of these pre-canonical manuscripts. The manuscripts we have — discussed in this Report — are the later editions, produced by people from the rival camp. They wanted to be patronised. We have different establishments, different *derā*-s, different *gurdwārā*-s, where they kept their own Pothī-s, their own version, so that these should be worshipped and so that their business may flourish. This is the production of the rival camp and unfortunately we do not have access to any of the early manuscripts.

Jash:
I would like to know what are the main issues in your area of research at this moment which require further investigation.

Ahluwalia:
I should like to put several issues before all the scholars present here. 1. What are the documents that have been used for the compilation of the *Ādi-Granth*? 2. Do these documents belong to the pre- or the post-canonical period? 3. If these documents have

been prepared by the rival camp, who borrowed from whom and which one is thriving on the other?

Ānandghan, Broughton and Tulsīdās: Report on Three Years' Research

IMRE BANGHA

In the past three years I have mainly worked on the life and works of a Brajbhāṣā poet from the 18th century, Ānandghan (who is today erroneously known as Ghanānand). He wrote both simple Bhakti poetry — songs (*pad*-s) as well as longer poems (*nibandha kāvya*-s) based on couplets (*dohā*-s and *caupāī*-s) — and ornate quatrains (*kabitta*-s) that reflect the style of the *rītikāl*, the 'period of mannerism'. His works were published in a good edition by Vishvanath Prasad Mishra in 1952.

Unparalleled language, deep psychological insight and a touch of individuality give Ānandghan's *kabitta*-s such intensity that today they are considered to be among the best Hindi literary products of the 18th century. Their peculiarity is that the beloved, who is usually addressed as Sujān, can either be interpreted to be the divinity (usually Krishna), or a real woman (she was probably a Muslim dancer). In this approach Ānandghan seems to have been influenced by Persian and Urdu poetry, although many of his quatrains are set into a Krishna-Bhakti context.

It may not come as a surprise that the first point to be discussed was the poet's name. Almost all scholars and writers of the 20th century refer to him as Ghanānand or Ghan Ānand. It was convenient to distinguish him in this way from the other — Gauḍīya Vaishnava, Jaina, Sikh etc. (!) — Ānandghan-s of Hindi literature. It is also true that the poet included his name as Ghana ānãda [घन आनँद] into the dactylic or anapaestic rhythm of his *savaiyā*-s. However, all colophons of the several dozen manuscripts available today give the name as Ānandghan.

It is very difficult to put some of the most outstanding Hindi poets into a historical context as for instance is the case, in spite of many efforts, with Kabīr, Mīrā Bāī and even Sūrdās. Regarding Ānandghan, however, we are more fortunate. In the *Harikalā Belī* by the poet 'Uncle Hita' Vṛndāvandās expresses his grief over the killing of ascetics in Braj, including Ānandghan, in *vikram samvat* 1813. On the basis of Vṛndāvandās' poem it can be said that

Ānandghan died as a Vaishnava ascetic on or around the 6th of March 1757 in or around Vrindavan in the massacre of Braj at the hands of Ahmadshah Abdali's soldiers.

Although it is not possible to establish many independent events from the poet's life there is some material to investigate how his contemporaries received his poetry. The three earliest dated manuscripts — from AD 1727, 1729 and 1743 — show that Ānandghan's twofold approach to Sujān was clearly understood, since the scribes changed the word either to *su pyārī* 'that beloved woman' or the like, putting the poem into a secular context, or to *ju syām* '(that) Krishna' etc., indicating a Krishna-Bhakti context. However, orthodox Vaishnavas rejected this double approach, and Ānandghan acquired such a bad reputation that he had to give up the *kabitta* forms, and he wrote simple Bhakti poetry for the rest of his life. In spite of the fact that his quatrains were popular at royal courts his disrepute was so strong that even the respected courtier Brajnāth got into trouble by expounding Ānandghan's quatrains and made bitter remarks on those who tried to simplify them. This infamy was the result of his alleged contact with Muslims, and of considering his poetry to be less Vaishnava than it seems to be at first sight.

A close examination of the relationship between the two most popular collections of Ānandghan's quatrains, the *Sujānhit* and the *Ghanānand-kabitt* shows that the latter is based on the former. The *Sujānhit* reflects Ānandghan's development from mundane love to Krishna-Bhakti. Brajnāth, the compiler of the *Ghanānand-kabitta*, considered Ānandghan's poetry to be less based on Krishna-Bhakti than the *Sujānhit* suggests. By discarding many Bhakti poems from the *Sujānhit* he gathered a collection that puts more emphasis on the complexity of the object of love.

I also argued that Brajnāth is identical with Brajnāth Bhaṭṭ, a poet of Sanskrit and Braj, and a courtier of Sawai Jaisingh. He probably compiled the *Ghanānand-kabitt* in Rupnagar around 1748; as two of the manuscripts that tend to give substitutes for the word Sujān were written there, and Brajnāth stayed in Rupnagar that year as the dating of one of his works indicates.

Ānandghan was most successful in his quatrains, *kabitta*-s. *Kabitta*-s were popular in Braj literature since the time of Tulsīdās. According to traditional descriptions, Hindi verse forms either follow a prescribed sequence of poetic units (morae), or simply count them, or count the syllables irrespective of their length. An examination of the role of the accent in *kabitta*-s demonstrates that poets were aware of this role and the poet Ratnākar wrote about it, although he did not use the word 'accent'. An awareness of this aspect of the *kabitta*-s is indispensable in critical editions that aim to present a text with the smallest number of corruptions. (Unfortunately the published form of my article on this problem does not contain my footnotes.)

The text editions I am working on at the moment already take the role of the accent into consideration. One of them is a new edition of Thomas Duer Broughton's *Selections from the Popular Poetry of the Hindoos* of 1814, which is the first printed anthology of Brajbhāṣā poets. Its author was a British army officer, who published and translated poems that his soldiers knew by heart. On the basis of this anthology, therefore, one can get a glimpse of the most widely memorised and recited Braj verses in the early 19th century. Surprisingly enough these verses were not folk poems, but products of court poetry in the most refined period of Hindi literature, the *rītikāl.* Thus this anthology shows that the poetry enjoyed in princely courts had a wider audience then some of the modern critics would imagine. The importance of Broughton's book is not restricted to the Hindi literature. Though his translations were far from being hailed as good poetry even in his own time, his anthology serves as a remarkable source of popular interest in Oriental literature in the era of the romantics. Apart from Broughton's text, the new edition contains a reconstructed Hindi version of the poems with their new English translation.

Another text edition I have started work on is Tulsī's *Kavitāvalī*, a collection of 325 Braj quatrains. Its first half depicts scenes in the Rāma-story, whilst the second half is a collection of devotional poems to the supreme god, Rām, and to other gods and goddesses. The delicacy of certain scenes, and the personal touch, make this collection an outstanding work of Hindi literature, which has already been translated into English twice. However, the text available in print is based on an edition from the 1850s. No study of its manuscripts has been made since. For the critical edition I have already collected several copies of manuscripts (dated from between AD 1692 and 1894). The relatively small number of textual variants, and the same order of quatrains in each manuscript, suggest that, unlike in the case of the songs of Mīrā Bāī, Sūrdās or Kabīr, the manuscripts go back to one or more written sources, and as there was not a period of oral transmission prior to writing down these texts, we can come very close to what the poet originally wrote.

I also started to collect the manuscripts for a critical edition of the quatrains of the so-called '*rītimukta*' Ṭhakur, a court poet from the turn of the 18th and 19th century, who blended poetic refinement with the use of idioms taken from everyday language.

DISCUSSION

Pauwels:
I wonder whether those differences in variants have to do with the genre or the fact that the *kabitta* does not allow in itself as much variation in its recitation as a *pada* would do. In a *pada* all the lines can be switched and moved around easily, or be left out. Do you have any thoughts on that?

Bangha:
It is true that *kabitta*-s and *savaiyā*-s do not allow so much variation, although sometimes we find entire lines changed, and then we have to look into the reasons for that change. Usually the variations are only of a few words. *Kabitta*-s and *savaiyā*-s can have either a Bhakti or a mundane content.

Horstmann:
Sundardās is replete with *savaiyā*-s of the richest kind, and with a deep theological content.

Bangha:
I pointed out that *kabitta*-s and *savaiyā*-s can be both mundane and transcendental. I did not come across any *pad*-s that are mundane.

Horstmann:
What about Thakur, from where was he?

Bangha:
He was from Bundelkhand, attached to the Jaitpur court.

Report on My Published Writings on the Bhakti Literature in Medieval Gujarati

H.C. BHAYANI

1. Devotional lyrics in oral tradition

Three collections of Gujarati devotional poems that were preserved in the oral tradition and were sung two generations back, but now being forgotten fast even in rural areas were published: *Hari Veṇa Vāya Che Re Ho Vaṁna-māṃ* (30 lyrics; 1988); *Gokul māṃ Ṭahukyā mor* (30 lyrics; 1989); *Jharmar Meh Jhabūke Vīj* (25 lyrics; 1991). They represent various song-types: *Dhoḷ* (customarily sung by the Vaishnava women of advanced age sitting every night in a small group in the courtyard of their small resedential tenements to perform *santsaṁg*); *Rās* (sung with dance movement on festive and religious occasions); *Garbā* (sung with dance movement during the nine days of Śakti worship); *Bhajan* (customarily sung by *santa bhakta-s*). The distinctions are in some cases blurred because they rest much more on characteristic mode and occasion of singing rather than on subject-matter.

These lyrics derive their subject matter (1) from the Puranic tradition relating to Krishna's *bāla-carita*, (2) from the *Rāmacarita* or they pertain to *bhakti* or *vairāgya*. The chief aim was to record the specific musical mode (*deśī*) in which these songs have been sung traditionally. Specimen musical notation has been provided for each song by Hasu Yajnik and Pravinsimh Jadeja.

2. Medieval Gujarati poems on Krishna's life edited from manuscripts for the first time

1. *Bhāgavatadaśamaskandha* by Premānanda (18th century, in collaboration with U.J. Joshi), 1966, 1972.
2. *Thāl* attributed to Narasiṃha Mahetā, in *Kṛṣṇa-kāvya*, 1986.
3. *Rāsalīlā* (1988) contains *Kṛṣṇakrīḍita* by Rāula Kāhna; *Harivilās*, anonymous; *Rāghava-rāsa* and *Hari-cuākharā* by Vāsaṇadāsa (poems written in the 15th-16th centuries).

4. *Paṁḍavalā* by Rāghavajī and Vīracaṁda. This is a verse rendering of the Mahābhārata story. Vīracaṁda's part deals with the *Kṛṣṇa-viṣṭi* occurring in the Udyoga-parvan.
5. *Kṛṣṇa-bālacarita* (1992) contains *Kṛṣṇa-bālacarita* by Kīku Vasahi, *Kṛṣṇa-caritra* from the unpublished Jain *Pāṁḍava-caritra* in prose, datable to the 15th-16th centuries. Some noteworthy poems on Kṛṣṇa-Bhakti belonging to this period are still unpublished and require to be edited.

3. *Kṛṣṇa-bhakti* of medieval Gujarat in historical perspective

1. The following articles published earlier have been republished in the collection *Kṛṣṇa-kāvya* (1986). The titles are given here in English translation: *Kṛṣṇa* in the *Mahābhārata*; *Kṛṣṇa* in the Buddhist *Jātaka-kathā* (*Jātaka* 454; *Ghṛta-jātaka*); *Kṛṣṇa*'s boyhood in Prākṛta and Apabhraṁsa poems; On earlier literary sources of Kṛṣṇa-Bhakti of Gujarat prior to the 16th century; Precedents of several themes recurring in the poems of the 16th century poet Narasiṃha Mahetā on *Kṛṣṇa*'s boyhood.

2. In the introduction to *Rāsalīlā* (1988) is given a brief reference list of Sanskrit, Prākṛta and Apabhraṁsa and Old-Gujarati poems relating to *Kṛṣṇa-caritra.* The list is chronological.

A systematic, detailed account of Bhakti in medieval Gujarat (from the 15th to the 19th century, based on literary sources) remains a desideratum.

In the Company of Bengali Mediaeval Literature

FRANCE BHATTACHARYA

At the end of twenty-two years spent in India teaching French in various universities, I felt that I had acquired sufficient knowledge of Bengali language and literature to write a *doctorat de troisième cycle* on the Bengali *rūpakathā* or fairy tales. That was in the seventies, when the intellectual life in France was dominated by the champions of the Structuralist School, both in anthropology and in literary studies. I attempted to analyse the stories compiled by Dakshina Ranjan Mazumdar in his famous book *Thākurmār Jhuli*, with the help of a methodology borrowed from Vladimir Propp, Levi Strauss, Greimas and Barthes. I wrote the dissertation under the supervision of Madeleine Biardeau, one of our foremost scholars of Sanskrit who has specialised in the study of the epics. As is obvious from my choice of methodology, what interested me was the narrative process and what it revealed of the inner content of the stories.

Later on, while engaged in the teaching of Bengali language, literature and culture at the Institut national des langues et civilisations orientales in Paris, I undertook a comparative study of the *Manasā* and the *Caṇḍī maṅgal*-s: two very long narrative poems in honour of these deities, with a *doctorat d'état* as my objective. The *maṅgal kāvya*, as a literary genre, is a storehouse of information about Bengali religion, society, customs and way of life in the mediaeval period. Each version of the main *maṅgal*-s constitutes a kind of encyclopaedia of Bengali life that makes its study very rewarding. We also find many references to epic and Puranic myths, that are of pan-Indian persuasion, concerning for instance the birth of the goddesses or the cosmogony, as well as original stories that, apart from Bengal, can only be found, if at all, in neighbouring regions. This intermingling of what some call the "Great tradition" with the local Bengali imagination for creating myths is a peculiar charm of these compositions.

This time, I did not intend to keep structuralism as my single methodological option, although the usefulness of some of its concepts is obvious to me even to this day. At first, I intended to study only the *Caṇḍī maṅgal*, being attracted by the fact that one of its authors, Mukundarām Cakravartī, called also Kavi Kaṅkan, was a major mediaeval poet in Bengali. Once again, in the beginning, it was the narrative process that interested me, along with the structure of the theogony as revealed in the story. While analysing the different episodes and main characters, human as well as divine, I felt that the remarkable parallelism with those in the *Manasā maṅgal* called for a more thorough comparison between the two poems. As I proceeded in the study, the Manasā story, and particularly the version composed in 1495 by Vipradās Pipalāi, appeared to me particularly interesting.

We are fortunate enough to possess a critical edition prepared by one of the most erudite scholar of Bengali literature, the late Professor Sukumar Sen, published by the Asiatic Society of Bengal in 1953.

The *Manasā maṅgal*, as Vipradās tells it calling it *Manasā Vijay* — and his is one of the two oldest existing versions — can be read as the story of the triumph of Bhakti over yoga. The human hero, Cāndo, is a king who has obtained from Śiva, after a great deal of mortifications and exercises, the Great Knowledge, the *mahājñāna*. So, he has himself become immortal and can at will revive the dead. He thus has nothing to fear from anyone, least of all from the goddess of snakes Manasā. Therefore, not only does he refuse to worship her, but he misses no occasion to insult her. The goddess knows that the spreading of her cult among humans cannot happen as long as Cāndo does not worship her. So, by means fair or foul, she forces the king to accept defeat by offering *pūjā* to her feet. Yoga, as presented in the Nāth legends, which allows a man to obtain immortality through his own efforts and practices, is shown to be inoperative in front of a goddess who insists on an attitude of devotional surrender. The fight between Cāndo and Manasā is a re-enactment of the Vedic and epic struggle between, respectively, the carriers of *amṛta* and *viṣa*, the bird and the serpent. Cāndo's real name is Candrapati, the lord of Candra, that is the moon, receptacle of *amṛta*, and Manasā is surrounded by the *nāga*-s The defeat of Cāndo is achieved in a gradual process: at first, the destruction of his beautiful garden, the death of his six sons — garden and sons being symbolic representations of his kingly prosperity, the wreck of his fleet, his own near-drowning and miserable condition, and finally the death of his last son through snake bite. But even more significant is the defeat and death of snake bite of another character in the story: the *ojhā* Dhanvantari, possessor of *amṛta* and of the knowledge obtained through yoga that gives him complete control over poison, *viṣa*. Before Cāndo, and as a first enactment of the same drama, Dhanvantari, Cāndo's counterpart, is vanquished by Manasā and her *nāga*-s. In this story, the character that epitomises devotion to Manasā is a woman, Behulā. Thanks to her, Cāndo, her father-in-law, gets back his riches, his sons and his boats once he has accepted to worship the goddess. Behulā is a *bhaktā*, but one of a special, heroic kind: she threatens, fumes and kicks to obtain from Manasā what she wants. As a devotee, she demands that her husband be restored to life, and the goddess has no option but to comply. She would otherwise be guilty of the murder of a woman. To a fierce deity a fierce devotee!

The *Caṇḍī maṅgal* appears to be built on a similar narrative pattern. The goddess, this time Caṇḍī, insists on obtaining the worship of the merchant Dhanapati who is a devotee of Śiva and does not appreciate female deities. By giving him many trials she forces him to yield and offer her his *pūjā*. But in this poem, there is no question of anyone having obtained any power through yogic practices. The final hero who redeems his father is a child, Caṇḍī's devotee. Indeed, the perfect *bhakta*, the one who surrenders totally and unconditionally to his chosen deity, can only be a child. There can be no better *bhakta*.

Before ending with this topic, I would like to stress that, contrary to what has been written here and there, neither the *Manasā* nor the *Caṇḍī maṅgal* are *śākta* texts. Except for a rhetorical flourish and devotional hyperbole, these texts do not claim for their respective goddess the status of the Supreme Being, and Vaishnavism seems in most cases to have been the personal preference of the poets. Can one read the shifting from the triumph of yoga to that of Bhakti as an historical process or should one understand it structurally as two possible attitudes of man inevitably confronted to decay and death? I shall not attempt an answer in this short communication.

In later years, I have pursued the study of the *maṅgal kāvya*-s and have written on the *Dharma maṅgal* two articles: one on Bhakti and human sacrifice, that was published after the Paris Bhakti-conference, and recently one on the place and importance of the low castes in this particular *maṅgal*. It is out now in an Homage to Professor Dusan Zbavitel published by the University of Prague.

Besides, in all these years, I have had time to write on tantrism as the *śākta* practice in Bengal, as well as on the construction of the Saint in Caitanya's hagiography written by *Brindāvan Dās*.

Later, I studied, both in West Bengal and in Bangladesh, the construction of a cultural hero in the person of Lālan Fakir, a famous Baul who died in the final years of the 19th century. Taking interest in the non-sectarian approach of the Bauls and recognising in their songs a mingling of tantrism, *sahajiyā* Vaishnavism and Sufism, all these approaches being characterised by the accent put on the body as a microcosm, I tried to decipher the metaphors of the body as they are expressed in the Baul songs. From this, my interest in mediaeval Islam grew and I went over to study Saiyid Sultān, a mediaeval Muslim poet who wrote a history of the prophets called *Nabī Vaṃśa*, in which he gave a place to Krishna. As far as mediaeval literature goes, I am now working on the fusion of yoga and Sufism in a 17th century text, entitled *Yoga Kalandar*, and have presented a paper on this subject at the Edinburgh Conference: "Yoga and Sufism. The confluent of two rivers – a mediaeval Bangali text".

BIBLIOGRAPHY

Kavi Kaṅkaṇ Caṇḍī, by Mukundarām Cakravartī, ed. Sukumar Sen, New Delhi: Sāhitya Akademi, first ed. 1975, 2nd ed. 1986.

Vipradās Manasā Vijay, ed. Sukumar Sen, Calcutta: Asiatic Society of Bengal, 1953.

DISCUSSION

Shima:

Bhakti has nothing to do with tantrism. In your case, apparently, tantrism (*siddha yoga*) and Bhakti are connected. Can you please tell me when and how these two trends were connected?

Bhattacharya:

In my opinion tantrism has been evidently present in Bengali life, for quite some time and in various forms. In the *Maṅgal Kāvya* there is no question of Śakti as the primaeval goddess. The *Maṅgal Kāvya* are not Śākta texts, contrary to what some scholars have written, e.g. in the *History of Indian Literature*, published by

Harrassowitz[1]. The background of the period during which the *Maṅgal Kāvya* were written, was the triumph of Vaishnavism. That question interested me too, to see how against the background of Vaishnavism you have the place and the role of the goddesses, and how the goddesses remained firm in that context. I do not think that tantrism as a practice was at all present in the *Maṅgal Kāvya.* It was even condemned.

Shelke:

My question relates to what you said about Puranic material and local traditions being mixed in the texts. When we see the Puranic material and the local traditions of those days, how can you distinguish the two?

Bhattacharya:

When we look at the goddess Caṇḍī as represented in the texts, we see that the first part is about the birth of the goddess. When that event is being narrated, it is totally borrowed from the pan-Indian tradition.

---

[1] Goudriaan T. & Sanjukta Gupta, *Hindu Tradition and Śākta Literature.* A History of Indian Literature, vol. II, fasc. 2. Wiesbaden: Harrassowitz, 1981.

Beginnings: Legends of Origin in the *Kṛttivāsi Rāmāyaṇa*

MANDAKRANTA BOSE

My current work is on the impulse of Bhakti in the *Kṛttivāsi Rāmāyaṇa* as part of a much larger project on the *Rāmāyaṇa*. That project, entitled "Mediating Cultures: The Foundational Role of the *Rāmāyaṇa* in South and Southeast Asian Societies", deals with the epic as the expression of an entire civilization's psyche, spreading throughout India and Southeast Asia, and even other Asian regions. I began the project last year at the University of British Columbia with a two-day conference on problems of the text, iconography, performance and gender. This led to a slim volume comprising five studies on South and Southeast Asian *Rāmāyaṇa*-s.

As a follow-up, I organised, also in June 2000, a more ambitious gathering of some of the most active *Rāmāyaṇa* scholars for a week-long intensive workshop, and I expect its outcome to be a substantial collection of essays.

As I began to look closely at the enormous influence of the *Rāmāyaṇa* in terms of the vast number of its regional versions and renderings, I focussed in particular on the *Rāmāyaṇa* of the mediaeval Bengali poet *Kṛttivāsa*, placed by most scholars today in the last half of the 15th century (Smith, 229). It became immediately apparent that despite its widespread and enduring influence, and its departure from *ādi kavi* Vālmīki's text in both narrative and thematic design, concerning which scholars are generally in agreement, relatively little attention has been paid to the *Kṛttivāsi Rāmāyaṇa*. Two impressive instances of recent scholarship are John Brockington's *Righteous Rama* (1984), and William Smith's *Rāmāyaṇa Traditions in Eastern India* (1988), but these, like investigations by earlier scholars such as Dinesh Chandra Sen and Sukumar Sen, contribute more to the survey of the textual problem than to thematic and narrative matters.

The textual problem has proved to be virtually impenetrable in the absence of an alpha text. Since no complete text has survived from antiquity, the mass of 1500 or so fragments and versions seems to preclude any possibility of constructing a systematic recension, as admitted by scholars from D. C. Sen and Sukumar Sen to Smith and Tushar Kanti Mahapatra. In Dinesh Chandra Sen's opinion, "What the original poetry of Kṛttivāsa was like, can now be only dimly guessed" (178). Sen was convinced, though, that Kṛttvāsa did base his narrative on Vālmīki's poem because the older the manuscript of the *Kṛttivāsi Rāmāyaṇa*, the closer it proves to be to Vālmīki's text. The first printed edition of Kṛttivāsa's poem was published in 1802-3 by the Serampore Press and subsequent editions have not departed from it in any radical way. But just how faithful that text is to the presumed original of Kṛttivāsa cannot be gauged, which led Bhabatosh Datta to state that "scholars even doubt whether the present text of Kṛttivāsa's *Rāmāyaṇa* contains a single line composed originally by the poet" (Datta 546). This may be unduly gloomy because, despite the vast number of versions that claim to represent Kṛttivāsa's work, the main elements of his distinctive treatment of the Rāma tale remain clear. These were the elements that seem to have been gathered together in the Serampore Press edition. No essential variation from this appears in the second Serampore edition of 1830, nor in the edition of Nrittalal Sheel in 1884 or that of Akshay Kumar Datta in 1901. The same holds true for the modern edition I possess, published by Akshay Library, Calcutta in 1954. What we have, then, is a composite text that the Bengali reading public has known as the *Kṛttivāsa Rāmāyaṇa* for at least the past 200 years, and it is this text on which current work, including my own, is based. As Dinesh Chandra Sen declared, to the average reader it does not matter — though it certainly does to the textual critic — that the present *Kṛttivāsi Rāmāyaṇa* is situated rather far from the Vālmīki text, for it represents the evolving thought and feeling of the Bengali speaking people (Sen, 178).

As we consider the narrative and thematic departures the *Kṛttivāsi Rāmāyaṇa* has made from the Vālmīki text, we may see a number of cultural and ideological innovations. Among the many instances of this, tales of miraculous birth are particularly notable for reasons that I hope will become clear as I continue. For this presentation I have chosen to examine the episode of the birth of Bhagīratha, son of King Dilīpa and ancestor of Rāma.

The story, briefly and shorn of minor variations, is this: King Dilīpa dies leaving his two wives childless, which causes them and the gods great anxiety about the continuation of his line. But after Dilīpa's wives consort with one another on Śiva's advice and with his special blessing, one of them conceives, delivering a male child by this biologically impossible stratagem. However, the child is born without any bones, which compels its mothers to place him on the path taken by the sages to the river, where the child gains proper human form and health by a boon granted by the misshapen *ṛṣi* Aṣṭāvakra. The poet attempts to lend credence to this marvellous story etymologically by deriving the name Bhagīratha as that of one engendered from two *bhaga*-s or pudenda.

This lexical explanation suggests that the poet is deliberately drawing attention to the miraculous nature of the birth. We may remember that miraculous births are by no means uncommon in the *Rāmāyaṇa*, or in other legends for that matter. In the *Kṛttivāsi Rāmāyaṇa* we hear of Māndhāta being born from Yuvanāśva's thigh after the latter drinks consecrated water meant to cause his queen to conceive. Rāma himself and his brothers are born after King Daśaratha's three queens ingest a magic *caru*, and so removed is Rāma's birth from ordinary human birth that his mother feels no labour pain, nor does any polluting blood taint the birth process. Still more marvellously, in the *Kṛttivāsi Rāmāyaṇa* Sītā is not even born from a mortal female body, but out of the earth's womb.

The Bhagīratha story stands out for two reasons. First, it is a significant departure from Vālmīki's epic, which merely states in the 7th *śloka* of the 41st *sarga* of the Bālakaṇḍa that Dilīpa is succeeded by his "most righteous son" Bhagīratha, but does not mention the circumstances of his birth. The emphasis there is on Bhagīratha's feat of bringing the waters of Gaṅgā to flow over the ashes of his 60,000 uncles to revive them. By contrast, the *Kṛttivāsi* version makes a special issue of Bhagīratha's birth.

Secondly, the focus on that birth at once underscores the supercession of natural laws, and thereby emphasises the critical role of the authors of that miracle, compelling us to question the place of the miracle in the larger scheme of the poem. Dilīpa's death threatens the extinction of his line, which would of course prevent Rāma's birth and — let us not forget — the completion of the poem. It is therefore essential that somehow Dilīpa's line be revived even if it means forcing a miracle upon the plot by the direct intervention of the gods in human affairs and the laws of nature.

Yet, other questions arise at once. Why must this *Rāmāyaṇa* depart from the Vālmīki narrative so strikingly? Why must Dilīpa die without issue? And why must the absurdity of same-sex reproduction be countenanced, instead of solving the problem by adopting the *śāstrīya* practice of *niyoga*? Given these alternatives, we must take the narrative choice made in the *Kṛttivāsi Rāmāyaṇa* as deliberate and purposeful. I would argue that the purpose is one of affirming for the reader an absolute faith in the divine will to save humanity. The deliberate departure from the Vālmīki narrative implies that within the cosmic design a particular plan has been laid down for life in the human world, which is to come to fruition in the redemptive presence of Rāma in the world. Dilīpa's death is an accident that threatens to disrupt that plan and compels divine and holy beings to step in to save it. The miracle is a narrative device that conveys a sense of that plan and tells the reader/audience that the gods are always on hand to save humankind from evil. Dilīpa's childless death is, then, a thematic necessity, for without it the poet would have no opportunity to invent a miracle nor to create an occasion for the affirmation of faith in the gods. This is the necessity that also precludes the *niyoga* solution to the problem of the childless widows.

The poet further asserts the redemptive aspect of spiritual power by the second miracle attendant upon Bhagīratha's birth, that is, the reconstruction of his shapeless body by Aṣṭāvakra's boon. This extension of the story casts it in the common pattern of the poor and the helpless throwing themselves upon the grace and mercy of superior beings. In this case, curing the child is an insoluble problem for its mothers and no action is possible except to place the child such that some compassionate rishi's gaze might fall upon him. That a devotee's utter helplessness should be answered by a holy being's compassion is a thematic point which commonly coincides with the happy climax of the plot in popular legends of gods and sages, particularly in the numerous *pāñcālī* narratives that became a central part of popular worship practices in eastern India from mediaeval times as Bhakti-cults took hold there. The narrative paradigm as well as its Bhakti-implications date back to the Mahābhārata episode of Draupadī's disrobing where she is saved by Krishna only when she throws herself entirely upon his mercy.

The Bhagīratha episode is, of course, only one clue to the Bhakti-orientation of the *Kṛttivāsi Rāmāyaṇa*, which has notable *rākṣasa*-s such as Taraṇī-sena and Vīrabāhu dying at Rāma's hands, but raising their last breaths in adoration to him because in their devotion to him they had chosen this short-cut to *mokṣa*. These, like the Bhagīratha story, are *Kṛttivāsi* embroideries upon the Vālmīki base and are transparent strategies for asserting the supremacy of the godhead as Viṣṇu and constitute a message that leaves the reader/listener no option but to subscribe to the worship of Viṣṇu as Rāma.

The distinction from the Vālmīki *Rāmāyaṇa* may seem slight at this point, but it is actually substantial. The earlier work primarily creates a cosmic drama of the contest between good and evil, each turn in its narrative structure demonstrating the inevitable victory of the righteous. In Kṛttivāsa's hands the story takes on a different urgency, that of the absolute surrender of the human to the divine. The tale of Bhagīratha's miraculous birth is a small but telling piece of evidence in discovering that urgency.

REFERENCES

Editions:

Bṛhat Saptakāṇḍa Rāmāyaṇa, Published by Akshoy Kumar De, Calcutta, Lakshmibilas Press, 1308 B.E. (1901 CE).

The *Rāmāyaṇa*, translated into Bengali by Krittee-bas, 2nd ed. Serampore [Serampore Mission Press], 1830.

The Ramayun, Published by Nrittalal Sheel, printed by Ramlal Sheel, Calcutta, 1291 B.E (1884 CE).

Vālmīki Rāmāyaṇa: *Bālakāṇḍa*, ed. G. H. Bhatt, Baroda, Oriental Institute, 1960.

Critical Studies:

Banerjee, Asit K., ed., *The Rāmāyaṇa in Eastern Asia*, Calcutta, Prajñā, 1983.

Brockington, J. L. *Righteous Rama*, Delhi, Oxford University Press, 1984.

Datta, Bhabatosh, "The Rāmāyaṇa in Bengal", In Raghavan, 546-560.

Mahapatra, Tushar Kanti, "A Critical Recension of the Rāmāyaṇa by Krittibas", In Banerjee, 136-141.

Nagar, Shanti Lal, transl. *Kṛttivāsa Rāmāyaṇa*, Delhi, Eastern Book Linkers, 1997.

Raghavan, V., ed. *The Rāmāyaṇa Tradition in Asia*, Delhi, Sāhitya Akademi, 1980.

Roy, S.B.C., *The Ramayana of Krttibas and Tulsidas*, Calcutta, Indian Progressive Publishing, 1996.

Sen, Dinesh Chandra, *History of Bengali Language and Literature*, Calcutta, Calcutta University, 1911.

Sen, Sukumar, *Bangala Sahityer Itihas*, 4th ed., Vol. 1, Pt. 1, Calcutta, Eastern Publications, 1963.

Smith, William, "Krttibās and the Pandits: The Revision of the Bengali Rāmāyaṇa", In Proceedings of the Nordic South Asia Conference, 1980, Studio Orientalia, Vol. 50, Helsinki, 1981, pp. 229-240.

Smith, William, *Rāmāyaṇa Traditions in Eastern India*, Stockholm, Department of Indology, University of Stockholm, 1988.

Word-Indexes, Text-Editions and a Dictionary

WINAND M. CALLEWAERT

Śrī Guru Granth Sāhib, With Complete Index,
Motilal Banarsidass, Delhi, 1996;
Part 1, 1430 pp.; Part 2, 1-205 pp.; 967 pp.

An analysis of the *Ādi-Granth* of the Sikhs, compiled in 1604, in no way suggests a lack of respect for the sacredness of the scripture. Human hands and memories were needed to give a form to the divine inspiration which started with Gurū Nānak early in the 16th century. It was the genius of a human medium that put that inspiration in writing. It was not only an inspiration of a moment or of a few months, but of several centuries, as is testified to by the numerous hymns of Bhagats prior or contemporary to Gurū Nānak.

Nearly 400 years after the compilation, a formatted reprint and a complete index should enable both devotees and scholars to have easier access to this enormous and inspiring scripture. The purpose of this two-volume publication that took me five years to complete is 1) to give a reprint in Devnāgarī of the complete text of the *Ādi-Granth*, in such a way that the structure of the *pad*-s is easily visible and a reference system can be added; 2) to give a complete word-index, with reference to the pages and lines where the words occur.

The standard reprints of the *Ādi-Granth*, in both Gurmukhi and Devnāgarī, respect the initial layout of the first manuscript commissioned by Gurū Arjan: on each page a standardised number of lines is given, and on each line a standardised number of words. (For thise page-break, however, there is no uniformity in the different editions.) As a result, the structure of the hymns, the stanzas and the end-rhymes cannot easily be observed. In view of the Index I ignore this layout and reprint the text in such a way that the structure of the hymns is visible and at the same time an easy reference system can be created. The layout of each page, however, is respected, in such a way that each page starts or ends with the words found in the original.

In Part 1, the line reference numbers and the abbreviations for the Gurū or Bhagat, are given in the left margin, to the left of a vertical line. In Part 2, I give an Introduction with:

The Hagiographies of Anantadas. The Bhakti Poets of North India, Curzon Press, London; 2000, 414 pp.

Some time before or around AD 1600 an ascetic of the Rāmānandī order in Rajasthan felt inspired to bring together in a poetic composition the different legends he had heard about the great *bhakta*-s of his times. He most probably did not use ink or paper, but sang and composed as he recited, convinced that he earned great merit doing that. It is not unlikely that the story he himself sang a couple of years later was slightly different, because of a particular need or bias in an audience or because he had learnt something more in the meantime. But the purpose was always the same: to sing the praises of the saint and proclaim the supremacy of devotion (*bhakti*) to God (called Hari, or Rām).

He sang about Nāmdev, Kabīr, Raidās, Dhanā, Angad, Trilochan and Pīpā. More famous *bhakta*–s he could not have chosen and four of them (Kabīr, Dhanā, Pīpā and Raidās), he says, were initiated by Rāmānanda. Nāmdev, Angad and Trilochan were too faraway in the past, even for his sense of history to call them disciples of Rāmānanda. The association with Rāmānanda was repeated by Nābhā and Rāghavdās in their *Bhaktamāl*-s, and by later tradition, but doubted recently by Parśurām Chaturvedī (1964) and modern scholarship. In fact, it may have been Anantadās who was responsible for this association, possibly along with the growing tradition of fashioning Rāmānanda, in the seventeenth century, as the founder of the Rāmānandī sect, as suggested by Burghart[2].

Many legends about the saints must have been at the disposal of Anantadās. Already in his days dozens of legends about the famed Kabīr and Raidās of Banaras were circulating in Rajasthan. For the other *bhakta*–s he had to be satisfied with just a couple of legends.

These *parcaī*–s composed by Anantadās became very popular matter for travelling singers and *bhakta*–s who drew great inspiration from the miracles, the encounters of the saints with Brahmins and Qazis, their unfaltering trust in God never deserting them. The travelling singers who memorised the *parcaī*–s of Anantadās were themselves also poets, capable of adding or changing a line or two. The result of their genius and creativity is a headache and a challenge for the text critic who looks at manuscripts and tries to restore what Anantadās originally must have recited.

A study of the *parcaī*–s of Anantadās gives not only an insight in a very creative period of oral transmission. These *parcaī*–s are also like a video of late 16th century social and religious thinking.

The Millennium Kabīr-Vāṇī, 1. *Pad*-s,
Manohar Publ., New Delhi, 2000, 629 pp.,
(with Swapna Sharma en Dieter Taillieu)

Kabīr is probably the most frequently quoted poet-saint in North-India, but at the same time he is probably also one of the most wrongly quoted saints. Rabindranath Tagore translated 100 of his songs, early in the 20th century, and thus made Kabīr known all over the world. But, having now prepared a critical edition of the songs of Kabīr I dare to propose that hardly any of the Tagore songs was composed by Kabīr. I can understand that a translator of Kabīr, or a devotee finding inspiration in Kabīr's beautiful sayings may look for a nice song without bothering about its authenticity.

---

2 See Richard Burghart, "The founding of the Ramanandi sect", in *Ethnohistory* 25 (120-139), p. 134. See also Peter van der Veer, *Gods on Earth: The Management of Religious Experience and Identity in a North Indian Pilgrimage Centre*. Delhi, OUP, 1989, pp. xii and 89; and William R. Pinch, *Peasants and Monks in British India*, Berkeley, UCP, 1996, pp. 48-66.

But let us not start writing commentaries on Kabīr and on fifteenth century Banares quoting those songs.

David Lorenzen of Mexico City, eminent specialist in the Kabīrpanth and its literature, made a recent survey of the twenty most popular songs of Kabīr in the Kabīrpanth today[3]. What did I see? Only one of these most popular songs is found in the earliest written repertoires I studied. Of course, Kabīr's songs continued to be passed on in an oral tradition, along with the scribal tradition.

I argue two points:

One: Kabīr very soon was 'appropriated' by interested parties (from the Gorakhnāthīs and the Rāmānandīs in the 17th century to the Brahmins like Hāzārī P. Dvivedī in the 20th century, and even Mahatma Gandhi). Kabīr was appropriated for their own ideological purpose or benefit. And thus, as time passed, the corpus of songs with Kabīr's name increased. Two: Among the songs in the earliest manuscripts of Kabīr we can earmark those that may have been popular in the repertoires around 1556, that is two generations after the death of Kabīr and one generation before the first manuscripts still preserved now were written. The norm is 'occurrence' in Punjab and/or Rajasthan.

When everything is said and done, one question remains: how could Kabīr become so charismatic that many devotees, possibly during his lifetime and definitely after his death, were happy to insert his name as *bhaṇitā* or 'identity-card' in their own compositions and let those songs circulate with his name, not their own name? What was his genius that eventually was changed into a social consciousness strongly influencing later generations?

If in the 20th century many singers may perhaps not even know who the *original* Kabīr was, why are they too happy to include their own good, sometimes excellent compositions in the repertoires that are performed in his name? What we have here is a social strategy by which certain ideas are promoted using the charismatic name of a person who as such ceased to exist long ago, who may not even have supported the very ideas that are now spread in his name.

It is the search for that charisma that keeps haunting me and encourages me to look for a 'Kabīr' we may still be able to define, that is the person who was popular in 1556. I do not claim I can go back to the original Kabīr. The only exercise I can reasonably make is to look at the songs that were popular in 1556, 40 years after

---

3 *Praises to a Formless God*, 1996, pp. 205-223.

Kabīr's death, and may have a chance of having been composed and sung by Kabīr.

Now I should only like to briefly refer to my second argument, that among the songs in the earliest manuscripts of Kabīr we *can* earmark those that may have been popular in the repertoires around 1556, that is two generations after the death of Kabīr and one generation before the first manuscripts still preserved now were written. The norm for this earmarking is 'occurrence' in Punjab and/or Rajasthan. To put it very simply, we have basically three regions where the written tradition of Kabīr has been preserved: Banaras, Punjab, and Rajasthan.

In the Banaras region, the *Bījak* collection is the most popular text based on manuscripts, however, not older than the 19th century. One reason given for this fact in sectarian Kabīrian circles is the tradition of immersing and destroying old manuscripts on certain occasions. I do not want to go into this, but the regions where we do find early manuscripts are Punjab and Rajasthan. In Punjab we have the Sikh tradition of the *Ādi-Granth* of 1604 and its antecedent the Mohan Volumes of 1572. In Rajasthan we have basically three traditions, which are rather different and therefore interesting from a textcritical point of view.

Again saving you the details, depending on the occurrence in a number of repertoires, I have marked songs as more or less 'popular' around 1556, that is one generation after the death of Kabīr.

Songs earmarked with three [***] have, according to me, a high probability of belonging to a very early core. These three [***] songs are found in

[1] the *Ādi-Granth* and/or *Mohan Pothī* of the Punjabi tradition, and in at least one of each of the three Rajasthani traditions:

[2] at least one *Pañcavāṇī* manuscript,

[3] at least one *Sarvāṅgī*,

[4] at least C and/or J.

Two [**] are given if the *pad* is found only in three of [1] [2] [3] [4], but including the *Ādi-Granth* and/or *Mohan Pothī*, while one [*] is given if the song is found only in each of the three Rajasthani repertoires [1] [2] [3], not including the *Ādi-granth* or *Mohan*

Pothī. Thus looking at the occurrence of a *pad* in repertoires of both Rajasthan and Punjab, we have

48 songs with [***]: found in Punjab and in most Rajasthani repertoires

97 songs with [**]: found in Punjab and in some Rajasthani repertoires

95 songs with [*]: found only in Rajasthan.

TOTAL: 240 *pad*-s.

Summing up

In the manuscripts/repertoires dated between 1570 and 1681 I found a total of 593 *pad*-s with the name of Kabīr. Of these *pad*-s only one is found among the 'Twenty popular songs' recorded by David Lorenzen in Banaras in 1991.

Kabīr's songs have had a long life of nearly five centuries. The first major event in that life was not that they were written down, but that they travelled. They travelled in different directions and they did so in different companies, in different memories. Of one thing we are certain: the songs of Kabīr very soon travelled west and became popular in Rajasthan and in Panjab. They were not popular in, e.g. Vrindavan where a revival of devotion for Krishna started after Caitanya came there around 1500.

The repertoires reflected in the manuscripts we studied, do not go back to one archetype of one generation before. These repertoires underwent changes several generations earlier and a comparison of these repertoires takes us to at least the year 1556. And, if a song is found in more repertoires, it has a better chance of belonging to a basic core of songs popular around 1556. It is hard to explain how a song popular around 1556 would become a stray song and would eventually continue to exist only in one repertoire. Thus, if a song is found in more repertoires, it has a better chance of belonging to a basic core of songs popular around 1556.

Rāmānanda and his Hindī Works

PINUCCIA CARACCHI

Recently, my research has been dominated by a figure as great as he is mysterious: Rāmānanda. My interest in Rāmānanda goes back to more than twenty years ago, at a time when I was studying in Banaras with a scholarship granted by the Indian Government. I then requested Shuk Dev Singh to help me in translating Rāmānanda's Hindī works edited by Baḍathvāl[4]. By the end of June 1978, the first translation into English and Italian was completed, but I was deeply dissatisfied with it, on both linguistic and interpretative grounds. Therefore I clearly felt it did not deserve to be published and, considering this work as an unripe fruit, I turned my attention toward the *Rāmānandajanmotsava*. This Sanskrit text claims to be part of the *Agastya-saṃhitā* and may be considered a *Rāmānanda-mahātmya*, containing also a brief biography of Rāmānanda, whose authority is unquestionably accepted by his followers. I thought this to be the best starting point for a research on Rāmānanda and in 1989 I published a little book regarding this subject, with the Italian translation of the *Rāmānandajanmotsava*[5]. In the introduction I pointed out some problems concerning the authentic origin of this text, since there are several *Agastya-saṃhitā*-s, but the *Rāmānandajanmotsava* does not appear to belong to any of the above mentioned texts. Therefore, I had to conclude that either the *Rāmānandajanmotsava* is part of an unpublished or unknown (at least unknown to me) *Agastya-saṃhitā* or it must be considered an apocryphal text. As far as I know, the question still remains unsolved, although my opinion is that the second solution is probably the right one.

In truth this is not the only problem that remains unsolved: after long research centred on the life, the thought, the works and the personality of Rāmānanda, the issues that have been raised and not

---

4 *Rāmānanda kī hindī racnāeṁ*, ed. P. Baḍathvāl, pradhān saṃpādak H. Dvivedī, Nāgrīpracāriṇī Sabhā, Kāśī, 1955.

5 Vita di Rāmānanda – Il Rāmānandajanmotsava dell'Agastya-saṃhitā, Promolibri, Torino, 1989.

answered appear to be more than the resolved problems. The results of this research has been published in a book printed in 1999, which also contains the translation of the songs attributed to Rāmānanda, based on the first proof prepared in collaboration with Shuk Dev Singh[6]. In fact, the research pursued two different directions: 1) the examination of the songs edited by Baḍathvāl both from the linguistic and the interpretative point of view; 2) the figure of Rāmānanda and its position both in the *santa* and in the Vaishnava tradition.

As far as the songs are concerned, in order to penetrate and unveil their symbolism and their *sādhukkaḍī bhāṣā* I perused all the available works belonging to both the Nāth and the *santa* tradition. Thus I also discovered many passages identical or very similar to passages contained in the songs attributed to Rāmānanda, a discovery which shed light on their interpretation and enabled me to get a clearer elucidatory vision[7].

Regarding the problem of the attribution to Rāmānanda of the songs edited by Baḍathvāl, I came to the conclusion that there is no irrefutable evidence to prove its certainty. If, after all, this can be stated regarding almost all the *santa* songs — since they have long been orally transmitted[8] — in the case of Rāmānanda's songs the doubts have indeed several far more grounded reasons to exist. One of such reasons is that their themes often appear to be in contrast with the figure of Rāmānanda as an *ācārya* of a *vaiṣṇava sampradāya.* Most of them are probably due to some poet of the *tapasī śākhā,* a Rāmānandī branch that was deeply influenced by the doctrine of Gorakhnāth. Notwithstanding the fact that their attribution to Rāmānanda is unreliable (at least in most of the

---

6 P. Caracchi, *Rāmānanda e lo yoga dei sant,* con una traduzione dei canti hindī in collaborazione con Shukdev Singh, Edizioni dell'Orso, Alessandria, 1999.

7 In some doubtful passages, another help came to me — at a linguistic level — from examining the manuscripts of the Kabīr Caurā Maṭh, which contain different versions of *Rāma rakṣā* and *Gyāna tilaka,* manuscripts whose photographs I received from David Lorenzen, who has catalogued the manuscripts present in the Kabīr Caurā Maṭh and has photographed many of them. See D. N. Lorenzen, *A Catalogue of Manuscripts in the Kabīr chaurā Monastery,* El Colegio de Mexico, 1994.

8 On this subject see *The Hindī Padāvalī of Nāmdev.* A critical edition of Nāmdev's Hindi songs with translation and annotation by W. M. Callewaert and M. Lath, Motilal, Delhi, 1989, pp. 3-4.

cases), I deem that they deserve all the same to be translated and studied as a little, but precious contribution to the *santa* literature, to which they unequivocally belong.

The results of the research conducted on the songs are contained in the wide commentary following their translation, where for each verse both linguistic and interpretative issues have been examined in the light of the *santa* and Nāth traditions and of the Hindū tradition as well. The problems concerning the existence of manuscripts, the presence of other versions and their differences from the Baḍathvāl's edition, and the related questions of attribution have been discussed in an introduction pertaining to each song.

As far as the figure of Rāmānanda is concerned, my research mainly followed three tracks:

1. the biographical sources, both written and oral;
2. the works attributed to Rāmānanda (besides the Sanskrit works also the few Hindī compositions not included in Baḍathvāl's edition): problems of attribution and doctrine;
3. the history of the Rāmānandīs, in so far as it is related with Rāmānanda himself.

Besides dealing with the customary and well known biographical problems regarding dates and places which are related with almost all great men in the context of Indian history, my primary aim was to shed light on the various problems concerning the true personality and thought of Rāmānanda and his position within the Bhakti movement. For instance, was he the guru of all the twelve disciples attributed to him by the tradition? Was he truly a *vaiṣṇavācārya* belonging to the *paramparā* of Rāmānuja? And if so, is it possible to conciliate the Vaishnava doctrine of his Sanskrit works with his teaching as a guru of Sants? In the beginning of the 20th century scholars such as Grierson and Farquhar exalted him as one of the greatest reformers in the history of religion, while nowadays many scholars refute, totally or partially, the extraordinary role which has long been attributed to him in the diffusion of the Rāma-Bhakti in North India, the role he played within the *santa* movement and even the role of founder of the Rāmānandī Vairāgī. Now what has been the real importance of Rāmānanda's role?

In the context of my research I've tried to answer these and other questions and even though it may not always be possible to give an exhaustive solution and interpretation to all such issues, I have tried to formulate a few hypotheses or at least to draw a picture of the *status quaestionis*. I am aware of the fact that in some cases my research does not arrive at certain conclusions, but they may nevertheless be taken as starting points for further research. In any case, to my knowledge, this has been the only research on the figure and the work of Rāmānanda since a long time, probably the first one after that of B. Śrīvāstav, which has been published in Hindī in 1957[9]. In fact also the aforesaid affirmations of today's scholars concerning Rāmānanda do not seem to be based on serious and deep studies[10]. Therefore I've tried to fill a gap pertaining to one of the most fascinating and mysterious figures of the Bhakti movement.

---

[9] See B. Śrīvāstav, *Rāmānanda-sampradāya tathā hindī sāhitya par uskā prabhāv*, Hindī Pariṣad, Prayāg, 1957. It is a very precious book for any research on Rāmānanda especially because it examines books and documents which are either not available at present or very difficult to find.

[10] As far as the *santa* movement is concerned, these critical positions seem to start from a hypothesis formulated for the first time by P. Caturvedī and then subsequently supported by a great scholar as C. Vaudeville. According to her the attribution to Kabīr of a guru like Rāmānanda is simply due to an attempt to 'hinduise' Kabīr. See P. Caturvedī, *Uttarī Bhārat kī sant-paramparā (saṃśodhit tathā parivartit)*, Bhārtī Bhaṇḍār, Ilāhābād, 1972, II ed., pp. 155-161; C. Vaudeville, *Kabīr*, Clarendon Press, Oxford, 1974, pp. 110-116 and C. Vaudeville, *A Weaver Named Kabir*, Oxford University Press, Delhi, 1997, 1st ed., 1993, pp. 87-92.

Positions in the Field of Mediaeval Indian Culture

THOMAS DE BRUIJN

This paper presents current research projects and publications in the period since the last session of this conference in Venice, 1997. The trajectory of my research in this period involved some drastic changes in direction and focus. There is a point where the various topics of my research converge, however, and I hope to say more about that in this paper.

My research activities at the time of the Venice conference were part of the aftermath of finishing my Ph.D. dissertation on the poetry of Malik Muhammad Jāyasī, in 1996. A few years later I can look back at not only the rounding off of some publications on mediaeval Sufi poetry in Hindi, but also at the start of a completely new project which focuses on the literary sociology of the Nayī Kahānī movement in post-Independence Hindi and Urdu fiction. The sociological perspective of the latter project introduced me to new approaches in dealing with literary texts. In turn, this also influenced my perceptions of the mediaeval material and new research initiatives in that field.

A workshop on 'Emblematic figures, orality and identity' which was organised by a research group of CEIAS/EHESS in Paris, provided the opportunity to rework much of the material I had gathered for my thesis on the social and cultural position of the mediaeval Sufi poet, his patrons, and his audience. My paper for this workshop focused on the link between the literary themes and the historical, social and cultural context of mediaeval Sufi poetry in Indian vernaculars. In the case of Muhammad Jāyasī, there is scant but significant information on his background, which allows an interpretation of his poetry that relates it directly to the political and religious circumstances of 16th century North India.

The position of a Sufi poet such as Muhammad Jāyasī was determined by a complex of social and cultural forces. One element was the local ruler or nobleman as patron of the poet or the Sufi congregation (*dargāh*) he belonged to. Another important factor was the audience of Hindu and Muslim devotees who came to the shrine of the Sufi *pīr* to partake of the *barakat* of the holy man. This audience brought the poet in contact with Indian devotional traditions and popular Islam. This influence was balanced by the connection with the doctrinal traditions of classical 'textbook' Sufism, which was present in the form of the leadership of the local Sufi *khānqāh*, and the overall framework of Islamic orthodoxy enforced by the *'ulamā*.

Many interpretations of Jāyasī's work have relied heavily on the notion of religious syncretism and are based on a typically modern, monolithic concept of religious identities. These interpretations fail to see the influences of contemporary social, political and religious discourses in his works which later layers of transmission and ideologically biased re-interpretation have disregarded or distorted. A reading which separates the various layers of meaning in Jāyasī's poetry and relates them to the spheres in which the poet operated reveals a surprisingly rich connection between the themes that structure Jāyasī's poetic work and the position of Sufis in the fields of religion and power — where exemplary figures reigned and religious identities were forged. The main themes of the poems, such as mystical love, the sacrifice of the lover, the roles of the rulers and their feudal allies and the exemplary behaviour of the princess Padmāvatī as described in the *Padmāvat*, can thereby be seen to refer to a real world of religion and politics at the time of the composition of these works.

The relation between the social function of the Sufi poet and the poetics of his work was also a topic in my contribution to the Venice conference, which has now appeared in the proceedings. The paper dealt with Jāyasī's *Akharāvaṭ* and discusses the prominence of the didactic element in the rhetoric of the Indian Sufi poet. The work of the Sufi poets, who operated on the borders between cultural groups and were living examples of the amazing richness and complex nature of mediaeval Indian culture, demands intense scholarly attention from South Asianists who are well-versed in the cultural idiom of Indian Islam in its many forms. Careful study of this material, together with historical studies of the period, will yield much more in the future and can assist in correcting communal stereotypes or idealist notions of tolerance that are projected onto the mediaeval period.

One of the most challenging tasks in this respect lies in the further exploration of the links between the poetic concepts of the various traditions of mediaeval religious poetry — the Sufis, the *saguṇa* and *nirguṇa* Bhakti poets. These agents operated in contiguous fields of cultural production and it may be challenging to say this, but the argument can be put forward that none could have done what they did without mutual influences and crossovers which led to the exciting experiments with content and form we find in the mediaeval texts.

To explore this thesis further, I have devised a research-project which investigates the use of Krishna-imagery in a remarkable text: the *Kanhāvat* of Malik Muhammad Jāyasī. While there are indications that similar texts must have been extant, it is the only preserved retelling of the Krishna-story from the perspective of an Indian Sufi poet. The scenes from the life of Krishna follow the account in the *Bhāgavat Purāṇa*, but the way they are described reveals strong influence from miracle tales and popular hagiographies of *pīr*-s and other 'holy men'.

A study of the use of Krishna imagery in this poem and a comparison with important sources of Krishna poetry could reveal how images that have become standardised in later traditions of Krishna-Bhakti were in active use and subject to shifts in religious and cultural association in the 16th century in the milieu of the Sufi poets. Such evidence is very relevant for an evaluation of the monolithic image of the tradition of Krishna poetry that is put forward in later sectarian sources and would corroborate evidence for alternative meanings of this poetic repertoire in different social and cultural contexts. Verses attributed to Sūrdās have been found in early collections of Bhakti poetry with a distinct *nirguṇa* character. The use of the Krishna story by Sufi poets could present another example of alternative semiotic paradigms for this well known material.

A serious problem for research which involves sources of Krishna poetry is of course the fact that an authoritative edition of the *Sūrsāgar* is still under construction. Comparison with the presently available collections aided with previews of the critical edition can, however, shed light on Jāyasī's angle on images that in later sectarian codification have been solidified into stereotypical concepts of devotion to Krishna, but might have had a less uniform semantic potential in an earlier phase. Comparisons with Krishna imagery in Jāyasī's other texts and with Sufi poetry by other Avadhi poets and the works that were produced at Muslim courts in Bengal, can reveal interesting parallels. So far, it has not been possible to raise funding for this project, so it has to be left for when better days come around.

The intense research effort that has in the last decades been devoted to editing, translating and interpreting the collections of Sūrdās, Kabīr and other Bhakti poets have made all scholars in the field aware of the complicated problems of fixing the chronology and semantic orientation of the canon of mediaeval Indian religious texts. My recent shift towards a new area of research — from mediaeval poetry to post-Independence Hindi and Urdu literature — has made me review my own perspective on the mediaeval material. On the European Conference on modern South Asian Studies in Prague in 1998, I convened a panel on Indian Islam and Sufism. In this panel I presented a paper which explored a new approach to the many awkward problems that arise when the contemporary social and political constellation in India is compared to the mediaeval situation, especially where communal relations and the interpretation of mediaeval texts are concerned. In this comparison, categories and judgements that are typical of the history of modern India are easily projected on the mediaeval situation. The religious syncretism that is often proposed for the poetry of Kabīr and Jāyasī is a good example as it is based on a modern concept of religious identity as a monolithic entity which does not allow for hybridity or polyvalence.

A good understanding of the mediaeval should be based on a direct analysis of contemporary situations and the transitions that link the past with the present. This is not only relevant in historical or social science research, but can also have an interesting dimension to add to textual studies. In many cases the transmission of texts in manuscripts or other forms is understood and described as a mechanical chain of unspecified instances of reproduction of a literary text. Even in the case of the transmission of the work of Muhammad Jāyasī, which is much less problematic than the reception of other mediaeval material, the editors have paid little attention to the specific circumstances of reception and reproduction. Sociological approaches to modern literature have made considerable progress on this point by trying to define how a literary work emanates from a position that is determined by the push and pull of social, economic and cultural forces that constitute a field of cultural production in a certain period. Analysis of these forces and the underlying structure and ideology of that field and of the conversions of capital that are involved in the consumption and production of literature, can give a better view on the place of a literary work — a new text or an expensive copy of a manuscript — in a particular social or cultural context.

It would be interesting to review our perspective on the mediaeval sources for text-editions in this light. In Jāyasī's case, there is sufficient evidence to argue that the various instances in which his work was received and reproduced in the form of new manuscripts connect a series of stages in the development of a literary field rather than that they represent a more or less straight and mechanical line of textual transmission in which every reproducing agent attached the same value and meaning to the literary work that was transmitted. The great variety in the nature of the manuscripts — illustrated, commissioned, simple copies or elaborate versions — is an obvious sign in this direction.

By focusing on the value of a literary work and the various forms of capital — economic, cultural, symbolic — invested in it during each of the successive reproductions and by analysing how this process is related to the various periods of pre-modern Indian history, it will be possible to describe the journey of texts through the history of the field of literary production. This will allow an assessment of the changes in the texts that takes into account the changes in the social and cultural circumstances in which they are transmitted.

It will not be easy to find the right sources for such a project. Yet, there could be much information in what we already know, but tend to overlook. It could prove interesting to investigate in detail the workings of the mechanism that is somewhat uncritically subsumed under the header of sectarian influence. Re-examining what we know of sectarian organizations or Sufi *khānqāh*-s as social institutions that operate conversions of economic and political power into cultural capital could also yield a better understanding of the value of texts in this process.

Patronage of religious poetry, manuscripts, and institutions was a major force in the establishment of a field of cultural production in the mediaeval period. This phenomenon could be an interesting starting point for research which would benefit from cooperation with historians and art-historians. The present progress of research into collections of Bhakti poetry could also contribute to this and allow a new research perspective which is not so much focused at the religious semantics of mediaeval poetry or formal reconstructions of transmission trees, but rather on the role of the mediaeval material as 'stake in the game', to use an expression of Pierre Bourdieu. It will be of special interest to follow the transmission of texts as they pass the thresholds of modernity, when the mediaeval poetry — in the form of textbooks and compilations — enters the public sphere of modern Indian culture. To go back to the example of the poetry of Muhammad Jāyasī, a question which might come up is: what made people take up Jāyasī's texts at the end of the 19th century and produce them in much larger numbers than ever before through Naval Kishor's lithograph press? Which image of the mediaeval tradition inspired the editions of R.C. Shukla, M.P. Gupta and V.S. Agravala? The same goes for the position of the other modern forms of the mediaeval materials.

The mediaeval materials have come to us because people saw that they represented a capital of some sort that was worth the investment for preservation and reproduction. Much has been discarded because its value could no longer be converted into capital that was fit for the field it passed through. In this sense, what we have in the form of manuscripts and prints is the reflection of the genesis and development of a field of cultural production. Instead of focusing exclusively on the religious hermeneutics of this material, it also makes sense to look at the history of the field that produced this material.

In the near future I hope to elaborate these ideas with reference to the role of patronage in Indo-Muslim culture for a seminar in Paris, next year. Methodology and case studies for this endeavor need to be further worked out for that occasion, but it is evident that they will benefit from the experience of research into the sociology of modern literature. A history of the field of Indian literature can span a wide range of topics and periods and connects Nayī Kahānī with mediaeval religious poetry.

DISCUSSION

Zelliot:

There is a young Slovakian scholar, Dushan Deak, in Pune now working on Muhammad Sheikh, a poet who apparently was fully integrated in the Maharashtrian Varkari tradition. I do not remember the particular Sufi order to which he belongs, but I wonder whether we have here too a certain Sufi order more interested in becoming part of a chiefly Hindu tradition then the other orders. What order did Jāysī belong to?

de Bruijn:

He belonged to a local branch of the Chistiya order.

Zelliot:

I was wondering whether we can acquire some pan-Indian knowledge, looking at this Muslim poet who was fully integrated in the Hindu tradition.

de Bruijn:

If you look at it from the perspective of a local Sufi institution, it appears to be very involved in quite a few local institutions, with devotees coming from all kinds of groups. It is more an exception if a Sufi institution — e.g. at the Mughal court, or of intellectual Sufis — is totally cut off from the local context. These texts do not come from the Mughal court, but from a very local background where everything was interconnected, where even perhaps Hindu Rajas were employed by the Mughals and to find some justification for their authority by employing a Sufi poet. Thus, in a Sufi narrative the name of a king could easily be Hindu. It is not hard to imagine that the patronage of a Sufi poet was used as a foundation for the authority of a Hindu king, who was part of the system of the Mughal empire. These are the very intriguing local dynamics that emerge from a study of these texts.

Abstract and Review

BALWANT SINGH DHILLON

Although in recent years several scholars have taken up textual studies of the Ādi Granth, the state of transmission of Bāṇī has not come into their focus. The history of the Sikh scriptural text, as asserted by some critics, is not of obscure nature. Its origin can easily be traced back to Gurū Nānak Dev whose experience of the 'Numinous' formed its very core and basis as well. Truly, in order to popularise the message of *Gurbāṇī*, oral transmission in the form of musical tradition has been a popular mode, but it was not the only way to preserve the Sabad for posterity. Our sources confirm that beginning with Gurū Nānak Dev, the Sikh Gurūs were not averse to recording the Sabad on its very manifestation. Before Gurū Nānak Dev left the mundane world, the first redaction of his sacred writings had been compiled into a codex, popularly known as the Pothī. The successive Sikh Gurūs not only contributed to the Sikh sacred writings, but took a keen interest also to prepare and circulate the codices of *Gurbāṇī* among the Sikh Saṅgats. Subsequently, a tradition of *Gurbāṇī* in scribal form had flourished under the watchful eyes of the Sikh Gurūs. Early Sikh sources belonging to the period of Gurū Rām Dās reveal that public reading of *Gurbāṇī* had become an essential part of the Sikh liturgy. Subsequently, the scribing of Pothī-s of *Gurbāṇī* had developed into a pastime for pious Sikhs. The codices that had been prepared had been duly installed in the Dharamsālās. Even the practice to to read the first hymn from the Pothī when opened (*vāk*), had come into vogue. Evidence at hand indicates that a well-nurtured mother tradition of *Gurbāṇī* in scribal form had come down to Gurū Arjan Dev on his succession.

Another mode to transmit *Gurbāṇī* which had developed in close proximity to the scribal tradition, related to public reading of the sacred texts. Similarly, musical traditions have developed into a very popular and powerful mode for the transmission of Bāṇī among the Sikhs. The musical or oral tradition of *Gurbāṇī* which was prevalent among mainstream Sikhs did not have an independent origin, but had thrived purely on the mother tradition, i.e. the scribal tradition. Looking back at the pre-Ādi Granth milieu, there is no reason to doubt that to compete with the main stream Sikhism, at least three other traditions of *Gurbāṇī*, namely the Udāsī, Bhallā and Mīnā had come to stay among the Sikhs. Even the Hindālī, a heretical tradition had emerged on the scene to pollute the Sikh tradition. The Sikh Gurūs were impelled to defend the originality and authenticity of their mission vis-à-vis what their rivals claimed it to be. Nevertheless it is a fact that the rivals were also producing their own codices on the pattern of the Sikh Gurūs, ostensibly to establish and run their respective gurudoms. We can well imagine that codices were being produced by different scribes for different reasons and purposes. The role of the Janamsākhī-s and that of the scribes engaged in copying was quite significant in the transmission of Bāṇī. Evidence at hand suggests that in the pre-Ādi Granth period, transmission of Bāṇī continued through various means and traditions. The point that we intend to make here is that before using any source as an evidence for textual studies of the Ādi Granth, a text critic has to evaluate the historical scenario out of which a particular source had originated. Besides, one has to unravel the process through which it had been composed, the sources employed for it and the very purpose of its origin. Moreover, a text critic has to give scrupulous attention to discern from which of the above-mentioned traditions of *Gurbāṇī*, a particular source has originated, otherwise the conclusions drawn on its face value will not be valid.

Review of *Ahiyāpur Wālī Pothī* (Punjabi)
Vol. 1, ed. Prof. Pritam Singh
Amritsar, Guru Nanak Dev University, 1998, pp. 321, price Rs 350

The Gurū Granth, the scripture of the Sikhs, is primarily concerned with the 'numinous' experience. Although a number of authors have contributed to it, the whole literature is essentially religious in nature. Ever since its first codification in the form of Ādi Granth in 1604, its text has been looked upon as the most authentic and original repository of the divine 'word'. A dominant section of the scholars of Sikh studies believe that since the Ādi Granth writings have come down in an authenticated form from the Sikh Gurūs themselves, there is absolutely no need of textual studies. Perhaps this is the only reason that so far they have given scant attention to locate and evaluate the sources, which are said to be of earlier origin than the Ādi Granth. On the other hand, working largely on the basis of a few deletions and variant readings found in the old manuscripts of the Sikh scripture, some scholars have shown keen interest in the textual studies, so that a sure and certain text could be fixed. For any meaningful textual analysis (of the Ādi Granth) access to documents, especially the sources which are said to be the basis of the Ādi Granth, is a pre-requisite. It is believed that while compiling the Sikh scripture Gurū Arjan Dev, the fifth Gurū, had some sources at his disposal besides the corpus that he had inherited from his father Gurū Rām Dās, the fourth Sikh Gurū. Some of the traditional Sikh sources describe that before compiling the Ādi Granth, Gurū Arjan Dev approached Bābā Mohan at Goindwal requesting him to lend the Pothī-s of Bāṇī that were said to have been prepared during the Gurūship of the third Master, Gurū Amar Dās. Presently, two volumes popularly known as the *Goindwāl Pothī*-s are extant, of which one is known as the Ahiyāpur Pothī and the other as Pinjore Pothī. It is claimed that these are the same volumes that Gurū Arjan Dev had utilised to compile the Ādi Granth. Ahiyāpur Wālī Pothī by Prof. Pritam Singh, the book under review, deals with one of the above volumes. It is the product of a research project that Guru Nanak Dev University, Amritsar had assigned to the author in 1990 with a specific purpose to investigate whether the extant Pothī-s are ancestral to the Ādi Granth or not.

Scholars working in the field of manuscripts know well that in order to secure access to the documents lying in the privạte and public collections is an uphill task. Usually the custodians are found to be highly secretive and often they do not even allow scholars to examine their manuscripts from an academic point of view. We are informed that the interest of the author in the Pothī-s is not of recent origin but dates back to the 1950s. The first part of the book describes Prof. Pritam Singh's quest and the difficulties that he had to encounter to have access to these volumes. On being denied access to the original manuscript, largely due to the evasive attitude of its custodian, the author was obliged to conduct his study with the help of a photographed copy of the said Pothī. For his study he takes into account the 18th and 19th century Sikh sources which hold that Gurū Arjan Dev had borrowed the Pothī-s from Bābā Mohan to compile the Ādi Granth. Similarly he takes note of the 20th century Sikh writers who have commented on the

Pothī-s, especially their status vis-à-vis the Ādi Granth. The author has come to the conclusion that though these volumes have been a much talked about source of the Sikh canon, yet no scholar had examined them thoroughly to test their authenticity. The author feels that the majority of the scholars have not scrutinised these documents for themselves. The scholars who had the opportunity to examine them from close quarters were too occupied with one or another issue of their immediate interest. Consequently, full and faithful analysis of their contents has remained a mystery.

The second part of the book is most significant as it presents in detail the contents of the Pothī under study. The author describes in it the distinctive features such as the edict recorded at the outset; the headings ascribed to the *rāga*-s, authors and their writings; the musical modes and their tunes; the sequence of *rāga*-s and their internal patterns; the authorship; the serial number of the writings; folio numbers – old and new; the textual variants; and the orthographic style of the Pothī. Besides, putting the data step by step, the author points to the similarities as well as the differences that he has noticed between the Pothī and the Ādi Granth. It helps the reader to judge for himself the merits of the Pothī from a textual viewpoint. The study reveals that the Ahiyāpur Pothī spread over 300 folios is an anthology of 293 hymns (pp. 84, 105) that have been arranged according to the *rāg* pattern. The scribe of the Pothī has employed six forms (p. 74) of invocation (*mūlmantra*), which differ radically from that of the Ādi Granth. In the opinion of the author it may be due to the sectarian purpose of the Pothī.

Besides a hymn each in Waḍahaṁs, Malār, Āsā, Bilāwal and Gūjarī, the Ahiyāpur Pothī comprises eight *rāga*-s in the order of Sūhī, Parbhātī, Dhanāsarī, Basant, Bhairo, Māru, Kedārā and Tilaṅg. Obviously, the sequence of *rāga*-s of the Pothī does not conform to the Ādi Granth pattern. Another distinctive feature of musicology that has come to light, is the employment of composite modes such as Sūhī Dakhaṇī Jiguru, Sūhī Jiguru, Parbhātī Lalatā, Dhanāsarī Dakhaṇī, Dhanāsarī Pasato Māru Gaḍāū, Basant Dakhaṇī, Bhairo Dakhaṇī and Māru Kedārā (pp. 83, 85, 88). These modes are quite alien to the musical tradition that has been preserved in the Ādi Granth. On the other hand composite modes of the Ādi Granth namely Parbhātī Bibhās and Basant Hindol are absent in the corresponding *rāga*-s of the Pothī. Similarly, the tunes mentioned in the Pothī for singing have found no mention in the Ādi Granth (p. 87). Moreover, contrary to the Ādi Granth, the Pothī does not carry reference to the beat (*gharu*). A comparative look at the arrangement of writings in each of the *rāga*-s of the Pothī with their counterparts in the Ādi Granth, confirms that with the exception of a few similarities, differences are more pronounced (p. 150). Another category of musical variants, which deserves the attention of the critics, is 'fillers' and 'vocatives' that have crept into the text of the Pothī. Similarly there are a number of hymns, which take off from different lines than those in the Ādi Granth. These two types of musical variants have not found adequate attention in the study. Anyway, all these factors point to the fact that the Ahiyāpur Pothī belongs to a different musical tradition than that of the Ādi Granth (p. 103).

On comparing the text of the Pothī with its counterpart in the Ādi Granth, the author has observed that the corresponding *rāga*-s of the Pothī neither have the writings of the first three Sikh Gurūs nor of the mediaeval Bhagats in their entirety. Instances of verses missing from the text are also noticeable (pp. 198, 199). On the basis of these facts, the author has come to the conclusion that the text of the Pothī has never been a basis for compiling the Ādi Granth (pp. 196, 202). He remarks that Gurū Arjan Dev had access to an incredible source, otherwise the text that we have in addition to the Ahiyāpur Pothī would not have been possible in the Ādi Granth.

The author points to the fact that as many as 17 authors have contributed to the text of Ahiyāpur Pothī. Although, in order to differentiate the writings of different authors, the terms such as Mahallā or Mahallu, Bābā or Bābā Pātshāh, Gulām or the names of the Bhagats have been employed, yet there are as many as 128 hymns (p. 105), which are without any indication of authorship. Consequently, the reader finds himself clueless to determine the authorship of such writings. In the opinion of the author there are at least 18 hymns (p. 111) in the Pothī on which its scribe differs over the issue of authorship with that of the Ādi Granth. The study has brought into limelight another important feature of the Pothī, which relates to apocryphal writings. The author has noticed three extra-canonical writings attributed to Gurū Nānak (pp. 90, 102) and Gurū Rām Dās (p. 94) that form part of the Pothī. According to the author as many as 13 compositions authored by Gulām/Sadā Sewak using the pseudonym of 'Nānik' are present in the Pothī from its very beginning (p. 128). Similarly 9 *pada-s* of extra-canonical nature attributed to the mediaeval Bhagats and Sufis namely Kabīr

(3), Nāmdev (4), Tirlochan (1) and Sharaf (1) are also available in the Pothī (pp. 195-196). All these writings have found no acceptance with Gurū Arjan Dev for inclusion in the Ādi Granth. On the basis of above factors, the author remarks that Gurū Arjan Dev has not followed the Pothī in any manner to compile the Ādi Granth.

While discussing the textual variants, the study makes reference to two *pada-s* of Nāmdev — *hindū gardani mārаū tohi* and *sulatān pūchai kahu re nāmā* — in *rāg* Bhairo (p. 197), which in the opinion of the author are found merged into one hymn in the Ādi Granth. One may easily disagree with the above observation as, except for the theme, the text in both sources is quite at variance. On comparing the text on seven folios of the Pothī with its counterpart in the Ādi Granth, the author has found as many as 122 variants relating to the use of syllables and their spellings (pp. 189-191). He feels that the total variants of the above category may be more than twelve thousand (p. 192). Arguably all these wide ranging divergences between the contents of the Ādi Granth and Ahiyāpur Pothī can only be explained by accepting the fact that both are parallel entities and owe their origin to different sources and the theory that Gurū Arjan Dev has borrowed the material from the Ahiyāpur Pothī, finds no validity as far as the internal evidence is concerned.

The study also provides a brief introduction to the authors whose writings are preserved in the Pothī. Though it is of little use for the specialists, yet the discussion on Gulām/Sadā Sewak and Sharaf deserves their attention. The writings of Gulām, according to the author, are not hymns composed by Gurū Rām Dās before he assumed the Gurūship, as wrongly believed by some scholars (p. 125). These are fake compositions (kachī-Bāṇī), which the rival and schismatic group of Bābā Mohan tried to place at par with the hymns of the Sikh Gurūs. On the basis of internal evidence the author unfolds the mystery surrounding the identity of Gulām, which is quite convincing. He argues that Gulām is none else but Sahansar Rām (p. 136), the son of Bābā Mohan who has prepared the Pothī to establish a hereditary seat at Goindwal. However, his remarks that Gulām and Sadā Sewak were two personalities and the latter seems to be a trickster who has played the mischief to circulate the poetry of Gulām as that of his own (p. 137), are hard to believe. It may be noted that Gulām and Sadā Sewak are synonyms and secondly the composition (p. 124) on which the author has built his argument, alludes to Sewak half a dozen times.

It appears strange that instead of referring to the original folios (in or outside the margin) the author has invented another set of folio numbers. In the absence of the second volume of the study which will have the facsimiles of the Ahiyāpur Pothī, a reader sometimes finds himself confused as a comparison of the references that have been made in the earlier studies, has become quite cumbersome. Secondly, the change brought in by the author to arrange the writings of the Pothī afresh, is liable to blur the vision of a reader who is interested in its original or present format. The author also attempts to explain the physiognomy of the Pothī. Methodologically, it seems to be unrealistic to comment on the physical features with any certainty on the basis of a photocopy.

The study also devotes a section to the orthography of the Pothī. In the absence of a colophon, the author has taken recourse to it to determine the age of the Ahiyāpur volume. He concludes that its recording may have taken place somewhere between AD 1580 and 1620 (p. 226). It is noteworthy that the orthography of the primary and secondary scribe (excluding the hand in Tākarī) carries identical features. In how far the orthography of the primary scribe differs from that of the secondary scribe, no indication has been offered. On close perusal of various sections and sub-sections, one finds that the study under review is an honest presentation of the contents of the Ahiyāpur Pothī. The author has rare occasion to falter in his observation. He wrongly attributes a hymn in *rāg* Sūhī (*jo dīsai gur sikhaḍa*) to Gurū Nānak (p. 90) to find it absent in the Pothī. Since the hymn in question belongs to Gurū Arjan Dev, it is futile to locate its occurrence in the Pothī.

The age of the Pothī has been a debatable issue. The edict that refers to its recording date having been placed at the beginning has gone brittle and subsequently it has been repaired. According to Dewan K.S. Puri, the handwriting expert whose opinion the author has sought to resolve this ticklish issue, the date 'might have also been overwritten or there is some ink spread' (p. 256). At the same time he states that the main portion of the edict is in the hand of the primary scribe. Consequently, the very mention of the blessings of the first three Gurūs in the edict, has led the author to refute the traditional theory that the Ahiyāpur Pothī has been prepared during the period of Gurū Amar Dās (pp. 73, 231). The presence of writings attributed to Gurū Rām Dās and Gurū Arjan Dev suggests that it belongs to post-Gurū Amar Dās period. On the basis of orthography the author argues that its recording might have been completed between 1610-1620 (p. 231). In fact while dating the Pothī the date, i.e. *samvat* 1652, *māgh vadī* 1 (7 January 1596) cannot be ignored. The suggestion does not look plausible that instead of enhancing its antiquity the custodian has indulged in post dating.

In a nutshell the study stresses that the Ahiyāpur Pothī owes its origin to the sectarian developments in the Panth. It has been prepared to establish the ancestral line of gurudom that has its origin with Bābā Mohan, the son of third Gurū. The notion that it has been prepared under the direction of Gurū Amar Dās finds no validity. The study straight away rejects the borrowing theory to remark that the Ahiyāpur Pothī has never been a source of the Ādi Granth. It argues that both anthologies owe their origin to different sources and represent two parallel entities (p. 239). It also highlights the role of the schismatic trends in Sikhism, which were transmitting as well as using the vehicle of *Gurbāṇī* to further their vested interests. The study takes note of the Pothī to remark that it is an important document of mediaeval devotional literature produced in Gurmukhī as it has preserved some writings which are not found in any other source nor are these known to the critics of Punjabi literature. Though microfilms and photographs are widely used in research studies yet to criticise the present work, one can safely say that to comment upon the Pothī on the basis of photographs is not a reliable methodology. However, the author has not demonstrated any undue haste to arrive at his conclusions, but has shown utmost care to observe historical and literary norms. It would have been much better if the companion volume of the book containing the facsimiles had also been made available along with it. It is a welcome addition to the scholarly literature on Sikh scripture and will stimulate the readers to have a fresh look at the textual issues that have come to the fore in the recent past.

The Lyrics of *ṭhumrī*: Hindi Poetry in a Musical Genre

LALITA DU PERRON

My doctoral thesis is on the lyrics of a vocal genre of North Indian (Hindustani) art music, *ṭhumrī*. There are three major vocal genres in the Hindustani tradition: *dhrupad*, *khyāl*, and *ṭhumrī*, often termed 'semi-classical' as its music is lighter, more accessible and less strictly adhering to the rules of *rāg* (musical mode) than that of *dhrupad* and *khyāl*. *Dhrupad* texts have been the subject of linguistic analyses, most notably by Françoise Delvoye 'Nalinī' (1987) and Lucy Rosenstein (1997). Although *ṭhumrī* texts have been discussed as part of musicological studies, they had not prior to my work been treated as an area worthy of research in its own right. I felt that *ṭhumrī* lyrics deserved to be the focus of a dedicated language-based study. Although my thesis contextualises the lyrics in their performance setting, it is primarily a textual analysis in which musical observations are based on existing studies, augmented by my own experiences studying and living with Hindustani musicians.

These *ṭhumrī* texts tend to be concise, using limited vocabulary primarily drawn from Braj Bhāṣā. They are almost invariably written from a female perspective. The predominant mood of the lyrics is romantic, usually describing formulaic situations in a Krishnaite idiom. The combination of this idiom with the romantic mood and the female gaze has led to an increased perception of *ṭhumrī* as an essentially devotional genre. The deconstruction of this perception lies at the heart of my thesis. In contemporary received views, *ṭhumrī* is a light song form whose primary function is to provide some diversion at the end of a serious *khyāl* concert. The *ṭhumrī* music is accessible; its language is sweet and mellifluous; its mood is romantic. As one musician put it: everybody loves *ṭhumrī*. This rather reductionist view belies *ṭhumrī*'s original function as a vehicle for dance, and its slightly later role as the primary avenue for emotional expression in songstress-courtesan (*tavāyaf*) performance. We know that *ṭhumrī* was integral to the courtesan tradition, a fact which is not commonly acknowledged in the modern construct of its meaning, even though its connection with courtesan life has affected both its musical and textual shape. It is a testament to *ṭhumrī*'s integrity as an art-form that, in spite of its original context, it has survived the transition to modernity. In the process its meaning has been changed, its tradition has been re-invented, its history has been denied.

Certain claims notwithstanding, *ṭhumrī* is not an ancient form: its origin and development can be traced back to a confluence of folk and art music in the 18th century. We know that *ṭhumrī* flourished in the middle of the 19th century, when the aristocracy of Lucknow favoured it greatly over the more serious offerings of *dhrupad* and *khyāl*. Following the exile of Wajid Ali Shah and the subsequent consolidation of colonial rule, changes in patronage structure as well as in indigenous attitudes to dance resulted in the gradual decline of the courtesan tradition. As a dance form in *tavāyaf* performance *ṭhumrī* lost currency, and as courtesans began to entertain in private salons, a new style of *ṭhumrī* emerged and eventually became the most prominent form of *ṭhumrī*. This form of *ṭhumrī* is called *bol banāv ṭhumrī*, as the emphasis is on *bol banānā* using phrases extracted from the text as a vehicle for melodic improvisation. Short phrases are repeated many times, with a view to emphasising a different shade of meaning with each repetition. It therefore follows that in this form of *ṭhumrī* the texts ideally have strong emotive qualities, providing singers with ample scope for melodic elaborations.

Bol banāv ṭhumrī emerged at a crucial time in the history of Indian performance art. The end of the 19th century spawned a movement directed towards appropriating indigenous art to nationalist ideals. Cultural artefacts were invested with religious and traditional meaning and were reconstructed as sources of pride in the motherland, no longer symbols of decadent feudal life and the hedonistic lifestyles of the princely rulers who had given the British so much cause for contempt. The erotic and manneristic courtesan genre *ṭhumrī* was extremely problematic as it did not easily lend itself to this shift of focus. However, as male singers became interested in the possibilities presented by *ṭhumrī*'s emotive character and as, in the context of North Indian art, the interpretation of the erotic as devotional posed no major obstacles, *ṭhumrī* managed to outgrow its sole function as a vehicle for entertainment by *tavāyaf*-s. Whereas in the private space of the *mujrā* the courtesan performed *ṭhumrī* with the appropriate emphasis on emotional expression, voicing the heroine's longing for her lover as she charmed and enticed her male audience, in the public sphere of music festivals and recordings — both in their infancy in the first decades of the 20th century — *ṭhumrī* was performed by increasingly well-known male singers and by women who insisted on being known on concert announcements and record labels as 'amateurs', i.e. not 'professional women'. Whereas the desire expressed by *ṭhumrī*'s lyrical heroine could readily be enacted by the *tavāyaf* in relationship to her prospective clients, the same desire easily lent itself to a devotional interpretation when the context demanded it. Minor alterations to certain texts combined with a selective choice of material resulted in somewhat sanitised versions of the original songs, which retained their emotive and romantic expression even if they were now primarily interpreted in a Krishnaite idiom.

Although at the outset of my research I had intended to investigate the — now seemingly unverifiable — link between *ṭhumrī* texts and folk songs, the emphasis gradually shifted as I realised that the primary characteristic of the texts was that they appeared to be impossible to define. From considering this a nuisance situation destined to frustrate the weary Ph.D. candidate's research objectives I moved on to realise that this ethereal quality was not only the defining characteristic that I had been looking for, but was exactly what had provided *ṭhumrī* with the route into its present-day status as a major genre of Hindustani music. The linguistic register of *ṭhumrī* conspires to locate the texts in a space which is insulated from mundanity; the frequent reliance on diminutive forms is but one component of this, augmented by narrowly defined lexical choices, which tend to avoid Perso-Arabic and *tatsama* vocabulary as well as the more functional components of Khaṛī Bolī such as pronouns and auxiliaries. The combination of *ṭhumrī*'s linguistic register, its use of imagery reminiscent of earlier Bhakti poetry, its female perspective and its romantic and implicit if not explicit Krishnaite idiom, contribute to the modern construction of its meaning in a devotional framework.

Exploring the effect of the change in performance milieu on the lyrics of *ṭhumrī* raises the question of who actually motivates such reconstructions; although it is seemingly the performer who is in control of alterations to her genre, she is ultimately motivated by the desire to keep her art form compatible with the demands of patronage. The question of 'selling-out' thus arises: is the performer who adjusts her art to suit the needs of her audience merely suitably accommodating, or actually compromising her artistic integrity for the sake of survival or commercial success? The last chapter of my thesis explores the avenues open to an art form whose traditional performance environment ceases to be relevant. I suggest that an art form may be viewed as a commercial commodity, whose value partly depends on market forces and is determined by external circumstances, consumer perception and fashionability. The reliance of *ṭhumrī* on formulaic language and imagery is highly significant: I argue that the predictable nature of the texts allows the audience to be instilled with a sense of recognition, which invests the genre with an aura of traditionality that is crucial for its survival in the modern age.

DISCUSSION

Callewaert:

What are the sources of the texts? Have you used mediaeval Persian sources, more specifically the manuals for music?

du Perron:

All of the texts that I based the thesis on were texts I had recorded or had evidence of being used during the last 100 years. What I found in terms of manuscripts was that there were quite a lot of manuscripts, dating from probably the beginning of the 19th century. It does not go much further back than that. My research is very much based on the living tradition. What seems to happen in the 19th century is that a lot of *ṭhumrī*-s were written, perhaps by people who just sat down to write a *ṭhumrī*, without really fitting in with anything else. Looking at the way the language was used and the way the subject matter went, it is often very hard to see how they even actually have been performed. I decided in the end, as part of my methodology, to stick with performed sources.

Offredi:

Is it possible to know something about the differences between the *ṭhumrī* in Banaras and Lucknow? Did you focus your research mainly on the Lucknow *ṭhumrī*, which is much more refined, with the Banaras *ṭhumrī* which is more popular?

du Perron:

I think that the Lucknow *ṭhumrī* was more related to dance, while the Banaras *ṭhumrī* is slightly later and more related to the emotional expression that came after the dance. Thus, one could speak of a time-frame difference. Hence perhaps we speak of the Lucknow *ṭhumrī* as being more refined, as it was more narrative in function. There was more text and therefore there was more scope to bring in various facets. The Banaras *ṭhumrī* which is much more a 'seated' *ṭhumrī*, had to rely more on emotional expression and so it was more about the way language is used.

Horstmann:

I would like to know about the milieu in which the *ṭhumrī* was performed. How did they manage to avoid each other, I mean the *ṭhumrī* performing milieu and those performing *ghazal*-s? In that Nawabi milieu, did the circles form consciously, or did they have nothing to do with each other?

du Perron:

They were exactly the same milieu, the very same people singing *ghazal*-s as *ṭhumrī*-s, perhaps with a slight change of emphasis. The *ṭhumrī* would have been more dance-oriented, more emotional, while the *ghazal* would be more intellectual, with a stronger emphasis on poetry. As someone remarked: with a ghazal, where the poetic genius is very important, we might say '*vāh*' and with the *ṭhumrī* you say '*āh*'.

Horstmann:

Who were the agents trying to keep the language pure? You were emphasising that the language was Braj. How did they manage to stay clear of the Urdu of the *ghazal*-s? Is there any contemporary debate about this?

du Perron:

I am not aware of any such debate, and this is something I would like to look into, in time to come.

Bangha:

I have a question about the purity of the language too. I observed something similar in the 18th century Hindi poetry of, e.g. Ānandghan, who tried to get rid of the *tatsam* and the Persian vocabulary. I am looking for the reason. Do you have any suggestion there?

du Perron:

In terms of *ṭhumrī* I feel that it has very much to do with an effort to make it timeless in some way; it embodies a timeless realm and it really does not want to be linked with anything real, something that we can pin down. That is the beauty of it as an art form: it exists somewhere in the middle. I feel that there is a kind of linguistic manipulation going there, even if I am not sure that it is very conscious.

Old Sants and New Traditions

DANIEL GOLD

As with a number of us, I think my first encounter with India and with Bhakti was the result of happenstance — or destiny, or fortuitous *karma.* I went to India in the late 60s in the Peace Corps. I mentioned India as one of the countries I was interested in, but I was thinking of the Himalayan foothills, not the plains. Peru might also have been nice. If things had been different perhaps I would now be talking to a group of Andeanists, or perhaps not.

I was in a Madhya Pradesh group and landed in Gwalior, where with my recent B.A. I initialised long time teachers into then current methods of teaching English, which I had enthusiastically learned in a three month course. On the side, I got mixed up with some very unorthodox Radhasoamis with whom I am still in touch. Since they weren't in a major lineage, they tended to use texts of the older Sants. And since some of the principal people involved really did use those texts as a guide for internal practice, they commented on them, as well as on some mainline Hindu texts, in terms of yogic experience. This led me to see the Sants as a kind of loose tradition and the *nirguṇa* texts as actually having esoteric meaning. Moreover, since this was an active group, it also led me to see the weight the figure of the guru could have in a devotional tradition with no other ionic image for deity.

This exposure eventually led, after graduate training in history of religions and more years of fieldwork based in U.P. to two books on the Sants as a tradition of holy persons. In addition to examining experience of guru devotion, those books looked at problems of tradition itself:

> the flexibility of lineages without a lot of institutional baggage, which can change dramatically as new gurus take over;
> what happens when baggage does accumulate;
> the inevitable crises at the time of succession;
> the ways in which different lineages regard and relate to one another;

> the ways lineage identify is reflected in texts and collections of texts.

The first book, which presented most of the historical content, was published by Oxford, New York, and was reasonably well distributed. The second, which elaborated on some of the issues of tradition using a specific, rather obscure, U.P. lineage, which included Bhikha and Paltu, was published by a U.S. Academic Press and probably hasn't made it in quantity into European libraries. That book also took up some problems on writing about religion, which have continued to haunt me over the years.

Having become familiar with the Sants, I continued to think about them and write about them now and then over the years since that work was done. This has usually been when cogitating some general question in Indian religions, where the Sants have been a point of reference and favored example. The latest work in this genre is an article soon to appear in the latest of Steven Katz' anthologies on Mysticism and Scripture. Under the rubric of Mysticism and Scripture it deals with issues for contemplative experience posed by the great scriptural diversity found in different Hindu traditions. It is reckoned with differently in different ones, and more interestingly, seems to have different experimental impacts in them. In that article, *nirguṇa* Bhakti figures as a foil for the really *nirguṇa advaita* Vedanta, which the editor wanted covered, and, on the other side, with the Hindi *saguṇa bhakti*, with which it is continuous. As in that article, my forays into Hindi Krishna-Bhakti have generally been to show points of contrast and continuity with the Sants; specialised work on Krishnaite tradition has been left to others who can speak with more authority. But I have also worked on the Nāths, the other main tradition from whom the Sants are said to draw, and that work has been more substantial.

Getting to know a little-studied version of the Nāth tradition was also a matter of happenstance. During the time of my fieldwork on the Sant project, I had the occasion to visit the Rajasthan field site of my future wife, the talented and very prolific anthropologist Ann Grodzins Gold. There I was struck by the songs sung by householder Nāth yogis and their followers. They were similar in many ways to those of the *nirguṇa* repertoire with which I was familiar, but they were often interpreted differently and were given a very different delivery, sung with gusto and ganja to a rural community. Pursuing these songs in their different contexts seemed like an interesting project, and one, moreover, that I could pursue in the same place as Ann.

My work was in part shaped and certainly made easier by the anthropological history of the village. An enterprising folklorist, Joseph Miller, had first come to live there, drawn by a regional epic bard. He then enlisted Ann with the idea that they could share some of the basic ethnographic work. Joe had trained a number of young village men in folkloric methods of exact transcription from tapes. So when I expressed an interest in the songs there was a crew ready who knew just what to do in ways I wouldn't have thought to have asked. One of Joe's old assistants was himself a respected Nāth singer who could explain the Rajasthani in nice Hindi. I visited a few times in the eighties and settled for a half a year in 1993. The last stretch yielded many neatly written files of Nāth *bhajan*-s and key interviews, mosty annotated. The *bhajan*-s still remain mostly unworked and unpublished-folkloric data that I don't quite know what to do with, but to which I occasionally return.

Most of my work then on the Nāths was less on the texts themselves, which I took at face value along with their given explanations, than with the contexts of the songs: on the cultic traditions in which they were used, on the singers and their performances. I was interested in the relationship of the householder Nāths to their ascetic counterparts, and in the ways in which they appropriated the common Nāth tradition. I've written several articles on these topics, and have thought to put them together with some more into an ethnography of the householder Nāths in southeastern Rajasthan, but my enthusiasm for that project is not, at the moment, at one of its peaks. But I may well get back to it some day. A number of intriguing angles remain unexplored.

In the meantime, though, I have since got involved in another project, one that brings me back to my initial Indian roots in Gwalior. A little restless, I confess, with rural Rajasthan, I thought I would look at what's going on in the city I knew from thirty years ago. The project, started in 1997, was to look at urban religious institutions in an ordinary city, and their links to one another and to others in North India. As it naturally turned out, a number of the institutions to which I was drawn were ones with which I felt familiar. I could see old threads of *nirguṇa bhakti*, but they were now taking new institutional directions that if not exactly global were at least regional and interregional.

Most visible to me were issues of succession, change and explosive North Indian expansion at the old unorthodox Radhasoami establishment that I knew earlier. What had been a very local establishment now had vital outputs in several North Indian areas — Banda, U.P., the Jodhpur area; and all over Himachal Pradesh. People of different distinct regional identity — not to mention social strata — were mixing and intermixing. We have sometimes talked about Sants as integrators of traditions; now I was seeing the inheritor of a Sant movement as vehicle of national integration in modern India.

Just down the road from that establishment was the Anandpur *maṭh*. It was very much a Sant lineage like the Radhasoamis, originating in U.P., spreading in the old Northwest provinces, and developing an establishment in the forests of Guna, in the hinterlands of old Gwalior state. At both establishments, verses of Sants are publicly read. With different lineages, though, they tend to ignore one another, serving different functions in separate North Indian networks.

Gwalior has established Nāths, but here Maharashtrian ones, who came with the Scindia rājā-s. Like the Rajasthani Nāths, they too sang *bhajan*-s and told stories, but different ones in an imported regional style. Notable religious figures in town, they maintain close ties to a local Maharashtrian elite.

Also noteworthy is the efflorescence of *qawwālī* in this predominantly Hindu city, where *dargāh*-s are often managed by largely Hindu committees. If Sants sometimes represented points of popular religious contact between Hindus and Muslims in earlier times, *qawwālī* at Sufi *dargāh*-s seems to do in the new India.

I have not yet written up much from this project. I mentioned that issues of writing about religion have haunted me from the beginning. After doing this research I set myself the task of finishing a book on the subject I had started before I left. Since its ideas have been germinating for so long it represents — for those of you familiar with current U.S. religious studies battles — what is by now a rather retrograde position. But it's also a little different, focusing on the aesthetics of the writing. It's tentative title is The Fascinating Science: Modern Dilemmas in Writing on Religion.

Then I will very happily return to my Indological work: first the Gwalior project, and maybe some more on the Nāths. Together, these can keep me busy for quite a few years. But sometimes what I really feel like doing is just translating Sant poetry — some of the more striking songs of less well known Sants. And maybe the stashed–away Nāth *bhajan*-s, too. This may be left for the work of advancing professional, as they say, maturity: I dream about doing the translations poetically, paying attention to rhythm and trying to make nice natural rhymes.

Report on Bhakti Research

JOHN S. HAWLEY

Over the years I have noticed that when it's my turn to speak in these triennial gatherings, the more experienced of you shudder a little and look away, I can see it in your eyes: "Here it comes: the latest lament about the incalculable width of the *Sūrsāgar*. How long has he been working on that thing, anyway? Still not arrived at the other side?"

You're right — still not (at least, not quite) — but I believe I can now see the shoreline. Years ago Kenneth Bryant and I, having collaborated on the collection of manuscripts that would serve as the basis of a new critical edition, decided it would be best to divide the work ahead. With generous help from others (Mandakranta Bose, for example, is present here today), Ken took responsibility for the edition itself and I focused on producing an English verse translation and commentarial essay for each poem. We drew the line at poems that could be shown to have been in circulation in the 16th century, where the manuscript trail ends with the fabulous Fatehpur manuscript of 1582 (now in Jaipur) and when the original Sūrdās (if I may speak in this way) quite probably lived.

Critical editions are an endangered species, and perhaps rightly so: the guns, of course, are postmodern and postcolonial, and the quarry Orientalist. But as Ken suggested when he spoke on this topic in Seattle six years ago, our aim has not been to discover the *ipsissima verba* of the "real" Sūrdās, but to display the process by which the *Sūrsāgar* came to be in its earliest stages. The process of creating this edition — and this translation, I might add — has actually had the opposite effect from reifying an essential or essentialist Sūr. In many cases, thankfully, it's provided a way to reconstruct lost utterances, lost meanings, lost cadences, even lost poems, as an edition ought to do. But it has also demonstrated the extent of variation in this importantly oral tradition even in the 16th century itself, and has pointed to the agency of not one but many singers, audiences, editors, scribes. It's a rich texture — hardly a matter of one author and his one work.

No one number can be correct in stating how many poems are extant from the 16th century, but the Bryant edition now contains 417, with about a dozen others still to be processed. The final number should be either 428 or 430, but come what may, not *cār sau bīs.*

Some of you have waited a long time to know just which poems these are, so I've brought the list of 417 as a handout today. Let me reproduce the first ten entries here.

Bryant Edition / NPS Conversion Table

Crit. Ed.	NPS listing
1	629
2	638
3	642
4	693
5	709
6	710
7	717
8	720
9	733
10	749

Until the edition itself appears, it's the right-hand column that will be of use to you, since the numbers the Nagaripracarini Sabha [NPS] editors attached to the poems are listed there[9].

Comparing the two columns, you'll see that we have elected to order the poems narratively, yet beginning not with the *vinaya* poems, as the Vallabhite reconstruction of Sūr's life would suggest (in the *Caurāsī vaiṣṇavan kī vārtā*), but rather with the birth of Krishna, as is done in a number of 17th century manuscripts from which we draw. This already betrays an orientation toward what Sūr's poems were to become: the *Sūrsāgar*, as of 1640 (with U 1), with a definite narrative line. But a processual view of the corpus reveals that the dual past-and-present orientation of "history" makes this unavoidable in any case, and the narrative line both corresponds to the understanding of those who have treasured

[9] The Nāgarīpracāriṇī Sabhā [NPS] edition being cited is that published in V.S. 2029 (1972 CE). All primary references are to volume 1, published in that year. The appendix appears in volume 2, published in V.S. 2033 (1976 CE).

poems attributed to Sūr and helps along readers who are new to the world of Krishna, Rādhā, Rām, and all.

Once this narrative arrangement has been adopted, it becomes one of the first jobs of the commentary to undo the damage it causes by displaying the individual integrity of each poem. Most are situated within a frame of narrative and even explicitly intertextual awareness, but the secret of their success is their individual coherency. Sometimes it's almost jewel-like. You won't believe me when I tell you that I've pulled out a poem more or less at random to illustrate the sort of thing I hope to do in my essays on individual poems, but it's true. NPS 613, quoted below, which will be listed toward the end of our collection, happened to be where I was in my review process when I realised I might need an exemplar today. And apropos of getting to the other shore of the *Sūrsāgar*, the homecoming motif was attractive. You'll notice that I begin my little comment by saying something about how the poem is thrown into the audience's *medias res*, yet I imply something about the poem's coherency by pointing to how the poet manages to make himself part of his own audience by the time he's done. He becomes a spectator to the arrival of Sītā and Rām in Ayodhya along with the audience he constructs. I try to say something about the "gendering" of the poem along the way: *which* audience does it reconstruct?

NPS 613

1 Kausalyā, elated, rose and ran
2 While Sumitrā emerged from the palace, holding an *āratī* plate.
3 These two were like cows who'd been kept from their calves so the herders could graze them in the forest.
4 At evening, returning with their teats beginning to flow, the mothers were reunited with their little ones.
5 They placed sacred grass, fruit, and curd on golden plates and arranged them in a special way with *āratī* lamps.
6 As girls with trembling voices and lotus-like eyes began to sing auspicious songs.

7 The streets were carpeted with cloths of every hue,
the lanes filled with showers of fragrant flowers,
8 And hearing the sweet clamor of voices below, the
gods in heaven sounded deep *dundhubhi* drums.
9 Then they arrived at home, and then sat down, and
the Brahmins sang out blessings such as these:
10 "For the sake of those to whom you're closely
bound, you and Sītā must dwell in this city forever,
Master of Sūr."

Notes

This poem focuses on the immediate instinct of Kausalyā and Sumitrā, mothers of Rām and Lakshman, to celebrate the return of their sons after years of exile. The poet gives his audience a sense of this immediacy not just by means of what he says, but by what he leaves out. He makes no mention of Lakshman anywhere in the poem, and even Rām is introduced only in the last verse, through locutions that couple him either with the women's side of the family (*siyā sahit tum*, "you and Sītā") or with the poet (*sūr ke sāī*, "Master of Sūr"). Sūr even bypasses the key moment of *darśan* (cf. NPS 611, 614), when Kausalyā and Sumitrā first catch a glimpse of their sons. He rushes instead to its instant effects: how Kausalyā "rose and ran" (*uṭhī dhāī*, v. 1) and Sumitrā appeared at the door holding an *āratī* plate (v. 2). All this would catapult the knowing audience into the moment itself.

They would certainly know the significance of the *āratī* plate, which is used here, as on similar occasions (NPS 4803), to signal auspicious welcome. The informal *āratī* ceremony involves the decoration of a metal plate with various well-omened substances and little cruses that can be lit as lamps (v. 5). Women — especially the senior woman of the house — then wave the tray before the guest or homecoming family member with a clockwise, roughly circular gesture as an act of blessing. The *āratī* 's ritual specificity and its strong associations with women and the home heighten its emotional associations, especially for any women in the audience.

It is indeed noteworthy that so much of the poem is occupied with women (vv. 1-6). Their actions are evidently what catches the gods' attention (v. 8), and even when Brahmin males seize the verbal and ritual reins to utter their own words of blessing, the only name they actually employ is Sītā's. Of course, we know that Rām is also present, for he is addressed with the pronoun "you" (*tum*, v. 10); and Lakshman very likely comes to mind when the poet uses the generic masculine plural to say "they arrived at home, and then sat down" (*nivāse baiṭhe*, v. 9). But just who "they" are is never actually specified.

Perhaps this is Sūr's way of deferring to women's speech patterns by avoiding the actual mention of a man's name. But this absence of strict definition also enables us to envision a whole throng accompanying the protagonists. Then when the Brahmins urge Rām and his companions to stay in Ayodhya "for the sake of those to whom you're closely bound" (*bandhu hit*, v. 10), we can feel that they may have in mind not just the immediate family, but the whole kingdom that is drawn together under Rām's suzerainty. The most common meaning of the word *bandhu* is "relatives" — naturally, we think first and foremost of Kausalyā and Sumitrā — but "friends" may also be implied, and indeed anyone who feels the bond (*bandhu*) of connection.

The poet seems to press this point by placing himself in the crowd. He inserts his own name at an emphatic point, right at the end of the poem, and makes it grammatically impossible for anyone to pass him off as a mere spectator or narrator. This he does by declaring the postposition *ke* (*sūr ke sāī*, "Master of Sūr", v. 10). For Sūr this is an unusual step, and it prevents the "Master" from floating in a self-contained narrative realm that is merely imprinted with his signature. Rām is thus bound to Sūr, who in turn serves as a link between Rām's realm and ours. Is it then for all our sakes that the Brahmins speak as they do?

I hope the act of putting forward a little essay about each poem will suggest to readers that translation is inevitably a split-level process. To represent something of the way the poet anticipates and structures his audience's involvement in the poem often requires — for Sūr, at least — more than translation itself. Luckily, readers will be able to deal with these commentarial essays on a take it or leave it basis. No notes hang like shingles (or vines) from the translation itself.

Time has flown. In closing, let me just tick off some major conclusions that have emerged — for me, at least — in approaching the "other shore" of "Sūr's Ocean."

It is both historically and formally correct to speak of composite authorship in the case of the *Sūrsāgar.* Biologically speaking, there are more "Sūrs" than one, even in the 18th century. But the level of achievement in much of the collection does point, for me, to a distinctive "original" Sūr at the fountainhead of the Sūr tradition, much as it's hard to imagine the Kabīr corpus without an original Kabīr. Nothing has caused me to throw over my earlier conclusion that this Sūr was made to be a pupil of Vallabhācārya only well after the fact. As far as I can see, the 16th century *Sūrsāgar* is not a Vallabhite text.

I doubt that its medium of performance was *dhrupad.* Few poems parse out to four units, and the history of *dhrupad* itself becomes quite hard to reconstruct when one gets back as far as the 16th century. Instead, I'd follow Premlata Sharma in suggesting we think of the musical metier of the early *Sūrsāgar* as *sthāyī antarā,* or as she liked to call it, *pad gāyan.*

Was Sūr in any sense "translating the *Bhāgavat*"? No, not translating, but many poems do show that he knew it well — or at least its legacy-and sometimes he was pleased to stand it a bit on its head for especially attentive and knowledgeable listeners.

Was he blind? Here I'd want to stick with my old conviction that it was the echo between physical and spiritual impairment that overwhelmingly interested him — a trope of its own. And there's no question but that he became blinder and blinder as the *Sūrsāgar* grew into the 17th and subsequent centuries. But the rhetoric of one poem in particular (NPS 135), especially in its critically edited form, makes it hard not to think the "original", biological poet did become blind in old age. This poem goes back to the earliest manuscript (J1).

In my *Sūr Dās* book of 1984, I showed why I didn't think "our" Sūrdās could be the same as the one listed by Abu'l Fazl and Badaunī as belonging to Akbar's entourage. I stick by that. But what about the Sūrdās who appears at the court of Islām Shāh Sūrī, according to the *Afsānah-i-Shāhāṅ* of Muhammad Kabīr? It's tantalising to think of Sūr at the Afghan court, and historically more probable than at the Mughal one — but again I remain skeptical. To me, this passage, where Sūrdās is set alongside

Manjhan, Muhammad Farmūlī, and Mūsan, sounds more like a 17th century proof-text for the excellence of Islām Shāh's taste in "Hindavi" than a family memory to be literally trusted. There's just too much rhetorical intention in the rest of the *Afsānah-i-Shāhān* to see it any other way. One might have hoped that this one chance mention of Sūrdās would have proved the key to unlocking the performative ambiance of the historical Sūrdās — and Aditya Behl thinks it has. Alas, I don't believe we can go that far. When it comes to "the historical Sūrdās" we ourselves remain all too blind.

DISCUSSION

Zelliot:
Your handout with the translation is very handy, precisely because Bhakti poets are so subtle. Since you are somehow inside the mind of Sūrdās, can you tell us why he casts this in the voices and attitudes of women?

Hawley:
Yes, many *Sūrsāgar* poems are phrased in just that way. The male poet speaks in the voice or voices of women. Why? It's certainly not just Sūr, as your question suggests. This is a tradition that goes far back behind the moment when it surfaces in Hindi literature. I once proposed a psycho-genetic explanation for this propensity of the male poet to assume the female role and then address a male deity, but the social or historical answer is probably more persuasive. This tradition of performance existed for a millennium before Sūr.

Zelliot:
It does not seem normal to put a poet in a woman's role in order to pay tribute to the masculine god. And in any case, it does not read like that in this particular poem.

Hawley:
Ah yes, you're right. This is a moment where the poet's interest in the perspectives of women is expressed in "attitudes", as you initially put it, not in "voices". Here he describes how Kausalyā and Sumitrā react, rather than acting it out in their own words. This particular poem actually hinges around the word *vatsa*. It is a poem about *vātsalya bhāv* and the exemplar of *vātsalya bhāv* in the literature of Sūr and many other poets is the mother. In poems about Krishna, this role is usually taken by Yaśodā, or occasionally

by Devakī or even one of the *gopī*-s, but here, since the son in question is primarily Rām, the motherly exemplar is Kausalyā. Because Lakshman is also present, Sumitrā is also included, but she is somewhat ancillary, not mentioned in the title line. Very lovingly, Sūr carries their intense involvement for their "calves" from the boys' childhoods into their full maturity. In this way, the *vātsalya bhāv* becomes even more striking.

For the poet to project that *bhāv*, he projects himself into the primary role of the woman involved and then moves from there to generalise at the end of the poem. In the penultimate line he has Brahmins singing. With this, he separates himself from the attitudes of the women he has been describing and retraces the steps he took implicitly when the poem began. He rejoins the men, in this case the Brahmins who sing. That provides him with a natural place for inserting himself into the poem, which he does with the phrase *sūr ke svāmī*. His explicit use of the postposition *ke* forces his audience to reckon with the fact that he is doing this. It's not just a designation of Rām as "Sūr's Lord" by means of an implicit genitive, the compound *sūr svāmī*. No, he actually marks himself off from his lord by the *ke*, giving himself direct access to the poem.

That postposition makes us reconsider any assumption we may have had about this poem being the production of a disinterested narrator. Just a moment ago, I alluded to the fact that it's far more usual for Sūr to take cover in the persona and voice of one of the characters in Krishna's (or here, Rām's) world than to stand back from it. But in the first nine verses of this poem that's what it sounds like he is doing — just narrating, lah dee dah. And then, with this reference to the position of singer via the Brahmins and with the insertion of the postposition, we realise that the poet really imagines himself as part of the narration after all, not just its mouthpiece.

All this has a gender dimension. The poet uses the Brahmins as a link, but shows us in the end that when he was describing the moods — the attitudes, as you said — of the mothers in question, he was also taking part in what they felt. The lord he was describing is Sūr's Lord: *sūr ke svāmī*. The fact that he is a poet allows Sūr to cross the line between this world, the Bhakti world, into the Lord's world, the luminous world he is describing. The fact that the Lord's world is experienced primarily from a woman's point of view normally shows that this line is something to be reckoned with. Rām's realm — or Krishna's, even more — is experienced from a female point of view, whereas the poet in this world, the person through whom the audience sees them, is male. In this poem that female/male chasm and the *līlā/bhakti* chasm it represents are not so wide. But still it's something to be reckoned with: we need the "Brahmin link" and the explicit postposition to negotiate it. It's always an interesting mix, intimacy (as in *vātsalya bhāv*) and otherness (as in the distance between the immediate realm of performance and the imagined realm of Krishna or Rām). In Sūr's poetry, at least, it's very typical to experience this mix through the language of gender and sexual transposition.

Kabīr Oral Traditions: A Research Proposal

LINDA HESS

[As part of a book that documents the contours of the Kabīr tradition from oral forms through manuscript collections, printed works, mass media, and globalization, I will spend approximately the first eight months of 2002 in India studying living oral traditions. The following research proposal describes the project.]

1. Not bounded, not boundless

We reach the small market town of Maksi after driving five hours from Bhopal. Prahladji and relatives are there to meet us. We must walk through the town first, he says smilingly, it's market day, we shouldn't miss it. A short tour, then we pile into two cars and begin to drive down no-road — just fields, occasionally displaying rutted, rocky, muddy trails. Our city driver with his impeccably curtained white Ambassador is nervous, but within ten minutes we stop at a beautiful village house. The first creatures to greet us are two cows and their calves. A soft white thing just a few days old goes to drink from the wrong mother, and Prahladji gently moves it to the right one, explaining that the other cow will kick it if it gets too close.

We have come to meet Prahladji and get a taste of his singing. It's already 4 p.m. and we must return to Bhopal tonight. From three small buildings, occupied by three brothers and their families, children, women and men pour out — there are fifteen or twenty people, they say, the exact number doesn't seem to matter. Women smile under not-too-strict *ghūnghaṭ*. Prahladji's sister greets us, her face uncovered. Fields, houses, animals, family, wide blue sky, bright afternoon light — to speak of the singing without describing all this would be impossible.

They spread mats and quilts outside the house. Musical instruments appear: harmonium, *dholak*, wooden clappers with bells attached, a tall five-string drone. The three brothers put on colored turbans — at least this much decorum, this much change of costume, is required for the moment of singing Kabīr.

They begin with homage to the guru. Voices are quiet. Prahladji's eyes close. Next comes *maṅgal gīt*, a joyful tune with festive imagery, in the voices of *sahelī*-s, young women. The two brothers on either side of Prahladji sing in perfect unison with him, but always his voice leads. There follow half a dozen songs in different styles and moods, but all in the center of Kabīr tradition as I understand it. No trace of *saguṇa* Bhakti — there is love, but no story of lovers. Prahladji converses with us briefly between songs, telling about themes and styles, answering questions. They sing of the transiency of life:

> A leaf flies from the branch,
> no one knows where the wind will blow it,
> but it won't go back to its old place.
> The tree speaks to the leaf: listen!
> When you go, another sprouts.

They sing of the arrogance of pandits and qazis. They sing *ulaṭbāmsī*, the "upside-down language" of paradoxes and haunting humor. They sing of a state beyond duality:

> Man, bounded
> Saint, boundless.
> Kabīr, not bounded, not boundless.

Their songs touch the deepest modes of Kabīr's *nirguṇa* truth but are still full of earth's imagery.

As they sing, the light changes. A three-quarter moon rises over the house, stars appear. The air is dark but filled with moonlight, and they keep singing. Our conversation enters the darkness and moonlight. Someone lights a fire. The cows and calves seem to be listening, their white coats glowing. Silently, more people have joined the circle, materialising from somewhere. Prahladji ends the concert with an *ulaṭbāmsī* and goes off to see that dinner is being prepared.

We're told that two other parties have arrived — men from a neighboring village who want us to hear their singing. New accompanists slide into place. The younger one starts. His voice is not so full, and our companion from the Madhya Pradesh Adivasi

Lok Kala Parishad in Bhopal advises him in a friendly way to open up his throat. The next singer is excellent. We observe the dynamic nature of oral tradition: Instead of the arrow of the Word (*śabda*), we hear that the bullet of the Word may strike us. Instead of a bullock cart as image for the body, there is a railway train.

Prahladji's songs have no bullets or railway trains. But he hands us a dozen commercially recorded cassettes, some of which we have seen in a store on the way here. His presence will support no easy dichotomies between "tradition" and "modernity."

A village schoolteacher in his 40s, Prahladji cultivated a talent and a love for singing Kabīr *bhajan*-s and in ten years became something of a regional star. Successful performances in the region led to tours of increasing frequency and length. Invitations to Bhopal and Delhi, radio and TV appearances, and cassettes followed. His business card, Hindi on one side and English on the other, says, "P.S. Tapaniya, Radio and TV Artist. Kabīr singer, Malvi folk style, bhajan, folk music." He still teaches school, despite his busy schedule and growing prominence.

In the mid-90s Prahladji began to produce an annual Kabīr festival on open land near his house, with many singers and audiences that run in the tens of thousands. He has built a monument, a Kabīr Smarak, celebrating the great sage's multifaceted wisdom. The all-night festival is held at the end of April, intentionally correlated with Buddha Jayanti. Pictures of B.R. Ambedkar are seen on the walls of Prahladji's house, along with hand-painted couplets of Kabīr.

When I ask if the women also sing Kabīr, Prahladji says, "Oh yes", adding that his wife has performed on All India Radio. But for our eyes, on this occasion, the women sit with the children, they cook the food, they smile under their sari-ends. A longer stay here will enable me to become friends with them, to learn their ways of singing and participating in the culture that I have just glimpsed.

2. My Previous Kabīr Work and the Present Project

I began studying, translating, and writing about Kabīr in 1976, always working from published texts. With Prof. Shukdev Singh of Banaras Hindu University I translated the *Bījak*, the eastern tradition of Kabīr texts; our translation, with my scholarly essays and notes, was published in the U.S. and India in 1983, is still in print in India, and is under contract with Oxford University Press for reissue in the U.S. An abridged version was published by Shambhala in 1994. This work has received wide use and recognition.

From the mid-80s to the late 90s I worked on Tulsīdās and the Rāmlīlā performance. During this period my interest shifted from the exclusive text-centeredness of my early training to reception study and performative practice and experience. Intimate study of the literary text did not disappear, but became part of this larger picture.

Several special scholarly meetings were held in 1998-99 in honor of Kabīr's 600th birth anniversary; I was invited to participate in such meetings in San Francisco, London, Heidelberg and Banaras. Contacts there stimulated new thinking and opened up new work for me. After meeting poet and professor Kedar Nath Singh, I translated his long poem *Uttar Kabīr.* The eminent Hindi critic Namvar Singh introduced me to other modern poets who had written on Kabīr-related themes and encouraged me to translate them. In London, Mukund Dvivedi, the son of Hazari Prasad Dvivedi, approached me and said he had been looking for me for years. A number of people had asked for permission to translate his father's famous book *Kabīr* into English, but he wanted me to do it. I have started this project.

In 1998 an unusual request inspired me and launched the present project. Christopher Rouse, a Pulitzer Prize-winning American composer, had been commissioned by the Minnesota Symphony to write a song cycle. Drawing on exposure to Indian music years earlier, he chose to write *Kabīr Padāvalī* — six Kabīr songs, to be sung in Hindi, woven together in a half-hour piece for soprano and 80-member orchestra. Rouse called on me for help in transliteration and translation of the Hindi texts. The experience of working with him and the singer, Dawn Upshaw, to prepare for the premiere in Minneapolis (which I attended) stimulated a great deal of fresh thinking about the nature of the Kabīr tradition in particular and of cultural movement in general. I gave several conference papers with "Kabīr Goes Global" in the title, and I conceptualised the book to which the proposed research will contribute — *Kabīr Says: From Oral Tradition to Globalization.*

The book will examine the nature of transmission in the Kabīr tradition, considering what may be meant by "oral tradition" and how the process of cultural spread becomes gradually more complex, including oral forms, manuscript collections, print, cassettes, CDs, TV, film, the internet, and the global market — with each of these processes modifying, but never eliminating the others.

2.1. Oral Traditions

Kabīr oral traditions are so abundant that an attempt to "cover" them would not be wise. In deciding to draw deeply on a particular place, with emphasis on a single performer in his cultural context, I draw inspiration from Kirin Narayan (1997) and Ann Gold (Raheja and Gold 1994, Gold 1995, Gold 1992). I intend to stay in or near Prahladji's village (Lunakhedi, Dist. Ujjain) for several months, sometimes going on tour with him, learning about the network of Kabīr traditions in the region, getting to know the family and the gendered aspects of this tradition. I intend to stay in or near Prahladji's village (Lunakhedi, Dist. Ujjain) for some time, sometimes going on tour with him, learning about the network of Kabīr traditions in the region, getting to know the family and the gendered aspects of this tradition. I also intend to learn to sing this music, from Prahladji and from the women. The period of research in M.P. will culminate with the Kabīr festival at the end of April.

While the study of Prahladji will be the centerpiece of this section, there will also be other components. Since Kabīr's lifetime, his songs have traveled in India through local folk music forms, classical music, and sadhu singing, and his *Bāṇī* is dynamically present in people's memory and conversation. I will present a larger picture of oral transmission, historically and in the present. There will be a chapter on classical music, focusing on the famous renditions of Kabīr by Kumar Gandharva. My attention was drawn to Kumar Gandharva's Kabīr by U.R. Ananthamurthy, who, on a visit to Berkeley in the early 90s, urged me to collect, study, and translate the songs Kumar sang. As president of the Sāhitya Akademi at that time, he said that the Akademi would be interested in publishing such a study along with cassettes of the songs. Kumar Gandharva lived in Dewas, not far from Prahladji's village. An innovative and experimental classical singer, he was deeply influenced by local folk music styles. On my recent visit I learned that Kumar's son lives nearby and performs; his widow also continues to perform and possesses a large archive of Kumar's performances and collections. Ashok Vajpeyi, current Vice Chancellor of Mahatma Gandhi International Hindi University, knew Kumar well, has written extensively on his art, and is ready to help me in this undertaking.

Additionally, in fall 2001, I will travel to various Kabīr Panth *maṭh*-s in Madhya Pradesh, Uttar Pradesh, and Bihar to listen to *bhajan*-s and *dohā*-s as sung by Kabīr Panth sadhus. A chapter or section on Kabīr Panth performers will be incorporated into this part of the book.

2.2. Written Traditions

This section will give a comprehensive account of the manuscript and print history of works attributed to Kabīr. My 1987 article, "Three Kabīr Collections: A Comparative Study", presents the histories and analyses the contents of the three major regional/sectarian manuscript sources — the Sikh tradition in Punjab, the Dādū Panthī tradition in Rajasthan, and the Kabīr Panthī tradition in U.P. and Bihar). It discusses the different "Kabīr" personalities that emerge in eastern and western traditions and theorises on the core characteristics of Kabīr's personality and style. That article is still considered a significant contribution to Kabīr textual studies. However, important new manuscript work has been done since then, providing earlier dated texts than were previously available and ways of distinguishing between earlier and later layers of manuscript sources. G. S. Mann has published the ca. 1572 manuscript precursors to the Sikh *Ādi Granth* (1604), previously the earliest attested source. J.S. Hawley has reported on fifteen Kabīr poems in the 1582 Fatehpur manuscript. And Winand Callewaert has brought all this and much more together in the "Millennium Edition" of Kabīr, based on the earliest dated manuscripts from the western (Punjabi and Rajasthani) sources. For many years Callewaert has been collecting manuscripts and preparing editions of North Indian *nirguṇa* poetry. The "Millennium" Kabīr includes 593 poems, with variants, from manuscripts dated ca. 1570-1669. Callewaert has asked me to do a book of translations based on this edition. I have selected 145 of the earliest poems and have begun the translation work. Since the *Bījak*, which I translated earlier, represents the eastern tradition, this project will give me a thorough familiarity with all the early sources of the written Kabīr.

2.3. Globalization

My first conference paper to broach this topic had "From Sadhus to CDs" in the subtitle. Sitting in the Minneapolis Symphony Hall on January 7, 1999, I found myself in a state of *adbhuta rasa* — absolute wonder that the illiterate, abrasive weaver of 15th century Banaras should have arrived at this place and been interpreted and performed in this way. Was something of the original Kabīr present here? How did he get here? What does it mean that cultural "products" from all over the world have entered global flows and markets? When did this process start? What stages should be distinguished in the big transmission picture? What aspects of this process are benign, what aspects pernicious, what aspects simply wondrous? For now, many questions. The answers will come from study of cultural globalization theory and from my unfolding experience and reflection as I research and write *Kabīr Says*.

BIBLIOGRAPHY

Appadurai, Arjun, 1996, *Modernity at Large: Cultural Dimensions of Globalization.* Minneapolis: University of Minnesota Press.

Callewaert, Winand & B. Op de Beeck, eds., 1991, *Devotional Hindi Literature: A Critical Edition*, 2 vols., New Delhi: Manohar Publications.

Callewaert, Winand, Swapna Sharma & Dieter Taillieu, eds., 2000 *The Millennium Kabīr Vani*, New Delhi: Manohar Publications.

Chaturvedi, P., 1964, *Uttarī Bhārat kī sant paramparā*, Allahabad: Bharati Bhandar,

Dvivedi, H.P., 1971, *Kabīr* (Hindi), Delhi: Rājkamal Prakāśan.

Gold, Ann G., ed., 1995, "Mother Ten's Stories", in *Religions of India in Practice*, ed. Donald S. Lopez, Princeton: Princeton University Press.

Donald S. Lopez, 1992, *A Carnival of Parting*, Berkeley: Univ. of California Press.

Hawley, John S., 1998, "Kabīr in His Oldest Dated Manuscript", Paper presented at annual meeting of American Academy of Religion, San Francisco.

Hess, Linda, 1987, "Three Kabīr Collections: A Comparative Study", in *The Sants: Studies in a Devotional Tradition of*

India, ed. Karine Schomer and W.H. McLeod, Berkeley: Religious Studies Series & Delhi: Motilal Banarsidass.

Hess, Linda & Shukdev Singh, trans., 1983, *The Bījak of Kabīr*, Essays and Notes by L. Hess, San Francisco: North Point Press & Delhi: Motilal Banarsidass.

Lorenzen, David N., 1997, *Praises to a Formless God: Nirguni Texts from North India*, Albany: State University of New York Press.

Mann, G.S, 2000, *The Making of Sikh Scripture*, New York: Oxford University Press.

Manuel, Peter, 1993, *Cassette Culture: Popular Music and Technology in North India*, Chicago: University of Chicago Press.

Narayan, Kirin with Urmila Devi Sood, 1997, *Mondays on the Dark Night of the Moon: Himalayan Foothill Folktales*, New York: Oxford University Press.

Raheja, Gloria G. & Ann G. Gold, 1994, *Listen to the Heron's Words: Reimagining Gender and Kinship in North India*, Berkeley: Univ. of California Press.

Vajpeyi, Ashok, 1982, *Kumar Gandharva* (Hindi), New Delhi: Rājkamal Prakāśan.

Vaudeville, Charlotte, 1974, *Kabīr*, vol. 1, Oxford: Clarendon Press.

— 1994, *A Weaver Named Kabīr*, New Delhi: Oxford Univ. Press.

Research Report

NASEEM HINES

Locating and duplicating the manuscripts of *Cāndāyan*, a 14th century Sūfi text composed in Avadhi, by Maulānā Dā'ūd, a disciple of the saint Nizām al-Dīn Auliā (d. 1325) has kept me busy for the last few months. The *Cāndāyan* manuscripts play a key role in my preparation and carrying out within the next two to three years, a critical study and English translation of *Cāndāyan.*

Dā'ūd's *Cāndāyan* belongs to a genre of mediaeval Hindi literature generally known as the 'Sūfi Masnavī' or 'Literary Allegorical Romance', of which the most well known example is Malik Muhammad Jāyasī's 16th century *Padmāvat.* Although *Cāndāyan* is perhaps not as well known as *Padmāvat,* it is nevertheless a work of comparable artistic merit and historical importance, and scholars, including Mataprasad Gupta, Shyam Manohar Pandey, Parashuram Caturvedi, Shiv Kumar Shandilya, and Charlotte Vaudeville have studied various aspects of the work. Several published editions of the work have appeared in Hindi, but to my knowledge, no full translation of *Cāndāyan* into a European language has as yet been published.

Cāndāyan is generally considered to be the earliest Masnavī written in Avadhi, the eastern most dialect of Hindi, and for this reason alone, *Cāndāyan* is often considered an important landmark in the development of North Indian vernacular literatures. The genre of the Masnavī possesses a long history even before its appropriation by Dā'ūd for his *Cāndāyan.* In terms of its contents, the Masnavī can be characterised as an allegorical romance involving elements of love, quest, adventure, suffering, and subsequent transformation and/or redemption.

From the *Cāndāyan* of Parmeshwarilal Gupta, and from the critical edition of *Cāndāyan* of Mataprasad Gupta, published in 1964 and 67 respectively, I gathered the basic information regarding the location, condition, and script of some of these manuscripts. As valuable as the above studies are, it may be pointed out that there are several weaknesses that stem from the fact that both the editions of *Cāndāyan* are Hindi editions, printed in Devanāgarī, filtering the text through a Hindi language perspective. The majority of early manuscript texts of *Cāndāyan*, however, are in Perso-Arabic script. In the process of transcribing manuscripts of *Cāndāyan* into a Devanāgarī format numerous errors and misinterpretations have been introduced which have some bearing on the precise nature of my own research.

For example, consider these opening lines of *Cāndāyan*, followed by Mātāprasād Gupta's explanation from his edition of *Cāndāyan*:

पहलै गाउं सिरजनहारू
जिनि सिरज्या यह देस दयारु
सिरजसि धरती और अगासू
सिरजसि मेर मंदर कबिलासू

First of all I praise the Creator
who has created this country and this region;
who created the earth and the sky,
and gave form to Meru, Mandar and Kailās
(M. Gupta 1967:73)

A few years ago in the course of studying *Cāndāyan*, which led to my dissertation *The Sufi Elements in the Indo-Sufi Masnavī with Specific Reference to Maulana Daud s Cāndāyan*, I first read the above lines and Mataprasad Gupta's explanation.

In my mind's eye, I could see the word कबिलासू written in the Arabic script, and although in terms of orthography, in the Devanāgarī script, the letters ब and व are very similar, in the Arabic script, the grapheme representing the above consonants are very different. Additionally, taking into consideration that the short vowels are not always indicated in the Arabic script, it was hard for me to accept that कबिलासू should be interpreted as mount Kailāsa. Moreover, in terms of linguistics also, the transformation of कबि to कै appears to be far-fetched.

The question then is what are the other possible words that may fit the context? Could it be, once the meaningless words are rooted out किबलासू? Considering the fraternal customs of the Sufi teachers, the above does not seem to be outside the realm of possibilities. Scholars of *Cāndāyan* agree that in rewriting the folk-tale of *Lorik-Cāndā* as a vehicle for presenting Sufism to the uninitiated general public, Maulānā Dā'ūd selected a very popular indigenous oral epic. His goal was to present an entertaining narrative in which Sufi thought may blend with more familiar elements. To put Meru, Mandar and *qibla*, the holy places to the Hindus as well as the Muslims, in a compact poetic line of only four words made perfect sense because the reexamined poetic line is in absolute conformity with the harmonising practices of the Sufis.

If, momentarily we hypothesise that the word in question is किबलासू, let us examine the changes that occur in the *kaḍvak* (a stanza like composition) in terms of poetics. If *qiblāsu* replaces *kailāsu*, the following pattern appears:

> पहलै गाउं सिरजनहारू, जिनि सिरज्या यह देस दयारु
> सिरजसि धरती और अगासू, सिरजसि मेर मंदर *किबलासू*

The first seven words of the first line are derived from the Avadhi lexicon. However, the eighth word, *dayāru*, which completes the line, is from the Perso-Arabic lexicon. In conformity to this pattern, the next seven words again are from the Avadhi vocabulary. The sixteenth and the last word *qiblāsu* comes from the Perso-Arabic lexicon. If the changes are found to be correct, this *kaḍvak* would confirm Maulānā Dāūd's brilliant craftsmanship.

This raises two major questions. First, how can we confirm that the word in question is indeed किबलासू? Secondly, if other substitutions, alterations or distortions have been introduced to accommodate a political agenda in the text or interpretation of the existing editions of *Cāndāyan*, namely the first edited by Dr. Parmeshwarilal Gupt in 1964, and the second by Dr. Mataprasad Gupt in 1967, also known as the Vārāṇasī edition.

Going back to the need to clear up incorrect information with regards to *Cāndāyan*, it may be pointed out that former scholarship claimed that *Cāndāyan* is composed entirely in the Hindi language. Nevertheless, it is very apparent that this statement also needs to be reexamined.

It is my sincere belief that the only way to clear up many of these misinterpretations and wrong representations is to go back and directly examine the original manuscripts, paying particular attention to those in the Arabic script and particularly noting cases where the original Avadhi as recorded in Perso-Arabic script is amenable to multiple interpretations. It is in the study, interpretation, and translation of *Cāndāyan* with particular reference to Arabic script manuscripts that I see the major contribution of my research project at hand.

BIBLIOGRAPHY

Gupta, Mataprasad, ed. *Cāndāyan*, Agra: Durga Printing Works, 1967.

DISCUSSION

Horstmann:
To what extent will the readings vary from the critical edition that we have now? Even having looked only at certain pages, what can one extrapolate from that?

Hines:
Mātāprasād reads कबिलासू and translates as 'Kailāś'. As short vowels were not accounted for in the Persian manuscripts I would rather read किबलासू. That makes perfect sense to me, thinking about the syncretic dimension of the Sufis.

de Bruijn:
Is the Manchester manuscript illustrated?

Hines:
Oh yes. One side of each folio has a colour miniature painting. On the facing side, in Persian prose, the episode is introduced.

The *kaḍvak*, a stanza-like poetic composition, follows in Avadhi. The *Cāndāyan* manuscript in the Manchester's John Ryland Library is very beautiful and well preserved. We still do not know what the end of Maulānā Dā'ūd's *Cāndāyan* would have been, if we had the entire text. The only basis on which we can build a hypothesis about the way it ends, is to be found in the oral tradition. The oral traditions of *Cāndāyan*, known as *Lorikī* or *Laur-Chandā* considerably differ from Dā'ūd's *Cāndāyan*, in the sense that there are two *sarpa-daṅśa* episodes in the written *masnavī*, while there is only one *sarpa-daṅśa* episode, at the very beginning, in the oral tradition. In Maulānā Dā'ūd's *Cāndāyan* (consists of 397 *kaḍvak*-s) the two *sarpa-danśa* episodes (308-329) are situated towards the end of the story, where Lorik, the protagonist or the mystic arrives at the pinnacle of his spiritual conquest[10].

de Bruijn:

Are you going to do anything with the illustrations?

Hines:

I asked permission of the Prince of Wales Museum and they said that I could reproduce the miniatures if I give them the credit. In Manchester it is different and I have to ask for permission for the particular paintings that I want to use for my book.

Callewaert:

These illustrations could perhaps be used for the poster of the Bhakti Conference you may organise in 2012 or earlier!

Hines:

I can further add that the *Masnavī* of Maulānā Rūmī (1258-1273) had a profound influence on *Cāndāyan*, which was completed in 1379. The next well-known work is Jāysī's *Padmāvat* (1540). Some of the *kaḍvak*-s of *Cāndāyan* are irregular in their metrical structure in terms of both the number of prescribed *mātrā*-s in a *yamaka* and the number of *yamaka*-s in a *kaḍvak*[11]. During the time that elapsed between 1379 and 1540, the poets had time to standardise the poetic form of *kaḍvak* which was still in a very fluid state in Dā'ūd's times. What makes the study of *Cāndāyan* most interesting and exciting to me, both in terms of subject matter, poetic style and prosody is that in terms of contents it offers the spirituality of Rūmī's *Masnavī* and in terms of language and poetry it is composed during the most interesting phase of the development of the Avadhi language and the *kaḍvak* meter.

---

[10] For more details, see Hines Naseem, "The Snake-bite Episodes in *Cāndāyan*: A Journey within a Journey", In Entwistle, Alan D. & Carol Salomon & Michael C. Shapiro, eds., *Studies in Early Modern Indo-Aryan Languages, Literature and Culture*, New Delhi, Manohar, 1999.

[11] For more details, see Hines, Naseem, *The Sūfī Elements in the Indo-Sūfī Masnavī, with Specific Reference to Maulana Daud's Candayan*, 1997, UMI Dissertation Services, Ann Arbor, Michigan.

Research Report, 1998-2000

MONIKA HORSTMANN

None of the research that I am engaged in presently or plan for the future fits the description of 'research on early literature in New Indo-Aryan languages'. Either my material is New Indo-Aryan allright, but then rather of an archival kind, or it is Bhakti-literature, but written in Sanskrit or a modern vernacular. I mention this because my case is rather than unique quite common. It only exemplifies that Bhakti studies have become more encompassing in several ways, but also, as one notices with regret, that a great number of genuinely early NIA Bhakti literary texts still desperately await a thorough study.

My research geographically focuses on eastern Rajasthan with occasional spill-overs into Braj. Over the years, I have moved away from literary studies in the narrower sense of the word to the study of historical documents relating to Bhakti. In my current projects, I am combining the study of literary texts with that of documents. My recent publications and ongoing interest can be put under the broad title "The relationship between religion and the state in eastern Rajasthan". In terms of sectarian orientation, I sustain interest in the Sant tradition, especially the Dādūpanth, but have for some time also pursued research pertinent to the Gauḍīya *sampradāya* (Horstmann, 1999) and, quite recently, the Rāmānandīs.

I will delineate the scope of my interest by taking my presently principal long-term project as an illustration and will also point out how my concluded research fits into my current projects. In 1999, I have started collecting archival material relating to the Rāmānandīs. Here it is specifically their Laśkarī (militant) branch that attracts my interest. This group is popularly called the Bālānandīs, after Bālānand who is credited to have conclusively organised the fighting Vaishnava sadhus in the 18th century. Bālānand (abbotship 1752-1794) lived in, and operated from, Jaipur. He rose to great political prominence in the regnal period of

Mādhav Singh (1750-1768) and was a contemporary of four Mahārājās of Jaipur. The military glory of the Vaishnava sadhus whithered in consequence of the Pax Britannica, though they recaptured some prominence at the time of the Mutiny. The status that they had acquired by their military support of regional powers, however, had enabled them to participate in a political network that outlasted their military activities. When in the first part of the 19th century circumstances compelled them to recast their role in the religious arena, they benefited from this network. So far, I have collected a fair amount (altogether ca. 2,200 microfilm frames) of letters, memoirs, revenue papers and also manuscripts of religious texts scribed for Bālānand himself and his successors, respectively; among the last-mentioned type of texts interestingly also a *paddhati* prior to the existence of the Laśkarī Rāmānandīs in Jaipur, but used by them and linking them with the wider Pāñcaratra tradition also adhered to by the Gauḍīya-s. From the esteem that these texts traditionally enjoy with the Bālānandī–s and from the fact that manuscripts thereof were commissioned by their abbots, we can conclude that they served their personal interest and actual requirements.

At present, I am attempting to tackle the historically and in some way also ideologically basic issue of how the militant Rāmānandīs acquired rank and status in the Jaipur kingdom, what vehicles serving this end they were able to mobilise, and how, in the process, they cast their role within the wider spectre of the religious groups active in the region. They had to compete and cooperate with religious groups already in ritual power at the Jaipur court. Foremost among these figured the representatives of the ancient Rāmānandī branch of Galtā (established by Kṛṣṇadās Payahārī in the 16th century) whose deities protected (and continue protecting) and legitimised the Jaipur dynasty. There were a number of additional Vaishnava groups who had direct access to the political sphere, most conspicuous among these the Gauḍīya–s who as custodians of the deity Govinddevjī since the beginning of the 18th century had become the representatives of the second Vaishnava deity protective of the Jaipur royal family (for the historical processes related to this, see Horstmann 1999 where I have studied the grants promulgated by the Kachavāhās in favour of that deity). The evidence so far available for Bālānand and his predecessor Vrijānand (d. 1752), who inaugurated the Laśkarī lineage of the Rāmānandīs in Jaipur around 1720, is limited and does not enable us to directly follow the debates going on during the period when these Rāmānandīs inserted themselves in the politico-religious field of Jaipur and the wider region. Vrijānand seems to have built on existing connections in Braj. For both him and Bālānand we have to reckon with personalities who took great care to religiously stabilise their position. They were alert to what this required, namely, above all ritual rank emanating from a *vigraha* or 'divine image as object of veneration' and a ritual bona fide status with the thence ensuing financial gains (royal grants, tax immunities, etc.).

This was all the more a pressing need because of the long-established ritual position of the Galtā Rāmānandīs who were in charge of vital royal cult objects. In the very beginning of the Bālānandīs' presence in Jaipur, no *vigraha* is mentioned. This is not to deny that it may have existed, but to state that it did not yet figure in establishing the Bālānandīs' rank at court. More precisely, the court, that is, the Mahārājā or his entourage are not yet recorded to have entertained a relationship with it that was sanctioned by the protocol. The springboard of their rise to rank and status (here I use the distinction usefully introduced by Emmanuel LeRoy Ladurie in *Saint-Simon ou le système de la Cour*, Paris 1997) was rather a *vigraha* of Krishna which they could acquire from Kṛṣṇadeva, Jaisingh's chief Gauḍīya theologian. In the years after Kṛṣṇadeva's death, this cult object was claimed back by his relatives. The deity had come to the Bālānandīs along with a comfortable royal grant that was, to their great advantage and in evidence of their by then unassailable position, not resumed by the state.

The Bālānandīs, like their Galtā confrères, traced themselves back to Rāmānuja, as was to be expected especially after Jaisingh's reform of the Vaishnava sects in the period of roughly the 1720s and 1730s. Within a fairly short span, they consolidated their status by giving prominence to specific Ramaite *vigraha*-s and by acquiring and building several important temples in the Jaipur State. Their fast consolidating rank and relations with the Jaipur court can be gleaned from the court protocol which, when examined in a comparative perspective that takes account also of their Galtā confrères, is here pertinent (in preparation); a preliminary essay on the court protocol needs methodological reconsideration (forthcoming).

The relationship between the Bālānandīs and Kṛṣṇadeva leaves us with an uneasy scope for speculation, but it certainly goes to show how close the newcomers were to the inner circle of

Vaishnava experts who helped Jaisingh formulate his unified system of Vaishnavism. In order to better understand this, I am presently also engaged in studying Kṛṣṇadeva's treatises commissioned by Jaisingh (a short preliminary essay is forthcoming).

It is in this way that I hope that the relations and debates sustained between the religious and political agents in prominence especially from around 1720 will gain sharper contours, especially if supplemented by more evidence on the activities of Jaisingh's theological counsellors. Much supplementary evidence — theological texts and ritual treatises — is contained in the library of the City Palace of Jaipur the authorities of which, however, over the last few years, have been adverse to its holdings being microfilmed.

The theological issues of the 18th and 19th century[12] were as much religious as political ones and were conducted by *śāstrī*-s within the frame of their systems. These concepts of Bhakti are so prominent and powerful that they tend to obscure other, equally important aspects of Bhakti as it has thrived in Rajasthan. Recently, in a book addressing problems surrounding the Rāmdev cult and related traditions[13], Dominique-Sila Khan has persuasively reminded us of this. These currents in the Bhakti-traditions have, for some sects at least, fallen into oblivion. As far as the present period is concerned, in some cases it would even be an exaggeration to talk of suppression of, or animosity against, existing counter-currents, for this would presuppose an awareness that is simply missing. This is why I wish to conclude my academic projects on Bhakti by the preservation and study of *guṭkā*-s of Dādūpanthī origin of which two to three hundred are preserved in the main temple of the sect in Naraina. These devotional compilations produced for private usage and thus reflecting personal preferences usually name their compilers/scribes along with their geographical and spiritual affiliation. In those *guṭkā*-s, texts of various traditions survive, be they Muslim, Nāth or of various other origin awaiting examination.This project is to start in 2002.

---

[12] For this see Catherine Clémentin-Ojha's superb *Le trident au palais*, Paris 1999.

[13] Dominique-Sila Khan, *Conversions and Shifting Identities*, Delhi, 1997.

As for the Dādūpanth, I have recently devoted a paper, based on hagiographical texts and historical documents that cover the period from the 18th century to the beginning of the 20th, to food transfer as a key symbol of group structure and solidarity as a central concept in the sect (forthcoming). It also shaped the code for conduct of the sect. Couched in the broader frame of the concept of food transfer as it prevails in Rajput society as a symbol of elitarian brotherhood, the concept had a strong economic and political impact. It attributed to the territorial expansion of the sect and, over the centuries, it has helped stabilise its structure.

To conclude, another project now nearing completion is concerned with a genuine piece of Bhakti-literature, this time from the 20th century. I am going to publish a study and translation of the spiritual autobiography of a woman saint from the Marwari community which was also composed in Marwari, in the year 1956, one year before she died and in anticipation of her demise. I am here especially intrigued by the way in which the author, who as a member of the mobile and modernising Marwari business community, meaningfully constructed her life largely by the example of popular theology and hagiography. Methodologically this requires a two-tier treatment, namely, a literary study of the text and its strategies and a separate, but complementary study of the discourses conducted on its author, either in biographical treatises composed by eye-witnesses or by relatives (for a preliminary essay, see Horstmann 1999).

Research on Various Traditions in Devotional Literature

BALWANT JANI

Devotional literature of the mediaeval Gujarātī tradition

Madhyakālin gūjarātī jñānmārgī kavitā, Ahmedabad: Pārśva Prakāśan, 1990.
Including an extensive article (70 pp.) on the history of 600 years of mediaeval Gujarati tradition of philosophical poetry, with 108 compositions and a bibliography. The Preface also focuses on the following topics: introduction to the important philosophical poets; the philosophical doctrines of the *jñān mārg*, seen in the works of the main poets; works by important philosophical poets; selection, rejection and additions to the traditional context; the form of path of philosophical knowledge; line of folk tradition; reflections on the criticism of mediaeval Gujarātī philosophical poetry.

Devotional cults based on the Vaishnava tradition

Praṇāmī cult

Prāṇanāth svāmījivan-kavanuṁ ākalan, in Svādhyāya ane saṁśodhan. Gandhinagar, Sāhitya Akademi, 2000.
A detailed introduction to the life and literature of Prāṇanāth Svāmī, the founder of the Praṇāmī cult.
Prāṇanāth svāmī kṛt bārmāsī. Samitpāni, Ahmedabad, Pārśva Prakāśan, 2000.
A study in the doctrines of the Praṇāmī cult in the form of Bārmāsī, and their application in the context of Krishna devotion.
Praṇāmī sampradāy ane kirantano, Samitpāni, Ahmedabad, Pārśva Prakāśan, 2000.
An introduction to the Praṇāmī cult's *sādhanā*, through *kīrtan pad*-s.

Svāmīnārāyaṇ cult

Re sagapaṇ harivaranuṁ sācu, Ahmedabad, Navbharat Prakāśan, 2000.
Comprehensive introduction to the collected poetry of Brahmānanda of the Swaminarayan Cult.
Kṛṣṇa caritramūlak bārmāsī, Mumbai, Forbes Gujarātī Sabhā, 1993.
A comprehensive study of 18 *Barmāsī*-s belonging to the traditions of Krishna devotion and mediaeval folk literature.
Bṛhat kāvyadohan 1. Padmālā Mūlak, Gandhinagar, Gujarat Sāhitya Akademi, 1999.
Detailed introduction (90 pp.) to the mediaeval Gujarati devotional literature, including an edition of some narrative poems from the *Bṛhat Kāvyadohan*.
Bṛhat kāvyadohan: 2. Kathāmūlak, Gandhinagar, Gujarāt Sāhitya Akademi, 1999.
Edition of narrative devotional poems, 110 pp.
Madhyaugīan Gūjarātī ūrmikāvyo, New Delhi, Sāhitya Akademi; 1998.
Edition of 108 devotional compositions from 900 years of mediaeval Gujarati literature.

Devotional narrative literature

Bhālaṇanāṁ kāvyo, Ahmedabad, Ādarś Prakaśan, 1985.
Fixing the date of Bhālaṇ this is a comprehensive introduction to the *upāsanā* devotion of Bhālaṇ, illustrated with extracts from the works of the poet; edition with annotations.
Rāmavivāh ākhyān by Bhālaṇ, Ahmedabad, Rāṇaḍe Prakāśan, 1991.
Editio princeps of the *Rāmavivāh ākhyān*, based on an old manuscript, including a prose translation into Gujarati, and a study on Bhālaṇ's contribution to Gujarati literature, in particular the context of devotional poetry of Pātaṇ (North Gujarat).
Rāmāvalā by Sri Hardās, Gandhinagar, Gujarat Sāhitya Akademi, 1992.
Compilation of oral Rāmāyaṇa traditions in *duhā* form, which is compared with other devotional currents.

Devotional literature of the folk-religious tradition

Pad-bhajan sūcī. Gandhinagar: Gujarat Sāhitya Akademi; 1994.
Index of ca. 10,000 *pada-s* of devotional literature, together with an authorwise classification.
Santavāṇī-tattva ane tantra. Gandhinagar: Gujarat Sāhitya Akademi; 1996.
A collection and study of the devotional literature belonging to folk-religious traditions, which focuses upon the *bhajan sant-vāṇī*, like *raveṇī* and *pyālo*, and the continuity of the devotional traditions of Mahāpanth, Nāthapanth, and Ravībhāṇapanth. A sketch of the lives of women saints, and their literature, complements this study.
Oral traditional Gujarātī literature, Ahmedabad, Pārśva Prakāśan, 1996.
A study of traditional oral Bhakti literature (songs), and the rituals associated with these.
Vahīvañcā bārot: Parīcay and pradān, Gandhinagar, Gujarāt Sāhitya Akademi, 1996.
A collection of genealogical records, and a critical study of their interpretation.
The Contribution of Women Saints to the Saint Literature of Saurāshtra.
A critical study on the works of women saints, in particular Amarbāi, Lirbāi and Toral.
Hagiography of Mahāpanthī Saints.
A critical study of the ritualistic and devotional compositions of the Mahāpanthī saints.
Indian Myths in Khojkī Narrative: Rājā Gopīcand Ākhyān by Pir Shams.
Lecture delivered on invitation by Prof. Mallison at the Ecole Pratique des Hautes Etudes, Paris.
Rupavela: A Chanted Narrative of Mahāpanth.
A comparative study of Rajasthani and Gujarati traditions, including an edition of the biographical sketches of Jesal-Toral, and Rupande-Mālde.
"A Unique Unison of the Saguṇa and the Nirguṇa in the *Agamnā Bār Mahinā* (the *Bārmāsī*) by Kāyamudīn Ciśtī", in Mariola Offredi, *The Banyan Tree*, Manohar, 2000, pp. 211-221.

Paper presented at the Fifth Bhakti Conference (Venice, 1997).

Research work
proposed to be undertaken (2001-2002)

A critical study of the ancient places connected with *santa* poets, their line of gurus or precepteros, their myths and the works of the saints of various traditions of folk religion.
A comparative study of *bhajan*-s of the Mahāpanth, *ginān* of the Khojā-s and the *bhajan*-s of the Nāth tradition.
Concept of the current Nakalank *avatār*; a critical study of the Nakalankī *bhajan*-s in folk religion.

Devotional literature
of the tradition of the converted community

Bohorā nasihat. Svādhyāy ane saṁśodhan, Gandhinagar, Gujarāt Sāhitya Akademi, 2000.
This is a collection and compilatin of all the Nasihat-s of Shekh Sādik Ali Sāheb of the Bohorā caste, a critical study and interpretation of his compositions, and a discussion of the use of Hindu cultural elements by converted Muslim poets.
Kayāmudīn Cistī's Āgamanā bār-mahinā. Svādhyāy ane saṁśodhan, Gandhinagar, Gujarāt Sāhitya Akademi.
A study on the use of the Guru-tradition by Kayāmudīn Cistī, and the form of inner experience of the *satcarka-bhedan* process applied in his *Āgamanā Bār-Mahinā*.
Khojākī narrative Gopīcand Ākhyān.
Unpublished article on the life of Khojā Pir Shams, including an edition of his *Gopīcand Ākhyān*, together with an interpretation and a glossary of this text.

Details of the research work
nearing completion (2000-2001)

Collection of the *ginān*-s (by Khojā Pīr), completed; indexing being completed.
These *ginān*-s were obtained from the hand-written diary obtained from an old Jamātkhānā, from old printed books, from oral

tradition (hearing), and from a book published by the Ismaili Association, Mumbai. These *ginān*-s are divided into two classes: myth based *ginān* compositions, and *pad*-based *ginān* compositions. The myth based *ginān* compositions are long. I have prepared a summary of these compositions, based on rituals and life-sketches of Indian saints and ordinary people.

I have also discussed the form of Bhakti emerging from this material. *Pad*-based *ginān* compositions are in the form of *prabhātīya*, *garbī*, *āratī*, *rās*, *bhajan*, etc. I have prepared an introduction to the subject matter of the above forms and I have also given an idea of the type of Bhakti that is appearing in these texts. Further, I prepared an introductory article on the details of the lives of the composers of these *ginān*-s and I made a comparative study of the various myths. Finally, I separated the *ginān*-s of the non-Pīr Khojā devotee poets, with a brief introduction about their Bhakti.

Devotional literature of the *cāraṇī* (bardic) tradition in mediaeval Gujarat.

Cāraṇ Sūdamācaritra, Ahmedabad, Pārśva Prakāśan, 1989.

Mediaeval Gujarati myth-tradition. Analysis of the *cāraṇī pad*-tradition in the context of the Bhakti *pad* literature, focusing on the following areas: Mālvā, Shrimāl, Rājasthān, north Gujarāt, Saurāshtra, and Kutch (Gujarāt State). Of special interest is the "friendly poetry" of the Gujarati *Sudāmā caritra* tradition, as opposed to the more philosophical currents, and the conflict between knowledge and action as revealed in the Rajasthani tradition.

Karsandās Bālia kṛt Kṛṣṇa bhakti kavitā, Rajkot, Saurāshtra University, 1992.

A comparison of the lives of Karsandās Bāliyā and Narasiṃha Mahetā.

Svarga bhūlavuṁ śāmalā, Rajkot, Saurāshtra University, 1998.

A discussion of the concept of *cāraṇī* devotion, as it emerges from the *duhā* poetry by Palaravabha and the author of the *duhā*-s still surviving in the oral tradition.

Cāraṇī bār-māsi, Rajkot, Saurāshtra University, 2000.

Research into the Krishna devotion delineated in the Gujarati Cāraṇī Bārmāsi.

Cāraṇī sāhitya pradīp, Part 2, Rajkot, Saurāshtra University, 2000.
Catalogues of the old manuscripts collected at the Gujarāti Bhāshā Sāhitya Bhavan, Saurāshtra University (Rajkot). The Preface discusses the forms of devotional poetry that are found in Cāraṇī, Gujarātī, Hindī and Braj.

Devotional literature of the Jain tradition of mediaeval Gujarat

Bhṛateśvar Bāhubalirās by Sālibhadrasūri, Ahmedabad, Pārśva Prakāśan, 1992.
Edition of the believed first work in ancient and mediaeval Gujarati literature, based on old manuscripts. Śālibhadrasūri's *rās* work is dated AD 1180.
Vastupālcarītra ane rāskṛtio, Ahmedabad, Pārśva Prakāśan, 1992.
Vastupāl, a Jain minister, became the subject of many mediaeval Gujarati works, which allows the researcher to reconstruct his biography. This study, including text editions of four small *rās* works by Samayasundar and Hīrānand, presents a detailed introduction to devotional traditions in Jainism and their authors.
Hīrānand sūri-jīvan kavannuṁ-ākalan. Svādhyāy ane saṁśodhan, Gandhinagar, Gujarāt Sāhitya Akademi, 2000.
Detailed study into the life and works of the Gujarati poet Hīrānand Sūri.
Dhāmmil Kumār Rās-Kathābodh Nimitte. Mūlyabodh-Svādhyāy ane saṁśodhan, Gandhinagar, Gujarāt Sāhitya Akademi, 2000.
Detailed study into the mythological elements and the Gujarati transformation of the *Dhammilkumār Rās* by Vīrvijajī.

Bhakti as Reflected in the *Caritāmṛta*

PRANABANANDA JASH

During mediaeval times, especially during the age of Śrī Caitanya (ca. AD 1485/6-1533)[14] the concept of Bhakti (devotion) played an important role in the creation of an egalitarian socio-religious order irrespective of caste, colour and sex. In fact, most of the religious teachers were preaching this powerful historical message for the reformation of the then degenerated society. Śrī Caitanya was one of the foremost personalities taking up divergent elements in society and making them relevant to the Bhakti phenomenon in view of social resuscitation. Adoration to Kṛṣṇa-Rādhā and the doctrine of Bhakti are woven round the texture of the Caitanya school of Vaishnavism in Bengal, popularly known as Gauḍīya Vaishnavism. The rudimentary principles of the Gauḍīya Vaishnavism centre round the spirit of sincere devotion (*bhakti*) of the worshipper, thereby growing into a deepening consciousness of the Infinite and Eternal. The concept of Bhakti during the time of Caitanya and afterwards added a new impetus to Vaishnava theology[15]. It plays an important role not only in the religious life of the Vaishnavas in order to achieve Ultimate Reality, but also remained concerned with the task of organising the followers through *samkīrtana* and *mahotsava*-s[16].

---

[14] See Krishnadāsa Kavirāj, *Caitanya haritāmṛita*, Basumati Publications, Calcutta, first repr. 1971.

[15] Pranabananda Jash, *History and Evolution of Vaishnavism in Eastern India*, Calcutta, 1982, pp. 202.

[16] It is well known that Caitanya adopted effective, though simple, methods to strengthen his movement by performing *saṃkīrtana* and *mahotsava*-s for the propagation of his faith, and also holding the comunity of his followers together. *Saṃkīrtana* is an informal mode of group-singing to the accompaniment of musical instruments, reciting the name of Krishna loudly with devotion. *Mahotsava* (grand festivals), also popularly known as *macchava* helped Caitanya to keep in touch with the Vaishnava devotees. Such festivals were generally organised at the time of the inauguration of temples or wealthy devotees volunteered to arrange them for the purpose of community gathering. These *mahotsava*-s were preceded and followed by *kīrtana* and attracted large crowds.

The followers as well as philosophers of Caitanya, especially the six Gosvāmīs Rūpa, Sanātana, Raghunātha Bhaṭṭa, Raghunātha Dāsa, Gopāla Bhaṭṭa, Śrī Jīva of Vrindavan, have discussed Bhakti in an exhaustive manner in their works[17], which were followed by the writings of Vṛndāvan Dās, Kṛṣṇadās Kavirāj and others. A close scrutiny of these works will reveal that the theology of the Gauḍīya Vaishnava school founded by Śrī Caitanya is characterised by certain distinctive features which distinguish it from other Vaishnava schools of thought. Besides, its concept of *acintya-bhedābheda* to explain the nature of Brahman, its ontology of Rādhā, its ideas on the values of human life or *puruṣārtha*[18], the doctrinal exposition of Bhakti accompanied by the *rasa* theory gives it a unique position in religious history. The Gauḍīya Vaishnavas accepted Bhakti as a doctrine and a part of theology. They thus evolved a system of practical, religious emotionalism and explained to intricate classification and nomenclature. Again, the *rasa* theory in relation to Bhakti and its various categories with special emphasis on the *madhura rasa*[19] not only exhibit the profound philosophical knowledge of the *ācārya*-s, but all these new and fresh ideas taken together amply demonstrate the exclusiveness and originality of Gauḍīya Vaishnavism.

According to Gauḍīya Vaishnavas Bhakti has broadly been classified as *sādhanā bhakti*, *bhava-bhakti* and *prema-bhakti* and each of these three is the representation of different stages of realisation.

Sādhanā-bhakti is attainable by the senses, like hearing the Lord's name, singing His *kīrtan* and seeing His beauty. It can be

---

17 *Bhakti rasāmṛta-sindhu*, *Ujjvalanīlamaṇi* and *Saṁkṣep bhāgvatāmṛta* by Rūpa Gosvāmī, *Bṛhad bhāgavatāmṛta* by Sanātana, the *Sandarbha*-s (Tattva, Bhagavat, Paramātma, Śrī Kṛṣṇa, Bhakti and Prīti) by Jīva Gosvāmī; *Haribhakti vilāsa* of Sanātana Gosvāmī and Gopāla Bhaṭṭa.

18 Caitanya considers love for god as the fifth or *pañcama puruṣārtha* instead of the traditional four, i.e. *dharma*, *artha*, *kāma* and *mokṣa*. According to the Caitanya school, *pañcamapuruṣārtha* or 'love for God' is the superior of all goals aspired for; and for that matter, they ignored the importance of *varṇāśrama-dharma* when compared to love for God.

19 *Madhura-rasa* or *ujjvala-rasa* is explained separately because of its prime importance in *bhakti-rasa*. The text consisting of fifteen *prakaraṇa*-s (divisions) deals with Krishna as a hero and his eternal consort Rādhā (*Rādhā-prakaraṇa*) exhaustively. The succeeding stages of *madhura-rasa* are also mentioned in an elaborate manner.

practised under some given circumstances when the devotee completely disregards the obligations of the *varṇāśramadharma*[20] and does not covet sensual enjoyment and liberation[21].

The Vaishnava *ācārya*-s prescribe sixty-four rites and rituals for a devotee to attain *sādhanā bhakti*, like submitting to the guru, accepting mantra or initiation and learning *bhakti* from him; serving the *guru* faithfully, performing *nāma-saṃkīrtana*, etc.[22] *Sādhanā bhakti* is also of two kinds: *vaidhi-bhakti* and *rāgānuga bhakti*. When a *bhakta* practises *sādhanā-bhakti* being inspired by the procedures of the scriptures, it is called *vaidhī*[23], but it is called *rāgānuga* when such a Bhakti flows spontaneously, without any scriptural injections or procedures. The *rāgānuga bhakti* is again of two types: *prema*, or *karma-rūpa*, and *sambandha rūpa*. The source of the former is the passionate desire to be Krishna's beloved like the *gopī*-s, while the latter seeks to establish a relationship with Krishna as His servant, friend or parents.

Bhāva-bhakti is the direct outcome of an inner emotion for Krishna, but this is something different from love. *Bhāva-bhakti* which is the ultimate stage of *sādhanā-bhakti* has been described by Rūpa Gosvāmī as follows:

> "When the *bhāva* for Krishna develops in one's mind, he becomes impatient; no one does waste his time unnecessarily. He begins to sing His name constantly and eulogises Him. He then longs for union with Him and starts loving his abode. Outward calm is followed by modesty and indifference to the sensual enjoyments. Yet, he remains firm in his hope of attaining Him"[24].

On attaining *prema-bhakti* which is considered as the final of devotion and the culmination point of all forms of Bhakti, the devotee feels that Krishna is something like his own possession which he would like to keep with love. This form of Bhakti reveals gradually in nine distinct succeeding stages with the cultivation of

---

[20] Rupa Gosvāmī, *Bhakti-rasāmṛita sindhu*, 2nd ed., Murshidabad, Bengali era 1925 (AD 1988), Pūrva II, p. 151.

[21] *Ibid.*, p. 44.

[22] *Ibid.*, pp. 73, 77.

[23] *Ibid.*, p. 33.

[24] Rupa Gosvāmī, *op. cit.*, Pūrva-III, pp. 196-197.

the following deeds: faith (*śraddhā*), holy company (*sādhu-saṅgati*), spiritual practice (*bhajana kriyā*), removal of constraints in the spiritual path (*anartha nivṛttiḥ*), devotedness (*syattate niṣṭhā*), the taste for the stage of devotedness (*rucistataḥ*), attachment to that state (*athaśakti*), emotional feeling (*bhāva*) and *prema*[25].

We have already mentioned that the Gauḍīya Vaishnavas regard Lord Krishna, the ultimate ideal, as an object of love and devotion. The devotee considers Him as the beloved. The exchange of loving reciprocation between the lover (devotee) and the beloved (Krishna) is called *bhakti-rasa* (love sentiment) which, according to the Vaishnava scriptures, are of twelve kinds: *Śānta-rasa* (quiet devotion); *prīta-rasa* (devotion as His faithful); *preya-rasa* (devotion as a friend); *vātsalya-rasa* (devotion as parents); *madhura-rasa/ujjvala-rasa* (devotion with erotic); *hāsya-rasa* (comic); *adbhuta-rasa* (marvellous); *vīra-rasa* (heroic); *karuṇā-rasa* (pathetic); *raudra-rasa* (furious); *bhayānaka-rasa* (terrible) and *vībhatsa-rasa* (ghastly).

Of these, the first five are *mukhya* (primary) while the remaining seven are considered as *gauṇa* (secondary)[26]. According to the Gauḍīya Vaishnavas, Lord Krishna can be realised by practising these twelve kinds of *bhakti-rasa* (love-sentiments). However, the primary *rasa*-s remain constantly within the heart of the devotees, whereas the seven others appear and disappear. A devotee adopts a particular devotion attitude according to his inclination and leaning. But *madhura-bhāva* (an attitude of conjugal love) is the best sentiment (*rasa*) for realising Lord Krishna. The expression of *madhura-bhāva* is distinctly projected in the concept of Rādhā and her love for Krishna. Her love for Krishna transcended all barriers of this mundane world. Śrī Caitanya introduced Rādhā as the idealised representative of bliss. From the philosophical perspective it may be said that Gauḍīya Vaishnavism presents *Rādhā tattva* in its most mature and developed form. A supramundane (*paramārthika*) is transferred semantically tothe empirical reality (*vyavahārika*). Such a form of an all-absorbing love advocated by the Caitanya School of Vaishnavism through *madhura-bhava* has been expressed in the following:

---

25 *Ibid.*, Pūrva IV, p. 218.
26 Rupa Gosvāmī, *op. cit.*, Dakṣiṇā V, p. 601.

Yuvaker ārti yathā yuvatī dekhiyā |
Sei rūpa ārti ār nā dekhi bhāviyā ||
E kāraṇe bhaktagā bhaje Yadupati |
Patnībhāva tār prati sthir kari mati ||[27]

as a young man yearns for his sweet-heart,
in the same manner, the human soul may yearn for Krishna.
In order to imbibe the same yearning,
the Vaishnavas worship Yadupati with an attitude of conjugal love.

However, it is very difficult to perform this kind of worship[28], because the love-sentiment entertained by Rādhā towards Krishna was entirely different from the ordinary earthly passion[29]. *Premam* (love for god) and *kāma* (lust or earthly passion) characteristically differ from each other as iron from gold, in colour and element. Earthly passion (*kāma*) denotes sensual enjoyment of one's self, while *premam* aims at making Krishna happy[30]. In order to practise *madhura-rati* (conjugal love-attitude to Krishna) the devotees have to undergo a series of succeeding stages, such as *rati*, *premam*, *sneha*, *māna*, *praṇaya*, *rāga*, *anurāga*, *bhāva* and *mahābhāva*. *Mahābhāva* is regarded as the supreme form of the realisation of love for Krishna. In fact, there are many other stages in between these succeeding stages, but we have no time here to analyse them in an amplified form[31].

Thus while dealing with the evolution of Bhakti it may said that earlier Vaishnava *ācārya*-s extolled Bhakti as a religious attitude, but it is the contribution of Mahāprabhu Śrī Caitanya and his disciples and/or followers to present Bhakti not only as a path: they interpreted it also as a *rasa*. They accepted Bhakti as a doctrine and a part of theology. The Gauḍīya Vaishnavas thus evolved a system of practical, religious emotionalism and explained its intricate classifications and nomenclature. Śrī Caitanya transformed the

---

27 Govinda Daser Kadea, p. 10.

28 *Ibid.* p. 13.

29 Krishnadas Kaviraj in his *Caitanya Caritāmṛta* (Madhya II, p. 68) mentions that love for Krishna is as the water of the Ganges and it is clearly distinguished from earthly love.

30 *Ibid.*, *Ādi*, Chapter 4.

31 For details, see *Ujjvala nīlamaṇi* of Rūpa Gosvāmī, pp. 225-291.

Bhakti form of ritualistic procedure into a devotional movement. To him love and devotion to Krishna would lead to the illumination of the mind and to ultimate salvation. He recommended dance and music to produce a state of ecstacy in which the *bhakta*-s could have a vision of god. No doubt, several Vaishnavites like Mādhavendra Pūrī, Advaitācārya, Śrīvāsa and others flourished before the advent of Caitanya, "but the advent of Chaitanya" as observed by S.B. Dasgupta, "was something like a fruition of all their devotional penances, and it was an event which was really epoch-making in the religion and literature of Bengal. Chaitanya, as he is interpreted by his followers, embodies in him the quintessence of both Rādhā and Krishna, and is both the realiser and the realised in the same personality"[32].

[32] S.B. Dasgupta, *Obscure Religious Cults*, Calcutta, pp. XV-XVI.

Oral and Written Traditions in Rajasthan (Pābūjī)

J. KAMPHORST

My on-going Ph.D. research centres upon the study of the development of the written and oral tradition of the peoples of western Rajasthan. I am particularly interested in the written and oral tradition about Pābūjī, a 600-year-old narrative tradition about the adventures of the Rajput warrior Pābūjī Dhandhal Rāṭhaur who, it is believed, lived in the first half of the 14th century. The written tradition about Pābūjī is part of the mediaeval bardic tradition of Marwar, the former kingdom of Rāṭhaur Rajputs. The contemporary oral tradition is part of a multi-story tradition of folk-epic and heroic songs as performed by various bardic castes of the Thar Desert.

The main questions I ask myself presently concern the manner in which the oral and written tradition about Pābūjī developed from ca. 1550 till now, though it should be noted that, as a historian, my primary interest lies in the mediaeval manuscript tradition. The questions I ask concern the form, content and function of both traditions and should result in a description of the historical context in which these Rajasthani traditions evolved. An important research theme is, of course, the manner in which the written and oral traditions have influenced each other or not, as the case may be. My study of the many different manuscripts versions of Pābūjī's adventures includes texts from the 16th century until the beginning of the 20th century. This selection gives an idea, however incomplete, of the 'chains of transmission' that formed the tradition. I also try to answer some longstanding questions about the nature of the mediaeval Rajasthani bardic institution. The study of extant oral genres through which Pābūjī's adventures are presently retold, illustrates the manner in which this Rajasthani heritage was transmitted.

Sources

The manuscript tradition about Pābūjī knows many different forms; apart from long heroic poems, the tradition also knows commemorative songs, wedding songs, miracle songs and prayers, as well as semi-historical Pingal prose stories. I am mainly concerned with different manuscripts versions of the 17th century *Pābūjī rau dūhā*, the 16th century *Pābūjī rau chand*, and versions of short songs like the *Gīt Pābūjī rau.*

Now I should say something about the oral sources which I study. I collected various stories, songs, epic performances as well as petitions or prayers dedicated to Pābūjī, as transmitted by various bardic castes, most notably the par (or story-cloth) Bhopos from village Kalmi, the Bhil Bhopos from Kolu who perform the *mātā* (drum) epic, and the Dholis and Motisars, who sing and chant short songs based on episodes of the Pābūjī folk-epic. Also part of my oral data are miracle stories as told by the Rebari and Rajput devotees of Pābūjī.

Approach

I approach my subject from three different angles, firstly through a descriptive study of the form content and function of the written and oral epic about Pābūjī. The first year of my research, I mainly studied the mediaeval manuscript tradition about Pābūjī. In October 1999 I collected several versions of the oral tradition about Pābūjī and I am now working on the transcription and description of these audio and video-recordings. My second approach is the comparative analysis of both traditions, based on methods as formulated by historians in the field like Shyal Mayaram, Jan Vansina and Wendy Singer. The third approach, the portrayal of the historical context in which both traditions evolved, is based on my analysis of the historical function of the written and oral traditions.

The interest of this research for the field of Bhakti studies lies in the many references to Nāth and Shakti influences found in both the mediaeval and extant traditions about Pābūjī. Another aspect which connects this historical research to Bhakti studies, is the fact that the extant oral tradition is clearly related to the primary Sanskrit epics, mainly through *avatār* linkage which renders the

Rāṭhaur warrior Pābūjī an incarnation of Rām's brother Lakṣmaṇ. Pābūjī's archenemy Jindarav Khinci is of course equated with Rāvaṇa. John D. Smith has described this *avatār* linkage in great detail. My contribution to the study of the contemporary epic of Pābūjī is that I show that many bardic as well as non-bardic castes, other than the Bhopo bards described by Smith, keep the memory of Pābūjī alive.

I furthermore try to see which layers of influence we may distinguish, when we study this tradition. The mediaeval tradition of Dingal *vīrakāvya* (heroic poetry), in which category the written tradition about Pābūjī is usually placed, is seen as a Great Tradition of Rajput martial ideals handed down to us by high caste, literate Cāraṇ bards and other court poets. This description, however, does not take into account the 'inclusive' aspects of the mediaeval written tradition. And this approach cannot account for the influence of the songs of illiterate, tribal Bhopo bards in the written tradition of Cāraṇ bards either.

Apart from the Sanskritic elements, which are stressed by Smith, the influence of mediaeval values and socio-political realities also stand out. The clearly a-historical role attributed to Gorakh Nāth in the Pābūjī tradition, as well as the indirect relation of this tradition with the regional cult of Cāraṇī Shakti-s, the living goddesses from the bardic Cāraṇ caste, still need to be accounted for. By seeing whether and to what extent we can assume that the mediaeval historical tradition still influences the contemporary epic I hope to add to the discussion about the so-called 'Sanskritisation' of folk-epics and show that Sanskritic elements form only one of the many layers of influence which shape Rajasthani narrative traditions. In very general terms, the Pābūjī tradition seems to belong to that ideological expression of Rajasthani culture which is described as 'inclusive', for it is not only part of a heritage which voiced the Rajput Great Tradition, but it is also, and has been so from an early stage onwards, a vehicle to voice the socially upward aspirations of nomadic and tribal caste-groups.

The most interesting results yielded by my study thus far, concern the historical continuities of form, content and function of both traditions. I am especially interested in continuities, which may throw light on the historical function of the Pābūjī tradition in defining mediaeval and present-day caste-identities of the epic community. Another noteworthy aspect of this particular Rajasthani tradition is the manner in which mediaeval martial values still inspires certain aspects of the extant tradition. By seeing all different influences that shaped this heroic tradition, I hope to eventually arrive at a description of both written and oral traditions as part of one 'multi-layered' tradition, inspired by a 'common imaginative pool', as Rāmanujan has put it. As far as I can see now, the comparison of the mediaeval and present-day data should give an idea of the course of text expansion, which especially the par-epic went through. And I try to establish whether the process of deification of Pābūjī can be accounted for through a study of both written and oral sources.

I will return to Jodhpur in November 2000 and sit again with local folklorists, historians and poets, as well as the patrons of Pābūjī's epic, to see how the translated text are best read and how their function and meaning are interpreted in Rajasthan.

REFERENCES

Shyal Mayaram, "Mughal State Formation; the Mewati Counterperspective", paper read at the Third International Seminar on Rajasthan (Jaipur 1994; unpublished).

A.K. Rāmānujan, "Three Hundred *Rāmāyaṇas*: Five Examples and Three Thoughts on Translation", in: Paula Richman (ed), *Many Rāmāyaṇas, The Diversity of a Narrative Tradition in South Asia*, University of California Press, Delhi, 1991, pp. 22-49.

Wendy Singer, *Creating Histories, Oral Narratives and the Politics of History-Making*, Oxford University Press, Delhi, 1997.

John D. Smith, *The Epic of Pābūjī. A Study, Transcription and Translation*, Cambridge University Press, Cambridge, 1991

Jan Vansina, *Oral Tradition as History*, University of Wisconsin, Wisconsin 1985.

DISCUSSION

Callewaert:

Let me first express my admiration for you and others who have to do their research listening to tapes. It must be much harder and more time-consuming than trying to decipher manuscripts. But where did you find the manuscripts you worked with?

Kamphorst:
My manuscripts are mainly from Chaupasani, Jodhpur. The earliest dated manuscript is from the 16th century, written around 1550. There is also a well-known published manuscript from Ladhraj.

Callewaert:
I may perhaps bring to the attention of all of you the wonderful manuscript collection made by Srī Kripalu Sharma, Jaipur. It is called the Shree Sanjay Sharma Museum & Research Institute, Thatheron ka rasta (off Chaura Rasta) in Jaipur (302 003), 428pp. More than fifty thousand manuscripts have been collected, on a great variety of themes. In 2000 an excellent catalogue was brought out, edited (and published) by Rām Kripālu Śarmā, *Granth Parijāt*, Vol. I. A Classified Catalogue of Hindi Manuscripts in Shree Sanjay Sharma Museum & Research Institute, 428pp.

Jani:
We have this type of chanted narratives also in Gujarat. It is a living tradition in tribal communities, e.g. *Rāṭhoḍ kī vārtā.* We also have a Gujarati version of Pābūjī, available in printed form.

Rousseva-Sokolova:
There are, you said, long songs and short songs which are episodes from the long songs. Can you say something more about this?

Kamphorst:
My material comes from epic studies, which are mostly story traditions. Therefore; even short songs are seen as part of an epic tradition. In the Pābūjī tradition you have epic changes with every bard, but the themes of these epics — like the wedding of Pābūjī, or the theft of a horse, or any other adventure — are remade into short songs. They are sung on any occasion.

Horstmann:
What were the occasions when you recorded?

Kamphorst:
Some occasions were created by me, others I encountered during fieldwork. For instance, I witnessed the Navrātri festival in Kolu, in Mārvār, where the Bhil *mātā* epic is performed. I returned the next day after the festivities were over, to record the *parvārau* performance of the Bhils again. But this time, I recorded the songs without the *mātā* drums, allowing me to hear and transcribe the text of the performance properly. The *par* epic performance by Bhopos, on the other hand, was organised by people I knew, in Gopal Bari, near Jodhpur.

Report on Research

CATHARINA KIEHNLE

Since long I have been working on a translation of Keśav Prahlād Atre's *Buvā tethem̩ bāyā*, 'Where there is a Guru there are Women', first staged in 1964 in Bombay. I hope it is ready for print before the end of 2001. Being an adaptation of Molière's *Tartuffe*, the play is of course about Bhakti only insofar as it shows what Bhakti is not. *Tartuffe* is said to be universally applicable, still the text had to be changed in several respects in order to become 'Indian'. The most important change is that Tartuffe has become a fake *guru*, accompanied by Āī, or 'mother'. A researcher on Bhakti recognises in the play a host of common-places of Indian religions, especially since mock *bhajan*-s and *kīrtan*-s are performed on stage. I hope it will be fun to read for those who want to improve their Marathi and for those interested in the mechanics of adapting theatre plays into foreign cultures. Friends of the late Prof. S.G. Tulpule will be reminded of him in many notes that supply local background information.

The reason why I have not been able to do much research recently is that I had to brush up my Hindi in order to be able to teach it, together with Hindi literature, etc. One way for me to combine Marathi and Hindi in future is to work on a subject common to both languages. From the innumerable possibilities I chose hagiography. Over the years I have collected about 70 books and booklets both in Hindi and Marathi on saints who have lived during the last 150 years. Since the Dattā *sampradāya* plays a very important role in religious Maharashtra, I selected a saint belonging to that tradition. He is called Śaṅkar Mahārāj and died in 1947 in Poona. He is fascinating for various reasons. Within the 50 years after his *mahāsamādhi*, he has risen from a marginal *guru* to the heights of a hero in a children's book that is theoretically available at every street corner. This can be surpassed now only by an Amar Citra Kathā volume and a movie. His *samādhi* at Sātārā Road has grown into a *maṭh* with regular festivals and three *artī*-s plus one *abhiśek* daily. His image has become an icon and his praise is sung in Marathi as well as in Hindi. So far he has three biographies (or hagiographies, depending on the aspect under which they are viewed) and his teachings are quoted in the fictional autobiograpy by G.K. Pradhān.

With regard to the biographies, several questions arise. For example, how did the present-day authors proceed, with eyewitnesses and audiences around that are (presumably) much more critical than those of the middle ages? To which extent do they make Śaṅkar Mahārāj fit into traditional patterns, and to which extent does he remain a real individual? What are the features that make him a saint, and what makes him so popular now, and with whom?

As to his individuality, he definitely has one because his devotees remember encounters with him, complete with date and place. He had his particular style of dressing (if at all he dressed), *dhotī*, *kurtā*, sometimes rings and necklaces, and from time to time Muslim headgear. He used to smoke and that is why during his *pūjā* a cigarette is lit. One thing which is quite touching and which no one would have invented is that he was crippled and of the size of a child. The authors gracefully sanctify this fact by calling him *aṣṭāvakra*, 'eight[fold] crooked', or 'crooked in eight [places]', like the famous sage Aṣṭāvakra. He is also called *ājānubāhu*, 'whose arms reach down to the knees', a feature reserved for exceptional personalities like the Buddha, and quite a number of saints enumerated in V. Joshi's *Sakala santa - citra gāthā*.

This leads to the less individual features which he shares with other gurus from the Dattā tradition and popular saints of Maharashtra, like Akkalkoṭ Svāmī, Sirḍī Sāī Bābā and Gajānan Mahārāj. These three are included in a painting that presents Śaṅkar Mahārāj and his tradition, linked up to the god Dattātreya. Thus, there is ample scope for comparing stories and motifs from various hagiographies, old and new. In this particular case it will be useful to concentrate on Maharashtra and the Dattā *sampradāya*, which, with its *Gurucaritra* — an account on the lives of its founders — has set its own standards for hagiography, and into which (as in Śaṅkar Mahārāj's *paramparā* Śirḍī Sāī Bābā and Gajānan Mahārāj) sometimes also such personalities are absorbed who originally had nothing to do with it. The latter phenomenon is not only due to endeavours to legitimise a certain tradition, but also caused by visions of the *bhakta*-s who contribute considerably to the tradition building. This is one reason why one should interview them about the motivations for their affiliation to Śaṅkar Mahārāj.

His *maṭh* is, of course, situated conveniently in the fastest growing area of Poona, but perhaps they experience the power of the teachers belonging to the Dattā *sampradāya*, a power that has kept the tradition alive for over more than five centuries. Since some of those teachers are also coming to the West, I hope that research into the present day Dattā tradition will be useful also for those dealing with contemporary religion in general.

REFERENCES

Atre, Pralhād Keśav, *Buvā tetheṃ bāyā*, Mumbaī: 1964.
Mī Pāhilele Śaṅkar Mahārāj, *nivedan*, Yogī Jñānanāthjī, Santacaritramālā 3, Puṇe, 1999 [= 1981].
Jośī, Pralhād Narhar, ed., *Saṭīp, savivaraṇ Śrīgurucaritra*, Thāṇe, 1981.
Jośī, Vāman, *Sakala Santa - citra gāthā*, Puṇe, 1993.
Mudhoḷkar, Rameś, *Śrīśaṅkaramahārājāṃcyā goṣṭī*, Puṇe, 1996.
Pradhan, G.K., *Towards the silver crests of the Himalayas*, Bombay, 1993 [=1963].
Tāṃdḷe, Jñāneśvar, *Śrīśaṅkaramahārāj*, Puṇe, 1985.

DISCUSSION

Bangha:
Would you call this the religion of a certain sect?

Kiehnle:
No, I would not. It is just a 'religion' of fake gurus in general. Atre was very interested in the social situation of India and he also felt he had to do something about the situation of Hinduism, which he considered as not good, because it was represented by people who had nothing to do with it.

Hawley:
With Shankar Maharaj, can you get back to a story of his life or are you forced to get your information only from the devotees?

Kiehnle:
The story of his life has been reconstructed mainly from information provided by the devotees, but it is difficult to say to what extent one can trust their accounts. Some events concerning his childhood may even have been told by Shankar Maharaj

himself, but they were embellished afterwards. For example, when he was found as a baby in the jungle, he is said to have been alone in the first biography. According to the most recent biography there were four tigers with him.

Zelliot:

Aren't there several gurus now with that name, and did Atre know this Shankar Maharaj?

Kiehnle:

Yes, there are quite a few gurus with that name, but the one under discussion — he died in 1947 — was among those Atre knew personally. It is said — of course by devotees — that he kept a picture of Shankar Maharaj with him. If that was so, Atre must have liked him. The Buva from the play was modelled after several other gurus bundled into one, among them a priest from Pandharpur who had killed a woman.

Purandare:

Didn't he rather criticise the blind faith in women, and women who get easily carried away by so-called gurus?

Kiehnle:

No. A critic wrote, when the play was staged for the first time, that it has a wrong title. The guru's female partner, an imposter herself, is the only woman who likes him, at least for some time. All the other women among the main characters of the play are not at all carried away, they hate him. In fact, those who are really taken in (apart from the general crowd of devotees) are the rich landowner and, only in the beginning, his father-in-law.

Research in Gujarat

FRANÇOISE MALLISON

I have studied Gujarat and the religious culture of mediaeval India — or maybe I should say it the other way round: the religious culture of mediaeval India as documented in Gujarat — in order to evaluate the specificity of a region within the general framework of the religious culture of mediaeval India, i.e. the contribution of this region to the general history, and the transformation undergone by the general pattern when applied to a local analysis.

My first entry into this field — after having received training in the mediaeval religious history of the West, more precisely concerning the economic life of a group of Cistercian monasteries many of whom were actually located not too far away from Leuven! — was an attempt to investigate the possibility of religious renunciation for women within Hinduism, and this in the Gujarati context. Thus I chanced on the Svāmī Nārāyaṇa movement. Svāmī Nārāyaṇa (1780-1830) was not a fashionable topic in the sixties. The movement was to attract the attention of western — mainly anthropological and sociological — scholarship later on, when an offshoot of the movement, the Puruṣottam Saṁsthā (itself subdivided), had spread into England (after the Gujarati migration from East Africa) and after it had become quite affluent. I dealt with its original literature of the beginning of the 19th century, and with the main movement. They were an example of Krishna-Bhakti with a reformist bend of mind, but for all that was said, Svāmī Nārāyaṇa was an imitator of the Puṣṭimārga even if he let the English officials pamper him, and it was only three decades later that I was able to realise that the reforms he was pushing probably had their roots in the deep layers of the traditional religious culture of mediaeval Saurashtra, that is in the *Santavāṇī* culture of Kathiawad.

I shifted to Narasiṃha Mahetā (1414-1477), a quite different sanctity. He is a kind of national poet welcomed by all, even by the Muslims as far as they are speaking Gujarati. Narasiṃha is sometimes compared to Sūrdās, although he was never taken over by any sectarian movement, except for the cult as a saint (not a god) rendered to him by a few people around his supposed home at Junagadh, at a place named Narasiṃha Mahetā no Coro. The case of the lifestory or hagiography of Narasiṃha appears as a kind of exemplary tool for the exploration of mediaeval religious life and mentality, and I proceeded to look at the lifestories of saints, either sectarian or mythological, and at the foundation stories of holy places in Gujarat, for a better understanding of the local religious culture. It appears from what I said that Vaishnavism, even Krishnaism, in its specific version of the Puṣṭimārga, but also pre-Vallabhite as well, was the subject of my research.

After this comparative study of hagiography I wanted to try comparative hymnology, this being the result of an encounter with the Muslim religious hymnology and literature written in Gujarati, especially the Ismā'īlī *gināna.* There I extended the field from Vaishnava Bhakti to Parsi, Jaina, Tantrika and Ismā'īlī movements, to discover that many religious groups used or use the same songs. I further also noticed that a type of folk regional culture nourished a popular mysticism unaware of orthodoxy or orthopraxis. What struck me most was the similarity of the *Santavāṇī,* a cluster of Tantric Mahāmārgī, Nāth, Kabirian lyrics, with the Satpanthī *gināna* of the Nizārī Ismā'īlī tradition of North Western India. There the *lokadharma,* (i.e. the local popular religions within the regions of Saurashtra, Kutch and Sindh on one side, and of North- and East-Gujarat and Rajasthan on the other, unexplored and ignored for so many reasons — untouchables, Adivasis, orality and esoterism) could suddenly explain even better than as a mere folk component, the deep unity of the Gujarati religious culture.

This point I have reached for the time being. We have built up a programme to save the Ismā'īlī *gināna* heritage of Gujarat, a difficult task among a closed community that has undergone so many changes since the 19th century. I must add that the 19th century with which I began, with Svāmī Nārāyaṇa, continues to occupy my mind as a period explaining both mediaeval and modem religious culture. As I said, Svāmī Nārāyaṇa appeared modern to the English contemporaries, but his targets as well as his models were exclusively the concepts and the praxis of the *Santavāṇī* adepts.

DISCUSSION

de Bruijn:
How would you explain the part played by the 19th century in explaining both mediaeval and modern religious culture?

Mallison:
When we want to study mediaeval religious traditions such as the *bhajan*-s and so on, we sometimes are able to find manuscripts and ancient documents, but at the same time we need to look at modern and contemporary material. The living tradition is in itself a source documenting the ancient tradition. Besides that, we see in the 19th century the emergence of the printing presses following the first lithographic prints. By the end of the 19th century Narasiṃha Mahetā's corpus had been printed at the Gujarati Printing Press of Bombay by Iccharam Suryadas Desai. Suddenly texts became available to a lot of people who no longer had to depend on oral transmission. It is these 19th century texts the Gujarati people are even now singing. If while working on these texts one tries to restore an original text, this "more authentic text" will not have the favour of the contemporary active followers who stick to their 19th century "vulgate". This passage from ancient tradition to modern times should make us reflect when we compare this type of "vulgate" with old manuscripts in order to reconstruct a more authentic text.

Research on Advaitācārya

REBECCA J. MANRING

I've been working with the surprisingly large body of works treating Advaitācārya, who, as most of you will know, is the person to whom the Gauḍīya Vaishnava tradition attributes the advent of Krishna Caitanya. Advaita was about 50 years older than Caitanya, already a recognised scholar with his own following long before Caitanya was born. His followers would come to be the only group to produce not a biography of Caitanya, the official sectarian leader, but multiple biographies of Advaita himself. Clearly there was some concern that Advaita would fade away into obscurity as the movement grew over time.

There are three major biographies, and another two treating Sītā Devī, Advaita's primary wife. A fair amount of mystery and even some controversy surround those compositions, and I've already published on that subject, and anticipate publishing the translation of *Advaitaprakāśa* in 2001.

Perhaps more interesting are a number of apparently *sahajīya* texts in which Advaita figures prominently. I have found three separate such texts, all called either *Advaita-kaṛaca-sūtra* or *Advaita-sūtra-kadaca*, each extant in several manuscripts. That fact in itself is unusual for the Advaita corpus. But what is even more unexpected, at least initially, is finding Advaita's name associated with *sahajīya* practices. For the texts, each with a slightly different content, all take the usual *sahajīya* form of dialogues.

Sahajīya materials in general tend to be very problematic for the likes of us. They remain unpublished texts, and while there are numerous extant manuscripts, we cannot clearly identify the provenance of most of them, either in terms of geography or even of doctrinal lineage. Many *sahajīya* texts appear to be copies of each other, with perhaps no more than a few name changes here and there. And there are the usual problems with trying to date the things. Clearly the vast majority are post-Caitanya. Some have asserted that the *sahajīya* movement is much older, and certainly we can find similarities in practice with older traditions, but there is really little solid evidence for placing the Vaishnava *sahajīya*-s any time before the death of Caitanya. And we do find a proliferation of these texts in the 17th century.

Aside from numerous *pada*-s, the vast majority of *sahajīya* texts are written in the form of dialogues between a guru and a disciple. For example, among the *sahajīya* materials bearing Advaita's name, the longest text, the one I've worked most extensively with so far, is a dialogue between Mādhavendra Pūrī[33], the guru, and his disciple Advaita. Mādhavendra takes Advaita step-by-step through the various stages of *sahajīya* initiation and practice, answering questions and providing further elaboration at each step along the way. As usual for such materials, the text is constructed in coded language so that the precise details of the sexual practices are not apparent to the casual reader. That language is quite similar to what we would find in other *sahajīya* texts, but unfortunately for me, there are some differences, so I cannot simply decode what I am working on, based on what someone else working with Bengali material has found. So right now I am at the stage where I have identified some of the code words, and am working to figure out what they mean. The most promising way to do this seems to be to step back from the trees and look at the entire forest, so to speak, and see what sort of metaphors carry throughout the text, and compare those metaphors with metaphors in other contemporary pieces. Many of these are fairly transparent, having to do with *rasa* and *rati* and swimming against the current. A smaller part of this project will be to attempt to compile some sort of glossary, and see how consistent it is throughout this admittedly very limited corpus I'm dealing with.

My working supposition for the time being is that Advaita was not actually involved in *sahajīya* practices (although frankly, I do not think that is an interesting or important question). What I strongly suspect we have in these alleged notebooks of Advaita's, is the appropriation of his good name by a group not nearly so highly respected in Vaishnava circles. In other words, what I *do* find interesting, is what his name is doing here.

---

[33] Mādhavendra Pūrī is a rather shadowy figure in Vaishnava literature about whom very little is known. Most likely he was originally from South India. The *Advaita Prakāśa* states that Advaitācārya first met him at "Madhav's place" in South India, and studied with him for some time. He is credited with the introduction of *yugal sevā* (worship of the divine couple, instead of the usual worship of a single deity, alone) into Bengali Vaishnavism.

On the other hand, just to play the devil's advocate for a moment, I also strongly suspect that the lines, the boundaries, between what we academics call different traditions, are very very fluid. In other words, I do not think we can say with any certainty that a member of the mainstream Gauḍīya community could absolutely not have also been a *sahajīya* practitioner. And in fact I do not think it the historicity of the material being reported is an issue. I think instead that the use of Advaita's name — and it is quite clear that the authors intend us to understand this as Advaitācārya, because of the mention of other names key in Advaita's life and mission — is simply a rhetorical strategy, intended to get our attention, to assure us that the practices discussed are legitimate, to make us perhaps not look too closely at them, and to expand the umbrella of Gauḍīya Vaishnavism to include still broader range of praxis and theory.

The late Sukumar Sen left a manuscript collection of over 900 pieces, which collectively comprise what has come to be considered Bengali literature. The collection is largely composed of *Maṅgala kāvya*, with many manuscripts of Bengali *Mahābhārata* and *Rāmāyaṇa*, some Vaishnava *Padāvalī*, some *sahajīya* works, a few Satya Pīr/Satya Nārāyaṇa stories, and numerous other works. Unfortunately, due to the vagaries of the Bengali climate, the manuscripts are rapidly deteriorating. The South Asia Microforms Project, based at the University of Chicago in the U.S., has provided funding, film and technicians to film the collection this winter so that these materials will remain accessible to scholars in the future. I have already catalogued the collection and expect to publish it, with some biographical material about Professor Sen, in India in the near future.

DISCUSSION

Callewaert:
Do I understand that these will be microfilmed as well as digitised?

Manring:
The South Asia Microfilm Project has microfilmed the entire Sen collection and is currently considering digitising it as well. The catalogue, which consists of an alphabetical listing of the manuscripts with brief descriptions, will be published sometime in

2001, probably in India, and once it is published the entries for the individual manuscripts will be accessible online through the World Catalogue (OCLC).

du Perron:

Besides representing the texts for others to use, are there also plans to do something to actually preserve the manuscripts themselves?

Manring:

Before we could begin filming we had to remove years of dust from the manuscripts. At that point I began investigating low-tech, low-cost ways by which we might leave the manuscripts in a better condition than we had found them. Subsequently, each piece has been first wrapped in handmade (i.e. low acid) paper. I pasted a label identifying the manuscript on the outside of the paper. Then I placed that bundle between two pieces of "pieceboard", and wrapped the entire "sandwich" thus formed in red cotton, *shālu,* the traditional manuscript covering. I pasted a second label to the outside of the *shālu,* and tied the entire bundle with white cotton tape. The manuscripts are now sitting in new bookshelves at the Sen family home in Barddhaman, covered to prevent dust from accumulating again. As an interesting side note, the late Sukumar Sen resisted his friends' efforts to convince him to have the collection treated with insecticide, mistakenly insisting that dust itself was the most effective insecticide available.

Burton:

Do you think the *sahajīya* materials in the Advaitācarya corpus are "authentic" or are they rather an example of the appropriation of Advaita's good name for the *sahajīya*-s' own purposes?

Manring:

I'm not even going to touch the question of what the word 'authentic' means! Clearly the *sahajīya*-s who produced these materials consider them authentic, as they represent a view which that group truly held and holds. Does Advaita's own family, his own descendants, consider them authentic? Probably not. But whose word counts here? It all depends on one's perspective. On the one hand it is not totally outside the realm of possibility that Advaita did indeed participate in *sahajīya* activities. We're beginning to discover that what we had originally thought to be solid lines between traditions are actually quite fluid, and people can and did adopt practices and doctrines from multiple sources. What I think was solid, was the concept of a lineage transmitted through a guru, but that guru may be drawing on a number of different sources for his teachings. That being said, I do think this material constitutes an attempt on the part of one *sahajīya* group to legitimate itself by demonstrating its connection with a man the community regarded as a veritable pillar of society, Advaitācārya, a man who was beyond reproach. Nothing the man did could be considered scandalous, so if he was *sahajīya* (as these texts purport to demonstrate) then *sahajīya* practice must be legitimate.

Zelliot:

Is there still a worship or honour today for Advaita, or has he passed out of practise?

Manring:

When I, was doing my dissertation research, I spent a lot of time in Shantipur, his hometown and I followed the festival season. In particular I was interested to see what they would do on his birthday. It is a tremendous festival and the images of Advaita and Sītā Devī were taken out of the temple and paraded around the town. What is interesting is the part when everybody sits in the temple courtyard and listens to the recitations. There is a little bit of recitation from the *Advaitaprakāśa*, one of the bigger biographies of him. Mostly they recite from the *Caitanya Caritāmṛtam*. His family continues to maintain the temple that he set up. He had a large family, so there are several other temples that are in the lineage of his sons. They are still being maintained and there are images of Advaita along with those of Rādhā and Krishna.

Interrogating the Oral and Written Traditions of Mīrābāī and Kabīr

NANCY M. MARTIN

Let me begin with a song from rural western Rajasthan sung by a highly regarded low-caste Meghwal singer named Padmarām:

> The bamboo pole of knowledge has penetrated my
>   body;
> The rope of love is pulled taught.
> Drunk with love, I climb up on the rope,
> And with utter concentration, perform the acrobat's art.
>
> *My love is only for Hari's name;*
> *I see only Hari's name; I hear only the Lord's name.*
> *My love is only for Hari's name.*
>
> I have thrown down the pot balanced on my head;
> Smashed the pot of ego;
> Now with a dancer's graceful steps, I fall at the feet of
>   God.
> I come, snapping out the rhythm with joy.
> *My love is only for Hari's name...*
>
> The spout of the pleasure palace will open,
> A thousand drops cascading down,
> Hari, a thousand drops cascading down.
> The cuckoo of love will begin to call.
> These are the things worth tasting.
> *My love is only for Hari's name...*
>
> Though I walk the path of past traditions —
> People say I go against them,
> Oh Compassionate One, people say I've gone astray.
> Wounded, I wander here and there,
> And no one asks what my heart feels.
> *My love is only for Hari's name...*

Ancient books, old scripts — why get hung up on
these?
Oh Compassionate One, why get hung up on such
things?
Mīrābāī's is the dear Mountain Bearer —
All fear of taking the final leap is gone.
My love is only for Hari's name…

Until we reach the *chāp* of Mīrā, it is not necessarily clear to whom this song might be attributed. There is a defiance here, but also a focus on concentration and the name of God and on the depths of love. A thread of logic connects the verses, but we could imagine them also appearing in other contexts surrounded by other verses or with a different refrain. Images from folk traditions and everyday life pervade the song — the *naṭ* or acrobat performing in a crowded public market, the ubiquitous pot of water balanced on the heads of countless women bringing water to countless homes. The song does not belong to any literary canon of Mīrā, not being found in any current published set of Mīrā songs or in any manuscripts, as far as I know. How might we come to terms with the nature of such a seemingly boundary-less tradition of religious poetry and the religious insights embedded therein?

One way to approach these questions is through a close comparative study of written and oral traditions of songs attributed to specific saints, and I have embarked on such a study of Mīrābāī and Kabīr, collecting oral traditions of both saints among predominantly low-caste singers in rural western Rajasthan (including both *jāgaraṇ* performers and professional caste musicians) beginning in 1993[34]. In addition to exploring the transmission of and reservoirs for such oral traditions (reported in my essay in *The Banyan Tree*[35]), I have begun a comparative study of these songs with the manuscript traditions of the saints. In so doing a picture of the wider traditions begins to emerge — traditions whose nature is fluid and dynamic rather than fixed,

[34] The working title of this project is 'The Renunciant Rāṇī and the Weaver of Protest: Mīrābāī and Kabīr in Rajasthani Folk Traditions'.

[35] Nancy M. Martin, "Kabīr and Mīrabai in Folk Traditions of Western Rajasthan: Meghwāl and Māṅganiyār Repertoires", in *The Banyan Tree: Essays on Early Literature in New Indo-Aryan Languages*, edited by Mariola Offredi, Delhi: Manohar, 2000, vol. II, 391-424.

coalescing at times around particular images in related families of songs and at other times drawing on images and phrases from a wider pool of folk and devotional materials to generate new and yet "familiar" songs in the accepted language of particular saints. And within the songs sung by these low-caste singers, I have identified what I would call a low-caste Hindu spirituality of liberation.

In the case of Mīrābāī, if we examine songs attributed to her in 17th and 18th century manuscripts in Rajasthan, we do not find a coherent or original core of songs, but instead what appear to be the repertoires of singers with overlapping imagery and in some cases overlapping phrases and verses, though not identical forms of songs, which have a distinct continuity with the oral performance traditions of the 20th century in the same region. Many are heavily marked by imagery from Vrindavan and Krishna's incarnation and the range of emotions encompassed by romantic love. What makes them distinctly Mīrābāī's is above all the appearance of her name in the final line which adds an additional layer of meaning to the songs by invoking her narrative and experience. With regard to these songs, the grounds for authenticity are the identification of Mīrā with Krishna's *gopī* lovers and the fact that the song is more often sung in her name than that of another saint, even as the singers draw from the broad pool of images of Vaishnava devotion.

We also find other families of songs that are thematically associated with Mīrā — those addressing Krishna as a *jogī*, for example, and songs addressed to the *rāṇā*, rejecting all he has to offer, embracing the life of the renouncer and of the poor, and recounting her persecution. And many of these songs also overlap with folk forms and genres of women's songs — recounting the ornaments of a bride to reject the traditional ones and take on the ornaments of devotion or offering sung dialogues between Mīrā and the *rāṇā* or her sister-in-law or her mother or mother-in-law in "chorused conversation"[36]. These forms and genres are here transformed into a language of devotion even as A.K. Ramanujan has so eloquently suggested of the images and tropes of classical Tamil love poetry used by the Āḻvārs and Nayanmars[37]. This

---

[36] Ann Grodzins Gold, in Gloria Goodwin Raheja and Gold, *Listen to the Heron's Words*, Berkeley: University of California Press, 1994, pp. 93-94.

[37] A.K. Ramanujan, "Afterword" in *Hymns for the Drowning: Poems for Visnu by Nammalvar*, London: Penguin, 1993.

continuity with folk and women's songs forms another boundary of the tradition.

In addition there are also a series of standard phrases that mark songs attributed to Mīrā — for example, "your servant in birth after birth" or "without you I cannot live" or "hunger does not come by day nor sleep by night" — and also set verses that appear in multiple song — of Mīrā being sent the cup of poison, for example, or standard expressions of *viraha*. These phrases and verses can be combined in innumerable ways to form familiar yet new songs, and the singers singing the songs (in the snapshots recorded in writing in manuscripts or caught through audio recording and transcription) understand themselves to be singing Mīrā, even if they are not singing a fixed song. Indeed a comparison of manuscript and oral sources suggests that there is no fixed form of any song attributed to Mīrā, although there are indentifiable families of song that move around specific sets of images.

In addition to deepening our understanding of the nature of the tradition through such an analysis, we can also explore the religious import of this material. My initial reflections appear in a recently completed article, focusing on Kabīr[38]. A distinctive voice emerges from the songs sung by low-caste singers that has clear similarities with the religious reflections of "the poor" broadly defined in other religious traditions. These songs are directed toward ordinary people and sadhus, both encouraging them and challenging them. In the case of Kabīr, the biting critiques of the *Bījak* give way to calls for respect of self and others and affirmations of embodiment and the dignity of all by virtue simply of a human birth, formed by God, the master craftsman, with the potential for liberation. The value of the things of this world is radically relativised, because of their transitory nature, and social distinctions evaporate in the face of death. Protest is embedded in what is praised and what devalued, and life's meaning is clearly shown to lie in the cultivation of devotion to God, a difficult path at best, but the only true choice. Songs of Mīrābāī, sung among the same low-caste communities, also reflect similar themes of self-respect, dignity, and survival, with particular emphasis on Mīrā's renunciation of privilege and affirmation of the dignity of the low-caste people with whom she

---

[38] Nancy M. Martin, "Homespun Threads of Dignity and Protest: Songs of Kabir in Rural Rajasthan", accepted for publication in a volume on Kabir edited by Monika Boehm-Tettelbach of the University of Heidelberg.

stands in solidarity. The deep parallels between the low-caste religiosity being articulated here and that found, for example, in the theological reflections emerging out of "poor" Christian communities suggests further that social positioning may shape theistic religious experience in distinct ways that cross the boundaries of religious traditions.

In addition to this ongoing project, I have also just completed a detailed study of the broader traditions surrounding Mīrābāī[39]. Comprehensive in nature, this work begins with an exploration of the manuscript traditions of story and song associated with the saint, but then turns to the academic construction of Mīrābāī in the late 19th and early 20th centuries, oral performance traditions of narrative and song surrounding her, and the role she plays for women who choose lives of independence and/or devotion outside of marriage.

Mīrābāī comes to the attention of nationalists and then Rajput historians as a shining example of Indian womanhood, but her story must be retold to eliminate those elements that might be offensive to Rajput honor and ideals of the *pativratā*. Elements enter the story not found in earlier tellings, reflecting the structure of the tales of Rajput heroines and seemingly emerging from a small group of men related to Mīrā's natal and marital family[40]. Vastly different stories of Mīrā are sung by low-caste singers in "Mīrā Janma Patrī" and in a second epic tradition called "Kumbhā Rāṇā rī Bāt"[41].

Mīrā's name is also used to describe particular women. At a superficial level, any girl or woman who shows unusual skill as a poet, dancer or singer or who demonstrates great devotion or fiery independence may be called "Mīrā." But other women become much more deeply identified with her, taking up the lives of devotional saints, singing and dancing in temples, and sometimes also composing in her name. I have located a number of such

39 Nancy M. Martin, *Mīrābāī*, forthcoming with Oxford University Press, New York, 2002.

40 Nancy M. Martin, "Mīrābai in the Academy and the Politics of Identity", in *Faces of the Feminine from Ancient, Medieval and Modern India*, edited by Mandakranta Bose, New York: Oxford University Press, 2000.

41 Nancy M. Martin, "*Mīrā Janma Patri* and Other Tales of Resistance and Appropriation", in *Religion, Ritual, and Royalty*, edited by Rajendra Joshi and N. K. Singhi, Jaipur: Rawat Press, 1999. I was able to record a group of Turi Bhats in the Sirohi region singing *Kumbha Rana ri Bhat* in 1996, though I have not yet published an analysis of this fascinating narrative.

women, who have come to understand their own life experiences and choices in terms of the saint, and the wider society has also made sense of their lives through an identification with Mīrā. Thus Mīrā opens up a space for women (generally upper-caste Rajput or Brahman women) to choose lives outside of the *pativratā* ideal[42].

In the end, how does one come to terms with the vast and dynamic set of traditions of story and song which surround such saints? Using the example of the actual life of Indira Devi (a disciple of Ram Mohan Roy and Sri Aurobindo who met Mīrābāī in trance for more than forty years) as a parable for the way such traditions function and grow, I propose that, particularly in the case of Mīrā, her narrative and songs function as a form of *līlā*, with each participant in the tradition entering into the narrative world of Mīrā's life and emerging both transformed by the encounter and transforming the tradition in the process. Such transformative encounters generate new yet "authentic" songs and stories as saints, like Mīrābāī, continue to live on in the imaginations and experiences of devotees.

DISCUSSION

Shelke:

Have you been able to determine the historical facts about Mīrā's life? More specifically, do you know with any certainty who her husband actually was?

Martin:

We do not have historical documentation regarding her life — only one reference in *Naiṇsī rī Khyāt* which says "People say she was married to Bhoj Rāj." But there is no way we can find out for sure whether this is the case. Bhoj Rāj is convenient — he did not do anything of any significance, and he died early. But I have not come across any source that can help us definitively decide whether Mīrā was his wife.

Shelke:

---

42 I first reported on such women in "Mīrābai: Inscribed in Text, Embodied in Life," in *Vaisnavi*: *Women and the Worship of Krishna*, edited by Steven Rosen, (Delhi: Motilal Banarsidas, 1996), pp. 7-46. I have followed their lives since that time and additional information appears in the finished work.

Have you found some of the same themes in the folk traditions of Kabīr that you have found in Mīrā?

Martin:

Yes. One of the reasons why I studied Kabīr and Mīrā together was that one cannot really tell what elements of certain songs might be identified as characteristic of Mīrābai in the folk traditions unless one also looks at what is being sung in the names of other saints. Then one can identify shifts in common styles and themes that are particular to a given saint. For example, there are songs called *fakīrī*, which are about renunciation, that are sung in both the Kabīr and Mīrābāī traditions, yet they are different in nature. *Fakīrī* songs of Mīrābāī are primarily an expression of solidarity as this high caste woman embraces the life of the poor and, in some, rejects everything that the *rāṇā* has to offer. Those of Kabīr have overlapping themes and speak more of the renunciation of the ascetic or sadhu and the passing nature of all worldly objects and sources of security. There is also a group of *fakīrī* songs which may be attributed to either saint and are, with only the *chāp* changing. However, to change the *cchāp* does shift the meaning, given the differences in each saint's narrative and character.

Bangha:

Is there any possibility that the event of Mīrā's having been poisoned can be found in any of the poems that can be attributed to Mīrā herself?

Martin:

My guess is that there is a historical basis for this incident, but there is no definitive evidence to prove it. I do not see any reason to doubt that Mīrābāī herself existed or to doubt that there is some truth to the story of her oppression because it is so fundamental to who she is as we know her. Yet it is very hard to tell what might be the facts of her life, even if we could assume that the most commonly attributed songs of Mīrā really belonged to this particular sixteenth-century woman (which we can't). There are songs which are absolutely beautiful poetically that have been preserved. And some are clearly very old. But whether they were composed by one particular woman, I do not know. I do not see any way to find this out, but I also do not think that it is absolutely necessary to do so.

Bangha:

Is the poisoning incident unique to Mīrā's story?

Martin:

Surviving poisoning is a common motif in the *stories* of a number of other saints, but I do not know whether these poisoning incidents appear in the *songs* of other saints. Many songs attributed to Mīrā make reference to this incident in her life, however. The two most fundamental identifiable characteristics of Mīrā are that she was a high caste woman and that she was poisoned. These elements define Mīrā (whether or not seemingly autobiographical songs can be traced back to her direct speech).

Zelliot:

Mīrābāī is often represented, for untouchables in Gujarat, as a symbol of oppression and misery, and as one in whom they can find comfort. Are you aware of Parita Mukta's book[43]? And, did you find any similar attitude among the low-caste people with whom you worked? Did they adopt Mīrā as the symbol of an oppressed person with whom they could identify?

Martin:

Yes, I am very much aware of this book. And, yes, but I would articulate this in a slightly different way. I would say that what she becomes is a way for them to articulate their own oppression and at the same time to resist it. We have all these songs that say: "Rāṇā, I do not want all the things that you can give me. Everything you have is in truth meaningless." By rejecting everything he has, the singers are rejecting the value of those things and affirming alternate values. And so I would say that it is not so much a negative identification with her suffering and oppression even as they are oppressed, but rather a positive affirmation of Mīrā's solidarity with them and willingness to take on the same life they live. She lifts them up, saying: "This is a good place to be, far better than the valueless world of the Rāṇā." If we look carefully at what the Kabīr of low-caste traditions also says, we find a sense that no matter whether you are wealthy or you are at the bottom of the social and economic hierarchy, the things of the world are all passing and they are not what count in the end.

---

[43] Parita Mukta, *Upholding the Common Life: The Community of Mirabai*, Delhi: Oxford University Press, 1994.

The *Romāvalī*, a Work Ascribed to Gorakhnāth Analysis of an Unpublished Manuscript from the Jodhpur Collection

MARIOLA OFFREDI

The text

The *Romāvalī* is a short work ascribed to Gorakhnāth, the systematiser (or, according to some scholars, the founder) of Haṭhayoga, who lived some time between the 9th and 13th centuries. The text of the *Romāvalī* I found in the Rajasthan Oriental Research Institute, at Jodhpur, covers folios 1-5 (from the last line of the verso of folio 1 to the fourth line of the recto of folio 5) of Codex 14396 in the Jodhpur collection stored in the Institute's library. The Codex is not dated. In the Institute's catalogue, it is marked as having been copied in *saṃvat* 19th century (AD 1743-1843).

The text of the manuscript differs from the one edited by Pītāmbardatt Baṛthvāl in *Gorakh-bānī*[44]. Baṛthvāl relied on three manuscripts containing various works: 1. "Pauṛī manuscript", or manuscript K, found in Jaipur by Paṇḍit Tārādatt Gairolā from Pauṛī (Garhwal). According to Baṛthvāl, the Pauṛī manuscript was copied around *saṃvat* 1715 (AD 1658), during the life of Rajjab, who himself collected works of Gorakh and other yogīs and sants, etc.,copied in the fourth part of the manuscript. 2. Manuscript GH, which he acquired from a bard, Śubhkaraṇ Cāraṇ from Jodhpur, containing various works, including those of Nirañjanī sadhus (and a Nirañjanī sadhu had, in fact, given Śubhkaraṇ the manuscript); Baṛthvāl states that the manuscript was copied in *saṃvat* 1825 (AD 1768). 3. An undated Sanskrit manuscript A, which contains the Sanskrit translation of works by the yogīs, and is kept in Sarasvati Bhavan at Varanasi[45]. The text published by Baṛthvāl is that of manuscript K. Variations in manuscript GH are given in footnotes. There is no translation or explanation of the text.

---

44 *Romāvalī*, in *Gorakh-bānī*, pp. 203-206.

45 *Ibid.*, *Bhūmikā*, pp. 12-14.

If Baṛthvāl is correct about the date of manuscript GH, the manuscript I found in the Oriental Research Institute should also be ascribed to around 1825 *saṃvat* (AD 1768). In *Gorakh-bāṇī*, Baṛthvāl published the *Romāvalī* of manuscript K, while also providing details of minor variations found in manuscript GH. Such variations often, but not always, agree, either totally or in part, with the text I am analysing in this paper. Baṛthvāl also states that, unlike manuscript K, manuscript GH's *Romāvalī* is in dialogue form. It should also be noted that he was given manuscript GH by a bard from Jodhpur. However, one of the most striking differences relates to the ending line. Baṛthvāl states that the text of manuscript GH lacks the closing line, which in manuscript K is: *etī ek romāvalī granth jog kathitā śrī gorakhnāth*; while the manuscript I found does include the closing line (*iti śrī gorakhnāthjī kī romāvalī sampūrṇ*). In conclusion, while it appears that manuscript GH quoted by Baṛthvāl is not the one I found, there is at least some evidence that the two manuscripts were copied from the same or a similar original, or from a copy of the original. We cannot know for certain whether Baṛthvāl donated the manuscript to the Rajasthan Oriental Research Institute. The manuscripts belonging to the Institute were either purchased or transferred from State Museums (where they were transferred from the Department of Annals of the former Jodhpur Princely State); several, however, were donated[46].

Although the *Romāvalī* is probably a manual for teaching disciples, its function changed across the ages. Manuscript GH was given to Baṛthvāl by a bard. Such works have entered the repertoire of bards (*cāraṇ*) in Rajasthan, by whom they are sung. In fact, many original manuscripts are still jealously guarded by the Cāraṇ families and within the "small estates" (*ṭhikānā*)[47].

In the text, *ṣ* is used instead of *kh*. However, since some words occur in which *ṣ* is not pronounced as *kh* (for example, *diṣṭiḥ*= *dṛṣṭi*, R 10; also written in the *tatsama* form *dṛṣṭi*, R 22), in this analysis I have transcribed it as *kh*.

---

[46] P.D. Pathak, "Oriental Studies and the Oriental Research Institute, Jodhpur (A Brief Appreciation)", in *Rajasthan Oriental Research Institute Jodhpur*, pp. I-IV.

[47] *Ibid.*, p. I.

The teaching

The teaching is, as is customary, founded on not only esoteric, but magical principles. The magical element of the teaching lies mainly in the fact that it is expounded in groups of 3 and 4, and their multiples 12 and 16. The groups sometimes seem to comprise non-homogeneous categories; however, with the possible exception of the 4 vulvas (*khāṇī*), a link among the constituents may be inferred. Grouping elements can be also a device to aid memorisation, since teaching was orally transmitted. The differences between texts may also be ascribed to oral transmission. Moreover, the Nāthapanthīs were wandering Yogīs, who in due course branched off into different sects. Nonetheless, the magical element should not be underestimated; in *Mahādev Gorakh guṣṭi* (dialogue between Mahādev and Gorakh — a manuscript of *saṃvat* 1794 published by Baṛthvāl), for example, living beings are grouped into 5, because the material body is considered to be made up of the 5 elements — earth, water, fire, air, and ether (see below).

Number 3. The definition of *AUM* given in the *Gorakṣa Śataka* attests to the importance of this number: *AUM* is the supreme light (*paramjyoti*), "in whose elements the world *bhūḥ*, *bhuvaḥ* and *svaḥ*, and the divinities moon, sun and fire exist (GŚ 84). In which the three times, the three Veda, the three worlds, the three accents, and the three gods are situated [...] (GŚ 85). In which action (*kriyā*) and desire (*icchā*) and knowledge (*jñāna*), Brāhmī, Raudrī, Vaiṣṇavī (the consorts of the three gods), the threefold *śakti*, are contained (GŚ 86). That *Oṃ*, in which these three letters *A*, and likewise *U* and *M*, which has the *bindu* as its mark, exist, is the supreme light (GŚ 87)"[48].

Number 4. Rather than originating from the 4 directions (6/8 directions are recognised in Indian thought), number 4 may derive from the classification of living beings in zoology, and specifically from the classification made by Caraka. To remain in key with number 4, 4 senses instead of five are enumerated: sight, hearing, smell, taste (touch is not mentioned). In my view, the omission of touch has nothing to do with its connection with the most material

48 *Gorakṣa Śataka*, in G.W. Briggs, *Gorakhnāth and the Kānphaṭa Yogīs*, pp. 300-301.

of the five elements, earth; since the external gross matter is also made up of the three *guṇa*-s (ultimate subtle entities), and according to the Sāṅkhya system, the material body is constituted of all 5 elements. In *Mahādev Gorakh guṣṭi* [49], for instance, 5 senses are enumerated, and to remain in line with number 5, living beings are classified in 5 groups, with a repetiton of the viviparous group under two different headings: *jeraj* (*raj*? see below) and *piṇḍaraj* (which does not appear in the *Romāvalī*, where living beings are grouped into 4 categories).

Beginning

The teaching begins with the definition of body, as made up of *sattva* which is considered as the father, *rajas* the mother, and *tamas.* The body, thus made up of the three *guṇa* groups of Prakṛti, dies (*gāḍe pāai*, "is buried"). The visible body originates from the union of 7 elements: 4 from the mother — blood, flesh, skin and vessels (*nāḍī*); and 3 from the father — semen, bone, and marrow (R 1).

Following the definition of body, the "eight-member-yoga" (*aṣṭāṅg jog*) is also explained as consisting of parts named after parts of the body: 2 hands, 2 feet, breast, forehead, 2 eyes (? *vāṭ* [? *bāṭ* = *mārg*, "road"] (R 2). In the manuscript edited by Baṛthvāl, the word is *ghāṭ* [? = *diśā*, "direction"]). This definition underlines the importance of body in Haṭhayoga, and also clearly differentiates Haṭhayoga from classical Yoga, whose eight members (*yogāṅga*) or parts are: *yama* (restraint/self-control [moral injunctions]), *niyama* (rules/observances), *āsana* (posture), *prāṇāyāma* (holding the breath), *pratyāhāra* (withdrawal of the senses from their objects), *dhāraṇā* (concentration), *dhyāna* (meditation), *samādhi* (absorption) (the last three parts constituting *saṃyama* or control/self-control).

The body is particularly important in the teachings and practice of the Buddhist Siddhas. On the one hand, compared with Buddhist Siddhas, Gorakh lays greater emphasis on the interior practice, and as such, his teachings may be regarded as a protestant movement in a period when Hinduism was struggling to assert itself. On the other hand, Gorakh's teachings also include such practices as *vajrolī*, *maithuna*, etc., which are typical of the Buddhist Siddhas.

---

49 *Gorakh-bānī*, pp. 233-235.

The elements of the teaching given in the *Romāvalī* may be subdivided into "external", or located outside the body, and "inner", or located inside the body. The only element outside the body is the guru. The *Romāvalī*, however, highlights the importance of this element, stating that the disciple without a teacher is blind (*gur jiskā lakhāvai nahī celā tiskā andh*, R 20).

The remaining elements are located inside the body. In the manuscript, the teaching is imparted in the form of a dialogue between Svāmījī (Gorakh) and an *avadhū* (the text edited by Baṛthvāl is not in dialogue form). In contrast with other works ascribed to Gorakh, where the *avadhū* is often Gorakh himself, in the *Romāvalī*, Gorakh is the master, Svāmījī, and the manuscript closes with the words: "End of the Romāvalī of Śrī Gorakhnāthjī".

The inner elements are grouped by 2 (one group), 3 (three groups), 4 (seven groups), and their multiples 12 (one group) and 16 (one group).

Group of 2

1. The master of the heart (*hīrad pīr* [subsequently *hirad pīr*]), the master of the vital element/life (*jind pīr*). In the text, these are defined as inner. Master of the heart is mind, master of the vital element-life is breath (*pavan*) (R 5).

Groups of 3

1. Binding/stoppage (*bind* = *bandha*), piercing (*bhed*), posture (*mudrā*). The person who practices them is called a *siddha* (R 3). They are not explicitly defined as inner in the text, their inner character is inferred from description. The mind binds, the breath (*pavan*) pierces, one must pratice the posture of the semen (*bind mudrā* [*bind* = *bindu*]) (R 4).

2. Mind, sun, moon. Described as inner, even if not openly stated as such. In Haṭhayoga, sun and moon are located in two different centres, namely the *maṇipūraka cakra*, situated in the region of the navel and the *sahasrāra*, the thousand-petalled lotus situated at the top of the skull. The mind thinks purely, the sun destroys, from the moon the nectar falls (*man vimal vicārai sūrya khirai candra jharai*) (R 5).

3. The aim or truth of body (*sarīrārath*), the highest truth (*paramārath*), the secret truth (*gūḍhārath*). Defined as inner (*ghaṭ bhītarī*). The aim of the body is knowledge of the body, the highest

truth is knowledge of the breath (*pavan*), the secret truth is gnosis (*gyān*) (R 7).

Groups of 4
1. *Khecarī*, *bhūcarī*, the secret (*gupat*), the visible (*pragat*). Described as inner, even if not defined as such. *Khecarī* (the posture: "moving in the sky", rolling the tongue backwards to seal the hollow in the top of the throat) is mind, *bhūcarī* (the posture: "moving on the earth") is breath (*pav* = *pavan*), the secret is gnosis (*gyān*), the visible is body (R 6).
2. The 4 masters (*pīr*). Defined as inner. Mind is Machindar, body is Īśvarnāth, consciousness (*cit*) is Cauraṅgīnāth, gnosis (*gyān*) is Gorakh (R 8). In this enumeration, Gorakh predominates.
3. The 4 instruments (*takbīr* = *tadbīr*)[50], i.e. the senses. Defined as inner. Sight, hearing (*surati*), smell (*nāsikā*), taste (*jibhyā*) (R 9). It may be observed that, in order to remain in key with number 4, only 4 senses are enumerated — touch is not included in the list.
4. The 4 quarters (*dasā* = *diśā*). Defined as inner. Sound (*sabad*) is north, breath (*pavan*) is west, sight south, hearing (*surati*) east (R 10). It may be seen that *surati*, equating to east, is pre-eminent. The holiest passage of the *Ṛgveda*, the *Gāyatrī*, a verse from a hymn addressed to the sun god Savitṛ, is whispered in the ear of the initiate by the brahman who officiates at the ceremony of investiture with the sacred thread. The pre-eminence of the *surati* demonstrates the importance of the practice of sound for the yogīs. In other works ascribed to Gorakh and the Nāthapanthīs, sound is often called *sabad*, the Word. In the philosophy of music (Nādabrahmavāda), the *nāda* is perceived through musical sounds (*śruti*). There is a direct link between the experience of the yogīs and the philosophy of music, but it must also be stressed that the yogīs' goal is to surpass the experience of sound in order to attain the state of absence of sound, a state in which reintegration into the Absolute is achieved. In this enumeration, however, *sabad* is not given an esoteric meaning. Its importance lies in the fact that it is the "word", i.e. the teaching of the master. On the other hand, none of the four categories — sound, breath, sight, hearing — can be overlooked, as they constitute a unity in the experience of a yogī: sound or teaching (*sabad*) is a determining factor because "a disciple without a guru is blind" (see above); breath (*pavan*) is

50 *Śabd-saṅgrah* (Glossary), in *Gorakh-bānī*, p. 262.

fundamental because, through breath control, the mind becomes still; sight (*diṣṭiḥ*) is the inner sight, which the yogī, following the master's instructions, obtains after withdrawing his mind from the sense objects — inner sight enables him to experience the Supreme Light (*paramjyoti*), which is *AUM* (GŚ 84); hearing (*surati*) is hearing the sound of *AUM*, which is one with the Supreme Light.

5. The 4 spiritual instructions (*pades = upadeś* — which, at the end of the text, reappear as the 4 constituents of the sun [*cyāri kalā sūrya kī*] — instead of the 4 spiritual instructions, the text edited by Baṛthvāl has the 4 constituents of the self [*āp kalā*]). Defined as inner. *Ūram* (also written as *uram*), *dhūram*, *jotī* (also written as *joti*, *jauti*), *jvālā*. *Ūram* (wave) is the mind, *dhūram* (dust) is breath (*pavan*), *joti* (light) is the eye, *jvālā* (flame) is hearing (R 11-12). When the mind is stilled by breath control, the yogī reaches the state in which the Supreme Light that is *AUM* (connected with hearing) can be seen and enjoyed.

6. The 4 vulvas (*khāṇī* [mostly written as *khānī*]). Defined as inner. These are: *setaraj*, *jeraj*, *īḍaraj*, *udavīraj* (also written as *iḍaraj* and *udabīraj*) (R 13-14). This group matches Caraka's classification of living beings (including vegetation) as originating from humidity (*svedaja* — for example, insects), from an egg (*aṇḍaja* — for example, fish, reptiles, birds), from the placenta (*jarāyuja* — viviparous or mammals), and from a vegetable organism (*udbhijja*). According to Caraka, these are all sexually generated (*kṣudra-jantu*, small animals, are non-sexually generated, and are classed as animals without bones, animals without blood, animals belonging to very prolific species, animals which cannot be crushed). This group of 4 *khāṇī*, as explained in the *Romāvalī*, is, however, devoid of logic, or has a logic of its own. They have been grouped into 4 mainly to fall in line with the number of the remaining groupings, and then adjusted to match Caraka's classification of sexually-generated living beings. According to the *Romāvalī*, bone derives from humidity, semen from placenta, the eye from the egg, and the *romāvalī* (a line of hair [above the navel]) from a vegetable organism (R 15). The eye and the line of hair respectively resemble an egg and vegetation; semen may also be interpreted as being produced during sexual intercourse (see below, under the 16 *kalā* of the moon). The explanation of the birth of bone from humidity would appear to lie in the medulla ossium, while, according to Caraka, insects are born of humidity. As a matter of fact, grouping these categories into 4 falls in line with the remaining groups of 4,

i.e. it is based on magic, and/or is a device to aid memorisation of the text. In *Mahādev Gorakh guṣṭi*[51], another work ascribed to Gorakh, living beings are instead grouped into 5 categories, according to the 5 elements constituting the material body in the Sāṅkhya system of philosophy. In order to enumerate the groups of living beings in accordance with the 5 elements, a fifth category of living beings is introduced in *Mahādev Gorakh guṣṭi.* This is *piṇḍaraj* (= *piṇḍaja*), or the viviparous category, which is, however, also given as *jeraj* (properly *raj*, and Baṛthvāl puts a question mark after this word — at any rate, it cannot be *raj=rajas*, menstrual fluid, as this would not make any sense).

7. The 4 teachings (*bā̃ṇī*). Defined as inner. These are: *sahaj* (born together/inborn), *sañjam* (control), *supāv* (= *svabhāva*, "own state"), *atit* (= *atīta*, detached/free). The 4 *bā̃ṇī* summarise the teaching and main points of Haṭhayoga: inborn is the body, control is air-breath (*pavan*), own state is vital breath (*prā̃ṇ*), detached/free is the Supreme State (*param pad*), i.e. Supreme Bliss (R 16-17).

The enumeration of the 12 constituent parts of the sun (the sun, situated in the *maṇipūraka cakra*, soaks up the *bindu* [nectar or semen] falling from the moon situated in the *sahasrāra*; the *maṇipūraka cakra* also contains the element fire, the *samāna* air whose function is digestion, and *rajas*, i.e. menstrual fluid which, like the sun, soaks up the *bindu*)[52] and the 16 constituents of the moon, is preceded by a definition of the *mahāmudrā* and a summary of the main concepts set forth in the 4 category groups (R 18-19). The *mahāmudrā* is defined as the "great city" (*mahā ujīni nagrī* [great city of Ujjaini?], unborn (*ajaunī* [not born from a *yoni*]), self-born (*simbhū* = *svayambhū*. The definition of the *mahāmudrā* as a "great city", synonymous with Supreme Bliss, recalls a *caryāpad* by Siddha Ḍombīpā: "That Mātaṅgī, driving the boat between Gaṅgā and Jamunā (= the two *nāḍī* Iḍā and Piṅgalā), without asking for any money, takes us to the City of the Buddha (synonymous with Supreme Bliss)".[53] The Mātaṅgī is a woman from the scavenger caste. In the works of the Buddhist Siddhas, who practiced ritual coitus, the *mudrā*, or, more often, the

---

[51] *Gorakh-bānī*, pp. 233-235.

[52] G.W. Briggs, *op. cit.*, p. 313.

[53] Ḍombīpā, *Caryā* 14. Quoted in Parśurām Caturvedī, *Uttarī Bhārat kī sant-paramparā*, pp. 42-43. For the text of the *caryā*, see Miśrabandhu Vinod, p. 49.

mahāmudrā, is frequently named after women from the low castes or tribes.

The definition of the *mahāmudrā* is linked, similarly, with its practice, consisting of meditation on a possibly interiorised ritual coitus and on Sound: the person who meditates on *khāṇī bā̃nī* is called Nirākār (without form, the Absolute), in *AUM* the light is perceived (*khāṇī bā̃nī kū̃ vicārai te nirākār bolīai ūkār madhe jotī jāṇīai*, R 18). As the 4 *khāṇī* are defined as the whole body (R 13-15), which is the microcosmic level of the macrocosm, and the 4 *bānī* are defined as states/conditions of the body (R 16-17), Supreme Bliss or liberation is attained through the body and in the body, i.e. not after death. It is worth mentioning at this point, that, as he becomes one with the Absolute (*nirākār* [without form]), the yogī perceives the light in the sound *AUM*, which is both Light and Sound. Thus, we have an extension of the meaning of *bānī*: besides the word/teaching of the master, *bānī* is the Sound, that is, *AUM*.

The 4 constituents of the sun (first as *riv* [= *ravi*] *kī cyāri kalā*, and subsequently, in the last line of the *Romāvalī*, as *cyāri kalā sūrya kī*, which were presented earlier as the 4 spiritual instructions (*cyāri pades* [= *upadeś*], appearing as the 4 constituents of the self [*cāri āp kalā*] in Baṛthvāl, p. 204, and, at the end, 4 constituents of the sun [*cāri kalā sūraj kī*], p. 206) are again explained here (R 19): *uram* ([*ūram*] a metaphor of the mind), *dhūram* (a metaphor of air), *jauti* (light, for the sight), *jvālā* (flame, for the hearing). The mind drinks pure water (the nectar or *bindu*), unites the two parts, i.e. the types of air known as *prāṇa* and *apāna*, the first of which normally ascends, and the second of which normally descends, and thus enjoys the 16 *kalā* or constituent parts of the moon, i.e. the nectar of immortality falling from the moon situated in the *sahasrāra*, thus reaching Supreme Bliss.

At the end, before the 12 constituent parts of the sun and the 16 constituent parts of the moon are enumerated, the relevance of the teacher (*gur=guru*, a word different from *pīr*, which appears in the group of 2 consisting of the mind and the air-breath-*pavan*, and in the group of 4 Machindar-mind, Īśvarnāth-body, Cauraṅgīnāth-consciousness, Gorakhnāth-supreme knowledge-*gyān* [*jñāna*]) is underlined: the disciple without a teacher who makes him see is blind (R 20).

Group of 12

The 12 constituent parts (*kalā*) of the sun situated in the *maṇipūraka cakra*. The 12 *kalā* of the sun share a common element in the *rajas*, i.e. energy, activity, as they all stem from desire; *buddhi* (consciousness) is also included, as it is the seed of the desire for rational knowledge. They are enumerated as follows: thought, mind (properly: wave [*traga* = *taraṅg*]), pride, illusion, taking, error, purpose, consciousness, passion, anger, greed, and sight (*ciu traga ṛibh* [sic!, a copyist's error for *ḍibh*] *māyā paragrahaṇ parapañc het budhi kām krodh lobh dṛṣṭi*, R 22).

Group of 16

The 16 digits of the moon (*kalā*, a digit or one-sixteenth of the moon's diameter, refers to Śiva, who bears one-sixteenth of the moon). In the manuscript of the *Romāvalī* analysed here, despite being called "16 *kalā* of the moon" 17 *kalā*, rather than 16, are enumerated — the word *niravāsīk* (= without desire) may either be a copyist's error or an attribute of *nirañjan*. According to Baṛthvāl, who appears to have seen, if not the same manuscript as the one analysed here, at least one that was copied, with variations, from the same source, in the list of 17, "air" (*bāī* in Baṛthvāl, *vāī* in the manuscript analysed) and "nectar" (*amṛt* in Baṛthvāl, *imratāī* in the manuscript analysed) are given as a single element of the group. Since the words enumerated are not separated by a comma (as they are in Baṛthvāl), another hypothesis may be advanced. It would seem more logical to connect *niravāsīk* with *nirañjan*. The word *niravāsīk* (missing in the manuscript published by Baṛthvāl, and quoted as *nivāsīk* in a footnote) might be an attribute of *nirañjan*. The two words share a similar meaning: *niravāsīk*, "without desire/passion", and *nirañjan* "without ointment", i.e. untainted or unsoiled.

There is not one common element linking the 16 *kalā* of the moon. In those pertaining to morality, the *sattva* element of the Substance-Prakṛti (for example calmness, detachment, forgiveness, purity) is prevalent; others, such as Supreme State (which is given simply as *pad*) and nirvana, cannot be made up of *sattva*, which is a constituent of both thought and gross matter (according to Sāṅkhya, *sattva* and *rajas*, i.e. intelligence-matter and energy-matter, are predominant in thought, while *rajas* and *tamas*, i.e. energy-matter and mass-matter, predominate in gross matter)[54]. The 16 *kalā* are enumerated as follows: calmness, detachment, forgiveness, purity, unwavering, gnosis, own (essential) nature, supreme state, nirvana, fearlessness (*niravikh* [*niraviṣ*] = *nirbhīk*; Baṛthvāl has *nṛbiṣ*, which he suggests should be interpreted either as *nirbhīk* or *viṣ rahit*), passionless, unsoiled (the two possibly constitute a single *kalā*), (moderate) food, (moderate) sleep, sexual intercourse (*mahīthan* = *maithun*), breath, nectar (*svānti niravartī chimā nṛmal nihacal gyān sarūp pad nirabāṇ niravikh* [*niraviṣ*] *niravāsīk nirañjan ahār nidrā mahīthan vāī imratāī*, R 24) (Baṛthvāl has the same enumeration, except for *niravāsīk*, with different word forms).

Like the Buddhists, Gorakh preached a middle path, as is displayed by the inclusion of food and sleep in the 16 *kalā* of the moon, in the sense that they should be enjoyed in moderation. Particularly noteworthy is the fact that sexual intercourse is included among the *kalā* of the moon. The *Romāvalī* does not appear to have been intended for married yogīs, who are expected to practice moderation in every aspect of life, including sexual intercourse. Instead, *mahīthan* recalls *vajrolī* and similar sexual practices common to Tantric Buddhism.

Conclusion

He who practices the 4 constituent parts of the sun obtains the 16 *kalā* of the moon (*cyāri kalā sūrya kī sādhai tau saulh kalā candramā kī pāvai*), i.e. he who reaches stillness of the mind by breath control enjoys the Supreme Light which is the Sound. "End of the Romāvalī of Śrī Gorakhnāth" (*iti śrī gorakhnāthjī kī romāvalī sampūrṇ*).

ABBREVIATIONS

R *Romāvalī*
GŚ *Gorakṣa Śataka*

54 Surendranath Dasgupta, *A History of Indian Philosophy*, vol. I, p. 242.

REFERENCES

Romāvalī, Codex 14396, folios 1-5, Rajasthan Oriental Research Institute, Jodhpur.

Rājasthānī-hindī hastalikhit granth-sūcī, IV, Jodhpur Saṅgrah, ed. Oṅkārlāl Menāriyā, Jodhpur: Rajasthan Oriental Research Institute, 1978.

Baṛthvāl, Pītāmbardatt, ed. (see *Gorakh-bānī*)

Briggs, G.W., *Gorakhnāth and the Kānphaṭa Yogīs*, 3rd ed., Delhi: Motilal Banarsidass, 1982 [1938].

Dasgupta, Surendranath, *A History of Indian Philosophy*, 5 vols., Delhi: Motilal Banarsidass, 1991 (reprint) [Cambridge: CUP, 1922-1954]

Gorakh-bānī, ed. Pītāmbardatt Baṛthvāl, 4th ed., Prayag: Hindī Sāhitya Sammelan, 1979.

Gorakṣa Śataka (Sanskrit text with English translation), in G.W. Briggs, *Gorakhnāth and the Kānphaṭa Yogīs*, 3rd ed., Delhi: Motilal Banarsidass, 1982 [1938], pp. 284-304.

Rajasthan Oriental Research Institute Jodhpur, published on the occasion of the XXXI All India Oriental Conference Jaipur, 29-31 October 1982, Jodhpur: Rajasthan Oriental Research Institute, 1982.

Rājasthā̃nī sabad kos, 9 vols., ed. Sītārām Lāḷas, Jodhpur: Rājasthānī Śodh Sansthān & Caupāsnī Śikṣā Samiti, 1962-1978.

Offredi, Mariola, *Lo yoga di Gorakh. Tre manoscritti inediti*, Milano: Cesviet, 1991.

— "Some Concepts of Gorakh Yoga through the Analysis of three Nāthpanthī Manuscripts", in *Studies on Early Modern Indo-Aryan Languages, Literature and Culture*, eds. Alan W. Entwistle and Carol Salomon with Heidi Pauwels and Michael C. Shapiro, New Delhi: Manohar, 1999, pp. 267-286.

— "The Concepts of Sound and Light in Gorakh Yoga through the Analysis of Three Nāthpanthī Manuscripts from the Jodhpur Collection", in *Religion, Ritual and Royalty*, eds. N.K. Singhvi and Rajendra Joshi, Jaipur: Rawat Publications, 1999, pp. 153-172.

— Miśrabandhu (Gaṇeśvihārī Miśra, Śyāmvihārī Miśra, Śukdevvihārī Miśra), *Miśrabandhu Vinod*, *khaṇḍ* 1-2, new ed. rev. & enlarged, Lucknow: Gaṅgā Pustakmālā, 1972.

— Parśurām Caturvedī, *Uttarī Bhārat kī sant-paramparā*, 3rd ed. rev. & enlarged, Allahabad: Bhārtī Bhaṇḍār, 1972.

DISCUSSION

Horstmann:
Does anyone know of any field research being done about the usage of the texts today? The system you have been describing is inconsistent in itself. Is there any didactic usage for the Naths today? We know that the manuscripts of these texts are fairly recent.

Offredi:
According to me the texts are mainly concerned with spiritual teaching, by the teacher to the disciple.

Hawley:
Regarding the manuscripts you just described, of the Oriental Research Institute, Jodhpur, is it explained how that manuscript came into the collection? Does it have anything to do with the important presence of the Naths in Jodhpur in the 19th century?

Offredi:
The catalogues of that Institute are very good indeed, but I am not aware of how the manuscript was acquired.

Horstmann:
It may be that Véronique Bouillier, Paris, is starting a study about the very strong Nath traditions in Rajasthan.

Research Report

HEIDI PAUWELS

I would like to talk about the current project I am working on and I would be very happy to have your feedback on it. My research has been going in two directions.

One is the non-dissertational research, on the TV *Rāmāyaṇa*, which has become much easier now as we have the transcription by Prof. Mizokami[55].

I have been looking at gender issues, especially at Sītā as she is portrayed as the ideal Hindu woman. My approach has been to select episodes in which Sītā is central, such as the *phulvārī* episode, the wedding, her decision to go to the forest with Rām, and so on. My method has been to look at what Ramananda Sagar has done with the main sources, Vālmīki and Tulsīdās. I was quite surprised by the result of this comparison and by the way Sagar leaves out or selects to incorporate or even adds (see Bibliography, pp. 298-300).

My dissertational research was on Harirām Vyās, a 16th Rādhā-Krishna *bhakta* from Orcchā, settled in Vrindavan. In my book I give an edition and English translation, as well as a glossary. The book focusses on the vernacularization of a Sanskrit text, and the changes that came with it. I also presented Vyās's case with reference to several topics that may be of interest to you, such as the goddess Rādhā and Vrindavan as centre of pilgrimage. Vyās describes not only the glories of Vrindavan, but also vents his anger at people who came there and started to use the place for commercial purposes. I may further refer to the different papers I presented on Vyās in the earlier Bhakti Conferences, on the topic of meter and anthology versions of Vyās' poems.

Recently, I have convinced one of my students at Seattle to look at the poems of a Krishna poet, Mādhavdās Jagannāthī, in the *nirguṇī* manuscripts now available thanks to Winand Callewaert's efforts.

---

[55] Girish Bakshi and Tomio Mizokami, eds. 1992. *Ramayana*: A TV serial by Ramanand Sagar. Osaka University of Foreign Studies.

My current project expands on what I presented at the Paris Conference. For the book I analyse all poems by Harirām Vyās about other *bhakta*-s. This sheds interesting light on the early Bhakti milieu of Vrindavan. These can be called hagiographic poems *by* Vyās, whereas in the second part of the book I look at hagiography *about* Vyās. In a total of about 50 poems Vyās mentions by name other *bhakta*-s, contemporaries from Vrindavan or the neighbourhood, some alleged disciples of Vallabha (like Sūr), Mīrābāī and also *nirguṇī* poets like Raidās, Nāmdev and Kabīr. This could become a '*Vyās Bhaktamāl*', although the title may be misleading, because Vyās did not write to create a systematic *Bhaktamāl*, and the poems are scattered throughout the manuscripts of the *Vyās Vāṇī*, usually under the heading *sādhu stuti* or *sādhu viraha*. Vyās lived about half a century earlier than Nābhādās and he comes from a different sectarian milieu. This Vyās collection sheds some light on the oral formulae that Nābhā used. I do not mean to say that Vyās was a source for Nābhā, but that what Vyās wrote down must have been current in the oral tradition in his time.

In Vyās's works we see a particular kind of 'remembrance' of facts about earlier *bhakta*-s. It reveals more about the perception in the 16th century Krishna-Bhakti milieu than about the historicity of certain facts regarding a particular *bhakta*. The main issue I look at is: what does he tell us about the 16th century milieu, who is considered to be "in" and who is "out", and so on. I should clarify that Vyās did not found a *sampradāy*, but he saw himself as part of a broader community of saints.

DISCUSSION

Hawley:
Can you say something about the second part of the book, the materials *about* Vyās?

Pauwels:
This study is partly based on my dissertational research. I look mainly at the issues: what is the ideal of a devotee in the post-16th century period, and what are the sectarian appropriations of Harirām Vyās.

Burton:
Does Vyās list low-caste saints?

Pauwels:

Yes, in Nābhā's *Bhaktamāl* we find a list of low-caste saints said to be followers of Rāmānanda. Vyās has a rather similar list. One poem with such a list is often quoted as evidence for the fact that Kabīr and Raidās were initiated by Rāmānanda. It looks as if the list itself was going around in the oral tradition at that time. The list also has a rhetoric force emphasising that Bhakti saves also low-caste people. Linking this list to Rāmānanda seems to be the major agenda of Nābhā and Anantadās. The fact that this list is also found in Vyās's songs should perhaps not be seen as proof for the historicity of the initiations, but only as an indication that in Vyās's time these *bhakta*-s were considered to belong toegether and that it was said that Kabīr was initiated by Rāmānanda.

Svāmī Rām Tīrtha in Punjab

ROBIN RINEHART

My research has focussed on the geographical area of Punjab, on Hindi, Urdu, Punjabi and some Braj materials. I am trained in the history of religions (Hinduism) and the fact that I work on Punjab has led me to look at some Sikh and Muslim materials as well. The first area of my research was hagiography and I was especially intrigued by what everyone finds: the similarities we find in the stories that are told about saints' lives. I was also interested in the question why accounts of saints' lives change over time. I first looked at this in my dissertation which was on the life and teachings of Svāmī Rām Tīrtha, a Punjabi saint (1873-1906) and I went on to do some further work about him as a 19th century-early 20th century reformer of Indian religions, who was interested in promoting more clearcut definitions of religious traditions and to a certain extent also in drawing a connexion between religious identity and nationalism, a theme that has become much more important since India became independent.

After all that work I still had a lot of questions about how hagiographical traditions develop. Why, e.g. were there over 25 different hagiographies written about Svāmī Rām Tīrtha in just 80 years, particularly given that his community is relatively small? Why did the stories about his life become more mythical, considering that Svāmī Rām Tīrtha himself portrayed himself as a great champion of science and objectivity? In his early 20th century lectures he stated that he did not accept miracles, and yet if you talk to his followers, let us say in the 1980s, one of their favourite stories about Svāmī Rām Tīrtha concerns his pre-svāmī days when he was a mathematics professor and apparently would become so absorbed in his devotional activities that he would forget to show up for his classes. Krishna himself, it is said, would come in and give very compelling lectures on mathematics.

Thinking about all those questions took me back to the same materials that I had looked at for my dissertation and the result was a book that was published by OUP. There my approach was, rather than trying to establish a definitive account of Svāmī Rām Tīrtha's life (about which in fact there is enough information to do), to try to understand why the stories about his life should change and expand so dramatically in the course of less than one century.

I argue that the best way to understand hagiography is to look at it not so much as a record of the saint's life, but really more as the record of how people experience that life. That is an experience that necessarily changes, based on the hagiographer's particular relation to the saint. The observer may be actually a close follower, or not close; or somebody who becomes a follower long after the saint has lived. Each particular experience of the saint will reflect the particular historical, religious and political context. Essentially, what I was arguing is that mythologising is not something that is separate from history, which is the way it is often been characterised in critical literature on hagiography, but that in fact it is very much a historical process and that if you look at that interaction, you can learn so much more about how hagiography develops.

My interest in Svāmī Rām Tīrtha has led me also into other areas. He was said to be an advocate of practical Vedanta, like Svami Vivekananda. At the same time I was also intrigued by his frequent statement that his favourite poet was a Punjabi Sufi saint, Bullhe Shāh. That led me to look at Bullhe Shāh's life and poetry, where I discovered that there is a wide range of opinions in scholarship in India, Pakistan and the west, on who he was and what he wrote. Some people say he was a Sufi; others say he was an early advocate of the programme of Pakistan's Islamization; that he was a Vedantic Sufi, a Vaishnava Vedantic Sufi; or that he was the precursor of Radhasoami's theology.

In looking at this literature, I found that just very much as with Svāmī Rām Tīrtha, the most interesting questions for me were not necessarily about critical biography, or a critical edition of Svāmī Rām Tīrtha's work, but in figuring out the different ways that people rendered Svāmī Rām Tīrtha's life and work. What I found is that while there is a wide range of claims made about Bullhe Shāh, virtually all these claims are based on a strategy that involves a selective use of the rhetoric of textual criticism and historiography in order to make effectively religious and theological assertions. These are claims that revolve first around problematic assumptions about 1) the nature of authorship in biography and their relationship to one another, and 2) about religious categorizations. People typically have either taken 20th century conceptions of religious identity and projected them uncritically unto the past, or they have tended to invent categories that are not in any way well defined, such as 'Vedantic Sufism'.

Issues such as the debate about Bullhe Shāh's religious affiliations, the fact that Svāmī Rām Tīrtha is now seen as the great champion of Hinduism, but was in fact very fond of a Sufi saint, along with my field experiences in India and Pakistan have fuelled for me an ongoing interest in the categorization of religious traditions. In the Punjab this is an especially salient issue because, while it is common to talk about Hinduism, Sikhism and Islam as the main religious traditions of the area, the boundaries between them are not always clear-cut. There is abundant evidence from the past and the present that many Punjabis participate in religious activities that cross the currently accepted boundaries of the three religious traditions. This categorization is far more complex then we typically understand. We need to think about the methods we use for analysing these traditions. It is, e.g. problamatic to use the term 'Hinduism', particularly in pre-colonial South Asia. Further, we know that Sikhism has only gradually taken the form in which we see it today, and it is controversial how exactly you characterise that. There is also an enormous diversity in South Asian Islam, and conversion to Islam in South-Asia itself was typically a gradual process. Yet, we still tend to use the terms Hinduism, Islam, Sikhism when talking about religious literature in the Punjab. The use of these categories and what comes with them, and the particular ideas about what constitutes a religion shapes the kind of questions that we ask about the materials that we study. This often leads us to explain why the categories we use do not work and takes us away from what might be more interesting to study.

From that point of view I am now also looking at the *Daśam Granth*, a text associated with Gurū Gobind Singh, which involves all the issues that I just described. What does it reflect about Sikhism of its time, why is there all the material derived from the *Purāṇa*-s, why does it talk about goddess worship, and so on? Until very recently the literature on the *Daśam Granth* tended to focus really on questions of authenticity.

DISCUSSION

Hawley:
Are you trying to analyse the circumstances that lead to the compilation of the *Daśam Granth*?

Rinehart:
At this moment I am mainly looking at the different ways people have been looking at the *Daśam Granth*. There are different editions, some of which include far more material then others: Especially the editions like *caritropākhyān* that are considered to be controversial. How do people construct arguments about whether this was entirely the composition of Gurū Gobind or may be that he wrote only some parts, and how it all fits together. Also the question why some material is there at all.

Zelliot:
Kiehnle's Keśav Prahlād Atre [see above, p. 117 ff.] was given legitimacy by putting him in a particular tradition (*sampradāy*). How did Svāmī Rām Tīrtha get his legitimacy?

Rinehart:
He is not part of an established lineage. He initiated himself into *sannyās*, taking Svami Vivekananda as his model. Later biographies in fact link him directly to Svami Vivekananda, even describing spectacular meetings between the two.

Svāmī Haridās and the Haridāsī *Sampradāy*

LUCY ROSENSTEIN

My work on Braj has been focussed on the Haridāsī *sampradāy*, which, as you all probably know, is a religious community based in Vrindavan. Like the Radhavallabh *sampradāy* it is a *rasik* sect which worships the joint form (*yugal svarūp*) of Radha and Krishna, and concentrates on their eternal amours (*nitya vihār*).

Despite the abundance of hagiographic material, little is known about the instigator of the sect, Svāmī Haridās. His life probably spanned the last three quarters of the 16th century and the beginning of the 17th century. He is still venerated as a most skillful *dhrupad* singer and the legendary teacher of Tānsen. Two works are attributed to him: the rapturous *Kelimāl* is a collection of 110 verses, dedicated to the love-play of the divine couple Radha and Krishna, while the didactic *Aṣṭādaś Siddhānta*, which comprises 18 poems, expounds general Bhakti doctrines. However, despite Haridās's fame, his works have remained largely neglected. Even members of the Haridāsī *sampradāy* are often not familiar with his compositions since their complexity, obscurity, obsolete and untraceable regional (*deśī*) vocabulary and poetic liberties are a hard test even for the most ardent devotees.

It is precisely these qualities which triggered my interest in Svāmī Haridās's *pada*-s. The first time I read *Kelimāl* I understood very little. I accepted the challenge and started the work on my doctoral thesis, later turned into a book, entitled: *The Devotional Poetry of Svāmī Haridās: a Study of Early Braj Bhāṣā Verse*, published by Efbert Forsten in 1997.

The first problem I faced was the lack of critical edition of Haridās's texts. I spent six months in Vrindavan collecting manuscripts and reading through the printed editions with members of the Haridāsī *sampradāy*. I came back with a wealth of material: sixteen manuscripts (the earliest dated 1755) and copies of five sectarian commentaries to Haridās's texts. When I attempted to produce a *stemma codicum* of the manuscripts I realised that 'classical' textual criticism could not be applied to these texts for two reasons. First the oral transmission of Haridās's poetry for possibly two centuries meant a large-scale contamination. Second the usual criteria on which editorial decisions are based — meter and grammar — could not be applied here: neither the grammatically flexible dialect of Braj nor the metrically elastic style of *dhrupad* were of any assistance in trying to establish the direction of change in the text's variants.

I analysed the data presented by the manuscripts with the use of two computer programmes developed by biologists concerned with uncovering relationships between living organisms. The cladistic method makes implicitly historical assumptions regarding the origin of shared differences between the objects to be classified (in our case manuscripts). The phenetic method assesses overall similarities and differences between objects without making any assumptions about the historical relationships between the objects to be classified. Any physical measurable phenotypic property can be used, in our case these are the ones and noughts of having/not having the indicative variant. If we imagine co-ordinates where every axis represents one of our indicative readings, each of the witnesses would be designated by a point in a multi-dimensional space, and the aggregate distance between the manuscripts could be measured by the distance between the manuscript points. With the help of these two methods (particularly the phenetic one) I came to the conclusion that there were at least two recensions of Haridās's verses: one which might offer a glimpse of the pre-canonical period of oral transmission and the other which constituted the vulgate. Because of the two difficulties mentioned above I decided to settle for a scholarly, rather than a critical edition: to give the oldest and the most faithful to the canonised version manuscript as the basic working text and record all variants in the *apparatus criticus.*

Now that I had a text to work with, I turned my attention to the main task: interpretation and translation, and linguistic analysis of *Aṣṭādaś Siddhānta* and *Kelimāl.*

My observations on Haridās's language confirmed the general structure of Braj Bhasha, but Haridās's text also showed some salient features: extreme poetic liberty in creating rhyme-forms, abundance of Perso-Arabic vocabulary (and use of several non-Braj Bhasha forms) and partiality for (odd) relative-correlative constructions and repetitions.

To put the text into a context I also looked at the way sectarian commentaries have interpreted Haridās's *pada-s* and at their symbiosis with a singing tradition. The latter was proven by the connection of the verses with a *rāg*; the inclusion of a *chāp*, and the lack of any apparent metrical structure (apart from the regular four-line arrangement) which suggests association with the musical style of *dhrupad*. I further pursued the connection of Haridās's composition with *dhrupad* in an article entitled rather unimaginatively 'Svāmī Haridās and *dhrupad'* which I published in the *Journal of Vaiṣṇava Studies* in 1996.

Turning my attention to the sectarian commentaries I investigated the way they have re-interpreted Haridās's message to fit the theological views of the sect developed after his death. Three tendencies were clearly prominent: Haridās's preference for the eternal love-play of the couple (*nitya vihār*) had been made exclusive of any other motifs of Krishna's myth; his view of Radha as part of the *yugal svarūp* had given way to a preoccupation with her primacy; and Haridās's devotional persona as one of Radha's *sakhī*-s had been 'identified' as being a reincarnation of Lalita. The sectarian re-interpretation of Haridās's text proved to be a fascinating topic and I also dedicated an article to it: "From Kṛṣṇa's Mistress to the Mistress of Kṛṣṇa. The Evolution of Rādhā in the Haridāsī *sampradāy*", published in the spring 2000 issue of the *Journal of Vaiṣṇava Studies*.

While working on the Haridāsī *sampradāy* I was alerted to the similarities of its theology and that of the Radhavallabh *sampradāy*: both sects worship the joint form, *yugal svarūp* of Radha and Krishna, but give primacy to Radha. Both concentrate on the *nikuñja līlā* to the exclusion of *vraj līlā*. Both adopt erotic love (*mādhurya bhāv*) as their favoured devotional approach. In both sects the devotees are to emulate the role of a confidante, a *sakhī*, who promotes, but does not participate in the eternal amours. In my article "The Rādhāvallabha and the Haridāsī *sampradāyas*: A Comparison", published in the Fall 1998 issue of the *Journal of Vaiṣṇava Studies* I attempted to establish if there were any differences between the two sects on the basis of which they could claim separate identity.

This brief overview covers my research in the field of Bhakti so far. In the last two years I have unfortunately lost my single-minded dedication to the Haridāsī *sampradāy* and shifted the focus of my research from Braj-related topics to contemporary Hindi poetry. However, — "Once Brajvāsin for ever Brajvāsin" — I am sure I will keep returning to Braj; there is still plenty of work which waits to be done, even on the Haridāsī *sampradāy*. Apart from Haridās there are seven main *ācārya*-s of the sect; all of them have composed *vāṇī*-s, none of which has been studied yet. I am particularly fascinated by the second *ācārya*, Viṭṭhal Vipul, an ecstatic mystic who is said to have died within a week of Haridās's death, grief-stricken. Another project which has been discussed between Heidi Pauwels, Rupert Snell and me is a popular book on Hari *trayī* which would make their believes and poetry accessible to the general public.

DISCUSSION

Hawley:
Have you reconsidered your opinion in your book about Haridās and Tānsen?

Rosenstein:
Still I do not consider Haridās as the musical teacher of Tānsen.

Hawley:
How do Haridāsī-s imagine the association of Haridās and Tānsen?

Rosenstein:
I do not think it is very different from what we find in other hagiographical material. The (small) picture I have on my book is of the meeting between Akbar, Haridās and Tānsen. If you look at the age of the persons, it looks very improbable that this refers to a historical meeting, because Akbar is depicted as the oldest of all, which could not possibly be true. It is the typical topos about the emperor coming to visit, about the mundane power being subjugated by the power of devotion. In addition, of course, we have the interesting fact of Tānsen being present at the meeting. There are beautiful stories about how Tānsen started to sing, because Haridās would not sing in front of Akbar. Tānsen deliberately made some mistakes and then Haridās started to sing, in, e.g. *rāg malār*, with the result that it started to rain in the middle of summer.

Krishna Bhakti from a Playful Perspective

GALINA ROUSSEVA-SOKOLOVA

I would like to present to you the work I have finished as a Ph.D. thesis, which was defended in the Ecole Pratique des Hautes Etudes in Paris in 1999 and should be published soon by a Swiss editor, Labor et Fides, with the French title *Jeu et dévotion*: *Aspects ludiques de la bhakti krishnaïte au Braj*, or 'Devotion and Play: some ludic aspects of Krishna-Bhakti'. It is based mainly, but not exclusively, on texts by Sūrdās. The subject is more an anthropological than a strictly philological one, and the texts are presented not for their own sake, but rather as evidence material for the religious experience that lies behind them.

First, I want to express the uneasy feeling I have when speaking about my subject in English. That is because the word "play" has a more restricted sense in English than its equivalents in other European languages. The English language has two words, "play" and "game", where others have one and it makes it somewhat hard for me to convey the more abstract sense I have in mind when I speak about "play and devotion" or "play in devotion". An escape would be to use the word 'ludic' (from Latin *ludus* or 'play'), which I did not find in my dictionaries at home, but which I saw used in an article by Friedhelm Hardy.

Now I will go briefly through the table of contents of my book, focusing on the logical articulations of the text. It starts with a summary of what has been said about play as a theoretical concept in European anthropological thought, starting from J. Huizinga in the thirties. He saw 'play' as the origin of culture itself and though he has been much criticised for that, his focus on the ludic has inspired several generations of anthropologists, philosophers, sociologists and psychologists. The main criticicism against him was that his concept of the ludic was too vague, encompassing too many types of behaviour without a common denominator. Accordingly, few have dared after him to step out with a global theory of play. What we rather find is a focus on particular sorts of play, for instance children's plays, which have been a constant interest for psychologists.

Still, a few went in the opposite direction, like Eugen Fink, a German philosopher and a phenomenologist, who published in the early sixties *Das Spiel als Weltsymbol*, where he sees play as an ontological principle. His perception of play (to put it very simply) is like a sort of random Brownian movement of particles, free of all necessity, which underlies the structure of the universe. He also sees, though, a direct link between this abstract ontological principle and the play of children, or, for that matter, the play of gods.

From here we go to things Indian and in particular to the theological concept of *līlā*, which Fink would probably have found most inspiring if he knew about it. I do not go into a thorough analysis of *līlā*. What is important to me is that it makes theologically acceptable the analysis that follows, since in a way the plays and playing involved in the devotional activities in Braj prolong and develop the initial ludic act of the divinity.

From there we go to Sūrdās and his *Sūrsāgar*. Sūrdās's verses were chosen as reference material both because of their poetic quality and the immense popularity of their author, deemed an exemplary saint and an emblematic figure of the period. Through the analysis of a number of *pada*-s several points are made:

1) Compared to the manner in which different episodes of the myth are related in the *Bhāgavat Purāṇa*, in the *Sūrsāgar* a shift of perspective shows up. Sūrdās adopts a down-to-earth and deeply subjective point of view, which makes possible a truly empathic experience of the audience.

2) From the point of view of play Sūrdās's vision transforms the somewhat abstract theological principle of *līlā* into a play more tangible and concrete. By imitating the humans the divinity has transformed the universe into a playground. More than the Creator of the play, he is now presented as a participant — a particularly joyful and mischievous one. Not only is he playing, at times his passivity is an invitation to be played with. By playing with him the mythical Brajvāsī-s attain their salvation. By imitating the Brajvāsī, devotees in Braj will attain theirs. Play is where God and men meet and participating in the play becomes a soteriological necessity. Thus play and playing is part of the devotional strategy of Krishna Bhakti.

The next step is to elucidate what kind of play the devotees cultivate by analysing the behaviour of the *gopī*-s as role models. Thus the importance of imitation and identification is brought to light, as evidence comes both from the texts and from the reality of temple life.

Then I go one step further from the texts to religious experience itself. A brief discussion is included on how play coexists with the sacred in different contexts. In search for a larger perspective I have turned to the tradition of hymnaries (*nitya* and *varṣotsava pad-saṅgrah, kīrtan saṅgraha*, etc.) to check the observations made on the basis of the *Sūrsāgar*. A brief philological presentation is included on what these hymnaries represent and how they are used in temples and private homes. I have taken these hymnaries (which contain many *pada*-s signed 'Sūrdās') as one logical step further from the myth of the *Bhāgavat Purāṇa* to the reality of temple life in its yearly and daily cycles. In my pursuit of the ludic I have searched in these extremely voluminous collections for poems related to different sorts of plays and games, like the swing, the kites, the play of *causar* between Rādhā and Krishna on the eve of Divālī, and the celebration of Sāñjhī, which is also considered a playful event. These are often late inclusions, but what I wanted to find out is whether play as a devotional strategy would be present in them. What I actually discovered is that the subject matter is of little importance to the presence or absence of play as a devotional strategy. Often, when a theme which has been part of the imagery of Krishna-Bhakti for a long time (e.g. the swing) is being treated, the *pada*-s are long, descriptive and static. They do not trigger the religious emotion independently, they are more like verbal icons illustrating and complementing the ritual context. They contain little or no trace of that 'invitation to join' the play which was detected in Sūrdās's verses. On the other hand, play may reappear, together with the mischievousness of the divinity and the deeply subjective point of view, for instance, in the songs, devoted to Sāñjhī.

What can be suggested is that the longer a theme or a mythological element has been part of the Krishna cult, the more stereotyped and ritualised its poetic treatment is. On the other hand, when it comes to the incorporation of traditions originally alien to Krishna-Bhakti, play is often resorted to as an integrating mechanism. Before being incorporated the foreign element is reworked and permeated by the general playful spirit of Krishna-Bhakti.

To conclude I should like to say that the ludic line of force is certainly not the only one to shape the devotion to Krishna. It is nevertheless a thread worth following and one which can possibly explain at least some of its paradoxes.

A Hindi Folktale Related with the Hindu Festival of *Bhaiyā Dūj*

TEIJI SAKATA

A study of an imaginary text produced by many variants[56]

Folktales are basically performed orally: they are told and heard among the members of the community in which the tales are traditionally enjoyed. Every storytelling is a live performance and the same performance of storytelling can never be made again in exactly the same way. One story told now will inevitably have some differences when told later, even if the same storyteller tries to perform it in precisely the same manner as he/she did it before. However, people often understand that they enjoy the same and familiar story having a definite form or text widely received in the concerned community. This kind of understanding is widespread in societies in which oral tradition is losing ground and folktales are usually enjoyed in written forms.

I argue that there is no definite form or text of a folktale. The seemingly definite form or solid text of a folktale is a comprehensive image produced by many variants of the storytelling. In order to demonstrate and explain this assumption, we are expected to have many versions or variants of a similar story. I will examine the issue selecting the example of Hindi story told on the occasion of the Hindu festival of *Bhaiyā Dūj*. The material of this story can be found in the books on Hindu festivals, in the collections of folktales and also in classical literature of Hindu myths and legends.

[56] I would like to thank Dr. Unita Sachidanand of Delhi University for getting me interested in the festival and folktale of *Bhaiyā Dūj*. While preparing for the seminars on folk traditions of North India with her in Tokyo in 1999, the idea to study the subject occurred to me. I would also like to thank Dr. Sachidanand for correcting and brushing up the manuscript of this paper.

1. Books on Hindu festivals and rituals

In the cities and towns of contemporary India, we may find many handy books bearing titles such as *The Book of Hindu Festivals and Ceremonies* [Bahadur 1998]. In small towns or bazaars of big cities, it is not uncommon to discover their counterparts in Hindi and other regional languages by the title of *Hiduoṁ kā vrat, parva aur tyauhār* [Tripāṭhī 1978], which can be roughly translated as *Hindu rites and festivals*. These books are usually meant to serve as a guide for housewives and other believers in performing annual religious festivals and ceremonies. However, they also throw some light on the origin of the festivals, offerings to be made to the god(s), appropriate methods of worship and related folktales and legends.

Tripāṭhi's treatise in Hindi on *Yam Dvitīya/Bhaiyā Dūj* festival, provides a complete guide to that festival. The author describes the origin of the festival by citing Puranic literature of classical Indian myths and legends. The food items (*bhoga*) offered to the god is specified by the material and the method of cooking. Also specified are the rituals associated with offering prayers. The author concludes by narrating the folktales (*lok-kathā*) and scriptural tales (*kathā*) generally recited on the occasion [Tripāṭhī 1978, 248-255]. But Tripāṭhī often neglects some of these important aspects while describing other festivals.

A similar book written by Bahadur in English, in the treatise on the *Bhaiyā Dūj* festival, gives a complete list of offerings to be prepared, comprehensive directions concerning the procedure of worshipping, and a rather long folktale with suggestions on the ceremonial performances to be observed on this occasion. But the book makes no mention of the origin of this festival [Bahadur 1998, 64-74]. Āśā Bahan's book in Hindi, on the contrary, explains the origin of the festival citing Puranic sources and myths/legends associated with the festival of *Bhaiyā Dūj*. However, it makes no attempt to incorporate folktales.

These examples show that the books on Hindu festivals, ceremonies and fairs are not always well organised, and very often they lack description of some important aspects of the festivals. A tentative survey of such sources, written both in Hindi and English, reveals that the folktales told on these occasions are not duly recorded.

2. Popularity and the sources of folktales related to Hindu festivals

Though not given due importance in general guides to Hindu fairs and festivals, the folktales associated with them seem to be very popular among the women folk. In a storytelling session performed by the members of a Hindu family at the request of the present writer, six members narrated thirty-two stories in all, among which four folktales told by two ladies related to Hindu festivals [30 August, 1 September, 1981 in Mathura City]. Fourteen selected folktales have since been published in the original Hindi with a Japanese translation [Sakata 1999].

In the published records of folktales related to Hindu festivals and ceremonies, we sometimes find such titles as *Avadhī vrat kathāeṁ* or *Ceremonial stories of the Avadhi dialect area* [Pāṇḍey 1967], *Rājasthānī vrat kathāeṁ* or *Ceremonial stories in Rajasthani language* [Purohit 1961]. Some other published records of folktales, though not bearing such titles, may include a section of ceremonial folktales. *Khaṛībolī kī lok-kathāeṁ* or *Folktales of the Khariboli dialect area* is a good example of this kind [Guptā 1979]. These sources, in most cases records of stories told by elderly ladies, offer excellent material for the study of ceremonial folktales which have not been given due recognition in the books found on Hindu fairs and festivals.

3. *Yama Dvitīya/Bhaiyā Dūj* described in Puranic literature

Yama Dvitīya/Bhaiyā Dūj is observed on the second day of the bright half of the month of Kārtik, and in some areas on the second day of the dark half of the month of Phālgun. The former, observed in the month of Kārtik or October-November, is more prevalent. The name *Yama Dvitīya* draws upon an ancient myth associated with Yama, the lord of Hell who was invited by his sister Yamunā to her house on this day. The festival in effect implies that the brother(s) are invited to their sisters' houses on this second day, and eat food prepared by the sisters. The origin of this festival is mentioned in various Purāṇas, huge sources of Sanskrit literature dealing with ancient Indian history, myths and legends. Kane describes the origin of the festival citing relevant Purāṇas such as

Bhavişyotara Purāṇa, *Padma Purāṇa* and *Skanda Purāṇa* [Kane 1994, 207-210]. The essence of mythological origin of this *Vrat* or festival/ceremony is found in *Skanda Purāṇa* [Book Two, Section III, Chapter 11, Nos. 44-53. English translation by Tagare 1994]. Important portions are cited below:

> 1. On this day, Yama, the son of the sun god Sūrya, was received with great hospitality by his sister Yamunā. Ornaments and cloths were presented to him.
> 2. The gentle lady Yamunā cooked sweet rice dishes and fed Yama.
> 3. After eating the delicious food, Yama honoured his sister with ornaments and clothes and asked Yamunā for a boon.
> 4. Yamunā requested that all sinners are to be set free from hell today, and that those who take food from the hands of their sisters should be happy.
> 5. Yama granted the boon to Yamunā saying that he who takes food in the house of his sister and worships her on this day shall never see the entrance of Yama's abode, hell.

All the Purāṇas quoted by Kane contain more or less a similar description as quoted above.

The main theme of the story given in *Skanda Purāṇa* is to strengthen the bond of close relationship between sister and brother. In the guidebooks to festivals and in the collection of folktales, most of the stories explaining the origin of this festival are similar to the above given story with slight differences. According to the notes to "The Story of a Brother and a Sister" (Uttar Pradesh) included in *Folktales of India* edited by Beck et al., the ceremony of *Bhaiyā Dūj* is specially popular in the Hindi speaking area of North India [Beck et al. 1987, 305]. The present writer has obtained sources containing stories of the *Bhaiyā Dūj* festival published from the Khariboli area [Guptā 1979, 12-16; Beck et al. 1987, 121-123] and from the Avadhi area [Pāṇḍey 1967, 190-201]. All these have sufficient information about the place and manner of recording.

The present writer also had the chance to listen to the story of *Bhaiyā Dūj* told by an aged lady of Jaipur city in March 1999. Dr. Unita Sachidanand, Associate Professor of Japanese language and literature at Delhi University, India informed us at a seminar that "she heard a story of *Bhaiyā Dūj* at her husband's native place near Chapra city, Bihar, located in the area of Bhojpuri dialect [Sachidanand, Unita. *Bhaiyā Dūj* as observed at my native place Garhwal and at the native place of my husband in the Bhojpuri dialect area", 26 June, 1999, Tokyo. Summary in Japanese was distributed to the participants.

Judging from the published records which contain information on the place of storytelling, and from personal observations, we may infer that, as also briefly mentioned by Beck et al., the stories of *Bhaiyā Dūj* are commonly told from Rajasthan in the west to the Bhojpuri area in Bihar in the east. In addition to the stories included in the books on folktales, we find some more related folktales in the books on Hindu fairs and festivals. Among the latter, the books by Tripāṭhī and Bahadur have already been mentioned above. Another popular book with many editions is *Bharatiya vrat tyauhār aur mahilā sangīt* by Āśā Bahan and Lāḍo Bahan [n.d.]. None of the authors of the books on fairs and festivals give any data concerning the place of storytelling or the name of the narrator.

4. Folktales of *Bhaiyā Dūj*: Three folktale types with many variants

Hereafter in this paper, the stories recited/narrated on the occasion of the festival will be mentioned as *Bhaiyā Dūj*, adopting the popular nomenclature by which the festival is known among the people. Folktales told on the festival are generally of three types:

> Type 1. A sister rescues her brother from many dangers, which may be similar to AT 707III "The children's adventures" and equivalent to Motif R158 "Rescue of brothers by sisters"[57]. Examples to be cited in detail later.

---

[57] AT = Arne & Thompson, *Types of the Folktales*, Revised Version, Helsinki, 1961.
Motif = S. Thompson, *Motif-index of Folk Literature*, Bloomington, 1936.

Type 2. Sister receives her brother once indifferently and later with respect, according to the cloth the brother wears, which is equivalent to AT1558 “Welcome to clothes”. Examples: Beck 1987, 121-123; Gupta 1976, 12-16.

Type 3. Sister's husband hates his brother-in-law/his wife's brother, and he tries to kill him when he comes to see his wife, which may have similar stories in Motif S0-S99 “Cruel relatives”. Example: Pandey 1967, 193-194 = *Bhaiyā Dūj* folktale No. 1.

Among these three types, type 1 has the greatest number of variants. Type 2 has a few variants, and type 3 appears seldom and no variant is found. I will now concentrate mainly on the stories belonging to type 1. This type has many variants which supplement each other, and as a result these variants may offer a comprehensive understanding of the festival and the story.

The detailed story recorded in Tripāṭhī's handbook on Hindu rites and festivals is given in summary below, highlighting the main events and actions. Tripāṭhī neither mentions the source of the stories nor does he give the place where he first heard it. But the story of *Bhaiyā Dūj* in his book is narrated in detail, and it contains most of the motifs we find in other rich variants. In this way, Tripāṭhī's version of *Bhaiyā Dūj* [Tripāṭhī 1978, 251-255] is expected to serve as the standard story for our study. In this study an effort will be made, by examining available records of the story told on the occasion of *Bhaiyā Dūj* festival, to demonstrate the assumption that there is no definite text of a folktale and that the ‘text’ is the imaginary product made of many variants of the storytelling. The story in Tripāṭhī's book goes as follows:

a) The youngest/younger <u>brother</u> is brought up so tenderly that he <u>has never been scolded.</u>
b) The <u>brother visits his sister</u> on *Bhaiyā Dūj* festival and is <u>received by her with honour.</u>
c) <u>The brother requests his sister to attend his marriage ceremony</u> to be held soon.
d) For the brother's return journey, the sister prepares lunch, which happens <u>to contain</u> <u>bones of a poisonous snake.</u> She, however, does not know this.

e) The sister, on learning the fact later, runs after her brother and succeeds in substituting the lunch before brother eats his meals. She, thus, protects her brother from a fatal death.
f) The sister goes to a nearby lake to draw water for her brother, and observes a carpenter collecting scattered spikes of porcupines.
g) Asked by the sister, the carpenter tells her that during the marriage ceremony her brother will be in danger of being bitten by a snake; of being pressed by a heavy door which would fall down on him, and, of being attacked by a lion.
h) The carpenter tells the sister the ways to protect her brother: to press the spikes of porcupines to the brother's face and to abuse him so as to save him from a snake bite; to hoist a golden flag on the door to keep him safe from the downfall of the door; and, to put some porcupine spikes and barley sheaves at the altar of marriage ceremony to protect him from the attack by a lion.
i) On returning to her brother, the sister presses the spikes on the face of her brother and abuses him.
j) Though not allowed usually, the sister interferes in every procedure of the marriage ceremony.
k) The brother/bridegroom faints during the marriage ceremony, the sister rushes to him and abuses him furiously.
l) During and after the marriage ceremony, the sister avoids all the dangers in the manner learned from the carpenter, and she even joins the bed of the newly wed couple, where the sister finds a snake crawling to bite her brother. She kills the snake.
m) Next morning, the sister tells the family about all the dangers and the way she protected her brother.

This is the digest of *Bhaiyā Dūj* folktale as presented in Tripāṭhī's handbook.

5. Obtaining an imaginary and comprehensive text: Tripāṭhī's version to be supplemented by other variants

We have the following versions/variants of the *Bhaiyā Dūj* folktale. Tripāṭhī's version/variant appearing in Section IV [Tripāṭhī 1978, 251-255].

T: The seventh sister rescues her only brother, who is younger than the sister. Āśā Bahan et al.'s two variants [Āśā Bahan et al., n.d., 150-151, 151-153].
Ā1: The only sister born after seven brothers rescues her husband, not her brother.
Ā2: The only sister rescues her only brother, who is younger than the sister. Bahādur's variant [Bahādur 1998, 66-74].
B: The only sister rescues her only brother who is younger than the sister. Guptā's variant [Guptā 1976, 12-16].
G: The only sister rescues her only brother, who is younger than the sister. Pāṇḍey's four variants [Pāṇḍey 1967, 194-197, 197-198, 198-200, 200-201]. Pāṇḍey's first story is about a relationship full of hatred between the husband and his brother-in-law/his wife's brother which belongs to the motif of "Cruel Relatives." Thus this story will not be included in the discussion to follow. For the convenience of examination, Pāṇḍey's stories Nos.1-5 will be renumbered Nos.1-4 here in this paper.
P1: The only sister born after seven brothers rescues her husband, not her brother.
P2: The only sister rescues her only and younger brother.
P3: The only sister rescues her elder brother, probably the youngest of seven brothers, with the help of lord Śiva.
P4: Lord Yama is invited to his younger sister Yamunā's house, and in return he grants a boon to the effect that those brothers and sisters who observe this ceremony will not be tortured by Yama.

For the reader's information, Purohit [1961] includes no story of this festival.

Among these nine, Ā1 and P1, being the story of a man and his wife, may be left out of this paper. Our main interest here is the stories in which sisters will rescue their brothers from imminent dangers. P4 may also be put aside, as it does not include the motif of a sister rescuing her brother. Thus we have six versions/variants of the main theme "Sister rescues her brother from many dangers" including T, the folktale recorded in Tripāṭhī's book and selected as our standard or basic version for this study.

While following the development of the folktale T — the version of *Bhaiyā Dūj* included in Tripāṭhī's book — we come across some motifs not very well explained in the story itself. To say it more directly, we feel that some points remain untold in the story and these untold points leave many unsolved questions. Important issues among them are listed below for a detailed analysis and explanation with the help of related variants[58]. As to the main characters, we may ask the following questions:

> 1a) Does the number of brothers and sisters carry any relevance?
> 1b) Does the seniority of brothers or sisters carry any significance?

As briefly described above, we have the variants introducing seven sisters and one brother as in the version of T, the variant with seven brothers and one sister as in P3, and we have the variants of one sister and one brother as Ā2, B, G, P2. In T and P3, seven brothers or seven sisters are introduced at the beginning of the story, but only one of them contributes to the development of the story. This fact makes it clear that the festival is meant for one sister and one brother.

Among the stories pertaining to the seniority of brother and sister, the variants of the elder sister and the younger brother

---

[58] While discussing *Many Rāmāyaṇas*, Ramanujan says that he has come to prefer the word *telling* to the usual terms *versions* or *variants* because the latter terms can and typically imply that there is an invariant, an original or *Ur*-text [Ramanujan 1991, 24-25]. The term *telling* will be useful in examining folktales, seeing the fact that they are enjoyed orally and usually do not have any definite text. The present writer may adopt, in future, the useful term and comprehension suggested by Ramanujan.

prevail with T, Ā2, B, G, P2. We have only one variant in which the brothers are elder and the sister is younger (P3). In the stories having a wife and her husband as characters as in Ā1, P1, the sister is younger to her seven brothers. The question whether the seniority of the main characters has any significance in the story of *Bhaiyā Dūj* or not, still remains unsolved[59]. As to the unpleasant actions taken by the sister against the brother such as abusing the brother and pressing spikes to him, its manner and effects are not made clear in the version of T.

> 2a) What are the effects of abusing the brother, and in what kind of words is he abused?
> 2b) What are the effects of pressing spikes on the brother?

We have two variants which may offer us answers to 2a: the question of abusing.

In P2, the sister is aware of the fact that the agent of lord Yama is looking for human skin with no holes for making a pair of shoes for Yama. For the shoes, only the skin of a young boy who has never been scolded is required. It is understood that once the boy is scolded, his skin will be damaged [197-198]. If not apparently stated as in this variant, there may be an understanding among the involved persons in this festival that a scolded man is not fit to be summoned to lord Yama's abode, and thus the person would never lose his life. B explains the effect of abusing differently. When the sister abuses her brother, the evil spirit possessing him felt uneasy and fled away [72].

The abusing terms are given in P2 [197]. The sister pronounces it twice to rescue her brother from Yama's agent: "Brother will die and his wife will become a widow." B quotes the abuses hurled by the sister extensively [71], e.g. "You scoundrel, it is you who is wishing me ill, you fit-for-nothing. You made me do all the hard work at my home and unnecessarily came to visit me. Now I will

---

59 Dr. Unita Sacchidanand wrote to the present writer in a personal communication on this issue to the effect that seniority of sister/brother bear no real significance in the development of the story; the number of brothers, greater than that of the sisters in many variants, signify the preference for a male child over that of a female in the regions where the institution of patriarchy has been strong and all encompassing.

definitely go to our village and tell our mother what a bad boy you are."

As an answer to the question 2b, P2 may offer a suggestion. When sharp spikes are pressed to the face of the brother, his skin is damaged bearing holes, which is not desirable for lord Yama. Freed and Freed, anthropologists who studied Hindu festivals in a village near Delhi, explain the reason and effects of abusing. According to them verbal abuse and physical pain are common methods for exorcising ghosts. Abuse is not directed at the victim of ghost possession. Rather, the intruding spirit is the target. The villagers hope that insults and threats in conjunction with mild pain or unpleasant measures would persuade the ghost to leave [282].

Judging from these variants and observations made by Freed and Freed, we understand that verbal abuse and physical pain given to the brother are meant to get rid of the dangerous and harmful being: Yama or evil spirit. By studying six variants of the story in which the brother is rescued by his sister from various dangers, we can now explain the reasons and the effects of abusing and giving pain, which are not told in the version of T. As examined above, we can deem that the whole group of variants cited here offers the image of a comprehensive and complete text of the folktale.

6. Discussion: Is comprehensive reading effective for understanding festivals and related folktales?

The variants examined above are told and enjoyed independently without any reference to similar versions/variants. Then a question is raised: should it be allowed to mix all the available variants and try to find answers to the curiosity of the people not involved in the storytelling session? It is quite clear that folktales, similar ones or the variants of one tale, should never be mixed up or supplemented by other sources so long as the folktales are enjoyed by the concerned community. As examined in this paper, the method to study relevant variants which have the same central theme and content developed by the characters performing the same function, will be fruitful in understanding the connotations not expressed in a single storytelling.

Before concluding this paper, it is necessary to mention the relationship of the folktale of *Bhaiyā Dūj* and the related myth. The myth recorded in *Skanda Purāṇa* is a story about lord Yama and his twin and younger sister Yamunā. Its main theme pertains to the relationship between the brother and sister. The folktale examined in this paper has partially the same theme, but the main concern of the sister in the folktale is to rescue her brother from various dangers, which is not found in the myth. Viewed from this perspective it becomes clear that this folktale is independent from the myth.

I previously observed a similar fact. In a North Indian village, a folktale with three episodes was told in one frame: while a merchant is out in connection with his business for a long time, some men try to seduce his wife. This frame is well known in Indian literature through the Sanskrit narrative *Śukasaptati.* The folktales and the narrative literature, though having the same frame and contents of seduction, are quite different: the wife in the folktale rejects the men at once, the wife in the narrative literature is always ready to have sexual relations with the men. The main theme in the folktale is chastity, in the narrative literature the theme is seeking pleasure [Sakata 1976]. This is an example of the folktale and the narrative literature having partially similar contents, but a different theme or intention of the central character[60].

The relationship of the written and oral traditions will vary if both written and oral traditions are living, as observed in India: there are examples as mentioned above, but there may also be a situation in which oral tradition may adopt some motifs from the written tradition. Many interesting topics told in the variants of *Bhaiyā Dūj* story remain to be examined in the future: the reason why the brother is exposed to the dangers, the place and the kind of various dangers and obstacles menacing the brother, the source from which the sister learns the proper way to rescue her brother, etc.

---

60 A minute study of similar interest is published in Barz and Yadav, "The Prince and the Vizir's Son" [1989], in which the relationship of two folktales and a related story in Sanskrit narrative literature, *Vetālapañcaviṃśati,* is examined. The authors conclude: it is more likely that the folk stories are derived from a living North Indian oral tradition than that they are retellings by different storytellers of the events of the Sanskrit story.

REFERENCES

Āśā Bahan and Lāḍo Bahan, *Bhāratīya vrat, parva, tyauhār aur mahilā saṅgīt*, Haridwār: Raṇdhīr Prakāśan, n.d.

Bahadur, Om Lata, *The Book of Hindu Festivals and Ceremonies*, New Delhi: UBS Publishers, 1998.

Barz, Richard K. and Yogendra K. Yadav, "The Prince and the Vizir's Son", in Barz, Richard K. and Monika Thiel-Horstmann, eds., *Living Texts from India*, Wiesbaden: Otto Harrassowitz, 1989.

Beck, Brenda E. F., Peter J Claus, Praphulladatta Goswami and Jawaharlal Handoo, eds., *Folktales of India*, Chicago: Chicago University Press, 1987.

Freed, Stanley A. and Ruth S. Freed, *Festivals in a North Indian Village*, Seattle, American Museum of Natural History, 1998.

Gupta, Satya, *Khaṛī Bolī kī Lok-kathāeṁ*, Illāhabād: Lok Bhāratī Prakāśan, 1976.

Kane, P.V., *History of Dharmasastra*, 3rd edition, Vol. V, Part 1, Poona: BORF, 1994.

Pāṇḍey, Induprakāś, *Avadhī vrat kathāeṁ*, Calcutta: Bhāratīya Jñānpīṭh, 1967.

Purohit, Mohanlāl, *Rājasthānī vrat kathāeṁ*, Bīkāner: Sādūl Rājasthān Research Institute, 1961.

Ramanujan, A.K., "Three Hundred *Rāmāyaṇas*: Five Examples and Three Thoughts on Translation", in Richman, Paula, ed., *Many Rāmāyaṇas*: *The Diversity of Narrative Tradition in South Asia*, Berkeley: University of California Press, 1991.

Sakata, Teiji, *Hindii-go Minwa-shuu* (*Folktales told in Hindi*), Tokyo: Daigaku Shorin, 1999.

— "A Parrot and the Wife of a Merchant. An Essay concerning the Relationship of Sanskrit Narrative Literature and a North Indian Folktale", *Shiso*, No. 623, May 1976.

Skanda Purāṇa, translated and annotated by G.V. Tagare, Delhi: Motilal Banarsidass, 1994.

Tripāṭhī, Rāmpratāp, *Hinduoṁ ke vrat, parva aur tyauhar*, Illāhābād: Lok Bhāratī Prakāśan, 1978.

On Editing the Songs of Lālan Fakir using both Oral and Written Sources

CAROL SALOMON

I am in the process of completing an edition and annotated translation of approximately 150 songs by Lālan Fakir, the most famous of the Baul poets of Bengal. In what follows I will discuss the edition component of my project — in particular my use of both oral and written sources to arrive at a text that is as close as possible to the original one.

Scholars editing Lālan's songs do not face the same problems as do those who edit the poems of earlier Bhakti poets such as Kabīr or Mīrā. It is possible to identify a core corpus of about 500 or so authentic Lālan songs and to establish a reliable text of them which we can be reasonably certain is close to that composed by Lālan. This is not only because of the comparatively recent date of the tradition — Lālan died in 1890 — but also because of the mode of transmission of the songs by Lālan-panthī fakirs and fakirs of other lineages in Kushtia and in surrounding districts in Bangladesh who use Lālan's songs extensively in their repertoires.

Lālan's songs which are short, usually no longer than three or four rhymed verses, are passed down orally from guru to disciple. Lālan-panthī fakirs clearly have a notion of a fixed authentic text. The fakirs memorise the songs and attempt to reproduce them as closely as possible to the texts taught by their gurus. They consider it reprehensible to change the words of a song by Lālan (Jhā 1995: 158) and will take a singer to task for placing Lālan's name in the *bhaṇitā* of a song they know to be composed by another poet.

Attention to preserving the songs in writing began during Lālan's lifetime, although the weight of evidence indicates that Lālan himself composed orally. According to an eyewitness account (anonymous *Hitakarī* obituary[61]) he could not read or write. His disciples, however, recorded the songs in notebooks.

---

[61] "Mahātmā Lālan Phakir", *Hitakarī* (31 October, 1890) 1:101. The obituary has often been reprinted. See, for example, Ābul Āhsān Caudhurī, *Lālan Śāh*, 2nd ed. (Dhaka: Bāṃlā Ekādemī, 1992), 117-119.

Several notebooks written by Lālan's direct disciples have recently come to the attention of scholars. Old notebooks of Lālan's songs are cherished by fakirs. They are handed down from guru to disciple and inscribed with the names of the successive owners. They are consulted when singers forget the words of songs and need to refresh their memories.

One of the earliest of these notebooks that is extant (V2), containing 317 songs transcribed by Jagat Biśvās, belonged to Bholāi Sā, Lālan's adopted son and one of his closest disciples[62]. Portions of it were copied down in 1893, only three years after Lālan's death. Maniruddin Sā, another of Lālan's close disciples, is said by fakirs to have played the role of scribe for Lālan[63]. I know of three extant manuscripts copied by him. (See the descriptions of V1a and b, Bh and K in the appendix[64].)

An interesting feature of K is that it contains a table of contents in Maniruddin's hand with the songs arranged in alphabetical order. A numbered list of Lālan's songs in Maniruddin's neat unmistakable handwriting, which seems to be a table of contents to a notebook that is no longer extant, has also come to light[65]. It names 520 songs. The songs contained in the old manuscripts and named in the unattached table of contents constitute the core of the Lālan corpus. One can be almost certain that they are authentic Lālan songs. Most of these songs also form a regular part of the repertoire of Lālan-panthī fakirs.

Versions of Lālan's songs sung today by Lālan-panthī fakirs are very close to those in the oldest extant notebooks, indicating that the songs have been transmitted with little change over the last hundred years and that they do not have different oral and written lines of transmission. Despite this, however, editions of the songs published to date are full of errors. In many places the texts make no sense and are obviously corrupt. In other places, as I learned in the course of my work, the mistakes are not so apparent. For the most part, the editors of these editions collected their songs by

62 The notebook was edited by Śaktināth Jhā (1995). See my review: Salomon, 1998.

63 Hosen 1998: 12.

64 I am grateful to Ābul Āhsān Caudhurī for providing me with xerox copies of Bh and K.

65 The list is in the possession of Ābul Āhsān Caudhurī who obtained it from a nephew of Ismāil Śāh Fakir whose guru was Bholāi Sā. I am indebted to Caudhurī for giving me a xerox copy of this as well.

copying them either from fakirs' notebooks or directly from performances. However, as I will explain, both these methods yield corrupt texts.

The notebooks are difficult to read for a number of reasons. They are, for the most part, written by semi-literate scribes who not only use nonstandard and inconsistent orthography reflecting Kushtia dialectal pronunciation, but also run words together, making them hard to recognise. In addition, the vocabulary of the songs is often difficult, including technical terms, uncommon Persian and Arabic words, which are often garbled in the manuscripts, and words from Kushtia dialect and from the distinctive jargon of sadhus. Moreover, even the oldest notebooks contain scribal errors. Finally, the songs are esoteric and can be difficult to understand even for seasoned scholars of Baul songs. Common mistakes made by editors include missegmentation of words and confusion of letters that have similar forms such as *k* and *ph*, and *s* and *m* or *n* and *l*.

The notion that the "performance is the text" does not apply to Lālan's songs since there is an "ideal text", i.e. the text taught by the guru, which may not match the text of the performance. When Lālan-panthī fakirs singing in public forget the words to a song, they will often ask another singer to prompt them. But if help is not available, they are obliged to cover up for lapses of memory as best as they can. Another reason not to collect songs directly from performance is the danger of mishearing words. The Lālan songs in Muhammad Mansur Uddin's famous folksong collection *Hārāmaṇi* were evidently obtained from singers during performance, since the texts are full of hearing errors.

I found the best way to obtain a reliable text of a song is to use both oral and written sources. The oral tradition serves as a check on the written tradition and vice versa. When the oldest notebooks are correctly deciphered, in most cases there are few significant variants from the current oral renditions of the songs. For each song I try to have at least one oral version which I have discussed for text and meaning with a singer respected for his or her knowledge of the songs, as well as one or more versions taken from the oldest surviving notebooks. Given the difficulty of the vocabulary, the nonstandard orthography of the notebooks, and dialectal pronunciation of the singers, it is easy to misconstrue what Lālan is saying on the literal level not to speak of the esoteric level. Even scholars who know the Lālan tradition well sometimes jump to the wrong conclusions. For example, Upendranath Bhaṭṭācārya, the author of the groundbreaking study *Bāṃlār Bāul o Bāul gān* incorrectly interprets Lālan's song "Āche ādi makkā ei mānab dehe" (The Original Mecca is in this Human Body). Bhaṭṭācārya (1971, song no. 43) gives the *bhaṇitā* as: *phakir lālan bale se ye gupta makkā ādi imām se miñe* ('Phakir Lālan says, "At the hidden Mecca the first imām was *miñe*"'). The correct interpretation of the entire song turns on an understanding of the word *miñe.* Bhaṭṭācārya (1971:325), taking it to be the Muslim honorific title, standard Bengali *miñā* (Persian *miyān*), says it means God himself (*svayaṃ khodā*). When I asked the Lālan-panthī fakir Khodā Bāksa for the words to this song, instead of *miñe* he gave *meye* "woman". After spending some time in Kushtia, I realised that *miñe* is actually the word *meye* "woman" spelled according to its pronunciation in Kushtia dialect. The song expresses the belief that the woman is supreme (*nārī śreṣṭhā*). This example underscores the importance of not taking anything for granted when working on these songs and of discussing each song word for word with knowlegeable fakirs.

The sample song in the appendix "Madināy rachul nāme ke elo bhāī" illustrates how I have used oral and written sources in tandem to arrive at the text that is as close as possible to that composed by Lālan. The most significant variants among the versions that I have collected occur in the final verse. These substantially affect the meaning of the song. The first line of that verse as given in K, the manuscript I have chosen as the exemplar, and in V2 "*kāyār śarik chāyā dekhi, yāro nāi sei lāśarikī*" ('I see the body's partner is its shadow. So he who casts no shadow has no partner') contains a clever play on words. Two pieces of information are needed to understand it. First, as stated explicitly in the song and in accordance with popular belief (see Schimmel 1985: p. 35 and p. 129; Rāzi 1982: p. 156), Muhammad has a body but no shadow. *Chāyā* 'shadow, shade' is the leitmotif of the song, repeated in the refrain (the verse given at the beginning of the song) and in all three verses. The song seeks to uncover Muhammad's true identity. Second, *lāśarikī* <Ar. *lā śarīk*) 'without a partner' or 'associate'[66] is

[66] *Lāśarikī* occurs in the form *lāśarikālā* (both *-i* and *-kālā* are suffixes used in forming nouns with the sense of 'possessing') in Lālan's 'Kon sukhe sā̃i karen khelā e bhabe' (Jhā 1995: 15, no.33) where it describes the *sā̃i,* 'lord' and is glossed as *ekelā* 'solitary, alone'.

an epithet of Allah who, the Quran states (e.g., 17:111) 'begets no son and has no partner'[67]. In the pun Lālan equates Muhammad with God by making an association between the lack of a shadow and the lack of a partner. He calls the shadow (*chāyā*) the body's partner (*kāyār śarik*). So if Muhammad has no shadow, it follows that he is *lāśarikī* 'without a partner', i.e. he is God[68]. (If A is B then the absence of A is the absence of B.)

Instead of *śarīk* in the phrase *kāyār śarik*, the other manuscripts I examined read *śarib* and *śarīr*. The oral version I obtained from Khodā Bāksa also has *śarīr*. The corruptions seem to have arisen from scribal rather than hearing error as the letters *k*, *b*, and *r* have similar forms. *Śarib* is meaningless and *śarīr* in the phrase *kāyār śarīr* 'the body of the body' makes no sense. The oral variant I obtained from Lāilī Begum, *chāyāhīn yāro dekhi śarik nāi se lāśarikī* ('that person whom I see is shadowless has no partner. He is *lāśarikī*'), may be a rephrasing by someone who did not understand the original pun or who tried to make sense out of the corruption of the original word *śarik*. However, it is clearly a *lectio facilior*, for the difficult pun on Muhammad as *lāśarikī* is lost. It would be highly unlikely for this pun to have been gained in transmission.

---

67 Abdullah Yusuf Ali, *The Holy Quran: Text, Translation and Commentary* (Parts I to XXX) (Lahore: Ashraf Printing Press, 1983), 726.

68 The belief that there is no difference between Muhammad and Allah is held by Bauls and many Sufi groups in Bengal (see Haq 1975:94), although, of course, such a belief is a cardinal sin in normative Islam. In other songs Lālan not only identifies Allah and Muhammad, but also equates them with the murshid.

It should not be taken for granted that Allah, Muhammad or the murshid or guru in Baul songs are masculine in gender, or that they are always considered one and the same. Depending on the context of the song, they can refer to any of the three sexes — the third being the androgyne — in any combination. Moreover, they do not stand for a supreme God or an abstract cosmic principle with no material reality, since Bauls do not believe in what cannot be perceived by tbe senses. Rather, they stand for man and woman, for the *mānuṣ* (person) produced from their union, or for their sexual fluids, either separately or in combination.

A further complication is that Bauls use *śarik* in the special sense of 'offspring'. Thus *lāśarikī* can also be translated as 'without offspring'. Bauls who are successful in *sādhanā* which involves sexual intercourse without seminal discharge do not have children and so they too are *lāśarikī*.

In the last line of the song the oral versions I collected transmit intact a phrase that is corrupt in all the old manuscripts I examined. The readings for this phrase as given in the manuscripts are: *tāo ohāri* (K) *tāo uhāri* (V2) *tāo ohaki* (V1) *tāhāohaki* (Bh) and *tao haki* (J). None of these readings makes any sense. The two oral versions have *tār hakikī* 'his true nature' (<Ar. *haqīqa*). *Hakikī* is an uncommon word in Bengali. The readings of the manuscripts are clearly garblings of this phrase.

What I have sought to demonstrate by this example is that neither oral nor written versions alone are sufficient to arrive at the text Lālan can be presumed to have composed. By comparing versions of both traditions, however, it is possible to obtain a text that one can be reasonably certain is close to that of the original.

REFERENCES

Bhaṭṭācārya, Upendranāth, *Bāṃlār Bāul o Bāul gān*, 2nd ed., Calcutta: Orient Book Company, 1971 (1378 B.S.).

Haq, Muhammad Enamul, *A History of Sufism in Bengal*, Dhaka: Asiatic Society of Bangladesh, 1975.

Hosen (Manṭu Śāh), Phakir Anoyār, ed., *Lālan-saṅgīt*, Tṛtīya khaṇḍa (3rd ed.), Kushtiya: Lālan Mājār Śarīph o Sebā Sadan Kamiṭi, 1998.

Jhā, Śaktināth, *Phakir Lālan Sā̃i: deś, kāl evaṃ śilpo*, Calcutta: Saṃbād, 1995.

Rāzi Dāyā, Nam al-Dīn, *The Path of God's Bondsmen from Origin to Return*, Translated from the Persian by Hamid Algar, Delmar, New York: Caravan Books, 1982.

Salomon, Carol, "Review of Śaktināth Jhā, *Phakir Lālan Sā̃i: deś, kāl evaṃ śilpo*", *JAOS* 118.1 (1998): 128-132.

Schimmel. Annemarie, *And Muhammad is His Messenger*, Chapel Hill and London: University of North Carolina Press, 1985.

Manuscripts

Vla and b: Visvabharati University, Rabindra Bhavan, no. 138A, 1 and 2. Collected by Rabindranath Tagore. Vla contains 126 songs and V1b, 172 songs. No date. In the same hand as Bh and K which were both transcribed by Lālan's disciple Maniruddin Sā.

V2: Visvabharati University, Rabindra Bhavan, acq. no.182, manuscript 480. Collected by Tagore. 317 songs by Lālan. Dated 1893. Transcribed by Jagat Biśvās. Lālan's disciple and adopted son, Bholāi Sā, was its first owner. A preliminary study of V2 and K indicates that they are essentially the same. Further study is needed to determine whether they are both copies of the same exemplar.

Bh: In the possession of Śamsuddin Śāh of Bhultiya, Cuyadanga District, Bangladesh. Contains 236 separate songs in Maniruddin's hand. No date. Includes a table of contents of the songs in the manuscript. Bound together with three short Sufi texts in the colophon of which Maniruddin's Bengali signature appears written according to colloquial pronunciation as Śrīmaniraddi Sā Phakir.

K: In the possession of Manṭu Śāh of Kushtia. Originally contained 328 songs of which 69 have been lost, leaving a total of 259 songs. Includes a table of contents with names of songs arranged in alphabetical order. Transcribed by Maniruddin Sā whose name appears in roman script written as Moniruddin Shah on pp. 3 and 4 along with the dates 1911 and 1917 respectively. Bound together with the first two Sufi texts contained in Bh. The second is incomplete. See the description of V2 above.

J: Belonged to the late Khodā Baksa Biśvās of Jaharpur, Kushtia. Contains 375 songs by Lālan; dated 1921; transcribed by Khodadad Hossain.

Oral versions

KhB: Khodā Baksa Biśvās recited the song and discussed it with me at the Shilpa Kala Academy, Dhaka, 1986.

LB: Laili Begum sang the song, which I recorded on tape, at a *pāllā gān* (song competition) in Gopinathpur, Magura District, Bangladesh, in 1986.

Sample text and translation of a song by Lālan's "Madināy rachul nāme ke elo bhāi":

madināy rachul nāme ke elo bhāi |
2 kāyādhārī haye keno tār chāyā nāi ||

ki dibo tulanā tāre khũje pāi ne e saṃsāre |
meghe raito chāyā dhare dhupero samay ||

chāyāhīn yāhāro kāyā tribhubane tāro chāyā |
e kathār marma laoyā abasya cāi ||

kāyār śarik chāyā dekhi yāro nāi se lāśarikī |
lālan bale tār hakikī balte ḍarāi ||

Underlined indicates emendation to the exemplar.
Exemplar: K no. 185; other manuscripts: V2 no. 188 (according to Jhā's edition); V1a no. 2; Bh no. 9; J no. 252; oral versions: KhB and LB.

3. LB adds *āmi* before *khũje.*
4. For *raito* V1a, Bh, J, and KhB *yāro*, LB *yeman.*
5. LB *yāro*, *trijagate*, and *tāri.*
6. LB *kathāri.*
7. V1a *śarib* which is probably a scribal error for *śarik.* Bh, J, and KhB *śarīr*, which does not make any sense. For *kāyār ... nāi* LB *chāyāhīn yāro dekhi śarik nāi.* For *yāro nāi* KhB *chāyāhīn.*
8. The emendation is based on the oral versions. The readings in all manuscripts I checked are corrupt: K *tāo ohāri*, V2 *tāo uhāri*, V1a *tāo ohaki*, Bh *tāhāohaki* and J *tāo haki.*

Brother, who is the man
they call the Messenger
who came to Medina?
He has a body —
so why no shadow?

What can I compare him to?
I can't find anything
in this world that equals him
whom the clouds shade
from the blazing sun.

His body has no shadow,
yet his shadow spreads
over the three worlds.

You've got to understand
what I'm saying.

I see, the body's partner[69]
is its shadow.
So he who casts no shadow
has no partner.
Lalan says; I'm afraid
to tell the truth about him.

DISCUSSION

Hawley:
How exceptional, even among the Bauls, is this attention to authenticity?

Salomon:
I think it is exceptional. I do not find this attention to authenticity as much in other Baul traditions and I have been thinking about how to explain this. The disciples were very attentive to preserve these songs in writing. Maniruddin was the scribe who copied these manuscripts several times.

Bhattacharya:
I understand that the Lālan-panthī fakirs are very keen on authenticity. Although the West Bengal Bauls sing Lālan's songs, they really belong to different traditions. It is clear to me now. Besides, you have explained beautifully all the variations in the actual wording of the songs. It is a very important work. About the word *hakikī*, I was wondering if it could not have been a later change since there is a continuous process of islamization that is going on in Bangladesh. Could it be a later substitution in an attempt to islamise the text?

Salomon:
Thank you, that's a good question. There are three reasons why I do not think that is the case here. First, it is scholars rather than fakirs who attempt to islamise the tradition, portraying it as an orthodox Sufi one. As I have stated, Lālan-panthī fakirs would not deliberately alter the words of a song by Lālan. Second, Lālan uses

[69] On the special sense in which the Bauls use *śarik*, translated here as 'partner', see note 71.

many Arabic and Persian words in his songs. The context of the song under discussion is Islamic and two other Arabic words are used in the verse in question. And third, the readings of the manuscripts do not make any sense. The only way to explain them is as garblings of *hakikī*, the variant of the oral versions collected from fakirs.

Research Report

WHITNEY SANFORD

1. Paramānand

In "Seeing Through Hearing: Paramānand's Synaesthetic Approach to Krishna" I deal with the question of the role of the poetry in *darśan*. How does hearing the poetry create *darśan* for the devotee in this ritual setting. Also while doing fieldwork, I had the opportunity to observe the *Aṣṭayāmalīlā* at Jai Singh Ghera. Poetry performed over a cycle over 8 days. This pushed me to consider how poetry fits with devotee homologising day to that of Krishna. Poetry is timed in temple performance, but the intensive 8 day performance drove it home.

Publications related to Paramānand's poetry:

"The *Gopīs* as Role Models: Understanding Paramānand's Function as a Saint", *Proceedings of the Sixth International Conference on Early Literature in New Indo-Aryan Languages*, 7-9 July, 1994 edited by Alan W. Entwistle and Michael C. Shapiro, New Delhi: Motilal Banarsidass, 1999.

"Real Men and Ideal Women: Gender Construction in the *Aṣṭayāma Līlā*", *Journal of Vaishnava Studies*, Vol. 5, No. 4, Fall 1997.

"The Emotive Body: The Role and Function of the Body in the Ritual of Transformation of *Laukika* to *Alaukika* in Paramānand's *Padas* and the *Aṣṭayāma Līlā*", *ARC. The Journal of the Faculty of Religious Studies*, McGill University, 25, 1997.

"An Evolution of Emphasis: A Comparison of the Story of 'Uddhava's Message' in the Bhramargīt in the *Bhāgavat Purāṇa* and the Bhramargīt of Nandadās", *Journal of Vaishnava Studies*, Vol. 1, No. 4, June 1994.

"Teaching the Teacher: The Sakhī's Role in Paramānand's *Māna* Poems", *Journal of Vaishnava Studies*, Vol. 1, No. 4, Summer 1993.

2. Balarāma

I later became interested in this significant yet background figure. At the Venice Bhakti-conference, I gave a paper on Balarāma and Krishna's role regarding the concept of the pastoral setting for the poetry: "Uneasy Partners: Balarāma as Embodiment of Wilderness", *The Banyan Tree, Proceedings of the Seventh International Conference on Early Literature in New Indo-Aryan Languages*, 6-8 August 1997, edited by Mariola Offredi, New Delhi, Manohar, 2000, pp. 363-387.

I also gave paper in Madison in which I looked at role of how Balarāma in sectarian circle as trope: interesting how Balarāma (and Krishna) have continuing sectarian roles through their leaders. This involves a process to resolve tensions and create hierarchy via familial strategy.

And further:

"Complementary Pairings: Balarāma and Krishna as Tropes". The 26th Conference on South Asia, 16-19 October 1997, unpublished paper given at the University of Colorado, Boulder Colloquium, February, 1998.

"Imagining Balarāma: Negotiating Braj Cultural Tensions through Poetic Vision". The 26th Conference on South Asia, 16-19 October 1997.

Upcoming Work and Presentations

"Holi through Daūjī's Eyes: Alternate Views of Krishna and Balarāma in Daūjī", in *Alternative Krishnas*, edited by Guy Beck (volume to be submitted to SUNY Press).

"*Yakṣas* on the Margin of Contemporary Practice", Annual Meeting of the American Academy of Religion, Nashville, TN, November 18-21, 2000.

Fieldwork

I spent the academic year 1998-9 in Dauj and Vrindavan on a Baldev project and looked at various sites for *nāga* and *yakṣa* worship. This portion will represent part of book. Two goals:

observed as much as possible of ritual cycle and collected local printed materials.

Balarāma and Krishna in an Idealised Braj: A Study of Inclusion and Symbiotic Hierarchy

The traditional images of Balarāma and Krishna — both in scholarship and in their religious depictions — are routinely portrayed as pastoral, yet these images assume Western romantic constructions of the pastoral, i.e. simple boys and girls populating an idealised rural landscape (Alpers, 134). Yet, despite the obvious parallels to German Romanticism, Braj pastoralization, ironically an urban phenomenon, encompasses a different set of conflicts, chiefly the disjuncture created by Balarāma's (anomalous) rusticity in relation to Krishna's rural persona that masks an urbane sophistication. Balarāma's earthy image conveniently frees Krishna to exist in that pastoral ideal in which nature never presents danger, and erotic dalliances have no unwanted consequences. The pastoralization process of the 16th century Braj seems to have concentrated in Balarāma those elements which do not easily fit into the pastoral ideal. Entwistle has observed that "pastoralization more adequately describes the dialectic between elite and folk cultures than Sanskritisation or Brahmanization", and this raises questions about the relationship of Balarāma to Krishna (Entwistle 1988, 88).

My hypothesis is that Balarāma is structurally necessary in a symbiotic but necessarily hierarchical relationship with Krishna, a complex of ideas which I will call an inclusive and symbiotic hierarchy. This family relationship appears in multiple dimensions, (e.g., theological, iconographic and communal) and provides a flexible structure through which divergent groups and practices can be related to the center, inevitably a form of Krishna. Association with Balarāma, as the elder brother, confers the pride of elder status while still acknowledging Krishna as dominant, giving implicit sanction to seemingly divergent actions — and this carries over in sectarian theology and practice. I propose to study the relationship between the subordinate deity Balarāma and the dominant deity Krishna of Braj in terms of what this *complementary pairing of siblings has to tell us about the larger issues of religous inclusion and the resulting symbiotic hierarchies.* To do this, I will parallel my reading of the 17th–18th century literature on the subject with direct observations of the ongoing Balarāma-Bhakti at the Daūjī Temple near Gokul in Braj.

Devotees of Balarāma, particularly those at the Daūjī (elder brother) Temple, elevate him to a position of centrality, a practice which contradicts textual accounts and challenges assessments of Balarāma as subordinate to Krishna. Balarāma's associations with *Nāga*-s (semi-divine serpent-like beings), for example, his irascibility, fondness of drink and connections to water, agriculture, and fertility, in relation to Krishna's tame pastoral image have determined both Balarāma's elevation and subordination. Importantly, this pattern is not only replicated in sectarian Vaishnavism, but can also be found in Jainism and Buddhism. For example, the relationship between Krishna and Balarāma-*Nāga* recapitulates Buddhism's subordination and incorporation of the *Nāgas* (Vogel, 2). Similarly, the Jaina Purāṇas reinterpret the Vaishnava account of relationship of Balarāma and Krishna to support the Jaina hierarchy (Jaini, 230). The qualities of Balarāma have historically been conflated with those of the *Nāga* cults which have been active in the Braj region since at least the 4th century BCE.

Texts

I have collected and am working with the following printed materials in this project on Daūjī. These texts are primarily in Hindi (with the exception of the *Garga Saṁhitā*), and many are in the form of pamphlets available to devotees at the the temple. Ghanshyam Pandey, a member of one of the more prominent Pandey families of Daūjī, is the head of the *Śrīhaladhar Śodhasaṁsthān* and has published several pamphlets which describe rituals at Daūjī.

Materials in Daūjī:
Garga Samhitā (Balabhadra Mahātmya).
Brajarāj Kṛṣṇakadeva (cultivating) Baldev anthology of devotional poetry regarding Baldev. Compiled by one of the local Pandeys.
Brahmarṣi Śrī Saubhari Carita (2 parts).
Saubhari Samhitā (2 parts).

Bhagvān Baldev: narrative of life of Baldev. Locally compiled: Sudarshansinh Cakra.
Bālakrishna, same author: discusses all the relatives of Krishna.
Maharishi Eminent Śrī Saubhari Maharaj and his First Gauṛ-Ahivasi Brahman Lineage by Pr. Madhvacarya.
Śrī Haladhar Nityārcan by Ghanashyam Pandey.

I am still searching for a text that is mentioned in the bibliography in Alan Entwistle's *Braj: Centre of Krishna Pilgrimage.* I have searched in libraries and have asked countless people in India about this two page text. I would be grateful for your help if anyone should come across this. The *Śrīdaūjī Prakaṭya Vārtā* is the final two pages (supposedly) of the *Śrī Gokul Mahātmyam*, edited by B.L. Sharma. Bombay: Venkatesvar Steam Press, 1940.

DISCUSSION

Gold:
Could you please expand a little more on the theme of pastoralization.

Sanford:
If you look at the figures of Krishna and Balarām, Krishna is represented as an urban figure. Often we conceptualise ideals of nature. A very urban construct is to look at nature as something restorative, something one goes to in order to relax. Krishna has a real element of that. In the 16th century people from both the Gauḍīya and the Vallabha traditions came with very urban ideas of what nature means. There we find traps against the evils of the city, admiring the way Krishna freely ramps around in nature. Balarām on the other hand represents a tradition where nature has to do with fertility and festivals (Holī is his festival!). For people living in the countryside, nature is not all that lovely.

Zelliot:
You spoke about Balarām being worshipped by low-caste people.

Sanford:
When I spoke about rusticity I argued that Krishna represents a very elite and urban idea of what it means to be rustic. In Venice I may not really have associated this with lower castes. Balarām is certainly important to a wide range of people. He spans all levels of society.

Virshaiva Pantha in 12th Century Maharashtra

SUREKHA SAWANT

During the mediaeval period society in Maharashtra was divided into the Varna system of Brahmins, Kshatriyas, Vaishyas and Shudras. The lower class people did not get respect in society and in order to eradicate this evil a revolution slowly developed through the Bhakti movement. New *sampradāya*-s or 'cults' and *pantha*-s based on religion, like Mahānubhāva, Vārkarī, Sufi, etc., were established. In the same period Virshaivism was established in Karnataka.

Bāsaveshvara was the founder of this Virshaiva Pantha. He was the son of a Brahmin. He was in conflict with his father about Brahminism and wanted to build a society based on truth, love and equality. It was strongly opposed by others because Basaveshvara was responsible for bringing about a great social religious revival. He was painfully conscious of the miseries of the downtrodden masses and knew very well how they were barred from all social and religious activities, so he declared that anybody could come and embrace his religion. The main theme of this religion was devotion to Shiva. Many people from the lower castes, like washermen, cobblers, etc., joined this religion.

Caste has always been a very important factor in the Hindu social structure. The untouchables were not allowed to enter temples. Basaveshvara said that the temple thus caused an estrangement between God and the devotee, but in the case of the 'Iṣṭa-Lingam' there is no mediation, the devotee has direct access to God.

The Lingayat Pantha was related to the 'Shivapantha'. These Pantha-s were respected in the south and devotees there were encouraged to play an active role in social affairs. The Virshaiva Pantha spread in Deccan Maharashtra, Andhra-Pradesh and Tamilnadu. The priestly class of the cult was called 'Jangam'. The cult encouraged women to pursue literary activities and thus they acquired self-confidence and leadership qualities through cult activities. The purpose of Virshaiva was to eliminate the Varna system and to boycot the Pūjā system. They wore the Shivalinga on their body and worshipped it. There was no temple system in this cult.

The research paper expects to explore literature and socio-religious traditions of the common people which were a by-product of the cult at that time. As I am still studying this movement/cult, I would like to answer the following questions and analyse them:

How, where and why was the cult established?

Why did the downtrodden masses join this cult and what was its social impact?

How popular was it and why?

Why were so many women interested in the cult and what kind of work did they do through the cult?

What are the reasons for the decline of the 'Virshaiva' cult?

Report

MICHAEL SHAPIRO

I am by training a linguist and most of my career has been spent doing research in the area of linguistics. I consider myself a friend of the Bhakti Conference, rather than a central player. Nevertheless there have been a few points in my career where my interests have intersected or come into contact with the interests of this conference. In my presentation I shall try to talk about those contact points. Earlier in my career I was solely involved in linguistic research in Hindi and Indo-Aryan languages, but because of the presence in my faculty ever since I joined of a Bhakti specialist, I could not stay away from texts, more specifically from Bhakti texts. Gradually I got involved in the history of Hindi texts and that is where I found the points of contact.

My primary interest was with Nānak, where my interest was primarily for linguistic reason. I did a number of studies on the fascinating Nānak material. The 'variation theory' became very useful here: there is not one way of saying things, there is a multiplicity of ways and the variability theory in linguistics provided some very helpful tools to characterise the style of language.

I did another published study on the vocative case in *Gurbāṇī*, because I believe there is in this body of texts a particular theological point in the repetitiveness of the grammatical structure. I also did two studies of what I could call the rhetorical aspects of *Gurbāṇī*. This is not yet published because at the time of this study, something like this about the *Japujī* proved to be controversial and I decided at the time to let it sit for a while. This is the area where my interest has overlapped with the interest of the Bhakti Conference.

What am I up to now?

1

For a number of years I have wanted to write a book providing an overview of the linguistic traits of the Hindi language. I am now working on such a book, which is to be published by Cambridge University Press under the title "*A linguistic Introduction to Hindi*". This is by no means to be a pedagogical or reference grammar of the language, but rather a broad synthesis of what a general reader would wish to know about the language as a linguistic, cultural, and historical entity. Broad areas to be covered include the cultural history of Hindi, dialect geography, orthography, phonetics and phonology, inflectional morphology, word formation, lexicon, syntax, pragmatics and stylistics, historical development, and the Hindi grammatical tradition.

2

I would also like to come back to my notes and the abundant material I have on Nānak's rhetoric in the the *Japujī* and *Āsā kī vār.*

3

Another project I have in mind is an Etymological Dictionary of Hindi. An elaborate proposal has been made for this, but so far funding has not yet been found. I had in mind not to trace the etymologies in the traditional way, from early Indo-Aryan onwards. My concern was rather that the material on Hindi be based on reliable editions of early texts in their earliest form. When I applied for funding years ago, the corpus of available texts was rather sparse. At this moment I can see there is a much larger database to draw upon. That is something I would like to re-examine.

Introducing Gadādhar Bhaṭṭ

SWAPNA SHARMA

सखी हों श्याम रंग रंगी ।
देखि विकाय गई वह मूरति सूरति मांहि पगी ॥
संग हुतो सुपनें अपनें पुनि सोइ् उही रस भोइ ।
जागेहु आगे दृष्टि परै सखि न॑ कु न न्यारो होइ ॥
एक जु मेरे नेंननि में निसि–द्योस रह्यौ करि भोन ।
गाइ चरावत जात सुन्यों सषि सोधों कन्हया कोंन ॥
कासों कहों को पत्याइ री मेरे कोंन करै पचि वादु ।
कैसे कै कह्यौ जात गदाधर गूंगे पै गुर स्वाद ॥

Friend, I am dyed in the colour of the Dark One.
I am lost looking at His image,
infatuated with the beauty of His face.
He accompanied me in my dreams,
and I fell asleep immersed in that pleasure.
When I awake, friend, and look around,
He is not away for a moment.
There is One who always dwells in my eyes,
day and night.
Friend, who may that Kanhaiyā be
who, people say, goes to graze the cow?
To whom shall I say this, who shall trust me?
Who shall argue it with surprise?
How can Gadādhar express this,
like a dumb person tasting sweet sugar?

Sources for the study

Recent research in the field of devotional literature and language of Braj have brought a number of important yet lesser known literary figures and their works to the attention of the academic world. One example of a poet of traditional lineage is the *gūṅgā* (speechless) Gadādhar Bhaṭṭ, who happened to see and sink in the beauty of the cowherd Kanhaiyā and craved to visit and live in his Land of

Dreams, the Braj-Vrindavan. An important source of information about him was obtained from the famous *Bhaktamāl*[70] of Nārāyaṇdās of Nābhā. The *chappayā*-s or six-line stanzas by Nābhājī form the foundation for the scarce information about this poet and his works. This information is supplemented by eight poems by Priyādās in his *Bhaktirasbodhinī*[71] commentary on the *Bhaktamāl*. Moreover, devotional poets like Dhruvdās[72], Nāgarīdās[73], Bhagvatrasik[74] and Cācā Vrindābandās[75] have been eloquent in their praise about his ecstatic devotion and great style when giving scholarly discourses on the *Bhāgavata Purāṇa*.

Drawing a biographical sketch

According to these sources Gadādhar Bhaṭṭ belonged to the Caitanya Sampradāya of the Vaishnava tradition. The religious and aesthetic teachings of Caitanya were projected in his Brajbhāṣā poetry. The *Baṁglā Bhaktamāl* of Lāldās suggests[76] that Jīv Gosvāmī, one of the founders of the Caitanya tradition in Vrindavan had introduced Gadādhar Bhaṭṭ to this viewpoint. In the absence of clear records, the family background of Gadādhar Bhaṭṭ cannot be established with certainty. Some records[77] in the Vidyā Bhavan at Kankraulī mention that he was a Brahmin of the Telangana region of Andhra Pradesh and that his native place is called Vellanad. From the works *Vallabh Vaṁś Vṛkṣa* and also the *Āndhra Telaṅg Bhaṭṭ Vaṁś Vṛkṣ* in the Vidyā Bhavan collection (Kankraulī) it would appear that the word *Bhaṭṭ* has been used for

---

[70] Rūpkalā Saṁskarā, 5th ed., Lucknow: Tejkumār Press Book Depot, 1969, p. 786.

[71] Cf. R.D. Gupta, *Studies in the Bhaktirasa-Bodhini of Priyadasa*, Ph.D. Thesis, University of London, 1967.

[72] *Bhaktanāmāvalī*, Vrindavan: Hita Sāhitya Prakāśana, [*samvat*] 2053, p. 78.

[73] *Granthāvalī*, vol. 2, Kāśi: Nāgarī Pracāriṇī Sabhā, 1968, p. 69.

[74] *Bhagavatrasik jī kī vāṇī*: *Bhaktanāmāvalī*, 4th ed., Vrindavan: Surendranath, [Samvat] 1995, p. 54.

[75] *Bhaktiras phuṭkar prasang*, compiled by Bābā Vishveshvar Sharaṇ, Vrindāvan: Braj Sevā Samiti, 1962, p. 265.

[76] *Śrī Bhaktamāl*, Durgā Prasād Lāhiṛi (ed.), Calcutta, [Bengali date] 1312, pp. 285-309.

[77] Cf. Nareshcandra Bansal, *Caitanya Sampradāy*: *Siddhānt aur Sāhity*, Agra: Vinod Pustak Bhandār, 1980, p. 293-298.

all classes of their lineage both in North and South India. The *karañjī* and the *śaṭ-bhrātṛ* lineages *kuṭumb* of Vrindavan which followed the Caitanya or Mādhva-Gauḍiy *sampradāy*, and the *Bhadarsā Brajiyā* of Nimarana and the *Mādhva Brajiyā* of Unchagaon also originated from the Andhra region. Gadādhar Bhaṭṭ is said to be the founder of the Bhaṭṭ families at Vrindavan.

The historians of Hindi literary tradition have often confused our Gadādhar Bhaṭṭ with Gadādhar Paṇḍit, who used to 'read' the *Bhāgavat Purāṇa* to Caitanya Mahāprabhu in Jagannāth Purī[78].

There is considerable disagreement regarding the dates of Gadādhar Bhaṭṭ. We propose: b.1515 - d.1610 (?). According to Gowri Shankar Duvedi[79] the year of his birth was *samvat* 1620 (AD 1563), while his main literary acitivity may be dated around *samvat* 1660 (AD 1603). Miśra Bandhu[80] mentions *samvat* 1632 (AD 1575). Dr. Śaraṇ Bihārī Gosvāmi[81] agrees with Miśra. The author of *Śiv Siṁh Saroj* is amusingly vague in his ascribing *samvat* 1580. Later Kiśorī Lāl Gupta[82] corrected the confusion between the different Gadādhar-s, and suggested "after [Samvat] 1592" as the time of his coming to Vrindavan. Naresh Chandra Bansal[83] determines *samvat* 1560 (AD 1503) as the year of his arrival in Vrindavan.

The most important piece of information comes from the testamentory document of Jīv Gosvāmī that is available in the Vrindavan Śodh Saṁsthān MS No. 79-A-B. It has a codicil in Gadādhar Bhaṭṭ's handwriting, as Jīv was unable to write or sign his own original testament. Gadādhar Bhaṭṭ puts his signature on

---

78 The confusion between the two Gadādhars arises as both were followers of Caitanya and both were scholars and preachers of *Bhāgavat Purāṇa*. More such examples are seen in Sengar Śivasingh, *Śivasiṁh Saroj*, Allahabad: Hindī Sāhitya Sammelan, 1970, p. 465sq.; and other accounts such as Hazārī Prasād Dvivedī, *Hindī Sāhitya: Uskā udbhav aur vikās*, New Delhi: Rāj Kamal Prakāśan, 1981, p. 369; and Ācārya Rāmcandra Śukla, *Hindī Sāhitya kā itihās*, 16th ed., Kāśī: Nāgarī Pracāriṇī Sabhā, 1968.

Other authors of the same name are Gadādhar Paṇḍit (a Bengali associate of Caitanya) and Gadādhar Miśra (a grandson of the poet Padmākar).

79 *Bundel Vaibhav*, Tīkamgaṛh: Bundel Vaibhav Granthamālā, 1957.

80 *Miśra Bandhu Vinod*, rev. and ext. ed., Lucknow: Gaṅgā Pustak Mālā, 1980, p. 352.

81 *Kṛṣṇa Bhakti kāvy meṁ sakhī bhāv*, Vārāṇasī: Caukhambā Vidyā Bhavan, [Samvat] 2023, p. 616.

82 Kiśorī Lāl Gupta, *Saroj Sarvekṣaṇa*, p. 234.

83 *Ibid.* (no. 77).

the document dated *samvat* 1665 (AD 1608). Jīv Gosvāmī was of 100 plus years of age then, passing away in AD 1610. Therefore we may surmise that Gadādhar Bhaṭṭ was a slightly younger contemporary of Jīv Gosvāmī and lived a good part of the 16th and at least the first decade of the 17th century.

Gadādhar's arrival was the beginning of a very creative relationship between him and the Caitanyaite Gosvāmīs, who had already settled in Braj a few decades earlier under Caitanya's projected renaissance of Krishna devotion. He was welcomed by Jīv Gosvāmī into the Caitanyaite philosophy and was formally initiated into the spiritual discipline by Raghunātha Bhaṭṭa. As a good disciple, he learned from his guru the art of giving religious discourses on the Bhāgavat Purāṇa. After the death of his guru, Gadādhar took the responsibility of giving *bhāgavat pāṭh* in the temples of Govinda, Gopīnāth, Madan Mohan and Rādhāramaṇ at Vrindavan. His reading and discourses grew into a continued institution, performed till today by his descendents.

In the famous line of Gadādhar quoted above we read: कासों कहों को पत्याइ री मेरे कोंन करै पचि वादु or "To whom shall I say this, who shall trust me? Who shall argue it with surprise?" Gadādhar's silent suffering was heard by a Brajavāsī. The famous Caitanyaite philosopher Jīv Gosvāmī, upon hearing this petition of Gadādhar from two *sadhū*-s, fell in love with its spirit of Bhakti and poetic power. He wrote through them to Gadādhar:

> अनाराध्य राधा पदाम्भोज युग्मं अदाश्रित्य वृन्दाटवीम्तत्पदांकाम् ।
> असम्भाष्य तदभाव गम्भीरचित्तान कुतः श्याम सिन्धोः रसस्यावगाहा [84]

or "Without worshipping both lotus-feet of Rādhā, and without enjoying the shelter of Vrindāvan marked by her feet, and without talking those earnest of heart/of the same feeling, how can you immerse yourself in the *ras* of the ocean of the Dark One?" It is said that Gadādhar received Jīv Gosvāmī's message when he was at a village well for his morning duties, and without even informing his family he left for his Dream Land. This may have happened around AD 1550.

---

[84] Raghunāth Dās, *Stavāvali*, Puridās, ed., Maimansingh: Sachinath Raychaudhuri, 1947, p. 41 (*ślok* 16.1).

His poetry

The corpus of poetry written by Gadādhar Bhaṭṭ, though not extensive, is very significant.

Padāvalī: the number of *pada*-s collected is 85, 4 of which have as *chāp* 'Kalyāṇ'[85].

Yogapīṭh or *Dhyānlīlā*. Besides this *Yogapīṭh/Dhyānlīlā* there is another independent composition. It is in *rolā* and *caupāī* style. It has a remarkable flow of Brajbhāṣā and is very effective. This very important work concerning the Caitanyaite devotional practice has a striking inter-textuality with two of his Vrindavan contemporaries: Kṛṣṇadās Kavirāj (writing in Sanskrit[86]) and Narottam Dās Thākur (in Bengali[87]). These Caitanyaites proceeded through *vaidhī bhakti* to *rāgānugā bhakti*. Their progress is from injunctional grammar to spontaneous loving devotion. At this stage, the practices move from an external to an internalised mode. Memory becomes the most important part of the process of keeping in touch with the object of devotion, which for the Caitanyaites is the divine couple of Śrīkṛṣṇa and Śrīmatī Rādhā in a loving union. The mode of relating to the divine is to meditate upon the divine name (*nām*), his dwelling (*dhām*), form (*rūp*) and play (*līlā*), while in each of these the meditator mentally participates in the divine play. Indian spirituality follows three levels of discipline: *chintan*, *manan* and *nididhyāsan*. Meditation of Yogapīṭh, the divine ritual seat, is a culmination of *nididhyāsan*. The temple of Govindadev[88] at Vrindavan was that Yogapīṭh in physical form.

Material for research

Most of Gadādhar Bhaṭṭ's collections are present in Vrindavan, the place of his creative life as a poet. A microfilm copy of his main works titled as *Gadādhar Bhaṭṭ kī Vāṇī* is available in the

---

[85] Bābā Kṛṣṇadās, *Gadādhar Bhaṭṭ kī vāṇī*, Vrindāvan: Rādheśyām Book Seller, [Samvat] 2015, pp. 11 (*pad* 11), 36 (*pad* 53) and 60 (*pad*-s 84-85).

[86] Cf. his *Govindalīlāmṛtam*. See S.K. De, *The Early History of Vaiṣṇava Faith Movement in Bengal*, 2nd ed., Calcutta: Firma K.L. Mukhopadhyay, 1961, pp. 54, n. 1, and 604-611.

[87] Cf. his *Prārthana*, Navadvipa: Sri Navinakrishna Dasa, 1963.

[88] Margaret Case (ed.), *Govindadeva Temple, A Dialogue in Stone*, New Delhi: IGNCA, 1995, pp. 74, 161, 200-201, 269 and 273.

Vrindavan Śodh Sansthān[89] while the undated yet complete manuscript of 69 *pada*-s is preserved in his descendants' collection at Śrī Rādhā Madanamohan temple (Bhaṭṭ jī kā Mandir). Two manuscripts, dated *samvat* 1800 (AD 1743) and *samvat* 1953 (AD 1897), containing some 40 *pada*-s, are from the personal collection of Dr. Naresh Bansal[90]. The popularity of his poems can be gauged from the fact that several *padsaṁgrah*-s include them: the MSS are found at the Vrindavan Śodh Sansthāna[91], Śrījī Mandir at Vrindavan and Śrī Kṛṣṇa Janmasthān Śodh Pīṭh, Mathura. Bābā Kṛṣṇadās was the first person to edit and publish the poetry of Gadādhar Bhaṭṭ under the title *Gadādhar Bhaṭṭ kī vāṇī*[92]. Viyogī Hari in his selection of Braj poetry, the famous *Braj Mādhurī Sār* has included 26 of his *pada-s* with an introduction[93].

His poetic genius

The poetry traditionally ascribed to Gadādhar Bhaṭṭ is rather intact because of two reasons: one, his poetry was preserved in his temple by his scholar-priest family descendents; and two, they were used in the musical ritual tradition of *samāj-gāyan*. Yogapīṭh being an esoteric religious meditation, its transmission was very tightly controlled. Hence the poet remained esoteric and his poetry less invaded by the spurious tradition of others using his signature! His poetry, despite its limited quantity, is rich in depth and offers a variety of themes. Within the scope of Krishna Līlā, the topics included *yamunā-stuti*, Nand-Yaśodā Vandanā, *vaṁśī* and *nām kī mahimā*, *vivāha-jyaunār*, *holī*, *śīt*, *vasant*, *pāvas*, *rituvarṇan*, *anurāg*, *rās*, *mān*, *kṛṣṇ-janma kī badhāī*, *kāliy-daman*, *gocāraṇ*, etc.

He wrote in classical Brajbhāṣā, which reveals his ability of mastering languages, as we know that his mother tongue was Telugu. Five verses in Sanskrit are also available. The maturity of style and depth in language show the height of his creativity. He imaginatively uses several figures of speech, simile-metaphors, illustrations, personifications, etc. He mainly dwelt upon *madhur*-

89 See note 73.
90 At Kasganj.
91 MSS Serial No. 590 (ACC No. 10489); Serial No. 753 (ACC No. 4461).
92 See note 85.
93 Prayāg: Hindī Sāhitya Sammelan, [Samvat] 1980, 1st ed., pp. 80-101.

ras, without neglecting *vātsalya* and *dāsya*. Like a bee, he collected nectar from the various *līlā*-s of Krishna and expressed their essence.

श्री गोविद पद पल्लव सिर पर विराजमानु ।
तिनु कैसे कहि आवै या सुख कौ परमानु ॥
व्रज नरेस देस वसत कालानल हूं न त्रसत ।
विलसत मन हुलसत करि लीलामृत पान ॥
भीजे नित नयन रहत प्रभु के गुन ग्राम कहत ।
मानत नहि त्रिविध ताप जानत नहि आन ॥
तिनके मुख कमल दरस पावन पद रेनु परस ।
अधम जन गदाधर से पावै सन मान ॥

When the lotusfeet of Govinda are placed on their head,
  how can they ever express the extent of that joy?
If they live in the region of the king of Braj,
  even the deadly fire cannot frighten them.
Their heart gets drowned enjoying the
  drink of the eternal nectar of *līlā*.
Their eyes remain wet when they
  relate all the qualities of the Lord.
They will not feel burning fires
  or be aware of anything at all.
Seeing their lotus faces and touching the dust
  of their feet, lowly Gadādhar finds honour.

His tradition

Gadādhar Bhaṭṭ's creativity was continued in Rasikottans and Vallabharasik, the former a Sanskrit poet and the latter a Braj poet. The family tree mentions Narhari Bhaṭṭ, Kṛṣṇarām Bhaṭṭ, and Bāl Mukund between Gadādhar Bhaṭṭ and these two. Govardhan Bhaṭṭ, Mannulāl Bhaṭṭ, Mādhav Bhaṭṭ were other well-known names in the family tradition of *Bhāgavat* scholarship, which continues uninterrupted till today. Tradition says that his deities, Śrī Rādhā Madan Mohan were found in the sands of the Yamunā on Vasant Pañcamī. This deity is now present in the Āṭhakhambā Mauhallā in Vrindavan and his descendants are now its caretakers. Many important festivals of the year are celebrated in this temple following the old traditions. Group *samāj* singing and *sām̐jhī*[94] are the great specialised devotional rituals of this family tradition. This temple is unique in the sense that it betrays an interesting synthesis of the Caitanyaite and Vallabhite nuances of Krishna worship. Bhaṭṭs and the Vallabhkul Gosvāmīs intermarry and both are Telugu-bhāṣīs committed to Krishna of Braj! The tradition of Gadādhar Bhaṭṭ and his family is a glittering gem in the great treasurehouse of Braj literature and culture.

---

94 Cf. Asim Kṛṣṇadās, *The Evening Blossoms: The Temple Tradition of Sanjhi in Vṛṇḍāvana*, New Delhi: IGNCA, 1996, esp. p. 33, for a detailed description.

Bhakti as a Vision

CHRISTOPHER SHELKE

The study of Bhakti for me is not merely an academic matter, but a *sādhanā* which helps me to form my personal life and allows me to contribute in a little way to the shaping of the society in the multi-religious atmosphere of India. According to my experience, in the conferences of the religious dialogue when the participants speak about the philosophies and theologies of their particular religion, often they have a dogmatic or apologetic attitude. They become defensive or aggressive. However, when they speak about Bhakti or mysticism, the participants are more docile, listening and even ready to change their attitude. Collaboration at such a stage is rather easy. On account of such an experience, I did my doctoral research at the University of Pune, entitled 'Comparative mysticism: Saint Ignatius of Loyola and Sant Rāmdās'[95]. It was awarded the prize of the best thesis in the Humanities for the year 1979. This thesis was for me the beginning of a *bhakti-sādhanā* that has inspired my academic teaching, my research and other activities.

Analysing his spiritual experiences, St. Ignatius of Loyola paved the path of spiritual discernment and proclaimed the maxim, the highest motivation for the activity, *ad maiorem Dei gloriam* or 'to the greater glory of God'. In the context of the middle ages he placed his service and the service of the members of the newly founded religious order, the Society of Jesus, at the service of the Roman Pontiff, who for him was the visible sign of the Kingdom of Christ, which he had sought and experienced in the Spiritual Exercises, which is the set of meditations and contemplations he first went through himself and later wrote down for his followers. For him the Kingdom of Christ was the Kingdom of Heaven, which was expressed concretely in justice, peace, unity and in loving service.

Sant Rāmdās, almost denying the Indian tradition of a Guruparamparā, sought spiritual knowledge by his own effort. He

---

95 *Don Sākṣātkāri*, Devi-Lakshimi Prakāśan, Pune, 1980.

realised the importance of *vivek* and of the destruction of *ahaṃkār* for the attainment of *moksha.* He perceived that *mokṣa* could be attained through the service of God and of *dharma.* The concretisation of the *dharma* for him was in Rāmarājya which consisted of freedom for worship, justice and the service of Rāma, of God. Rāmarājya for him was the unity of all men in righteousness. He proclaimed that every individual should direct his personal effort and activity along with all others for the service of the Mighty, *sāmarthe samaratha karūni sodavāve* ('by your power let others be powerful') and *sāmarthe samarpave* ('offer with your power'). Therefore, he gave his followers the *mantra* of *jaya jaya raghuvīr samartha,* or 'glory glory to the powerful one, the hero of the Raghuvamsha'. In this way Saint Ignatius and Sant Rāmdās proclaimed the service of the Kingdom of Heaven.

In order to introduce western thought to the students of religion in Maharashtra, I translated into Marathi two books, 'De visione dei' and '*De pace fidei*' of Nicholaus of Cusa with the titles 'Prabhudarśan' and '*Śraddhā-Salokh*'[96]. Nicholaus of Cusa (1401-1467) is known as a philosopher and a theologian. In these two books, I understand him as a real mystic, a real *bhakta.* He was for me almost like a guide showing what should be the aim of my research in Bhakti and of my activity. The primary assertion of the Vedic philosophy in the four Vedas and in the various Purāṇas could be said that it affirms that "the ultimate reality is one and we all participate by our being and consciousness in this reality". In the *ātman* is conceived the unity of *sat* and *cit.* Ascertaining the cause of various knowledge and opinions it is said, *ekam sat, viprāh bahusyām vadanti.* The Vedic philosophy also affirms that the Ultimate reality could be worshipped and honoured as God through various names. This understanding of God allows to every individual freedom of worship which is founded on his perception of the ultimate reality.

Nicholaus of Cusa has proclaimed in '*De pace fidei*' that knowledge is essentially and ultimately one. All our knowledge and opinions have their origin in this knowledge. He affirms that "this knowledge is eternal and it is the cause and origin of all beings. Therefore, God is knowledge and He alone is the eternal and origin

[96] The translation of '*De pace fidei*'.

of all beings"[97]. Vedic Bhakti, on which all movements are based in the Indian subcontinent, states that knowledge of God as the ultimate reality is given in human nature and this knowledge is the base for the Bhakti and for the fulfilment of human nature in achieving the unity with the Ultimate. Nicholaus of Cusa confirms this when he says: "all men according to their human nature hope for nothing less than the eternal life and they all have longing for the eternal life. All people perform according to their nature various rituals for the purification of the souls; and other venerations so that they may be worthy for the eternal life. Men strive continuously for happiness. Happiness means eternal life and its seed is contained in human nature. Man does not like to live like angels or any other being, but he would like to live like human alone. He would like to live like the happy man who has achieved ultimate happiness. Happiness is nothing else than joy or unity. Unity means going back to the same life from which he has been created. This is eternal divine life, with which the human desires to be united"[98].

For achieving unity with the Divine various Sants have proposed the way of *prapatti* ('dedication') or *śaranāgati* ('surrender') in their literature. The maxim, *uddhārаret ātmana ātmānām* ('save yourself through the self') does not say that man can attain *moksha* merely by self-effort. *Prapatti* as dependence on God is most necessary. Likewise, commenting on the New Testament, Nicholaus of Cusa has affirmed that "without faith one is unable to please God. However, it is important that faith be accompanied by actions; because without deeds it would be as good as dead"[99].

Vedic philosophy does not speak about God's commandments or divine injunctions, but rather proposes that the divine will is manifested in the very nature of man because the *ātman* dwells in human beings. I understand here that Nicholaus has explained the will of God in the context of Christianity in an excellent manner, which cannot be strange to any religion. He comments on the divine command saying:

---

[97] Shelke, Christopher, *Shraddhā-Salokhā*, Sphurti Prakashan, Ahmednagar, 1996, pp. 19-20.

[98] *Ibid.*, p. 45.

[99] *Ibid.*, p. 57.

> "I think that all have to admit that God's commandments are very pithy and are known by all. God's commandment is the common treasure of all nations (races). The light that gives us the knowledge of these commandments has been created along with the life giving soul; yes, because in the human person the Divine voice tells us that we must love Him, from whom we have received our existence. So also the golden rule which says that one should not do to others what one would not like to be done to himself. The perfection of God's commandments is nothing else but love. Ultimately, all commandments have their origin in love"[100].

Naturally, I need not remind here that the Bhakti theologian Nārada speaking about the nature of Bhakti says: "*sā prem svarūpā*".

In such thinking of Nicholaus of Cusa I find an excellent attitude of reconciliation and unity. Certainly such an attitude accepts the various modes and manners of religious worship, as Nicholaus himself would say, "if one cannot achieve and preserve uniformity, then rather without sacrificing unity and peace (Concordia) every nation (race) should have freedom to perform their own rituals and celebrations.

I think that by such variety real devotion will increase and each nation (race) will try to formulate their ritual in a more appropriate way and better than the others. This will be certainly more praiseworthy in the eyes of men and of God"[101]. This is exactly what is proposed in the Vedic philosophy when it states that God can be worshipped with diverse ways and names.

In '*Visione Dei*' Cusa stated that the highest perfection that man can ever attain is the vision of God, for God's 'seeing' means His 'being'. He sees everything and all things at the same time so He Himself is all things and everything at the same time., He is in all things and in everything by His own Word. According to him the knowledge of God begins with the knowledge of the world and the self, because everything is created in the Word of God. God can be seen only as the absolute Infinity and man can only strive after this vision.

---

100 *Ibid.*, p. 58.
101 *Ibid.*, p. 64.

In the writings of Nicholaus of Cusa I have found the real aim and motivation for the Bhakti and how Bhakti should contribute to the unity of the human race. Cusa studied the Quran and the other religions with an open mind and tried to raise and understand the good of these religions. He remains, in my opinion, a guide for dialogue of religion and by his mystical thought also a guide and motivation for Bhakti.

Many critics of Bhakti, especially D.Dandekar, R.D. Bhandarkar and G.B. Sardar, commenting on the Vārkarī Sampradāya, said that in the sphere of Bhakti, there reigns a spiritual democracy, meaning that the *bhakta*-s came together in the *satsang* and in the *kīrtan*-s, without looking at the caste and the differences. However, when one looks at the Bhakti literature in Maharashtra, one will notice that the writings of Tukārām, Nāmdev, Dñyāneśwar and Eknāth have been translated into English and other languages. There has hardly been any translation of the writings of Cokhāmelā and of other low-caste sants into English and other languages. Therefore, during the first year of my stay in Munich I translated the *abhaṅga*-s of Cokhāmelā into German with the title, "*Lobpreis des göttlichen Namens*" (Kosel, Munchen, 1991) and I also wrote for the Leiden conference an article on Cokhamelā. I have not failed to neglect the women Sants either. I wrote on Sant Janābāī and I have translated Sant Mīrābāī into German, which will be completed and published hopefully in 2002. In my teaching I have treated themes like 'Women mystics', 'Mysticism of the cross and the *ātman*' and 'St Teresa of Avila and Sant Mira'.

Certainly, Bhakti has the modern aspect of service which developed under the influence of Christianity and of Svami Vivekanananda. Naturally, Mahatma Gandhi has not been ranked among the *bhakta*-s and sants. However, as a student of theology and philosophy of comparative religion and mysticism, I cannot ignore Mahatma Gandhi and Ambedkar. The Gandhian search for truth and its application through non-violence for shaping human society bring us once more in a new vision of humanity which says that humanity can realise brotherhood of man by respecting the liberty of the individuals and by passive resistance, which means nothing less than the readiness of self-sacrifice. On the other hand, Ambedkar proposed a constitutional way of service. By proposing the safeguards and rights for the minority, whether it be religious, linguistic or cultural and by offering reservation facilities to the backward classes in the Indian Constitution, he has brought Bhakti thoughts of service in the functioning of the government. Democracy does not mean the rule of majority, but rather how the majority will serve the minority and by doing so it will serve the majority too. Here Mahatma Gandhi and Ambedkar implicitly agree on the idea that the politic is not meant for ruling, but for service. Naturally this idea is far away in the actual politic of India and many other countries. Therefore, in my teaching classes too I treat topics as 'The constitution religion of the Indian Constitution according to Ambedkar' and 'The religion of non-violence and of truth according to Mahatma Gandhi'.

I could say that while doing research and making a study of the various sants and *bhakta*-s in various religions, I have profited from their *satsang*. Their company has given me a broader perspective and vision and has motivated me to say *viśva eva kuṭumbakam*.

A Study of the Historical Development of Bhakti found in Five Commentaries on the *Bhagavadgītā*

IWAO SHIMA

One of the most important characteristics of the *Bhagavadgītā* is its attempt to combine three ways to salvation, i.e. *karman* (action), *jñāna* (knowledge) and *bhakti* (devotion). This attempt was, however, not completely successful. It contained many inconsistencies that left room for divergent interpretations by later commentators. In the various interpretations of the *Bhagavadgītā* by later commentators, we find various combinations of those three ways to salvation, which allow us to follow the historical development of salvation theories.

Among the many commentators, I select the following five, because they represent the major phases in the development of salvation theories in the interpretations of the *Bhagavadgītā*: Śaṅkara (700-750), Rāmānuja (1017-1137), Madhva (1197-1276), Jñānadeva (1275-96), and Tilak (1856-1920).

Śaṅkara interpreted the salvation theory of the *Bhagavadgītā* within the framework of *karman* and *jñāna*, that is the performance of Vedic rites and the knowledge of the identity of *brahman* and *ātman*. He insisted that final liberation could be attained only by the knowledge of the identity of *brahman* and *ātman*. With regard to Bhakti also, Śaṅkara interpreted it within the framework of *karman* and *jñāna* and took it as *jñāna* or as a means to attain *jñāna*. Śaṅkara thus interpreted the three ways to salvation in the *Bhagavadgītā* within the Upanishadic tradition of *jñāna*.

With the rise of the Bhakti movement in Tamil (7th-9th centuries), Bhakti began to occupy the central position in the three ways to salvation. Thereafter, this Bhakti was absorbed into the Brahmanical tradition and spread all over India. Three stages can be distinguished in the development of the Bhakti movement. During the first stage, the Bhakti movement, which had originated in a non-Aryan environment (Tamil), was absorbed into the orthodox Brahmanical tradition and was reconciled with the Brahmanical tradition of knowledge (*jñāna*) and meditation (*upāsanā*). Rāmānuja and Madhva are representatives of this stage.

They attempted to reconcile Bhakti with the Upanishadic tradition of *jñāna* and *upāsanā* and identified Bhakti with knowledge (*vedanā*) and meditation (*upāsanā*). Their Bhakti, however, came to lose, to some extent, the originally emotional character of Bhakti as a result of the reconciliation with the Upanishadic tradition of knowledge and meditation.

With the spread of the Bhakti movement to West- and North-India and among the lower castes, Bhakti became gradually free from the Upanishadic tradition of *jñāna* and *upāsanā* and recovered its originally emotional character. This is the second stage in the development of the Bhakti movement. This stage has two aspects. One is that Bhakti spread all over India through the Sanskrit language, which supported the Brahmanical tradition as the sacred language of the Brahmins; emotional Bhakti thus came to permeate the Brahmanical tradition itself. Vallabha, Nimbārka and others are representatives of this aspect. The other aspect is that Bhakti spread even among the lower castes through the local languages with the help of local sages who appeared in various parts of India. Jñānadeva is one of the representatives of this aspect.

Thus, in mediaeval India, the *Bhagavadgītā* was first interpreted by Śaṅkara to preach *jñāna* as the way to liberation. In contrast to Śaṅkara, most of the later commentators (except Bhāskara) interpreted the *Bhagavadgītā* to preach Bhakti as the way to salvation. In the modern age, however, we witness the revival of *karman* as a way to salvation, not in the sense of the performance of rituals or duties of one's own caste, but in the sense of social activities, such as the social movement for independence found in Tilak's interpretation.

This is my provisional rough sketch of the historical development of salvation theories found in commentaries on the *Bhagavadgītā*. The purpose of my study of these commentaries is to follow this historical development of salvation theories by modifying and amplifying my rough sketch on the basis of the original texts, and to make clear the significance of this historical development.

My plan to realise the purpose mentioned above

1. Establishment of an Asian Religious Studies Series, Kanazawa University (ARCS Kanazawa). Generally speaking, it is difficult to

find a place to publish Japanese translations of original texts, which usually do not sell well. Therefore, I would like to establish ARCS Kanazawa next year, in which I plan to publish my 2 of the three commentaries on the *Bhagavadgītā* as follows:

> A Japanese translation of Śaṅkara's commentary on the *Bhagavadgītā* (up to chapter 3; a rough draft is ready till the end).
> A Japanese translation of Rāmānuja's commentary on the *Bhagavadgītā* (up to chapter 3; a rough draft is ready till the end).
> A Japanese translation of Madhva's commentary on the *Bhagavadgītā* (up to chapter 3; a rough draft is ready till the end).

2. In July 1998 I restarted the journal *Maharashtra*, vol. 4, after a break of 18 years, in which I am now publishing my Japanese translation of Jñānadeva's Commentary on the *Bhagavadgītā* (chapters 1 and 2 have been published in *Maharashtra* 5-6; a rough draft is ready up to chapter 6 and will be published in *Maharashtra*).

3. Bhakti Study Meeting in Japan and Conference of South Asian Studies at Kanazawa in 2001.

4. Publication of a monograph on the historical development of Bhakti, in "Japanese Studies on South Asia" Series, in collaboration with Prof. T. Sakata.

Remarks on Some Aspects of Bhakti

BAHADUR SINGH

I should like to make some remarks on the aspects of Bhakti that interest me. First, Kabīr and Mīrābāī. In 1995-96 I went to Rajasthan to record the oral transmission of the texts attributed to these two Bhakti poets. I could do this in parts of north-, west- and south-Rajasthan. In the end I had collected about 500 texts, of which 300 are of Kabīr. About these texts I gave a report at the Venice conference (1997) and again at the Heidelberg conference (1999). At Venice I described the cultural and religious context of the process of transmisson, whereas at the Heidelberg conference I tried to show that we have hardly any criterion to prove that a text attributed to Kabīr is authentic or not, for the Bhakti idiom is substantially the same, whoever the author named in the signature line is. It would be great if this recording could in the future be extended to other parts of Rajasthan and if the material, vast though it will be, could be brought out in a truly critical edition, true in the sense that it discusses the relation between the oral and the written tradition.

II

In the 1980s I went to Rajasthan to record two major folk epics, namely Pābūjī and the Bagaṛāvat Devnārāyaṇ, both sung by devotees calles *bhopā*-s, belonging to the low-caste *thorī* who sing Pābūjī, and *kumhār* who sing the *Bagaṛāvat.* Till now, I have not found the time to publish anything on the Pābūjī epic, but I did publish two papers on the *Bagaṛāvat Devnārāyaṇ.* I hope to be able to prepare a critical edition of these works too.

III

Another aspect of Rajasthan that fascinates me is the Viṣṇoī tradition, both the written one and as it is lived today, all the more because this particular form of Bhakti is rooted in what we would call today 'ecological ethics'. At this moment I have been able to write only one article on this, but there too it would be of great indological and ethical significance if everyday life of the Viṣṇoīs could be studied.

The *Mahābhārata* in Eastern India

WILLIAM L. SMITH

The study deals with the *Mahābhārata* literature in eastern NIA languages with an emphasis on four full-length versions of the epic: the Assamese version (16th century), the Oriya version of Śarala Dāsa (completed 1475) and the Bengali versions of Kāśīrāmdās (17th century) and Kabi Sañjay (16th century?). Versions of the *Jaimini Bhārata* which are common in all three languages will be examined as well. The study focuses on the way in which the regional poets deal with the Sanskrit original as well as with apocryphal inclusions, especially stories which appear in several regional versions.

Preliminary research conclusions were discussed in several papers: "Rewriting the *Mahābhārata*", presented at the XI World Sanskrit Studies Conference, Turin, April 2000; "Battle Scenes in the Vernacular *Mahābhāratas*" at the 16th European Modern South Asian Conference, Edinburgh, September 2000; and "Why didn't Rāma Sarasvatī translate the *Mahābhārata*?", a lecture at Cotton College, Guwahati, Assam, February 2001.

Bhakti in Lexicography and Gurū Nānak *Bāṇī*

O.P. VASISHTA

My major areas of research are semiotics of literature and applied linguistics. My first interest relates to the study of the contribution of the Sikh Gurūs, especially of Gurū Nānak to the Bhakti movement. My second area of research relates to lexicography.

On the basis of the lexicographical experience gained through the years I have produced an original book in Punjabi entitled *Kosh Vigian ate Punjabi Koshkari* (i.e. Lexicology and Punjabi Lexicography) for which I was awarded Bhai Vir Singh award by the language department, Punjab. In this book, both the theoretical and practical aspects of lexicography are dealt with in detail, as also the critical evaluation of important lexicons including the ones relating to *Gurū Granth Sāhib* and *Daśam Granth*. The non-availability of an authentic up-to-date Punjabi Dictionary and an Etymological Dictionary of Punjabi Language was the major problem faced by us for the realisation of these projects. The shortage of funds was another obstacle, because in India applied linguistics is given secondary importance in the curricula of our country. And besides other numerous methodological, technical and non-technical problems faced in the preparation of bilingual dictionaries, we often came across the problems of giving a contextual meaning and finding exact equivalents due to the cultural variations in both the languages. For example, we find no equivalent for the lexical item आचमन करना or अँचवना in English and we have no other alternate but to explain its meaning as 'to sip water from the palm of the right hand (as a ritual)'. Similar is the case of *dhotī*, *dāl*, *gurmukh*, *khalsā* and numerous other lexical items.

Turning to my first area of interest, i.e. semiotics of literature, in my research work *Chinh-Vigiān ate Gurū Nānak Bāṇī* (i.e. Semiology and Gurū Nānak *Bāṇī*), I have tried to decipher the conceptual network of Gurū Nānak's poetry enshrined in the sign-system expressed in mediaeval idiom based on its binary oppositions of signifiers: *gurmukh* (person who obeys the Gurū) and *manmukh* (a self-centered person), *nām* (name) and *māyā* (illusion), *halāl* (money earned through honest means) and *harām* (money earned through deceitful means), *satiguru* (true guru) and *asatiguru* (false guru), exploiter and exploited, *mukti* (salvation) and *dāstā* (slavery), social values supporting the human existence (such as truth, patience, control, compassion, etc.) and social values opposed to man (such as ego, greed, anger, etc.).

After having analysed the surface structure of Gurū Nānak *Bāṇī*, I tried to decipher it at its immanent level: the signified of God (*wāhiguru* in Gurū Nānak's terms) appeared before me in the form of a perceptible and imperceptible conscious supreme power operating behind the material and socio-cultural phenomena; *jīva* as a dynamic social man; *gurmukh* as humane social man following the instructions of the Gurū; *manmukh* as inhuman social person not caring for the teachings of the Gurū; *nām* as true consciousness about God; *māyā* as a false-consciousness oriented way of life; *guru* as the awakened and enlightened teacher gifted with the knowledge of the Name of God; *sant*, *sādh*, etc. as the noble and learned man; *huqm* as the law of the supreme power; *razā* and *bhāṇā* as acting according to the law of the supreme power; ego, lust, anger, greed, attachment, pride, etc. as forces opposed to the social human existence; truth, contentment, patience, control, love, etc. as the qualities supporting the social human existence; and *mukti* as the salvation of humanity. Consequently, the hyper sign of Gurū Nānak's poetry at both its manifest and immanent levels manifested itself in the form of an action-oriented, dynamic and revolutionary humanistic world-view rooted in *bhakti* (devotion) and saturated by *giān* (knowledge).

I do not claim to be the first student to understand the Gurū Nānak *Bāṇī.* Much research work was done in this field before I took up this study. But the endeavour of my predecessors was confined to the manifest level, only giving the superficial meaning and paraphrase of the *Bāṇī*, except for the works of Prof. Sant Singh Sekhon and Prof. Kishan Singh. Secondly, their research was lacking a systematic and methodical approach. I have based my research on a semiological methodology introduced in Punjabi in the sixties by Prof. Harjit Singh Gill, former Chairman, Department of English and Linguistics, Jawahar Lal Nehru University, Delhi. Starting from the Saussurean concepts of semiology and structural linguistics, he introduced almost all the major concepts of structuralism, semiotics, deconstruction, post modernism, etc. The methodological insights enshrined in the works of these scholars were taken proper care of in this book.

For the study and analysis of the deep structure of Gurū Nānak's poetry, the actantial model presented by Greimas was aptly followed. Accordingly, this study produced very interesting results. On the one hand, the whole sign-system of the Gurū Nānak *Bāṇī*, especially the conceptual network consisting of major signs like God, *jīva*, *guru*, *nām*, *māyā*, society, *huqm*, salvation, etc. were deciphered on the basis of their binary oppositions as mentioned above. On the other hand, the whole sign-system was analysed in its mediaeval, feudal, socio-cultural perspective. It is not that the sign-system used by Gurū Nānak was absolutely new, but he used it in such a way — by transforming the meaning of signs — that I find in it the total transformation of the Bhakti movement in India. For example, the meanings enshrined in the signs of *janeu* (the sacred thread), *musalmān* (Muslim), *brāhman*, *sant* (saint), etc. were totally transformed in the Bhakti tradition. This transformation of the whole sign-system has proved to be an epistemological transformation of the established convention in the field of mediaeval language, literature and culture. As such, the Gurū Nānak *Bāṇī* stresses the total transformation of man, human society and the entire social milieu. For the transformation of human society it was obligatory to explore the insubstantial and empty signifiers relating to the traditional institutions and culture. Since the contemporary social, political and cultural conditions were not congenial for the growth of the human personality and the human society, Gurū Nānak had to transform each and every sign relating to the human society, giving birth to new cultural formations.

Besides, exploring the empty signifiers and giving them a revolutionary meaning, Gurū Nānak strongly criticised the nasty caste system, stressed the equality of man and woman and, more so, the relevance of woman to the society, salvation from slavery by criticising the prevalent feudal system, negation of the exploiting and persecuting system, raising a voice against political tyranny, exposing the deceitful religious institutions and characters, and suggested the inculcation of good deeds such as to make truthful labour one's ideal in life and share the earnings with fellow men, to bring a qualitative change in human life, to make their own *Bāṇī* the life support of their followers instead of following other religious Granths, to make a total change in the way of life and values of life, thereby creating parallel institutions, to establish Saṅgat, Paṅgat and and Laṅgar by the Gurūs with a view to abolishing the nasty caste system and inequality, to stress upon the essence of God in place of idol worship, to harmonise completely one's words and deeds, to establish the system of Gurūdom, to transform the tradition and heritage and, above all, to use the folk language and folk forms of poetry for the expression of his revolutionary and spiritual ideas.

To my mind, these are some of the salient characteristics of the Gurū Nānak *Bāṇī* which had strong impact on the national and global level. The contribution of Gurū Nānak has not only transformed the Bhakti movement, but also slowly and steadily changed the shape of Punjab and India. In this way, Gurū Nānak can be called a great thinker of India.

Future Plan

In the proposed project of Etymological Punjabi-English Dictionary of Gurū Nānak *Bāṇī*, I would like to synthesise both areas, thereby contributing a little to the research on Bhakti literature. I have submitted this project to the Panjab University during the tercentenary celebrations of the Khalsā in 1999.

Bhakti Literature in the Oral Tradition of Gujarat

HASU YAJNIK

Folksongs related to *Kṛṣṇacarit*

The Gujarat State Government Folklore Committee collected nearly 5,000 folkworks, containing folktales and stories, published in 14 volumes (1957 till 1979). At the time of its reprint I re-edited nearly 5,000 folktales and folksongs, subjectwise, under the guidance of Dr. H.C. Bhayani, in 7 volumes, with a folklore study. Of these I edited 606 folksongs which were connected with *Kṛṣṇacarit* and that has been published with folklore study in my *Lokgīto mā Kṛṣṇacarit*, Gandhinagar, Gujarat Sahitya Akademi, 1990:

> 18 on *kṛṣṇajanma*, 6 on lullabies, 5 on *Ādo* (child-persistance), 3 on *viśvarūpa darśana*, 68 on *bālakṛṣṇa*, 23 on Gopālakṛṣṇa, 12 on Vastraharaṇ, 18 on *nāgdamaṇ*, 29 on *dānalīlā*, 13 on *rāsalīlā*, 13 on Vādchhad or 'verbal competition', 4 on Holī, 179 on *gopī*, 49 on *muralī*, 52 on Rādhā, 5 on Chandrāvalī, 3 on Satyabhāmā, 11 on Rukīmaṇī, 32 related to Mathurā, 12 on Mās, 2 on Bāramasī, 31 various.

The paper based on these songs was published as 'Kṛṣṇa in Gujarati Folksong Tradition', H.C. Bhayani & Hasu Yajnik, in 'Devotion Divine' edited by D. Eck & F. Mallison, Paris, 1991.

Folksongs related to *Rāmcarita*

121 Folksongs based on *Rāmcarita*, published in '*Lokgito mā Rāmcarita ane Pāndav Kathā*', Gandhinagar: Gujarat Sahitya Akademi, 1992:

> 8 on Śravaṇa, 3 on Śabarī, 10 on Rām Kathā in brief, 18 on Vār and Tīthī, 70 on Sītā Svayamvara, abduction and abandonment, 12 on the Rām-Rāvaṇa battle.

The paper based on these songs was published in 'Studies in Early Modern Indo-Aryan Languages, Literature and Culture', edited by Alan Entwistle & Françoise Mallison, 1999.

Folksongs on Mahādev Śankar

In '*Ṛtucakra Samlagna Lokrachanāo'*, Gandhinagar: Gujarat Sahitya Akademi, 1995, I published 20 songs on Mahādev and in *Gujarati Lokgito mā Kathā-gito*, Gandhinagar: Gujarat Sahitya Akademi, 1994, I give 16 songs on Shiva-Bhiladī.

Devī-worship

In '*Ṛtucakra Samlagna Lokrachanāo'*, 1994 I published the following folksongs:

> 1 on Bahucharā, 4 on Mahi, 1 on Haramā, 3 on Rāndal, 1 on Jogmā, 7 Ashtaka, 5 on Garabā dance, 16 songs on the Māndavi-ritual of building a temporary small wooden temple of Devī, during Navrātri.

For the Saraju songs, I refer to my paper read at the Venice Conference, 1997, and published as 'A Living Tradition within the Devī-worship Ritual of the Vaiśya Sutār and Sorathiā and Bhopā Rabārī of Saurashtra', in M. Offredi, *The Banyan Tree*, 2000, pp. 223-234. In *Gujarati Loksāhitya ni Jīvancakra Antargat Rachanāo*, Gandhinagar: Gujarat Sahitya Akademi, 1996, I give 7 Rāndal (Rannādevī) songs.

Folksongs on Rāmdev cult

I published 4 songs on Rāmdev, 1 on Rupānde in *Ṛtucakra Samlagna Lok rachanāo*, Gandhinagar: Gujarat Sahitya Akademi, 1995.

Indian classical music & notation of Gujarati folk songs, Pad-Bhajan & Dhūn

My books on Indian classical music and instrument playing are published in Gujarati:

Violin Vadan, Ahmedabad: Gurjar Grantharatna Karyalay, 1997.
Śāstriya Rāgdarśan, Ahmedabad: Gurjar Grantharatna Karyalay, 1995.
Bānsarī Vadan, Ahmedabad: Gurjar Grantharatna Karyalay, 1998.

These books are on instrument playing and Indian classical music. The basic 55 classical *rāga*-s, their details, scales, *sargam*, *ālāp*, *jod-zālā*, *tān-palatā*, *gat* and traditional *chij*-compositions are given. In *Rāgdarśan*, there are 100 classical Indian *rāga*-s and their traditional compositions.

Notation of folksongs

Dr. H.C. Bhayani has collected and edited 90 Gujarati devotional songs which were in the oral tradition two generations ago. They include various song types such as Dhoḷ, Pad, Bhajan, Dhūn, Rās, Garbā. These songs are sung traditionally. I have given the musical notation of its traditional singing compositions. This work has been published as:

- *Hariveṇa Vāy chhe Re Ho Vanna Mā*, Gandhinagar: Gujarat Sahitya Akademi, 1998.
- *Gokul Mā Tahukyā Mor*, Gandhinagar: Gujarat Sahitya Akademi, 1989.
- *Zinā Zarmar Varse Meh*, Gandhinagar: Gujarat Sahitya Akademi, 1991.

Tracing Cokhāmelā

ELEANOR ZELLIOT

The 700 years of the Bhakti movement in Maharashtra have three unusual features: a great number of women poet-saints; a general family basis for saints' lives; and a congregation of saint-poets from as many as thirty castes in the Marathi language area. The life of Cokhāmelā exemplifies all these differences from Bhakti in other areas, and adds the fact that not only were he and his family of an untouchable caste, but they also sung in no uncertain terms against poverty and pollution concepts and practices.

My question is basically: how were the songs of this Mahār saint, and his wife, son, sister and her husband, carried through the centuries when they were illiterate, not allowed to enter the temple, and without a sect or cult center for written manuscripts. Not only were hundreds of songs recorded from this family of five — plus one or two other Mahārs about whom we know nothing — and kept somehow for posterity, but there is a new interest in this quite marginalised figure. There are three new inscriptions on Cokhāmelā's *samādhi* in the pilgrimage center of Pandharpur, adding to the one put up in 1954 when the *samādhi* was reconstructed. All three are dated 2000. There are four new books about Cokhāmelā and a new edition of the only separate collection of his *gāthā*, or songs, with an introduction by a highly respected novelist. Several Ph.D. theses are in progress or have been finished. Also the Bhakti tradition of other untouchable groups is ever-stronger, with one group: the Māṅg inventing their saint, the Puranic figure of Ajāmela, so that they could carry his footprints in their *diṅḍī* in the great pilgrimage to Pandharpur.

The only manuscript source I have found is in the *bāda*-s (notebooks) of literate Brahmin *kīrtankāra*-s, which V.L. Manjul has carefully collected from old *kīrtankār* sources. In one Joshi Bada (from Bijapur), there are three *abhaṅga*-s (songs) from Cokhāmelā, none of which are in print, and two of which are signed Kevalanāth Cokhā Mahār. The mystery is deepened. But what we know is that there were powerful voices of untouchables in the 14th century, somehow carried in a tradition that usually marginalised them, to emerge in the 20th century as cultural heritage for all.

BIBLIOGRAPHY*

Asani, Ali S., "The Khojki Script: A Legacy of Ismaili Islam in Indo-Pakistan", *Journal of the American Oriental Society* 107:3, 1987, pp. 439-49.

— "Sufi Poetry in the Folk Tradition of Indo-Pakistan", *Religion and Literature* 20:1, 1988, pp. 81-94.

— *The Bujh Niranjan: An Ismaili Mystical Poem in Medieval Hindustani*, Cambridge, MA: Center for Middle Eastern Studies (Harvard University), 1991.

— "The Ginan Literature of the Ismailis of Indo-Pakistan: Its Origins, Characteristics and Themes", in Eck, Diana L. & Françoise Mallison, eds., *Devotion Divine: Bhakti Traditions from the Regions of India. Studies in Honour of Charlotte Vaudeville*, Groningen & Paris: Egbert Forsten & EFEO, 1991, pp. 1-18.

— *The Harvard Collection of Ismaili Literature in Indic Languages: A Descriptive Catalog and Finding Aid*, Boston: G.K. Hall, 1992.

— "The Ismaili *Ginans* as Devotional Literature", in McGregor, R.S., ed., *Devotional Literature in South Asia: Current Research, 1985-1988*, Cambridge: Cambridge UP, 1992, pp. 101-12.

— "Bridal Symbolism in the Ismaili Ginan Literature", in Herrera, R., ed., *Mystics of the Book: Themes, Topics and Typologies*, New York: Peter Lang, 1993, pp. 389-404.

— "Folk Romance in Sufi Poetry from Sind", in Dallapiccola, A. & S. Lallemant, eds., *Islam and the Indian Religions*, Stuttgart: Franz Steiner Verlag, 1993, pp. 229-37.

— "A Testimony of Love: The *Git* Tradition of the Nizari Ismailis", in Giese, A. & C. Burgel, eds., *God is Beautiful and Loves Beauty. Festschrift of Annemarie Schimmel*, Bern & New York: Peter Lang, 1993, pp. 39-51.

— "The Bridegroom Prophet in Medieval Sindhi Poetry", in Mallison, Françoise & Alan W. Entwistle, eds., *Studies in South Asian Devotional Literature: Research Papers 1989-91*, New Delhi: Manohar, 1994, pp. 213-25.

— *Celebrating Muhammad: Images of the Prophet in Popular Muslim Poetry*, University of South Carolina Press, 1995.

— "In Praise of Muhammad: Sindhi and Urdu Poems", in Lopez, D., ed., *Religions of India in Practice*, Princeton: Princeton UP, 1995, pp. 159-86.

* In this list authors have given only their Bhakti-related publications.

— "Muslim Literatures of South Asia", in Nanji, A., ed., *Muslim Almanac: A Reference Work on the History, Faith, Culture and Peoples of Islam*, Detroit: Gale Research Inc., 1995, pp. 355-64.
— "Urdu Literature", in Esposito, J., ed., *Oxford Encyclopedia of the Modern Islamic World*, New York & Oxford: Oxford UP, 1995, pp. 289-96.
— "In Praise of Muhammad: Indigenizing the Arabic *qasida* in Urdu and Sindhi Literature", in Sperl, S. & C. Shackle, eds., *Qasida Poetry in Asia and Africa*, Leiden: E.J. Brill, 1996, pp. 351-61.
— "The Ismaili *Ginans*: Reflections on Authority and Authorship", in Daftary, F., ed., *Medieval Ismaili History and Thought*, Cambridge: Cambridge UP, 1996, pp. 265-80.
— "Arabic Literature in India", in Meisami, J.S. & P. Starkey, eds., *Encyclopedia of Arabic Literature*, vol. 1, London & New York: Routledge, 1998, pp. 395-6.
— "Propagating the Message: Popular Sufi Songs and Spiritual Transformation in South Asia", *Bulletin of the Henry Martyn Institute of Islamic Studies* 15:3-4, 1998, pp. 5-15.
— "Qazi Qadan: A Pioneer Sindhi Poet", in Offredi, Mariola, ed., *The Banyan Tree: Essays on Early Literature in New Indo-Aryan Languages*, Delhi: Manohar, 1999, pp. 3-13.
— "At the Cross-Roads of Indic and Iranian Civilizations: Sindhi Literary Culture", in Pollock, S., ed., *Literary Cultures in History: Reconstructions from South Asia*, Berkeley: University of California Press, [forthcoming].
— "Creating Tradition through Devotional Songs and Communal Script: The Khojah Ismailis of South Asia", in Eaton, R., ed., *Indo-Islamic Traditions 1000-1800*, Delhi: Oxford UP, [forthcoming].
— "Muslims in South Asia: Defining Community and the 'Other'", *Bulletin of the Royal Institute for Interfaith Studies*, [forthcoming].

Bangha, Imre, "The Harikalā Belī and Ānandghan's Death", *Annali dell'Istituto Universitario Orientale* (Napoli), 1997, pp. 231-41.
— "Kavitta chanda mẽ balāghāt [The accent in the *kabitta*-strophes]", *Nāgarī Patrikā* (Banaras), July-August 1998, pp. 10-2.
— *Saneh ko mārag: Ānandghan kā jīvanvṛtt* [The Path of Love: a biography of Anandghan], New Delhi: Vāṇī Prakāśan, 1999.
— ed., *The First Published Anthology of Hindi Poets: Thomas Duer Broughton's Selections from the Popular Poetry of the Hindoos: 1814*, New Delhi: Mahatma Gandhi Antarrashtriya Hindi Vishwavidyalaya and Rainbow Publishers, 2000.

— "Kāmpānī ke sipāhī tathā śṛṅgār-kāvya [The Sepoys of the Company and love Poetry]", *Vāgarth* (Calcutta) 65:November, 2000, pp. 78-80.

— "Mundane and Divine Love in Anandghan's Poetry", in Offredi, Mariola, ed., *The Banyan Tree: Essays on Early Literature in New Indo-Aryan Languages*, New Delhi & Venezia: Manohar Publishers & Universita degli Studi di Venezia, 2000, pp. 523-38.

— "Lover and Saint: The Early Development of Ānandghan's Reputation", *Journal of the Royal Asiatic Society* 11:2 (July), 2001, pp. 175-90.

— "Prem kiskā samān hai? – Ānandghan ke rupakõ mê prem tathā anya bhāv [What is Love Similar to? – Love and Other Sentiments in Ānandghan's Metaphors]", *Ras Nikunj* (Vrindaban), [forthcoming].

Bangha, Imre & Balázs Déri, *Távollét: Mirá hercegnö misztikus versei és legendája* [Separation: Mystic Poems and the Legend of Princess Mīrā], Budapest: Argumentum, 1997 – Hungarian prose translation, legend and explanations to the text by I. Bangha, and poetic translation by B. Déri.

— "Raszkhán versei [Raskhan's Poems]", *Lyukasóra* (Budapest), May 2000, pp. 12-3 – Hungarian verse translation.

Barz, Richard, *The Bhakti Sect of Vallabhacarya*, Faridabad: Thomson Press, 1976 – repr. New Delhi: Munshiram Manoharlal, 1992.

— "The Poetry of Guru Nanak", *Desh Videsh* (Journal of the India-Australia Association of Canberra) I:3 (January), 1977, pp. 15-8.

— "Kṛṣṇadās Adhikārī: an Irascible Devotee's Approach to the Divine", *Journal of Comparative Sociology and Religion* 14, 1987, pp. 35-54 – slightly altered repr. in Bailey, G. & I. Kesarkodi Watson, *Bhakti Studies*, New Delhi: Sterling Press, 1992, pp. 236-250.

— "Vallabhacarya", in Eliade, M., ed., *Encyclopedia of Religion*, New York, 1987, pp. 183-4.

— "Free Will in the Rāmāyaṇ of Bhānubhakti", in Thiel-Horstmann, Monika, ed., *Rāmāyaṇa and Rāmāyaṇas*, Wiesbaden: Otto Harrassowitz, 1991, pp. 29-46.

— "A Reinterpretation of Vaiṣṇava Theology: from the Puṣṭimārg to the Brahma Kumaris", in McGregor, R.S., ed., *Devotional Literature in South Asia: Current Research, 1985-1988*, Cambridge: Cambridge UP, 1992, pp. 298-313.

— "The Caurāsī Vaiṣṇavan kī Vārtā and the Hagiography of the Puṣṭimārg", in Callewaert, W.M. & R. Snell, eds., *According to Tradition. Hagiographical Writing in India*, Wiesbaden: Otto Harrassowitz, 1994, pp. 43-64.

Barz, Richard & M. Thiel-Horstmann, "Introduction", in Barz, Richard & M. Thiel-Horstmann, eds., *Living Texts from India*, Wiesbaden: Otto Harrassowitz, 1989, pp. 1-16.

Barz, Richard & M. Thiel-Horstmann, eds., *Living Texts from India*, Wiesbaden: Otto Harrassowitz, 1989.

Barz, Richard & Y.K. Yadav, *Contemporary Hindi Reader*, Canberra: Faculty of Asian Studies, A.N.U., 1978.

Bhattacharya, France, *Analyse structurale des contes de fées bengalis*, Paris: Université de Paris 3, 1978 – diss., 2 vols.

— "La déesse et le royaume dans le *Caṇḍī Maṅgal*", *Purusartha* (Paris) 5, 1981, pp. 17-53.

— "Les mets et la cuisine dans le *Caṇḍī Maṅgal*", in M.Cl. Porcher, ed., *Littératures de l'Inde* (*Purusartha* 7), Paris, 1983, pp. 131-75.

— "Viś, vaiśya et marchand dans le *Caṇḍī Maṅgal*", *Annuaire de l'EPHE* (Paris) Ve section, 1983, pp. 185-7.

— "Śīt Vasanta, les deux frères: essai de lecture idéologique", *Communications* (Paris) 39, 1984, pp. 64-77.

— "L'histoire de Śrī Vatsa d'après le *Mahābhārata* bengali de Kāśirāma Dāsa", *Communications* (Paris) 39, 1984, pp. 194-200.

— "Food Rituals in the *Caṇḍī Maṅgal*", *India International Centre Quarterly* (New Delhi) 12:2, 1985.

— "A propos d'une représentation du *Caṇḍī Maṅgal* au Bengale occidental", *Adyatan* (Paris) 3, 1986, pp. 7-26.

— *Etude comparée des Maṅgalkāvya bengali: Manasā et Caṇḍī*, Paris: Université de Paris 3, 1990, 3 vols – thèse de doctorat d'état.

— "The god Dharma, human Sacrifice and Bhakti in the *Dharma Maṅgal*", Entwistle, Alan W. & Fr. Mallison, eds., *Studies in South Asian Devotional Literature. Research Papers 1988-91*, New Delhi & Paris: Manohar & EFEO, 1994, pp. 345-52.

— "Le voyage dans la littérature médiévale du Bengale", in Salmon, Cl., ed., *Récits de voyage des Asiatiques. Genres, mentalités, conception de l'espace*, Paris: EFEO, 1996, pp. 39-52.

— "Hari the Prophet: an Islamic view of a Hindu god in Saiyid Sultān Navī Vaṃśa", in Hasan, Perveen & Mufakharul Islam, eds., *Essays in memory of Momtazur Rahman Tarafdar*, Dhaka: Centre for advanced Research in the Humanities (University of Dhaka), 1999, pp. 192-208.

— "Is Rūparāma's Dharma maṅgal an epic of the low castes?", *Archív Orientální* (Praha) 67:3 (August), 2000, pp. 359-86.

— "Is Rūparāma's Dharma maṅgal an epic of the low castes?", *Archív Orientální* (Praha) 67:3 (August), 2000, pp. 359-86.

Boltz, William G. & Michael C. Shapiro, eds., *Historical Phonology of Asian Languages*, Amsterdam & Philadelphia: John Benjamins, 1991.

Bose, Mandakranta, "Lāsya: Dance or Drama?", in Matilal, B.K. & P. Bilimoria, eds., *Sanskrit and Related Studies*, Delhi: Sri Satguru Publ., 1990, pp. 125-34.

— *Movement and Mimesis: The Idea of Dance in the Sanskrit Tradition*, Dordrecht (Holland): Kluwer Academic Publ., 1991.

— ed., *Nartananirṇaya by Pundarika Vitthala. A critical edition of a sixteenth century Sanskrit text on music and dance*, Calcutta: General Printers, 1991.

— ed., *The Dance Vocabulary of Classical India*, Delhi: Indian Books Centre, 1995 – 2nd revised ed. of *Classical Indian Dancing: A Glossary.*

— "The Lost Nāṭyavidhi of the Jaina Tradition", in Wagle, N.K. & Olle Qvarnstrom, eds., *Approaches to Jaina Studies: Philosophy, Logic, Rituals and Symbols*, Toronto: Centre for South Asian Studies (University of Toronto), 1999, pp. 348-59.

— "Rabindranath and the Poetic Heritage of Bhakti", in Entwistle, Allen D. & Carol Salomon & Heidi Pauwels & Michael C. Shapiro, eds., *Studies in Modern Indo-Aryan Language, Literature and Culture. Research Papers presented at the Sixth Conference on Devotional Literature in New Indo-Aryan Languages, Seattle, University of Washington, 7-9 July 1994*, Delhi: Manohar, 1999, pp. 57-69.

— "Textual Confrontations with Female Transgression in the Behula Legend", in Offredi, Mariola, ed., *The Banyan Tree: Studies in Modern Indo-Aryan Language, Literature and Culture. Research papers presented at the Seventh Conference on Devotional Literature in New Indo-Aryan Languages, Venice, 1997*, Delhi: Manohar, 1999, pp. 157-66.

— ed., *Faces of the Feminine in Ancient, Medieval and Modern India*, New York: Oxford UP, 2000.

— "Faith, Justice and the Feminine in the Manasamangala", in Bose, Mandakranta, ed., *Faces of the Feminine in Ancient, Medieval and Modern India*, New York: Oxford UP, 2000, pp. 153-61.

— "Satī: The Event and the Ideology", in Bose, Mandakranta, ed., *Faces of the Feminine in Ancient, Medieval and Modern India*, New York: Oxford UP, 2000, pp. 21-32.

— ed., *A Varied Optic: Contemporary Studies in the Ramayana Culture. Research papers presented at the Conference on the*

Ramayana Culture held at the Institute of Asian Research, University of British Columbia, 20-21 February 1999, Vancouver: Institute of Asian Research (University of British Columbia), 2000.
— "Uparupaka: A hybrid genre in the Sanskritic Tradition", *The International Journal of Hindu Studies* (Montreal, Canada), [forthcoming].

Brückner, Heidrun & Aditya Malik & Anne Feldhaus, eds., *Essays on Religion, Literature, and Law.* Sontheimer GD, New Delhi: Indira Gandhi National Centre for the Arts & Manohar, [forthcoming].

Burton, Adrian, *An Archival Study into the Text and Times of the Sarartha-varshini Commentary on the Bhagavad-gita by Vishvanatha Cakravarti.*
— *A Textual Study of the Prema-bhakti-candrika of Narottama Dasa.*

Callewaert, Winand, "Collating Manuscripts in Hindi with Computer", in *Computers in Literary and Linguistic Research. XIth International Conference ALLC* (*Louvain-la-Neuve, 2-6 April 1984*), 12, 1, 1984, pp. 5-8.
— "Life and Works of the Dadupanthi Rajab", *Orientalia Lovaniensia Periodica* 4, 1973, pp. 141-53.
— "Search for Manuscripts of the Dadupanthi Literature in Rajasthan", *Orientalia Lovaniensia Periodica* 4, 1973, pp. 155-67.
— "A 17th c. Anthology of Hindi Poetry", *Orientalia Lovaniensia Periodica* 5, 1974, pp. 187-96.
— "The Anabhay Prabodh of Garibadas", *Orientalia Lovaniensia Periodica* 5, 1974, pp. 163-85.
— "Manuscripts of some Bhaktamalas, Pañcavāṇīs and Sarvāṅgīs", *IA VRI Bulletin* (London) IV:Oct., 1976, pp. 5-12.
— "Key for Understanding Mystical Literature", *Orientalia Lovaniensia Periodica* 8, 1977, pp. 309-30.
— "The nirgun Bhakti of Rajab", *South Asian Digest of Regional Writing* (Heidelberg) 6, 1977, pp. 45-9.
— "Search for Manuscripts of the Dadupanthi Literature in Rajasthan II", *Orientalia Lovaniensia Periodica* 8, 1977, pp. 305-8.
— "Dadupanthi Sahitya ki Hastalikhit Granthom ki Khoj", *Shodh Patrika* (Udaipur) 28:1 (Jan.), 1978, pp. 5-24.
— "Microfilms of Hindi Literature", *Orientalia Lovaniensia Periodica* 9, 1978, pp. 185-8.
— *The Sarvangi of the Dadupanthi Rajab* (*Orientalia Lovaniensia Analecta*, 4), Leuven, 1978.

— "A Colloquium on Research in Devotional 'Hindi' Literature (Leuven, 1979)", *IA VRI Bulletin* (London) VII:Dec., 1979, pp. 36-7.

— "The Hindu-Christian Dialogue: A Bibliography", *Journal of Dharma* (Bangalore) IV:2 (April-June), 1979, pp. 186-211.

— "Catalogues of Manuscripts of 'Early Hindi' Bhakti Literature", *IA VRI Bulletin* (London) VIII:June, 1980, pp. 22-6.

— "A 'Dynamic Equivalence Translation' of the Bhagavad Gita", *Journal of Dharma* (Bangalore) V:1 (Jan.-March), 1980, pp. 52-63.

— ed., *Early Hindi Devotional Literature in Current Research. Proceedings of the International Middle Hindi Bhakti Conference (April 1979)* (*Orientalia Lovaniensia Analecta*, 8), Leuven, 1980.

— "God in 'Early Hindi' Bhakti: Male or Female?", *Journal of Dharma* (Bangalore) V:2 (April-June), 1980, pp. 190-8.

— "Microfilms of Hindi Literature in Private Possession", *South Asia Library Notes and Queries* (Chicago), June 1980, pp. 4-7.

— "Nirgun Literature in Rajasthan. A Report", in Callewaert, Winand, ed., *Early Hindi Devotional Literature in Current Research. Proceedings of the International Middle Hindi Bhakti Conference (April 1979)*, 1980, pp. 34-9.

— "The Sarvangi of the Dadupanthi Rajab and other Anthologies with Hindi Literature in Rajasthan", in *30th International Congress of Human Sciences in Asia and North-Africa (Mexico City, 1976)*, Mexico, 1982, pp. 98-104.

— "Text-analysis with Computer in Devanagari", in Thiel-Horstmann, Monika, ed., *Bhakti in Current Research*, Berlin, 1983, pp. 65-73.

— "The Leuven Text-Composition System in Devanagari", *Computer Science and Informatics - Journal of the Computer Society of India* 13:2, 1984, pp. 23-30.

— "Nirgun Literature. Lexicographical difficulties", in *Proceedings of the IVth World Sanskrit Conference (Weimar, May 1979)*, Berlin: Humboldt Un., 1985, pp. 361-4.

— "Rajasthani Literature without Autograph?", *IA VRI Bulletin* (London) XIII, 1986, pp. 9-18.

— "Dadu and the Dadupanth: The Sources", in Schomer, K. & W.H. McLeod, eds., *The Sants: Studies in a Devotional Tradition of India*, Berkeley: Religious Studies Series, 1987, pp. 181-9.

— "Indian Manuscripts without Autograph? A Computer Analysis", *Indo-Iranian Journal* 30, 1987, pp. 65-71.

— "Manuscripts, Archetypes and the Computer: A Report", *Literary and Linguistic Computing* 2:1, 1987, pp. 44-6.

— "Namdev's Repertoires and the Guru Granth", *Journal of Sikh Studies* (Amritsar) XIV:1 (Febr.), 1987, pp. 7-17.

— *The Hindi Biography of Dādū Dayāl*, Delhi: Motilal Banarsidass, 1988.

— "Raidas and the Guru Granth", *Journal of Sikh Studies* (Amritsar) XV:11 (Aug.), 1988.

— "Daduji Maharaj ki samanvay sadhna", *Gyananjali - Dadu Mahavidyalay* (Jaipur), 1988, pp. 22-3.

— "The Musical Arrangement in the Guru Granth", *The Sikh Courier* (London), Autumn-Winter 1989, pp. 25-7.

— "Namdev's Poems in Rajasthan and Panjab", *Annali ISMEO* (Napoli) 49:3, 1989, pp. 301-8.

— "Can the Bhagavad Gita be translated?", in Verma, C.D., ed., *The Gita in World Literature*, Delhi, 1990, pp. 89-100.

— "The 'Earliest' Song of Mira (1503-1546)", *Journal of the Oriental Institute* (University of Baroda) xxxix:March-June, 1990, pp. 239-53.

— "Critical Editions. A Waste of Time?", in Singh, Chandramani & Neelima Vashishtha, eds., *Pathways to Literature, Art and Archaeology. G.N. Bahura Felicitation Volume*, Jaipur, 1991, vol. 2, pp. 133-9.

— "Les poèmes de Namdev dans la littérature rajasthani", Mallison, F., ed., *Littératures médiévales de l'Inde du Nord*, Paris: Ecole Française d'Extreme-Orient, 1991, pp. 55-63.

— "Songs and Singers. Raidas and the Guru Granth", *The Journal of Religious Studies* (Patiala) xx:2, 1991, pp. 9-19.

— "Nirgun Literature on Microfilm in Leuven (II)", *IAVRI Bulletin* (London) xv-xvi, 1991, pp. 17-22.

— "Manuscripts, a Precious Goldmine", *The Journal of Religious Studies* (Patiala) xxii, 1993, pp. 158-73.

— *The Sarvāṅgī of Gopāl Dās*, Delhi: Manohar Book Publications, 1993.

— "Bhagatmals and Parcais in Rajasthan", in Callewaert, Winand & Rupert Snell, eds., *According to Tradition. Hagiographical Writing in India*, Wiesbaden: Harrassowitz, 1994, pp. 87-98.

— "Guru Ravidas: Teachings for the 21st Century", *Ravi Dass Jaikara*, Chandigarh, 1994, pp. 15-7.

— "The Name in Nirgun Bhakti", *Journal of Vaisnava Studies* (New York) 2:2, 1994, pp. 163-74.

— "The Sarvāṅgī of the Dādūpanthī Gopāldās", in *Studies in South Asian Devotional Literature. Research Papers 1988-1991, presented at the Fifth Conference on Devotional Literature in New Indo-Aryan*

Languages, held at Paris, Ecole Française d'Extrême Orient, 9-12 July 1991, 1994, pp. 449-54.

— "Guru Nanak: Ideal of Equality", *Indian Horizons* (New Delhi) 44:3, 1995, pp. 155-61.

— "Kabir. Scholarly Commentaries on Un-Critical Texts?", *Annali* (Istituto Universitario Orientale, Napoli) 56:1, 1996, pp. 88-104.

— *Shri Guru Granth Sahib* (*with complete index*), Delhi: Motilal Banarsidass, 1996.

— "Translating Santa Literature (North India, 1400-1700 AD)", in Garzilli, E., ed., *Translation, Translating, Translators. From India to the West* (*Harvard Oriental Series. Opera Minora*), 1996, pp. 1-10.

— "Kabir: Scholarly Commentaries on Uncritical Texts", Sinh Bedi, Haramahendra, ed., *Kalajayi Kabir*, Amritsar: Guru Nanak Dev Yunivarsiti, 1997, pp. 200-16.

— "Is the Poet behind the Texts?", *Journal of Indian Philosophy* 26, 1998, pp. 405-17.

— "On the Way to Kailash", in McKay, Alex, ed., *Pilgrimage in Tibet*, London: Curzon Press, 1998, pp. 108-16.

— "The Adi-Granth of the Sikhs. A Canon?", in Offredi, Mariola, ed., *The Banyan Tree. Essays on Early Literatures in New Indo-Aryan Languages. Proceedings of the Seventh International Conference on Early Literature in New Indo-Aryan Languages* (*Venice, 1997*), Delhi: Manohar Publications, 1999, pp. 523-34.

— "North Indian Bhakti Literature. Editions and Translations", in Mistry, P.J. & Bharati Modi, eds., *Vidyopāsanā: Studies in Honour of Harivallabh C. Bhayani*, Mumbai & Ahmedabad: Image Publications, 1999, pp. 13-27.

— *The Hagiographies of Anantadas. The Bhakti Poets of North India*, London: Curzon Press, 2000.

— (ed.), Swapna Sharma & Dieter Taillieu, collab., *The Millennium Kabīr vāṇī. A Collection of Pad-s*, New Delhi: Manohar, 2000.

— "Kabir's Pads in 1556", in [Proceedings of the Conference "The 600th Anniversary of Kabir's Birth" (Heidelberg, 15-18 June 1999)], [forthcoming].

Callewaert, Winand & B. Op de Beek, *Nirgun-bhakti sagar. Devotional Hindi Literature*, Heidelberg & Delhi: Süd-Asien Institut & Manohar Book Publications, 1991.

Callewaert, Winand & L. De Brabandere, "Nirgun Literature on Microfilm in Leuven, Belgium", *IAVRI Bulletin* (London) IX:Dec., 1980, pp. 24-48.

Callewaert, Winand M. & Philip Lutgendorf, eds., *Rāmcaritmānas Word Index / Mānas śabda anukramaṇikā*, Delhi: Manohar Publications, 1997.

Callewaert, Winand & Mukund Lath, *The Hindī Songs of Nāmdev*, Orientalia Lovaniensia Analecta, 29, Leuven, 1989 – also published by Motilal Banarsidass, Delhi.

Callewaert, Winand & P. Friedlander, *The Life and Works of Raidās*, Delhi: Manohar Book Publications, 1992.

Callewaert, Winand & Rupert Snell, eds., *According to Tradition. Hagiographical Writing in India*, Wiesbaden: Harrassowitz, 1994.

Callewaert, Winand & S. Hemraj, *Bhagavadgītānuvāda. A Study in Transcultural Translation*, Leuven, 1983.

Caracchi, P., *La presenza divina nella mūrti secondo i Purāṇa*, Indologica Taurinensia - Collana di Lettura, Torino, 1978.

— "The Divine Presence in the Mūrti according to the Purāṇa-s", *Purāṇa* XXIV:2 (July), 1982, pp. 261-85.

— "[review] Harivaṃśa Rāy Śarmā, *Sāhityik Muhāv'ra Lokokti Koś*, Delhi: Rāj'pāl & Sons, 1981, 315 pp.", *Indologica Taurinesia* X, 1982, pp. 303-4.

— "La Rāmlīlā di Rāmnagar (Banaras): vitalità di una tradizione", *Annali Dell'Istituto Universitario Orientale* 43, 1983, pp. 109-34.

— "L'India: religione e società", *Quaderni TMI - India Ieri e Oggi* anno XIV:4 (aprile), 1984.

— *Vita di Rāmānanda. Il Rāmānandajanmotsava dell Agastya-saṃhitā*, Torino: Promolibri, 1989.

— "[review] D.N. Lorenzen, Kabir Legends and Ananta-das's Kabir Parachai, State of New York Press, 1991, xiii+268 pp.", *East and West* 42:2-4 (December), 1992, pp. 539-40.

— *Grammatica hindī*, 3rd ed., Torino: Promolibri, 1999 – 1st ed. 1992.

— "I valori spirituali", in *L'insegnamento di Gandhi per un futuro equo e sostensibile. Atti del Convegno "Gandhi e il suo programma costruttivo 50 anni dopo la morte". Torino, 30 gennaio - 2 febbraio 1998*, Torino: ASSEFA e Centro Studi Sereno Regis, 1999, pp. 32-8.

— *Rāmānanda e lo yoga dei sant*. Singh S, trsl. & collab., Alessandria: Edizioni dell'Orso, 1999 – con una tradizione dei canti hindī.

— "[18 entries on Hindi literature and modern Hinduism]", in *Grande Dizionario Enciclopedico UTET*, 4th ed.

Caracchi, P. & S. Piano, *La saggezza hindū*, Cinisello Balsamo: Edizioni S. Paolo, 1998.

Chitre, Dilip & Günther-Dietz Sontheimer & Heidi Brückner & Anne Feldhaus & Rainer Kimmig, eds., *Tender Ironies: A Tribute to Lothar Lutze*, New Delhi: Manohar, 1994.

De Bruijn, Th., "The literary field and its margins: *Āṁcalika kahāniyāṁ* collected by Rājendra Avasthī" – paper presented at the 15th European Conference on modern South Asian Studies (Prague, 1998). Literature panel.

— "Nayi Kahani: Hindi short stories and the literary field of Hindi literature after 1947" – paper presented at the 6th Vishva Hindi Sammelan (London, September 1999).

— "Images of the Last Days: Jāyasī's *Ākhirī Kalām* and Indian Islam", in Entwistle, Alan W. & Carol Salomon & Heidi Pauwels & Michael Shapiro, eds., *Studies in Early Modern Indo-Aryan Languages, Literature and Culture*, New Delhi: Manohar, 1999, pp. 71-86.

— "Indianness as a category in literary criticism on Nayī Kahānī". Paper presented at the seminar "The Indian Character of Indian Literature" (Leiden, 9-11 March 2000), [forthcoming].

Deol, Jeevan Singh, "'Acceptable Poetry': Muqbil's Mystical *Qissah Hīr Rānjhā*", *International Journal of Punjab Studies* 3:2 (October), 1996, pp. 181-212.

— "'To Hell With War': Literature of Political Resistance in Early Nineteent-Century Punjab", *South Asia Research* 17:2 (Autumn), 1997, pp. 178-209.

— "The Mīṇās and their Literature", *Journal of the American Oriental Society* 118:2 (April-June), 1998, pp. 172-84.

— "[catalogue entries]", in Stronge, Susan, ed., *The Arts of the Sikh Kingdoms*, London: Victoria and Albert Museum, 1999.

— "Sūrdās: Poet and Text in the Sikh Tradition", *Bulletin of the School of Oriental and African Studies* 63:2 (June), 2000, pp. 169-93.

— "Eighteenth-Century Khalsa Identity: Discourse, Praxis and Narrative", in Shackle, Christopher & Gurharpal Singh and Arvind-pal Mandair, eds., *Sikh Religion, Culture and Ethnicity*, London: Curzon, 2001.

— "Non-Canonical Compositions Attributed to the Seventh and Ninth Sikh Gurus", *Journal of the American Oriental Society* 121:2 (April-June), 2001.

— "Text and Lineage in Early Sikh History: Issues in the Study of the Adi Granth", *Bulletin of the School of Oriental and African Studies* 64:1 (February), 2001, pp. 34-58.

— "Illustration and Illumination in Sikh Scriptural Manuscripts", in Goswamy, B.N., ed., *Art and the Sikhs. Images of a Community*, New Delhi: Marg Publications, [forthcoming].
— "Sex, Social Critique and the Female Figure in Vāris Shāh's *Hīr*", *Modern Asian Studies*, [forthcoming].

Dhillon, Balwant Singh, "Some Unknown Hukamnāmas of Gurū Gobind Singh", *Punjab History Conference Proceedings*, Patiala: Punjabi University, 1980, pp. 103-9.
— "Political Attitude of Gurū Nānak", *Journal of Sikh Studies* IX, 1982, pp. 45-58.
— *Śrī Gurū Amar Dās Abhinaṁdan*, Amritsar: Gurū Nanak Dev University, 1985 – a study into the image and personality of Gurū Amar Dās, as reflected in published and unpublished religious literature.
— "Development and Organisation of Sikh Panth Under Gurū Rām Dās", *Panjab Past and Present* (Patiala) XX, 1986, pp. 36-42.
— "Gurū Angad: A Study into Political Attitude", *Journal of Sikh Studies* XIV, 1987, pp. 17-22.
— "Gurū Angad on the Contemporary Political Milieu", in *Punjab Historical Conference*, Patiala: Punjabi University, 1988, pp. 96-101.
— "Guru Nānak and Institutionalization of Sikhism", *Journal of Sikh Studies* XV, 1988, pp. 35-42.
— "Religio-Political Institution of the Akal Takht", *Journal of Sikh Studies* XV, 1988, pp. 61-73.
— "Religion and Politics in Pre-Muslim India", *Journal of Religious Studies* (Patiala) XVI, 1988, pp. 106-14.
— "Organisation of Early Sikhism", *Panjab Past and Present* XXIII, 1989, pp. 30-41.
— "Gurū Nānak's Assessment of Muslim Rule in India", *Punjab History Conference*, Patiala: Punjabi University, 1991, pp. 41-9.
— "Myth of an Early Draft of the Ādi Granth", *Abstracts of Sikh Studies*, Chandigarh, 1993, pp. 75-92.
— "Gurū Nānak's Response to War and Violence", *Abstracts of Sikh Studies*, Chandigarh, 1994, pp. 24-34.
— "Myth of an Early Draft of the Ādi Granth", in Singh, Gianī Bachittar, ed., *Planned Attacks on the Ādi Śrī Gurū Granth Sāhib*, Chandigarh: International Institute of Sikh Studies, 1994, pp. 85-107.
— "Political Instability in the Early 16th Century Punjab", *Journal of Regional History* (Amritsar) NS II, 1994, pp. 112-26.

— "Evil of War: The Making of Sikh Response", *Journal of Sikh Studies* (Amritsar) XX, 1996, pp. 32-44.

— "Formation of Early Sikh Identity", in Singh, Kharak, ed., *Current Thoughts on Sikhism*, Chandigarh: Institute of Sikh Studies, 1996, pp. 75-84.

— "Gurū Har Sahāi Pothī: Myth of an Early Corpus of the Sikh Scripture", *Journal of Sikh Studies* (Amritsar) XX, 1996, pp. 33-53.

— "Foundation of the Tarn Tāran: Historical Perspective", *Journal of Sikh Studies* (Amritsar) XXI, 1997, pp. 17-24.

— *Parmukh Sikh te Sikh Panth*, Amritsar: Singh Brothers, 1997 – an exhaustive account of the composition and expansion of the Sikh mission during the early 17th century.

— "Gurū Nānak's Response to War and Violence", in Soch, H.S. & Madanjit Kaur, eds., *Gurū Nānak Ideals and Institutions*, Amritsar: Gurū Nānak Dev University, 1998, pp. 154-66.

— "The Institution of Dharamsāl: Origin and Development", in Soch, H.S. & Madanjit Kaur, eds., *Gurū Nānak Ideals and Institutions*, Amritsar: Gurū Nānak Dev University, 1998, pp. 183-201.

— *Early Sikh Scriptural Tradition: Myth and Reality*, Amritsar: Singh Brothers, 1999.

— "Guru Gobind Singh's Concept of Dharamyudha", *Journal of Sikh Studies* (Amritsar) XXIII, 1999, pp. 25-35.

— "[chapters I-IX]", in Singh, Kharak, ed., *Sikh History, Religion and Culture*, vol. 1, Amritsar: S.G.P.C., [forthcoming] – Contents: I. Socio-Religious Outlook of the Turkish Rulers; II. Early 16th Century Political Scenario of Punjab; III. Gurū Nānak's Mission: Socio-Political Implications; IV. Gurū Nānak and the Lodhīs; V. Gurū Nānak and the Mughals; VI. Gurū Aṅgad; VII. Gurū Amar Dās; VIII. Gurū Rām Dās; IX. Gurū Arjan Dev – these chapters present an exhaustive study of the consolidation, development and expansion of the Sikh Panth during the pontificate of the respective Sikh Gurus. Published in order to mark the Tercentenary of the Khalsa.

Dhillon, Balwant Singh & Amarjit Singh, "Myth and Reality: A Peep into the Goindwāl Pothīs", *Abstracts of Sikh Studies*, Chandigarh, 1995, pp. 24-34.

Du Perron, Lalita, "[review] Thomas Coburn, Encountering the Goddess: A Translation of the *Devī-Māhātmya* and a Study of its Interpretation (New York: SUNY, 1991)", *Asian Folklore Studies*, 1994.

— tr., *The Raga Guide.* J. Bor (ed.), Monmouth: Nimbus Records, 1999. Song text transcriptions and translations.

— "[review] Theo Damsteegt, *Girirāj Kiśor's* Yātrāeṁ*: A Hindi Novel Analysed* (Groningen: Egbert Forsten, 1997)", *Journal of the Royal Asiatic Society* 9:1, 1999, pp. 174-6.

— "The Role of Aesthetic Theory in the Interpretation and Performance of a Modern Genre", *SOAS Literary Review*, Autumn 2000 – electronic publication on the SOAS website.

— "*ṭhumrī*: A Discussion of the Female Voice of Hindustani Music", *Modern Asian Studies* 35:2, 2001.

— "[review] Simon Digby (tr.), *Wonder-Tales of South Asia* (Jersey: Orient Monographs, 2000)", *Journal of the Royal Asiatic Society*, [forthcoming].

Entwistle, A. & Carol Salomon & Heidi Pauwels & Michael Shapiro, eds., *Studies in Early Literature in New Indo-Aryan Languages. Proceedings of the Sixth International Conference on Early Literature in New Indo-Aryan Languages* (*Seattle*, *1994*), Delhi: Manohar, 1999.

Feldhaus, Anne, "The Mahānubhāvas and Scripture", *Journal of Dharma* III, 1978, pp. 295-308.

— "The *devatācakra* of the Mahānubhāvas", *Bulletin of the School of Oriental and African Studies* XLIII, 1980, pp. 101-9.

— "Bahiṇā Bāī: Wife and Saint", *Journal of the American Academy of Religion* L, 1982, pp. 87-100.

— "Foreword", in Ranade, R.D., Indian Mysticism: The Poet Saints of Maharashtra, repr. ed., Albany: State University of New York Press, 1982.

— "God and Madman: Guṇḍam Rāūḷ", *Bulletin of the School of Oriental and African Studies* XLV, 1982, pp. 74-83.

— "Kṛṣṇa and the Kṛṣṇas: Kṛṣṇa in the Mahānubhāva Pantheon", in Thiel-Horstmann, Monika, ed., *Bhakti in Current Research. 1979-1982* (*Collectanea Instituti Anthropos*, 30), Berlin: Dietrich Reimer Verlag, 1983.

— *The Religious System of the Mahānubhāva Sect: The Mahānubhāva Sūtrapāṭha*, South Asian Studies (University of Heidelberg), XII, New Delhi: Manohar Book Service, 1983.

— *The Deeds of God in Ṛddhipur*, New York: Oxford UP, 1984.

— "Introduction", in Abbott, Justin E., tr., *Bahiṇā Bāī: Wife and Saint*, repr. ed., New Delhi: Motilal Banarsidass, 1985.

— "Mahānubhāvāṃcā Mahārāṣṭra", *Abhirucī* XXVIII (Divālī), 1986, pp. 17-21 – in Marathi.

— "Maharashtra as a Holy Land: A Sectarian Tradition", *Bulletin of the School of Oriental and African Studies* XLIX, 1986, pp. 532-48.

— "The Destruction of Sins in the *Gautamī Māhātmya*", in Larivière, Richard W. & Richard Salomon, eds., *Festschrift for Professor Ludo Rocher* (*The Adyar Library Bulletin*, LI), 1987, pp. 104-22.

— "The Religious Significance of Ṛddhipur", in Israel, Milton & N.K. Wagle, eds., *Religion and Society in Maharashtra*, Toronto: University of Toronto. Centre for South Asian Studies, 1987, pp. 68-91.

— "The Gondhalī: Singers for the Devi", in Zelliot, Eleanor & Maxine Berntsen, eds., *The Experience of Hinduism*, Albany: State University of New York Press, 1988, pp. 73-81 – translation of an article in Marathi by R.C. Dhere.

— "The Orthodoxy of the Mahānubhāvas", in Zelliot, Eleanor & Maxine Berntsen, eds., *The Experience of Hinduism*, Albany: State University of New York Press, 1988, pp. 264-79.

— tr., *Pastoral Deities in Western India*. G.D. Sontheimer, New York: Oxford UP, 1989.

— "The Image of the Forest in the *Māhātmyas* of the Rivers of the Deccan", in Bakker, Hans, ed., *The History of Sacred Places in India as reflected in Traditional Literature* (*Panels of the VIIth World Sanskrit Conference*, III), Leiden: Brill, 1990, pp. 90-102.

— "Paiṭhaṇ and the Nāgas", in Eck, Diana L. & Françoise Mallison, eds., *Devotion Divine: Bhakti Traditions from the Regions of India. Studies in Honour of Charlotte Vaudeville*, Groningen & Paris: Egbert Forsten & EFEO, 1991, pp. 91-111.

— *In the Absence of God: The Mahānubhāvs' Early Years*. S.G. Tulpule, Honolulu: University of Hawaii Press, 1992.

— "Separation, Connection and Obedience among the Early Mahānubhāvs", in Entwistle, Alan W. & Françoise Mallison, eds., *Studies in South Asian Devotional Literature*, Paris & New Delhi: EFEO & Manohar, 1994, pp. 154-68.

— "Preface", in Sontheimer, Günther, ed., *Folk Culture, Folk Religion and Oral Traditions as Components in Maharashtrian Culture*, New Delhi: Manohar, 1995, pp. vii-ix.

— "Types of River Goddesses in Maharashtra", in Sontheimer, Günther, ed., *Folk Culture, Folk Religion and Oral Traditions as Components in Maharashtrian Culture*, New Delhi: Manohar, 1995, pp. 31-47.

— *Water and Womanhood: Religious Meanings of Rivers in Maharashtra*, New York: Oxford UP, 1995.

— "Goddess as Sister: The Case of Bhivāī", in Feldhaus, Anne, ed., *Images of Women in Maharashtrian Literature and Religion*, Albany: State University of New York Press, 1996, pp. 135-46.

— ed., *Images of Women in Maharashtrian Literature and Religion*, Albany: State University of New York Press, 1996.

— "Goddesses and the Domestic Realm in Maharashtra", in Glushkova, Irina & Anne Feldhaus, eds., *House and Home in Maharashtrian Culture*, New Delhi: Oxford UP, 1998.

— ed., *Images of Women in Maharashtrian Society*, Albany: State University of New York Press, 1998.

— *A Dictionary of Old Marathi*, Bombay: Popular Prakashan, 1999 – also New York: Oxford UP, 2000.

— "Hinduism: Religious Rites and Practices", in Young, Serinity, ed., *Encyclopedia of Women and World Religion*, New York: Macmillan Reference USA, 1999, pp. 424-5.

— "Rivers and the Death of Children", in Schömbucher, Elisabeth & Claus Peter Zoller, eds., *Ways of Dying: Death and Its Meaning in South Asia*, New Delhi: Manohar, 1999.

— "Mountains, Rivers, and Shiva: Continuity Among Religious Media in Maharashtra", in *Intersections: Socio-Cultural Trends in Maharashtra*, Hyderabad: Orient Longman, 2000, pp. 15-46.

Feldhaus, Anne & Aditya Malik & Heidrun Brückner, eds., *Essays on Khaṇḍobā.* Sontheimer GD, New Delhi: Indira Gandhi National Centre for the Arts & Manohar, 1997.

Feldhaus, Anne & Dilip Chitre, "[several articles on Marathi literature]", in Brückner, Heidrun & Rainer Kimmig, eds., *Literatur-Lexikon*, [forthcoming].

Feldhaus, Anne & Eleanor Zelliot, "Marathi Religious Traditions", in Eliade, M. et al., eds., *Encyclopedia of Religion*, New York: Macmillan Publishing Company, 1986, vol. 9, pp. 190-4.

Feldhaus, Anne & Vijaya Chitre, "The Pain, the Bier, & Eternity. A Story by Dilip Chitre [tr. from Marathi]", in Chitre, Dilip et al., eds., *Tender Ironies: A Tribute to Lohar Lutze*, New Delhi: Manohar, 1994, pp. 57-65.

— "Women Saint-Poets' Concept of Liberation", in Feldhaus, Anne, ed., *Images of Women in Maharashtrian Literature and Religion*, Albany: State University of New York Press, 1996, pp. 239-52 – translation of a contribution by Tara Bhavalkar.

Fenech, Louis E., "Persian Sikh Scripture: The Ghazals of Bhā'ī Nand Lāl Goya", *The International Journal of Punjab Studies* 1:1, 1994, pp. 49-70.

— "[review] Harjot Oberoi, The Construction of Religious Boundaries: Culture, Identity and Diversity in the Sikh Tradition", *The Middle East & South Asia Folklore Bulletin* (Ohio State University) 12:3 (Fall), 1995, pp. 2-4.

— "[review] Nikky-Guninder Kaur Singh, The Feminine Principle in the Sikh Vision of the Transcendent", *Journal of Asian Studies* 55:1 (February), 1996, pp. 199-200.

— "The Taunt in Popular Sikh Martyrologies", in Singh, Pashaura & al., eds., *Transmission of Sikh Heritage to the Diaspora*, New Delhi: Manohar Publications, 1996.

— "Martyrdom and the Sikh Tradition", *Journal of the American Oriental Society* 117:1, 1997.

— "Sikhisme", in Boisvert, Mathieu, ed., *Un monde de religions*, Montréal: Presses de l'Université de Québec, 1997.

— *Martyrdom in the Sikh Tradition: Playing the 'Game of Love'*, Oxford UP, 2000.

— "Martyrdom and the Execution of Guru Arjan in Early Sikh Sources", *Journal of the American Oriental Society* 121:1, 2001 [in the press].

— "Conversion and Sikh Tradition", in Robinson, Rowena, ed., *Conversion in Indian Religious Traditions*, Oxford UP, [forthcoming].

— "[review] Cynthia Keppley Mahmood, Fighting for Faith and Nation: Dialogues with Sikh Militants", *Lef History*, [forthcoming].

— "[review] J.P.S. Uberoi, Religion, Civil Society and the State: A Study of Sikhism", *Journal of the American Oriental Society*, [forthcoming].

— "[review] Nikky-Guninder Kaur Singh, The Name of My Beloved: Verses of the Sikh Gurus", *Religious Studies Review*, [forthcoming].

— "[review] Nirmal Dass, Songs of the Saints from the Adi Granth", *Religious Studies Review*, [forthcoming].

— "[review] Richard Saumarez Smith, Rule by Records: Land Registration and Village Custom in Early British Punjab", *Journal of the American Oriental Society*, [forthcoming].

Gautam, M.K. & G.H. Schokker, eds., *Bhakti in Current Research, 1982-85*, Kern Institute Miscellanea, 10, Lucknow & Ghaziabad & Delhi: Indo-European Publications, 2000.

Glushkova, Irina, "The Concept of Woman in the Poems of Tukaram", in Feldhaus, Anne, ed., *Images of Women in Maharashtrian Literature and Religion*, Albany: State University of New York Press, 1996.

— ed., *Indian Wife*, Moscow: Vostochnaya Literatura, 1996 – in Russian.

— "In Quest of Alandi-mahatma", *Annals of the Bhandarkar Oriental Research Institute* (Pune) 1997, 1998.

— "The Position of *Ghar* within the Marathi Speaker's World: a Paremiological Study", in Feldhaus, Anne & Irina Glushkova, eds., *House and Home in Maharashtra*, Delhi: Oxford UP, 1998.

— "Regional Studies; to be or not to be", in Vacek, Jaroslav & Jan Dvorak, eds., *Trends in Indian Studies. Proceedings of the ESIS* (*Studia Orientalia Pragensia*, XVIII), Prague: Charles UP, 1998.

— "The Banyan Tree of the Varkari Tradition: Transmission and Invention", in Assayag, Jackie, ed., *The Resources of History: Tradition, Narration and Nation in South Asia*, Paris & Pondicherry: EFEO & Institut Français de Pondicherry, 1999.

— ed., *The Tree of Hinduism*, Moscow: Vostochnaya Literatura, 1999 – in Russian.

— *Indian Pilgrimage: Metaphor of Motion and Motion of Metaphor*, Moscow: Nauchniy Mir, 2000 – in Russian.

— "Norms and Values in the Varkari Tradition", in Kosambi, Meera, ed., *Intersections. Socio-Cultural Trends in Maharashtra*, New Delhi: Orient Longman, 2000.

— "Vitthal: Sometimes Adored, Sometimes Rejected. Changes in Theological Pattern", in Offredi, Mariola, ed., *The Banyan Tree: Essays on Early Literature in New Indo-Aryan Languages*, New Delhi: Manohar, 2000, vol. 1, pp. 261-72.

— "Marital Conflicts in the Varkari Tradition", in Malik, Aditya, ed., [forthcoming].

— "Give Me Back My Blanket!: Metonimy and Metaphor in the Varkari Poetry", *BORI Annals 2000* (Pune), [forthcoming].

Glushkova, Irina & Anne Feldhaus, eds., *House and Home in Maharashta*, New Delhi: Oxford UP, 1998.

Glushkova, Irina & E. Vanina, "[review] A.R. Kulkarni, ed., *History on Practice: Historians and Sources of Medieval Deccan - Marathas*", *The Indian Historical Review* XX:1-2 (July-January), 1993.

Glushkova, Irina & Rajendra Vora, eds., *Home, Family, and Kinship in Maharashtra*, Delhi: Oxford UP, 1999.

Gold, Daniel, "Clan and Lineage among the Sants", in Schomer, Karine & Hew McLeod, eds., *The Sants: A Devotional Tradition of India*, Berkely: Berkely Religious Studies, 1987, pp. 305-32.

— "Comprehending Indian Devotional Religion: Cow-Love, Cowboys, and the Religio-Historical Imagination", *History of Religions* 26:4, 1987, pp. 401-21.

— *The Lord as Guru: Hindi Sants in North Indian Tradition*, New York: Oxford UP, 1987.

— "Approaching Some Householder Yogis: To Visit or Move In?", *Journal of Ritual Studies* 2:2, 1988, pp. 185-94.

— *Comprehending the Guru: Toward a Grammar of Religious Perception*, Atlanta (Ga.): Scholars Press, 1988.

— "Swadhyaya Parivar: Contemporary Religious Community in the Image of Traditional Family", in Srivastava, Raj Krishnan, ed., *Vital Connections: Self, Society, God. Perspectives on Swadhyaya*, New York & Tokyo: Weatherill, 1988, pp. 172-86.

— tr., "The Hindi Tradition", in O'Flaherty, Wendy Doniger, ed., *Textual Sources for the Study of Hinduism*, Manchester: Manchester UP, 1988, pp. 138-50.

— "Rational Action and Uncontrolled Violence: Explaining Hindu Communalism", *Religion* 21:4, 1991, pp. 357-70.

— "The Rise and Fall of Yogis' Power: Jodhpur 1803-1843", *Estudios De Asia y Africa* (Mexico) 87:1, 1992, pp. 9-27 – in Spanish.

— "What the Merchant-Guru Sold: Social and Literary Type in Hindi Devotional Verse", *Journal of the American Oriental Society* 111:1, 1992, pp. 22-35.

— "The Dadu Panth and Princely Power in Rajasthan", in Schomer, Karine & al., eds., *The Idea of Rajasthan: Explorations in Regional Identity*, Delhi: Manohar, 1994, pp. 242-64.

— "Guru's Body, Guru's Abode", in Law, Jane Marie, ed., *Religious Reflections on the Body*, Bloomington: Indiana UP, 1995, pp. 230-50.

— "The Instability of the King: Magical Insanity and Yogic Power in the Politics of Jaipur", in Lorenzen, David, ed., *Bhakti Religion in North India: Community Identity and Political Action*, Albany: State University of New York Press, 1995, pp. 120-32.

— "Naths; Gorakhnath; Kanphata Yogis", in *Harper's Dictionary of Religion*, 1995.

— "Experiences of Ear-cutting: the Significance of a Ritual of Bodily Alteration for Householder Yogis", *Journal of Ritual Studies* 10:1, 1996, pp. 91-112.

— "Nath Yogis as Established Alternatives: Householders and Ascetics Today", in Ishwaran, K., ed., *Ascetic Culture: Renunciation and Worldly Engagement* (*International Studies in Sociology and Social Anthropology*, 73), Leiden: E.J. Brill, 1999, pp. 68-88.

— "Nath Yogis as Established Alternatives: Householders and Ascetics Today", *Journal of Asian and African Studies* (Leiden) 34:1, 1999, pp. 68-88.

— "The Yogi Who Pissed from the Mountain", in Entwistle, Alan W. & Salomon Carol, eds., *Studies in Early Modern Indo-Aryan Literature and Culture*, New Delhi: Manohar, 1999.

— "Yogis' Earrings, Householder's Birth: Split Ears and Religious Identity among Householder Naths in Rajasthan", in Joshi, Rajendra, ed., *Religion, Ritual, and Royalty*, Jaipur: Rawat, 1999, pp. 35-53.

— "Experiencing Scriptural Diversity: Words and Stories in Hindu Traditions", in Katz, Steven T., ed., *Mysticism and Sacred Scripture*, New York: Oxford UP, 2000.

— "Kabir's Secrets for Householders: Truths and Rumors among Rajasthani Naths", in Boehm-Tettelbach, Monika, ed., *Papers from Kabir's 500th Anniversary Conference at Heidelberg*, [forthcoming].

Gold, Daniel & Ann Grodzins Gold, "The Fate of the Householder Nath", *History of Religions* 24:2, 1984, pp. 113-32.

Hawley, John Stratton, ed., *Devi: Goddesses of India*, Delhi: Motilal Banarsidass – South Asia edition.

— "Inner Sanctums: An American in Brindavan", *Bulletin of the Center for the Study of World Religions* (Harvard University), 1977, pp. 19-36.

— "The Butter Thief: Abstract", in Manmohan, ed., *Surdas Pancsati Samaroh*, Calcutta: Surdas Pancsati Samaroh, 1978, pp. 2.

— "The Early *Sur Sagar* and the Growth of the Sur Tradition", *Journal of the American Oriental Society* 99:1, 1979, pp. 64-72.

— "Krishna's Cosmic Victories", *Journal of the American Academy of Religion* 47:2, 1979, pp. 201-21.

— "Review and Prospectus of Research", in Callewaert, W.M., ed., *Early Hindi Devotional Literature in Current Research. Proceedings of the International Middle Hindi Bhakti Conference* (*April 1979*), Leuven: Katholieke Universiteit, 1979, pp. 77-80 – also Delhi: Impex India.

— "Solitude and Community among Sants and Vaisnavas", in Juergensmeyer, Mark & N. Gerald Barrier, eds., *Sikh Studies: Comparative Perspectives on a Changing Tradition*, Berkeley: Berkeley Religious Studies Series, 1979, pp. 91-4.

— "Thief of Butter, Thief of Love", *History of Religions* 18:3, 1979, pp. 203-20.

— "Krishna in Black and White: *Darsan* in the Early *Sur Sagar*", *Journal of Asian and African Studies* 15:1/2, 1980, pp. 43-58.

— "Pilgrims' Progress through Krishna's Playground", *Asia* 3:3, 1980, pp. 12-9, 45.

— "Scenes from the Childhood of Krishna on the Kailasanatha Temple, Ellora", *Archives of Asian Art* 34, 1981, pp. 74-90.

— "*Yoga* and *Viyoga*: Simple Religion in Hinduism", *Harvard Theological Review* 74:2, 1981, pp. 1-20.

— "The Joys and Despairs of Filming in Sarasvati's Treasurehouse", *South Asia Library Notes and Queries* 13 and 14, 1982, pp. 10-3 and 8-12.

— "The Boston Vinadhara Siva", *Journal of the Oriental Institute* (Baroda) 33:1/2, 1983, pp. 141-5 – with plates.

— *Krishna, the Butter Thief*, Princeton: Princeton UP, 1983.

— "The Sectarian Logic of the *Sur Das ki Varta*", in Thiel-Horstmann, Monika, ed., *Bhakti in Current Research, 1979-1982*, Berlin: Dietrich Reimer Verlag, 1983, pp. 157-69.

— "The Music in Faith and Morality", *Journal of the American Academy of Religion* 52:2, 1984, pp. 243-62.

— *Sur Das: Poet, Singer, Saint*, Seattle & Delhi: University of Washington Press & Oxford UP, 1984.

— "The Thief in Krishna", *Parabola* 9:2, 1984, pp. 6-13.

— "Echoes of Love and Creation in the Poetry of Sur Das", in Case, Margaret & N. Gerald Barrier, eds., *Aspects of India*, Delhi: Manohar, 1986, pp. 45-62.

— "Images of Gender in the Poetry of Krishna", in Bynum, Caroline Walker & Steven Harrell & Paula Richman, eds., *Gender and Religion: On the Complexity of Symbols*, Boston: Beacon Press, 1986, pp. 231-56.

— "Hindi Religious Traditions", in Eliade, Mircea & al., ed., *The Encyclopedia of Religion*, New York: Macmillan, 1987, vol. 6, pp. 330-6.

— "Krishna and the Birds", *Ars Orientalis* 17, 1987, pp. 137-61.

— "Krsna", in Eliade, Mircea & al., ed., *The Encyclopedia of Religion*, New York: Macmillan, 1987, vol. 8, pp. 384-7.

— ed., *Saints and Virtues*, Berkeley: University of California Press, 1987 – includes an introduction on the relation between sainthood and morality, and an essay, "Morality beyond Morality in Three Hindu Saints".

— "The *Sant* in Sur Das", in Schomer, Karine & W.H. McLeod, eds., *The Sants: Studies in a Devotional Tradition of India*, Berkeley & Delhi: Berkeley Religious Studies Series & Motilal Banarsidass, 1987, pp. 191-211.

— "Author and Authority in the *Bhakti* Poetry of North India", *Journal of Asian Studies* 47:2, 1988, pp. 269-90.

— "Bhakti", in Embree, Ainslie & al., ed., *Encyclopedia of Asian History*, New York: Scribner, 1988, vol. 1, pp. 154-7.

— "Mathura", in Ainslie Embree & al., ed., *Encyclopedia of Asian History*, New York: Scribners, 1988, vol. 3, pp. 510.

— *Songs of the Saints of India*. Juergensmeyer M, co-tr., New York: Oxford UP, 1988.

— "Tulsi Das", in *Encyclopedia of Asian History*, 1988, vol. 4, pp. 147.

— 125 color slides, with annotation, contributed to The Image Bank for Teaching Religious Studies, Harvard University: Center for the Study of World Religions, 1989.

— *Krishna, the Butter Thief*, Delhi: Oxford UP, 1989 – South Asia edition.

— "10 illustrations, with annotation", in Richmond, Farley & al., eds., *Indian Theatre: Traditions of Performance*, Honolulu: University of Hawaii Press, 1990.

— "Asceticism Denounced and Embraced: Rhetoric and Reality in North Indian *Bhakti*", in Creel, Austin & Vasudha Narayanan, eds., *Monastic Life in the Christian and Hindu Traditions*, Lewiston (NY): Edwin Mellen Press, 1990, pp. 459-95.

— "A Bhil Woman Tasted Them, Plum after Plum", in Tharu, Susie & K. Lalita, eds., *Women Writing in India*, New York: The Feminist Press, 1991, vol. 1, pp. 93-4 – a poem attributed to Mirabai, repr. from *Songs of the Saints of India*.

— "A Feast for Mount Govardhan", in Eck, Diana L. & Françoise Mallison, eds., *Devotion Divine: Bhakti Traditions from the Regions of India. Studies in Honour of Charlotte Vaudeville*, Groningen & Paris: Egbert Forsten & EFEO, 1991, pp. 155-79.

— "Naming Hinduism", *The Wilson Quarterly* 15:3, 1991, pp. 20-34.

— "Pilgrimage Out West", in Carman, John & Steven Hopkins, eds., *Tracing Common Themes: Comparative Courses in the Study of Religion*, Atlanta: Scholars Press, 1991, pp. 65-79.

— "Teaching the Hindu Tradition", in Juergensmeyer, Mark, ed., *Teaching the Introductory Course in Religious Studies: A Sourcebook*, Atlanta: Scholars Press, 1991, pp. 37-48.

— "Creative Enumeration in the *Vinaya* Poetry of Surdas", in McGregor, R.S., ed., *Devotional Literature in South Asia: Current Research 1985-1988*, Cambridge: Cambridge UP, 1992, pp. 225-36.

— "Every Play a Play within the Play", *Journal of Vaisnava Studies* 1:1, 1992, pp. 146-65 – also in Sax, William S. (ed.), *The Gods at Play: Lila in South Asia*, New York: Oxford UP, 1995, pp. 115-130.

— "Kṛṣṇa in the Performing Arts", in Rosen, Steven J., ed., *Vaisnavaism: Contemporary Scholars Discuss the Gaudiya Tradition*, New York: Folk Books, 1992, pp. 77-88.

— "Ayodhya and the Rubble of Religion", *SIPA News* 6:2, 1993, pp. 3, 16.

— ed., *Studying the Sikhs: Issues for North America*. Singh Mann G, co-ed., Albany: State University of New York Press, 1993.

— "Translations of poetry attributed to Mirabai", in Young, Serinity, ed., *An Anthology of Sacred Texts by and about Women*, New York & London: Crossroad & Pandora, 1993, pp. 297-8.

— "Why Surdas Went Blind", *Journal of Vaisnava Studies* 1:2, 1993, pp. 62-78.

— "The Bharat Kala Bhavan *Sursagar*", in Entwistle, Alan W. & Françoise Mallison, eds., *Studies in South Asian Devotional Literature*, Delhi: Manohar, 1994, pp. 480-513.

— "The Creation of Braj in the Poetry of Surdas", *Journal of Vaisnava Studies* 3:1, 1994, pp. 5-22.

— "Devotional Poetry of Medieval North India", in Miller, Barbara Stoler, ed., *Masterpieces of Asian Literature in Comparative Perspective*, Armonk (NY): M.E. Sharpe, 1994, pp. 78-93.

— ed., *Fundamentalism and Gender*, New York: Oxford UP, 1994 – contains an introduction (in part, with Wayne Proudfoot) and a chapter, "Hinduism: *Sati* and its Defenders".

— "The *Nirgun/Sagun* Distinction in Early Manuscript Anthologies of Hindu Devotion", in Lorenzen, David N., ed., *Bhakti Religion in North India: Community Identity and Political Action*, Albany: SUNY Press, 1994, pp. 160-80.

— "Poems of Tulsidas and Nanak", *The Kalyana-Kalpataru* 39:9, 1994, pp. 1071 – repr. from *Songs of the Saints of India.*

— ed., *Sati. The Blessing and the Curse: The Burning of Wives in India*, New York: Oxford UP, 1994 – contains an introduction and an afterword, "The Communities and Mysteries of Sati".

— "2 illustrations appearing in Margaret Case, *A Day in the Life of Krishna*", *Parabola* 22:1, 1995, pp. 16-20.

— "4 illustrations", in Smith, J.Z., gen. ed., *The HarperCollins Dictionary of Religion*, San Francisco, 1995, pp. 443, 445, 843, 862.

— "5 entries: Gopi; Krsna; Prema; Preman; Radha", in Smith, Jonathan Z. & William Scott Green & al., eds., *The HarperCollins Dictionary of Religion*, San Francisco: Harper San Francisco, 1995, pp. 392, 646-47, 856, 875.

— "Mirabai as Wife and Yogi", in Wimbush, Vincent L. & Richard Valantasis, eds., *Asceticism*, New York: Oxford UP, 1995, pp. 301-19.

— "The Saints Subdued: Domestic Virtue and National Integration in *Amar Chitra Katha*", in Babb, L.A. & S.S. Wadley, eds., *Media and the Transformation of Religion in South Asia*, Philadelphia: University of Pennsylvania Press, 1995, pp. 107-34.

— "Bhakti, Democracy and the Study of Religion", in Murty, K. Satchidananda & Amit Dasgupta, eds., *The Perennial Tree*, New Delhi: Indian Council for Cultural Relations, 1996, pp. 213-36.

— ed. & intr., *Devi: Goddesses of India*. Wulff, D.M., co-ed., Berkeley: University of California Press, 1996.

— "Translations of poetry attributed to Kabir and Mirabai", in Oxtoby, Willard G., ed., *World-Religions: Eastern Traditions*, Toronto: Oxford UP, 1996, pp. 72-3.

— "Dispatches from the Battlefield of Love", *Journal of Vaisnava Studies* 5:4, 1997, pp. 139-62.

— "Foreword", to Miller, Barbara Stoler, *Love Song of the Dark Lord*, new ed., New York: Columbia UP, 1997, pp. xi-xii.

— "Religious Studies: Medieval Hinduism", in Elder, Joseph W. & Edward C. Dimock Jr. & Ainslie T. Embree, eds., *India's Worlds and U.S. Scholars: 1947-1997*, New Delhi: Manohar, 1998, pp. 433-44.

— ed., *Encyclopedia of Religions*. Selby M, co-ed., Springfield (Ma.): Encyclopedia Britannica & Merriam-Webster, 1999 – sections on Indian religions, except Buddhism and Islam. These articles also contribute to the ongoing database upon which the *Encyclopedia Britannica* depends.

— "Fundamentalism", in Young, Serinity, ed., *Encyclopedia of Women and World Religion*, New York: Macmillan, 1999.

— "Fundamentalism", in Howland, Courtney W., ed., *Religious Fundamentalisms and the Human Rights of Women*, New York: St. Martin's Press, 1999, pp. 3-8.

— "Govardhan Puja, When Krishna Worships Krishna", *Journal of Vaisnava Studies* 7:2, 1999, pp. 37-63.

— "Krishna and the Gender of Longing", in Martin, Nancy & Joseph Runzo, eds., *Love and Gender in the World Religions*, Oxford: Oneworld Press, 2000, pp. 236-56.

— "Sur's Radha: Two Triptychs and a Double", *Journal of Vaisnava Studies* 8:2, 2000, pp. 95-117.
— "Who Speaks for Hinduism -- and Who Against?", *Journal of the American Academy of Religion* 68:4, 2000, pp. 711-20.
— co-ed., *The Life of Hinduism*. Narayanan, V., ed., Berkeley: University of California Press, [forthcoming].
— "Vrindavana", in *Encyclopedia of Hinduism*, [forthcoming].
Hawley, John Stratton & Donna M. Wulff, eds., *The Divine Consort: Radha and the Goddesses of India*, Berkeley & Delhi: Berkeley Religious Studies Series & Motilal Banarsidass, 1982.
— eds., *The Divine Consort: Radha and the Goddesses of India*, Boston: Beacon Press, 1986 – paperback edition.
Hawley, John Stratton in association with Goswami Shrivatsa, *At Play with Krishna: Pilgrimage Dramas from Brindavan*, Princeton: Princeton UP, 1981.
Hawley, John Stratton & Laura Shapiro, "Shiva's Manifestations of the Universe", *The Weekly* (Seattle), Dec. 1981, pp. 26.
Hawley, John Stratton & Mark Juergensmeyer, "Translations from the poetry of Sur Das, Ravi Das, Mira Bai, and Nanak", in Embree, Ainslie, ed., *Sources of Indian Tradition*, rev. ed. ed., New York: Columbia UP, 1988, vol. 1, pp. 358-67, 369, 376-8, 502, 504-5.
— "Translations of poems attributed to Mirabai", *Bulletin of the Center for the Study of World Religions* (Harvard University) 14:1, 1988, pp. 26-9.
— "Translations of poetry attributed to Mirabai", in Mack, Maynard, ed., *The Norton Anthology of World Masterpieces*, New York: W.W. Norton, 1995, vol. 1, pp. 2312-6.

Hess, Linda, "The Cow is Sucking at the Calf's Teat: Kabir's Upside-Down Language", *History of Religions* 22, 1983, pp. 313-37.
— "Ramlila: The Audience Experience", in Thiel-Horstmann, Monika, ed., *Bhakti in Current Research. 1979-1982*, Berlin: Dietrich Reimer Verlag, 1983.
— "Indian Religious Poetry", in Eliade, Mircea, ed., *Encyclopedia of Religion*, New York: Macmillan, 1986, vol. 11.
— "Kabir", in Embree, Ainslee, ed., *Encyclopedia of South Asian History*, New York: Columbia UP, 1986.
— "Kabir's Rough Rhetoric", in Schomer, Karine & W.H. McLeod, eds., *The Sants: Studies in a Devotional Tradition of India*, Berkeley & Delhi: Religious Studies Series & Motilal Banarsidass, 1987.
— "Three Kabir Collections: A Comparative Study", in Schomer, Karine & W.H. McLeod, eds., *The Sants: Studies in a Devotional*

Tradition of India, Berkeley & Delhi: Religious Studies Series & Motilal Banarsidass, 1987.

— "The Poet, the People and the Western Scholar: Influence of a Sacred Drama and Text on Social Values in North India", *Theatre Journal* 40, 1988, pp. 236-53.

— *The Ramlila of Ramnagar: An Introduction and Day to Day Description*, Berkeley, 1988 – rev. ed. 1991 – 55 pp. booklet, written at the request of the Maharaja of Banaras for use by visitors to the annual 30-day Ramlila performance.

— "Staring at Frames Till They Turn into Loops: An Excursion through Some Worlds of Tulsidas", in Humes, C.A. & B. Hertel, eds., *Living Banares: Hindu Religion in Cultural Context*, Albany: State University of New York Press, 1993.

— "Marshalling Sacred Texts: Ram's Name and Story in Late Twentieth-Century Indian Politics", *Journal of Vaiṣṇava Studies* 2:4 (Fall), 1994, pp. 175-206.

— "The Ram Legend as Theatre", in Dehejia, Vidya, ed., *The Legend of Rama: Artistic Visions*, Bombay: Marg Publications, 1994.

— trsl. & intr., *A Touch of Grace: Songs of Kabir.* Singh S., trsl., Boston: Shambhala Books, 1994.

— "Kabir in Translation", in Classe, Olive, ed., *Encyclopedia of Literary Translation*, London: Fitzroy Dearborn, 1999.

— "Rejecting Sita: Indians Respond to the Ideal Man's Cruel Treatment of His Ideal Wife", *Journal of the American Academy of Religion* 67:1 (March), 1999, pp. 1-32.

— "Lovers' Doubts: Questioning the Tulsi *Ramayana*", in Richman, Paul, ed., *Questioning Ramayanas: A South Asian Tradition*, Berkeley & New Delhi: University of California Press & Oxford UP, 2000.

Hess, Linda & Annemarie Schimmel, "South Asian Islamic Poetry", in Eliade, Mircea, ed., *Encyclopedia of Religion*, New York: Mcmillan, 1986, vol. 11.

Hess, Linda & Richard Schechner, "The Ramlila of Ramnagar", *The Drama Review* 21, 1977, pp. 51-82.

Hess, Linda & Shukdev Singh, trsl., *The Bijak of Kabir*, San Francisco & Delhi: North Point Press & Motilal Banarsidass, 1983.

Hines, Naseem, *The Sūfi Elements in the Indo-Sūfi masnavī, with special reference to Maulanā Dāūd's Cāndāyan*, 1997, UMI Dissertation Services, Ann Arbor, Michigan.

— "The Snake-bite Episodes in Cāndāyan: A Journey within a Journey", in Entwistle, Allan D. & Carol Salomon & Heidi Pauwels

& Michael C. Shapiro, eds., *Studies in Early Modern Indo-Aryan Languages, Literature and Culture*, New Delhi: Manohar, 1999.

— "In Quest for the Correct Combination: The Home-coming Episode in Maulana Daud's Indo-Sufi Masnavī *Candāyan*", in Offredi, Mariola, ed., *The Banyan Tree. A Volume of Papers read at the Seventh International Conference on Devotional Literature in New Indo-Aryan Languages*, New Delhi: Manohar, 2000, pp. 15-25.

Horstmann, Monika, "Dādūpanthī Sermons", in Thiel-Horstmann, Monika & R.K. Barz, eds. *Living Texts from Northern India* (*Khoj*, 2), Wiesbaden: Otto Harrassowitz, 1989, pp. 141-83.

— "Die Auffassung vom Dichter bei Hindi-Lyrikern des frühen bis mittleren 20. Jahrhunderts", unpublished paper of 1990.

— "Modes of renunciation in the Dādūpanth", unpublished paper presented at the Conference on Ascetics and Asceticism in South Asia, University of Florida, Gainesville, Fl., 13-16 February 1988.

— "Nirālā's approach to the Rāmāyaṇa and to Tulsīdās", paper presented at the Conference on Contemporary Rāmāyaṇa Traditions, St. Augustin, 21-24 September 1987.

— "On Grierson's rule of the short antepenultimate", *Anthropos* 65, 1970, pp. 858-66.

— "[review] Fürer-Haimendorf, E. von - Kanitkar, H., *An Anthropological Bibliography of South Asia*, Paris [etc.]: Mouton, 1970", *Anthropos* 65, 1970, pp. 1040-1.

— "Formelhafte Wendungen in einigen nordindischen Volkslied-Literaturen", *ZDMG* Suppl. III.2, 1977, pp. 984-91.

— "Hypothesen zur Datierung der Patolenweberei in Gujarat", *Asiatische Forschungen* 31:2, 1977, pp. 137-43.

— "[review] Archer, W.G., *The Hill of Flutes: Life, Love and Poetry in Tribal India. A Portrait of the Santals*, London: George Allen and Unwin, 1974", *Anthropos* 72, 1977, pp. 635-6.

— "[review] Ganeshan, V., *Das Indienerlebnis Hermann Hesses*, Bonn: Ludwig Roehrscheid, 1974; Id., *Das Indienbild deutscher Dichter um 1900*, Bonn: Ludwig Roehrscheid, 1975", *Arcadia* 12:2, 1977, pp. 218-21.

— "[review] Winter, H., *Zur Indien-Rezeption bei E.M. Forster und Hermann Hesse*, Heidelberg: Carl Winter, 1976", *Arcadia* 13:2, 1978, pp. 215-7.

— "[review] Sontheimer, G.D., *Birobā, Mhāskobā und Khaṇḍobā: Ursprung, Geschichte und Umwelt von pastoralen Gottheiten in Maharashtra*, Wiesbaden: Franz Steiner, 1976", *ZRGG* 31:3, 1979, pp. 298-9.

— "On a project of a verse and word concordance of Dādū Dayāl's *Padabhāg*", in Callewaert, W.M., ed., *Early Hindi Devotional Literature in Current Research. Proceedings of the International Middle Hindi Bhakti Conference (April 1979)*, Leuven, 1980, pp. 181-7.

— "Vergleichende Bemerkungen zum poetischen Verfahren in Dādū Dayāl's *Padas*", *Studien zur Indologie und Iranistik* 8/9, 1982, pp. 35-68.

— "The *bhajan* repertoire of the present-day Dādūpanth", in Thiel-Horstmann, Monika, ed., *Bhakti in Current Research, 1979-1982: Proceedings of the Second International Conference on Early Devotional Literature in New Indo-Aryan Languages, St. Augustin, 19-21 March 1982*, Berlin: Dietrich Reimer, 1983, pp. 385-401.

— ed., *Bhakti in Current Research, 1979-1982: Proceedings of the Second International Conference on Early Devotional Literature in New Indo-Aryan Languages, St. Augustin, 19-21 March 1982*, Collectanea Instituti Anthropos, 30, Berlin: Dietrich Reimer, 1983.

— *Crossing the Ocean of Existence: Braj Bhāṣā Religious Poetry from Rajasthan. A Reader*, Wiesbaden: Otto Harrassowitz, 1983.

— "[review] Pandey, S.M., *The Hindi Oral Epic "Candainī" (The Tale of Lorik and Canda)*, Allahabad, 1982", *East and West* 33, 1983, pp. 305-7.

— "Zu *Bhāgavata purāṇa* 10.16.32-59", *Wiener Zeitschrift für die Kunde des Morgenlandes* 27, 1983, pp. 65-95.

— "Gestalthaft - jenseits von Gestalt", in Klimkeit, H.-J., ed., *Heilige Schrift und heiliges Bild*, Bonn: Bouvier, 1984, pp. 137-59.

— "The Bhakti theology of the Dādūpanthī Sundardās", *Indologica Taurinensia* 13, 1985, pp. 199-212.

— "Jenseitsvorstellungen im Hinduismus", in Mensen, B., ed., *Jenseitsvorstellungen verschiedener Völker*, St. Augustin: Akademie Völker und Kulturen, 1985, pp. 67-81.

— *Nächtliches Wachen: eine Form indischen Gottesdienstes* (*Indica et Tibetica*, 6), Bonn: Indica et Tibetica Verlag, 1985.

— "[review] Morinis, E. Alan, *Pilgrimage in the Hindu Tradition: A Case Study of West Bengal* (Oxford University South Asian Studies Series), Delhi etc.: Oxford UP, 1984", *Asian Folklore Studies* 44:1, 1985, pp. 144-6.

— "[review] Singh, Pritam, *Sikh Concept of the Divine*, Amritsar: Guru Nanak Dev University, 1985", *East and West* 35, 1985, pp. 291-2.

— "[review] Tulpule, S.G., "Classical Marāṭhī Literature from the Beginning to A.D. 1818" in Gonda, J. (ed.), *A History of Indian Literature*, vol. IX, fasc. 4, pp. 309-471 [Wiesbaden: Otto

Harrassowitz, 1979]; Id., *Mysticism in Medieval India*, Wiesbaden: Otto Harrassowitz, 1984", *East and West* 35, 1985, pp. 292-3.

— *Symbiotic Antinomy: the social organization of a North Indian sect*, A.L. Basham Lecture, 1985, Canberra: Faculty of Asian Studies - Australian National University, 1986.

— "Baumwollbearbeitung und Weben als religiöse Symbole in der Hindi-Bhakti", in Brückner, Heidrun, ed., *Festschrift Wilhelm Rau* (*Studien zur Indologie und Iranistik*, 13/14), 1987, pp. 259-88.

— "[review] *Pada Sūradāsajī kā:The Padas of Sūrdās*, ed. with intr. and appendices by Gopal Narayan Bahura, with an essay by Ken Bryant (Maharaja Sawai Man Singh II Memorial Series, no. 6), Jaipur: Maharaja Sawai Man Singh II Memorial Trust, 1984", *Indo-Iranian Journal* 30, 1987, pp. 133-4.

— "Śrī Dādūjī Mahārāja kā eka ajñāta pada? [Ein unbekanntes Lied Dādūs? / An unknown song by Dādū?]", *Jñānāñjali* (Jaipur: Śrī Dādū Ācārya Saṃskṛta Mahāvidyālaya), 1988, pp. 19-20.

— "Forschungen zur nordindischen Bhakti am Indologischen Seminar in Bonn", in Eimer, H., ed., *Indology and Indo-Tibetology ...* (*Indica et Tibetica* 13), Bonn: Indica et Tibetica Verlag, 1988, pp. 21-6.

— trsl., *Leben aus der Wahrheit: Texte aus der heiligen Schrift des Sikhs* (*Klassiker der östlichen Meditation*, 3), Zürich: Benziger, 1988.

— "Pandey, Shyam Manohar, *The Hindi Oral Epic* Lorikāyan (*The Tale of Lorik and Candā*), Allahabad: Sahitya Bhawan Pvt. Ltd. / Napels: Istituto Universitario Orientale, 1987", *East and West* 38, 1988, pp. 334-5.

— "[review] Schreiner, P., *Begegnungen mit dem Hinduismus: Eine Einführung* (Herderbücherei 1143), Freiburg i.B.: Herder, 1984", *Orientalistische Literaturzeitnung* 88:1, 1988, pp. 98-9.

— "[review] *The Religious System of the Mahānubhāva Sect: The Mahānubhāva "Sūtrapāṭha"* ed. and transl. by Anne Feldhaus (South Asia Studies [New Delhi Branch, Heidelberg University], 12), New Delhi: Manohar, 1983", *Orientalistische Literaturzeitnung* 88:2, 1988, pp. 216-7.

— "[review] Schneider, U., *Der Holzgott und die Brahmanen*, 2 vols. (Freiburger Beiträge zur Indologie 16), Wiesbaden: Otto Harrassowitz, 1984", *Orientalistische Literaturzeitnung* 89, 1989, pp. 333-5.

— "[review] The Sants and other religious traditions [kumulative Rezension / key-review]", *Religious Studies Review* 15:4, 1989, pp. 319-24.

— "Bhakti and monasticism", in Kulke, H. & G.D. Sontheimer, eds., *Hinduism reconsidered*, Delhi: Manohar, 1990, pp. 127-40.

— "Die Kriegermönche Rajasthans, Jai Singh II. und das Bālānand-Problem", in Diem, W. & A. Falaturi, eds., *XXIV. Dt. Orientalistentag v. 26 bis 30. Sept. 1988 in Köln: Ausgewählte Vorträge*, Stuttgart: Franz Steiner, 1990, pp. 478-90.

— "In the defeat of time: the semantics of vigils in a North Indian Bhakti sect", in Eimer, Helmut, ed., *Frank-Richard Hamm Memorial Volume* (*Indica et Tibetica*, 21), Bonn: Indica et Tibetica Verlag, 1990, pp. 155-63.

— "[review] Van Skyhawk, Hugh (ed.), *Minorities on themselves* (South Asia Digest of Regional Writing, vol. 11), Stuttgart: Steiner-Verlag Wiesbaden", *ZDMG* 140:1, 1990, pp. 180-2.

— intr. & trsl., *Dādū: Lieder*, Stuttgart: Franz Steiner, 1991.

— "Dādūpanthī monastic rules", in Singh, C. & N. Vasishtha, eds., *Pathways to Literature, Art and Archaeology. Pt. Gopal Narayan Bahura Felicitation Volume*, Jaipur, 1991, vol. 1, pp. 95-113.

— "On the dual identity of Nāgās", in Bakker, H. & F. Mallison, eds., *Bhakti Traditions from the Regions of India. Studies in Honour of Charlotte Vaudeville*, Groningen & Paris: E. Forsten & EFEO, 1991, pp. 255-71.

— ed., *Rāmāyaṇa and Rāmāyaṇas*, Khoj, 3, Wiesbaden: Otto Harrassowitz, 1991.

— "[review] Entwistle, Alean E., *Braj: Centre of Krishna Pilgrimage* (Groningen Oriental Studies 3), Groningen: Egbert Forsten, 1987", *ZDMG* 141:1, 1991, pp. 197-200.

— "Dādū, *pad*-s (critical edition of the songs of Dādū)", in Callewaert, W. & Bart Op de Beek, eds., *Nirguṇa Bhakti Sāgara*, New Delhi: Manohar, 1992, vol. 1, pp. 14-21 and 201-279.

— "Gurū Nānak und der Sikhismus", in Antes, Peter, ed., *Große Religionsstifter*, München: C.H. Beck, 1992, pp. 115-32.

— "An oral theology: Dādūpanthī homilies", in McGregor, R.S., ed., *Devotional Literature in South Asia: Current Research, 1985-1988*, Cambridge: Cambridge UP, 1992, pp. 36-48.

— "[review] John, D. Smith, *The Epic of Pābūjī. A study, transcription and translation*, Cambridge: Cambridge UP, 1991", *ZDMG* 142:2, 1992, pp. 401-3.

— "Das Nachtgebet der Sikhs", in Sontheimer, Günther D. & H. Werny, eds., *Südasien-Anthologie*, Stuttgart: Franz Steiner, 1993, pp. 231-6.

— "Die gestalthaften Manifestationen (*avatāra*) von Gott Viṣṇu", in Mallebrein, Cornelia, ed., *Die anderen Götter: Volks- und*

Stammesbronzen aus Indien (*Ethnologia*, NF 17), Köln: Rautenstrauch-Joest-Museum, 1993, pp. 90-6.

— "Hochkulturliche Rezeption lokaler Gottheiten nach dem *avatāra*-Konzept: ausgewählte Typen", in Mallebrein, Cornelia, ed., *Die anderen Götter: Volks- und Stammenbronzen aus Indien* (*Ethnologia*, NF 17), Köln: Rautenstrauch-Joest-Museum, 1993, pp. 103-7.

— "Ein Kapitel nordindischer Religionspolitik im 18. Jarhundert: Jai Singh II. und die religiösen Orden", *Zeitschrift für Religionswissenschaft* 1, 1994, pp. 49-67.

— "Entfremdung und fundamentalistische Identitätskonstruktion im zeitgenössischen Indien", *Internationales Asienforum* 25:3-4, 1994, pp. 315-33.

— "Govinddevjī of Vrindavan and Jaipur and its Kachvāhā patrons from the mid 17th to the mid 18th century A.D.", in Entwistle, A.W. & F. Mallison, eds., *Studies in South Asian Devotional Literature*, New Delhi: Manohar & EFEO, 1994, pp. 82-93.

— "[review] Hawley, John Stratton - Mark Juergensmeyer, *Songs of the Saints of India* ..., New York and Oxford: Oxford UP, 1988", *ZDMG* 144:1, 1994, pp. 230.

— "[review] Lorenzen, David, *Kabir Legends and Ananta-das's* Kabir Parachai, Albany, N.Y.: State of New York Press, 1991", *ZDMG* 144:1, 1994, pp. 227-30.

— "Tradition und Moderne in A.S. Upādhyāya 'Hariaudhas' Roman *ṭheṭha hindī kā ṭhāṭa*", *Studien zur Indologie und Iranistik* 19, 1994, pp. 123-35.

— "An annual budget of Govinddevjī: a document of V.S. 1784 (A.D. 1728)", *ZDMG* 145:1, 1995, pp. 125-47.

— "Towards a Universal Dharma: *Kalyāṇ* and the Tracts of the Gītā Press", in Dalmia, Vasudha & Heinrich von Stietencron, eds., *Representing Hinduism: The Construction of Religious Traditions and National Identity*, New Delhi & London: Thousand Oaks, 1995, pp. 294-305.

— "Der Sikhismus", in Antes, Peter, ed., *Die Religionen der Gegenwart*, München: C.H. Beck, 1996, pp. 136-60.

— "Śrī Govindadeva and His Custodians from 1643 through the Time of Jaya Siṃha II (1700-1743)", in Case, Maragaret H., ed., *Govindadeva: A Dialogue in Stone*, New Delhi, 1996, pp. 185-93.

— "Les sermons du Dādūpanthī: Une forme de littérature orale liée aux écritures", in Champion, Catherine, ed., *Traditions orales dans le monde indien* (*Puruṣārtha* 18), Paris, 1996, pp. 147-57.

— "Einführung [zum Themenheft "Georges Dumézil"]", *Zeitschrift für Religionswissenschaft* 1998, pp. 119-24.

— ed., *Indian Diplomacy and Administration during the Mughal Period* (*The Indian Historical Review*, 25:1 (July)), 1998.

— "The preambles of official letters from Rajasthan: towards a stylistic typology", *The Indian Historical Review* 25:1 (July), 1998, pp. 29-44.

— *In favour of Govinddevjī: Historical documents relating to a deity of Vrindaban and Eastern Rajasthan.* Bill H, collab., Delhi: Indira Gandhi National Centre for the Arts & Manohar, 1999.

— "The Temple of Govindadevajī: a symbol of Hindu kingship?", in Singhi, N.K. & Rajendra Joshi, eds., *Religion, Ritual and Royalty*, Jaipur, 1999, pp. 162-75.

— "Weibliche Selbstverwirklichung: Die religiöse Autobiographie einer zeitgenössischen Heiligen", *Indien in Der Gegenwart* 4:3, 1999, pp. 35-51.

— "The debate on sati in the Rajputana Agency", in Malik, Jamal, ed., *Perspectives of Mutual Encounters in South Asian History, 1760-1860*, Leiden - Boston - Köln, 2000, pp. 79-92.

— "Ṣikh-Religion", *Theologische Realenzyklopädie* XXXI, 2000, pp. 263-6.

— "Südasien in kulturellen Globalisierungsszenarien: Indien als Fallbeispiel", in Bohle, H.G., ed., *21. Baden-Württemberg-Kolloquium 1999*, Stuttgart: Franz Steiner, 2000.

— "Religious dignitaries in the court protocol of Jaipur (mid-eighteenth to early nineteenth century)", in Kulke, H. & G. Berkemer & T. Frasch, eds., *Explorations in South-Asian History. Dietmar Rothermund Felicitation Volume*, Delhi, 2001.

— "[31 entries]", in Auffahrt, C. & H.G. Kippenberg & A. Michaels, eds., *Wörterbuch der Religionen*, Stuttgart: Kröner Verlag, [forthcoming].

— "Bhakti-Dichtung im Hindi-Sprachgebiet", in Hahn, Michael, ed., *Neues Handbuch der Literaturwissenschaft*, vol. 24: *Süd- und zentralasiatische Literaturen*, [forthcoming].

— "Charisma, transition of charisma and canon in North Indian bhakti", in Dalmia, V. & Angelika Malinar & M. Christoph-Füchsle, eds., *Charisma and Canon: The Formation of Religious Identity in South Asia [in Honour of Professor H. von Stietencron]*, Delhi: Sage, [forthcoming].

— "The flow of grace: Food and feast in the hagiography and history of the Dādūpanth", *ZDMG* 151, [forthcoming].

— "A paṇḍit among the modernists and a modernist among the paṇḍits", in Michaels, Axel, ed., *The Pandit: The Future of Traditional Sanskrit Scholarship*, Delhi, [forthcoming], pp. 165-75.

— "[review] Véronique Boullier, Ascètes et rois: Un monastère de Kanphata Yogis au Népal, Paris: CNRS Editions, 1997", *ZDMG*, [forthcoming].

— "Sikhismus", *RGG*, [forthcoming].

— "A theological statement by Kṛṣṇadeva Bhāṭṭācārya", in Krishna Naval, ed., *Anand Krishna Felicitation Volume*, [forthcoming].

— "Hazārī Prasād Dvivedī's Kabīr", in Horstmann, Monika, ed., *Images of Kabīr*, [in preparation].

— "Warrior-ascetics in 18th century Rajasthan and the religious policy of Jai Singh II", in Schokker, G H, ed., [forthcoming] – paper presented at the Third International Conference on Early Devotional Literature in New Indo-Aryan Languages, Leiden, 12-15 December 1985.

Horstmann, Monika & R.K. Barz, eds., *Living Texts from Northern India*, Khoj, 2, Wiesbaden: Otto Harrassowitz, 1989.

Kamphorst, Janet, "Rajasthani Narrative Traditions", *IIAS Newsletter* 21:February, 2000, pp. 12.

— "A Historical Approach to the Epic Traditions of Marwar", in *Proceedings of the 18th Rajasthan History Congress* (*10-12 February 2001, Rajasthani Research Institute, Chaupasni, Jodhpur*), [forthcoming].

— "The historical roots of the nomadic traditions of Marwar", in Mishra, Anita, ed., *Change and Continuity: Nomadic Culture in India*, New Delhi: Organisation for Applied Socio-Economic Systems, [forthcoming] – Oasis Seminar.

— "The Deification of Asian Epic Heroes: a historical perspective", in *Proceedings of the Ninth Seminar of The International Association for Tibetan Studies* (*Leiden University, 30th June 2000*), [forthcoming 2001].

— "The Poetry of War. A study of the oral characteristics of Dingal *vīrkāvya*" – unpublished paper, read at the South-Asia Institute, University of Heidelberg, 7th July 1999.

Kiehnle, Catharina, "A Vārkarī Bhajan Programme: Elements and Structure, Text and Translation", in Thiel-Horstmann, Monika, ed., *Bhakti in Current Research, 1979-1982. Proceedings of the Second Conference on Early Devotional Literature in New Indo-Aryan*

Languages, St. Augustin, 19-21 March 1982, Berlin: Dietrich Reimer Verlag, 1983, pp. 195-212.

— "Śivaismus und Viṣṇuismus in der Bhakti-Bewegung Mahārāṣṭras: Jñānadevas Saptapadī", von Schuler, Einar, ed., *XXIII. Deutscher Orientalistentag 1985. Ausgewählte Vorträge*, Wiesbaden: Franz Steiner Verlag, 1989, pp. 357-64.

— "Author- and Redactorship of the Jñānadev Gāthā", in McGregor, R.S., ed., *Devotional Literature in South Asia. Current Research, 1985-1988*, Cambridge UP, 1992, pp. 126-37.

— "Jñānadeva - Gott und Göttin - die Eltern des Universums", in Sontheimer, G.D. & Helma Werny, eds., *Südasien-Anthologie. 44 Übersetzungen aus Südasiatischen Literaturen* (*Beiträge zur Südasienforschung* (Universität Heidelberg), 140), Stuttgart: Franz Steiner Verlag, 1993, pp. 166-75.

— "Metaphors in the Jñāndev Gāthā", in Entwistle, Alan W. & Françoise Mallison, eds., *Studies in South Asian Devotional Literature. Research Papers 1988-1991*, New Delhi: Manohar, 1994, pp. 301-24.

— *Songs on Yoga: Texts and Teachings of the Mahārāṣṭrian Nāths* (*Alt- und Neu-Indische Studien*, 48.1), Stuttgart: Steiner Verlag, 1997.

— *The Conservative Vaiṣṇava: Anonymous Songs of the Jñāndev Gāthā* (*Alt- und Neu-Indische Studien*, 48.2), Stuttgart: Steiner Verlag, 1997.

— "The Lotus of the Heart", *Studien zur Indologie und Iranistik*, 1998.

— "The Vāsudev: Folk Figures and Vārkarī Bhakti in the Jñāndev Gāthā", in *G.D. Sontheimer Memorial Volume*, New Delhi: Manohar - Indira Gandhi National Centre of the Arts, [forthcoming].

— tr., *Where there is a Guru there are Women*, Atre [*Buvā tetheṃ Bāyā*], bilingual ed., [forthcoming].

Lorenzen, David N., "Kalamukhas of the Sakti-parisad", *Annals of the Bhandarkar Oriental Research Institute* 52, 1971, pp. 93-139.

— "La leyenda de Visvarupa y Ubhayabharati", *Estudios Orientales* 6, 1971, pp. 286-99 – from Mâdhava's *Sankara-digvijaya.*

— "La renunciació de Sankaracarya", *Estudios Orientales* 7, 1972, pp. 335-58 – from Mâdhava's Sanskrit *Sankara-digvijaya.*

— "La rebelión de los sannyasis", *Estudios Orientales* 9, 1974, pp. 1-13.

— "The Life of Sankarācārya", in Capps, D. & F. Reynolds, eds., *The Biographical Process*, The Hague: Mouton, 1976, pp. 87-107 – a revised version appears in F.W. Clothey & J.B. Long (eds.),

Experiencing Siva, Columbia, Mo.: South Asia Books & Delhi: Manohar, 1983, pp. 155-175.

— "Mattavilāsa", *Estudios De Asia y Africa* 12, 1977, pp. 208-24 – a Sanskrit play by Mahendravarman.

— "Warrior Ascetics in Indian History", *Journal of the American Oriental Society* 97, 1978, pp. 61-76.

— "Branches of the Kabir Panth", in Singh, Shukdeo & Vivek Das, eds., *Sādh matā hai sār*, Varanasi: Kabirvani Prakashan Kendra, 1981, pp. 75-9.

— "The Kabir Panth and Politics", *Political Science Review* (Jaipur) 20, 1981, pp. 263-81 – a second essay with this title, but based on different material, appears in Shukdeo Singh & Vivek Das (eds.), *Sâdh matâ hai sâr*, Varanasi: Kabirvani Prakashan Kendra, pp. 57-63; all the material appears in a Spanish version published in *Estudios de Asia y Africa* 18 (1983), pp. 427-451.

— "The Kabir Panth: Heretics to Hindus", in Lorenzen, David N., ed., *Religious Change and Cultural Domination*, Mexico: El Colegio de México, 1981, pp. 151-71 – this book was also published in Spanish by the same publisher (1982).

— ed. & intr., *Religious Change and Cultural Domination*, Mexico: El Colegio de México, 1981 – this book was also published in Spanish by the same publisher (1982).

— "Imperialism and the Historiography of Ancient India", in Mukherjee, S.N., ed., *India: History and Thought*, Calcutta: Subarnarekha, 1982, pp. 84-102 – a Spanish version appears in *Estudios de Asia y Africa* 12 (1977), pp. 186-207.

— "Sankaracharya y el Advaita Vedanta", *Estudios De Asia y Africa* 19, 1984, pp. 588-92.

— *La luna de la iluminación*. Alvarez M, Mexico: El Colegio de México, 1985 – a Spanish translation and study of Krsnamisra's *Prabodha-candrodaya*, a Sanskrit play.

— "Sankarācārya aur Kabīr kī sāmājik vichāradhārā [The Social Ideology of Sankaracarya and Kabir]", *Kabir Chaurā* (Varanasi) 1:3, 1985, pp. 241-4 – repr. in *Itihâs evam smârikâ*, Jaipur: Srî Kabîr Vichâr Mancha, 1988.

— "Sivaísmo: heterodoxia y ortodoxia", *Estudios De Asia y Africa* 21, 1986, pp. 258-72.

— "[7 entries:] Saivism: Overview; Saivism: Kāpālikas; Saivism: Pāsupatas; Durgā; Sankarācārya; Hathayoga; Gorakhnāth", in Eliade, Mircea, ed., *Encyclopedia of Religions*, New York: Macmillan, 1987.

— "The Kabir Panth and Social Protest", in Schomer, K. & W.H. McLeod, eds., *The Sants: Studies in a Devotional Tradition of India*, Delhi: Motilal Banarsidass, 1987, pp. 281-303 – a Spanish version appears in *Estudios de Asia y Africa* 17 (1982), pp. 338-368.

— "The Social Ideologies of Hagiography: Sankara, Tukârâm and Kabîr", in Israel, M. & N.K. Wagle, eds., *Religion and Society in Maharashtra*, Toronto: Centre for South Asian Studies - University of Toronto, 1987, pp. 92-114 – a revised Spanish version, "Las ideologías sociales del hinduismo: Shankara, Tukaram y Kabir", appears in *Estudios de Asia y Africa* 21 (1986), pp. 576-603.

— "Traditions of Non-caste Hinduism: The Kabir Panth", *Contributions to Indian Sociology* 21, 1987, pp. 264-83 – a Spanish translation is published in Saurabh Dube (ed.), *Pasados Poscoloniales*, Mexico City: El Colegio de México, 1999, pp. 485-512.

— "El *chauka* del muerto en el Kabir Panth", *Estudios De Asia y Africa* 23, 1988, pp. 445-68.

— "The Lakamukha Background of Virasaivism", in Maity, S.K. & Upendra Thakur & A.K. Narain, eds., *Studies in Orientology: Essays in Memory of Prof. A.L. Basham*, Agra: Y.K. Publishers, 1988, pp. 278-93 – a version of the essay is included as appendix in the reprint of *The Kapalikas and the Kalamukhas* (1991).

— "New Data on the Kapalikas", in Hiltebeitel, Alf, ed., *Criminal Gods and Demon Devotees*, Albany: SUNY Press, 1989, pp. 231-8 – a revised version is included as appendix to the reprint of *The Kapalikas and Kalamukhas* (1991); a Spanish version appears in *Estudios de Asia y Africa* 22 (1987), pp. 411-418.

— *Kabir Legends and Ananta-das's Kabir Parachai*, Albany: SUNY Press, 1991 – including an edition and translation (trsl. with Uma Thukral and Jagdish Kumar) of Anantadas's *Kabir Parachai*; co-edition by Indian Books Centre, Delhi, 1992.

— *The Kapalikas and Kalamukhas*, Delhi: Motilal Banarsidass, 1991 – reprint (1st ed.: Berkeley: University of California Press & Delhi: Thomson Press,1972) including two new appendices (articles from 1988 and 1989).

— "Evidencias tempranas de la religión tántrica", *Estudios De Asia y Africa* 27:2, 1992 – an English version will appear in a book on Tantrism edited by Katherine Ann Harper & Robert L. Brown, Albany: State University of New York Press, 2000.

— "Historians and the Gupta Empire", in Chhabra, B.C. & P.K. Agrawala & Ashvini Agrawal & Shankar Goyal, eds., *Reappraising Gupta History: For S.R. Goyal*, New Delhi: Aditya Prakashan, 1992, pp. 47-60 – a modified version appears in G.C. Pande & S.K. Gupta

& Shankar Goyal (eds.), *Political History in a Changing World*, Jodhpur: Kusumanjali Book World, 1992, pp. 44-56; and a Spanish version appears in *Estudios de Asia y Africa* 25 (1990), pp. 30-46.

— ed., *Bhakti Religion in North India: Community Identity and Political Action*, Albany: SUNY Press, 1995 – co-edition by Manohar Publishers, Delhi, 1995.

— "The Historical Vicissitudes of Bhakti Religion", in Lorenzen, David N., ed., *Bhakti Religion in North India: Community Identity and Political Action*, Albany: SUNY Press, 1995, pp. 1-32 – a modified Spanish version ("Bhakti, comunidad y política") appears in *Estudios de Asia y Africa* 100 (1996), pp. 319-356.

— "Lives of the Nirguni Saints", in Lorenzen, David N., ed., *Bhakti Religion in North India: Community Identity and Political Action*, Albany: SUNY Press, 1995, pp. 181-211 – a Spanish version appears in *Estudios de sia y Africa* 29:1 (1994), pp. 97-114.

— *Praises for a Formless God: Nirguni Texts from North India*, Albany: State University of New York Press, 1996 – co-edition published by Indian Books Centre, Delhi.

— *A Catalog of Manuscripts in the Kabir Chaura Monastery: Expanded Edition*, Mexico: Et Colegio de México, 1998 – 1st ed. 1994.

— "Studying Kabir Sahab and the Kabir Panth", *The Kabir Voice* (Kabir Association of Canada, Surrey, B.C.) June 1998, pp. 23-7.

— "The Life of Kabir in Legend", in Entwistle, Alan & Carol Salomon, eds., *Studies in Early Modern Indo-Aryan Languages, Literature and Culture*, New Delhi: Manohar, 1999, pp. 209-26 – a Spanish version appears in *Estudios de Asia y Africa* 28:2 (1993), pp. 196-215.

— "Who Invented Hinduism?", *Comparative Studies in Society and History* 42, 1999, pp. 630-59.

— "Bhakti", in Mitthal, S. & G. Thursby, eds., [forthcoming].

— "The Ideology of Gupta Kingship", in Goyal, Shankar & S.R. Goyal, eds., *The Wonder That Was Gupta India*, Jodhpur: Kusumanjali Book World, [forthcoming] – a Spanish version appears in *Estudios de Asia y Africa* 24 (1989), pp. 240-254.

— "Kabir Maths [and] Kabir Panth", in *Encyclopedia of Hinduism and Indic Religions*, University of South Carolina, [forthcoming].

— "Legend", in *Encyclopedia of Folklore in India*, Princeton UP, [forthcoming].

— "Marco della Tomba", in Boehm-Tettelbach, Monika, ed., [forthcoming].

— "A Parody of the Kapalikas in the *Mattavilasa*", in White, David G., ed., *Tantra in Practice*, Princeton: Princeton UP, [forthcoming].

— "Popular Hindu Movements", in Juergensmeyer, Mark, ed., *Thinking Globally about Religion*, New York: Oxford UP, [forthcoming].

— "A *Vajrasūcī* in Hindi", in Offredi, Mariola, ed., *The Banyan Tree. Essays on Early Literature in New Indo-Aryan Languages*, New Delhi: Manohar, 2000, pp. 441-455.

Lorenzen, David N. & B. Preciado, "Las dos alcahuetas", *Papeles De La India* 4, 1975, pp. 162-8 – from Somadeva's *Kathā-sarit-sāgara.*

Lorenzen, David N. & Benjamín Preciado Solís, *Atadura y liberación: las religiones de la India*, Mexico: El Colegio de México, 1996.

Lorenzen, David N. & L. Balmaseda, "El estado en la India antigua: inscriptiones de la época de los Gupta", *Estudios De Asia y Africa* 19, 1984, pp. 217-52 – a selection of Gupta Sanskrit inscriptions.

Lorenzen, David N. & M. Alvarez, "El edredón del conocimiento (*Jnan gudari*)", *Estudios De Asia y Africa* 23, 1988, pp. 166-87 – a religious poem in pre-modern Hindi, Hindi text included.

— "Las canciones populares de Kabir", *Estudios De Asia y Africa* 26:1, 1991, pp. 139-57 – poetic texts in pre-modern Hindi.

Lorenzen, David N. & Russell Maeth, "El *Liezi* y el *Satakatraya* de Bhartrhari: descubrimiento de una relación entre dos textos clásicos de China e India", *Estudios De Asia y Africa* 14, 1979, pp. 696-707.

Lorenzen, David N. & S. Devalle, "Nala y Damayantī", *Estudios De Asia y Africa* 11, 1976, pp. 34-47 – from Somadeva's Sanskrit *Kathâ-sarit-sâgara.*

Lorenzen, David N. & Uma Thukral, "Las canciones de Kamal", *Estudios De Asia y Africa* 29:2, 1994, pp. 259-71.

Lutgendorf, Philip, "[review] Wulff, Donna M., Drama as a Mode of Religious Realization, Scholars Press, 1985", *Asian Folklore Studies* (Nagoya, Japan) 47:1, 1988.

— "Ram's Story in Shiva's City: Public Arenas and Private Patronage", in Freitag, Sandria, ed., *Culture and Power in Banaras: Community, Performance and Environment, 1800-1980*, Berkeley & Los Angeles: University of California Press, 1989, pp. 34-61.

— "The View from the Ghats: Traditional Exegesis of a Hindu Epic", *Journal of Asian Studies* 48, 1989, pp. 272-88.

— "The Power of Sacred Story: *Rāmāyaṇa* Recitation in Contemporary North India", in *Ritual and Power* (*Journal of Ritual Studies* 4:1, a special issue), 1990, pp. 115-47.

— "Ramayan: The Video", *The Drama Review: A Journal of Performance Studies* 34:2 (T126), 1990, pp. 127-76.

— *The Life of a Text: Performing the Rāmcaritmānas of Tulsidas*, Berkeley & Los Angeles: University of California Press, 1991.

— "[review] van der Veer, Peter, Gods on Earth, Athlone Press, 1988", *Journal of Asian Studies* 50:4, 1991.

— "Words Made Flesh: The Banaras *Rāmlīlā* as Epic Commentary", in Burkhalter-Flueckiger, Joyce & Laurie Sears, eds., *Boundaries of the Text: Epic Performances in South and Southeast Asia*, University of Michigan: Center for South and Southeast Asian Studies, 1991, pp. 83-104.

— "The 'Great Sacrifice' of *Rāmāyaṇa* Recitation", in Thiel-Horstmann, Monika, ed., *Rāmāyaṇa and Rāmāyaṇas*, Wiesbaden: Otto Harrassowitz, 1992, pp. 185-205.

— "Indian Theatre and the Inside-Outsider. [review] Richmand, Farley P., & al., Indian Theatre: Traditions of Performance, University of Hawaii Press, 1990; [review] Bharucha, Rustom, Theatre and the World, South Asia Publications, 1990", *The Drama Review: A Journal of Performance Studies* 36:4 (T136), 1992, pp. 162-71.

— "The Secret Life of Rāmchandra of Ayodhya", in Richman, Paula, ed., *Many Rāmāyaṇas: The Diversity of a Narrative Tradition in South Asia*, Berkeley & Los Angeles: University of California Press, 1992, pp. 217-34.

— "Storysellers: Patrons and Performers in Contemporary North India", in Greenough, Paul, ed., *Redefining the 'Artisan': Traditional Technicians in Changing Societies* (*Occasional Paper*, no. 9-18), University of Iowa: Center for International and Comparative Studies, 1992, pp. 59-83.

— "The Quest for the Legendary Tulsīdās", *Journal of Vaiṣṇava Studies* 1:2, 1993, pp. 79-101 – published also as "La Busqueda del Tulsidas Legendario", *Estudios de Asia y Africa* (Journal of El Colegio de Mexico), 81 / 25:1, pp. 8-29 (Spanish trsl. by Mariela Alvarez).

— "[review] Hansen, Kathryn, Grounds for Play: The Nauṭaṅkī Theatre of North India, University of California Press, 1992", *Asian Theatre Journal* 10:2, 1993.

— "Banking on the Name", *Journal of Vaiṣṇava Studies* 2:2, 1994, pp. 147-62.

— *The Life of a Text: Performing the Rāmcaritmānas of Tulsidas*, Delhi: Oxford UP, 1994 – Indian ed.

— "My Hanuman is Bigger than Yours", *History of Religions* 33:3, 1994, pp. 211-45.

— "The Quest for the Legendary Tulsīdās", in Callewaert, W.M. & Rupert Snell, eds., *According to Tradition: Hagiographical Writing in India*, Wiesbaden: Otto Harrassowitz, 1994, pp. 65-85 – exp. version of "The Quest" (1993).

— "[review] Manuel, Peter, Cassette Culture, University of Chicago Press, 1993", *Journal of Asian Studies* 53:4, 1994.

— "Sundar kāṇḍ", *Journal of Vaiṣṇava Studies* 2:4, 1994, pp. 91-127 – complete translation.

— "All in the (Raghu) Family", in Babb, Lawrence A. & Susan S. Wadley, eds., *Media and the Transformation of Religions in South Asia*, Philadelphia: University of Pennsylvania Press, 1995, pp. 217-53 – rev. version of "Ramayan: The Video"; also in Allen, Robert C., ed., *To Be Continued ... Soap Operas Around the World*, London: Routledge, pp. 321-353.

— "Interpreting Ramraj: Reflections on the Ramayan, Bhakti, and Hindu Nationalism", in Lorenzen, David, ed., *Bhakti Religion in North India: Community Identity and Political Action*, Albany: State University of New York Press, 1995, pp. 253-87.

— "Rāmcaritmānas: From Book Five. The Beautiful Book", in Mack, Maynard, ed., *The Norton Anthology of World Masterpieces*, exp. ed., New York: W.W. Norton and Co., 1995, vol 1, pp. 2316-32 – translation.

— "Rāmcaritmānas", in McGreal, Ian P., ed., *Great Literature of the Eastern World*, New York: Harper Collins, 1996, pp. 235-8.

— "Blackburn, Stuart, Inside the Drama House: Rāma Stories and Shadow Puppets in South India, University of California Press, 1996", *BSOAS* 60:3, 1997.

— "Imagining Ayodhya: Utopia and its Shadows in a Hindu Landscape", *International Journal of Hindu Studies* 1:1, 1997, pp. 19-54.

— "Monkey in the Middle: the Status of Hanuman in Popular Hinduism", *Religion* 27, 1997, pp. 311-32.

— "[review] Lorenzen, D., Praises to a Formless God: Nirguṇ Texts from North India, 1996", *Journal of Asian Studies* 56:4, 1997.

— "Like Mother, Like Son: Sita and Hanuman", *Manushi: a Journal About Women and Society* 114, 1999, pp. 22-35.

— "City, Forest, and Cosmos: Ecological Perspectives from the Sanskrit Epics", in Chapple, Christopher Key & Mary Evelyn Tucker, eds., *Hinduism and Ecology*, Harvard UP, 2000.

— "Dining Out at Lake Pampa: The Shabari Episode in Multiple *Rāmāyanas*", in Richman, Paula, ed., *Questioning Rāmāyanas*, Oxford UP, 2000.

— "[four entries:] Hanumān, Mānas kathā folk, Rāma, Vyās", in Claus, Peter J. & Margaret A. Mills, eds., *South Asian Folklore: An Encyclopedia*, New York: Garland Publishing Inc., [forthcoming].
— "Medieval Traditions: An Annotated Survey of Recent Scholarship", in Sharma, Arvind, ed., *The Study of Hinduism*, University of South Carolina Press, [forthcoming].
— "Rāmacarita Mānasa (Tulsidas)", in Rao, K.L. Seshagiri & al., ed., *Encyclopedia of Hinduism and Indic Religions*, Columbia (South Carolina): University of South Carolina Press, [forthcoming].
— "Tulsidas", in Classe, Olive, ed., *Encyclopedia of Literary Translation into English*, London: Fitzroy Dearbon, [forthcoming].

Mallison, Françoise, "Sainteté - l'Hindouisme", in *Encyclopaedia universalis*, Paris, 1972, vol. 14, pp. 605-6.
— "[compte rendu] 'The Philosophy of Śrī Svāmīnārāyaṇa' de J.A. Yajnik. Ahmedabad: L.D. Institute", *Annals of the Bhandarkar Oriental Research Institute* (Poona) 53, 1973, pp. 277-8.
— *L'épouse idéale, la Satī-Gītā de Muktānanda, traduite du Gujārātī* (*Publications de l'Institut de civilisation indienne*, (série in-8°) 35), Paris: Institut de civilisation indienne, 1973 – texte en gujarati et traduction française.
— "Notes on the biography of Narasiṃha Mahetā", *Annals of the Bhandarkar Oriental Research Institute* (Poona) 55, 1974, pp. 189-201.
— "La secte krichnaïte des Svāmī-nārāyaṇī au Gujarāt", *Journale Asiatique* 262, 1974, pp. 435-71.
— "Saint Sudāmā in Gujarāt", in *Proceedings of the All-India Oriental Conference. XXVIIIth session. Karnataka University. Dharwar. Nov. 1976*, Poona: Bhandarkar Oriental Research Institute, 1978, pp. 427-38.
— "A note on holiness allowed to women: Pativratā and Satī", in *Ludwik Sternbach Felicitation Volume*, Lucknow, 1979, vol. 1, pp. 741-4.
— "Saint Sudāmā in Gujarāt: Should the holy be wealthy?", *Journal of the Oriental Institute* (Baroda) 29a, 1979, pp. 91-9.
— "Bhakti in Gujarāt: some problems", Callewaert, W., ed., *Early Hindi Devotional Literature in Current Research. Proceedings of the International Middle Hindi Bhakti Conference (April 1979)*, Louvain, 1980, pp. 88-102 – traduction partielle de cet article en gujarati par Candrakanth Sheth dans *Bhāṣāvimarśa* (Ahmedabad) 6:2 (1983), pp. 32-35; et par Rasiklāl Tripathi dans *Vidyāpīṭh* (Ahmedabad) 114 (ère Śaka 1903 [1981]), pp. 52-57.

— "The cult of Sudāmā in Porbandar-Sudāmāpurī", *Journal of the Oriental Institute* (Baroda) 29b, 1980, pp. 216-23.

— "[Traductions de *pada*]", in Patel, D. & J.N. Trivedi, *Devotional Songs from Gujarati*, Randheja, 1981, pp. 25-7, 39, 99-101.

— "Development of early Krishnaism in Gujarāt: Viṣṇu-Raṇchoḍ-Kṛṣṇa", in Thiel-Horstmann, Monika, ed., *Bhakti in Current Research, 1979-1982, Proceedings of the Second International Conference on Early Devotional Literature in New Indo-Aryan Languages*, Berlin, 1983, pp. 245-55.

— "[compte rendu] 'Au pays du roi vainqueur (Satruñjaya). Introduction au Jinisme laïque' de I. Armelin, Paris, 1983", *Journal of the Oriental Institute* (Baroda), 1984, pp. 109-10.

— "Gujarati [littérature]", dans *Encyclopaedia universalis*, 1ère ed., Paris, 1984, pp. 1221-2 – repris dans *Corpus* (Paris) 11 (1989), pp. 75-76.

— *Au point du jour: Les Prabhātiyaṃ de Narasiṃha Mahetā, poète et saint vishnouite du Gujarat, XV*[e] *siècle*, Publications de l'EFEO, 148, Paris: EFEO, 1986 – textes en gujarati et traduction française en regard.

— "Les chants *dhoḷa* au Gujarat et leur usage pour la dévotion vallabhite", *Bulletin de l'Ecole Française d'Extrême Orient* (Paris) 75, 1986, pp. 79-103.

— "[compte rendu] 'Sûr Dâs, Singer, Saint' de J.S. Hawley, Seattle, 1984", *Bulletin d'Etudes Indiennes* (Paris: Association Française des Etudes Sanskrites) 5, 1987, pp. 55*-61*.

— "Glimpses into Medieval Gujarati Devotional Literature", *Asmitā* (London: Gujarātī Sāhitya Akādami) 4:31 (August), 1988, pp. 185-92.

— "L'idéal féminin selon la tradition hindoue", *Viniyoga* (Liège), décembre 1988, pp. 31-6.

— "From Folklore to Devotion: The *dhoḷ* Songs in Gujarat", in Barz, R.K. & M. Thiel-Horstmann, eds., *Living Texts of India* (= *Khoj. A Series of Modern South Asia Studies*, vol. 2), Wiesbaden: Harrassowitz, 1989, pp. 87-101.

— "Hinduism as seen by the Nizārī Ismā'īlī Missionaries of Western India: The Evidence of the *Ginān*", in Sontheimer, G.D. & H. Kulke, eds., *Hinduism Reconsidered*, New Delhi & Heidelberg: Manohar & South Asia Institute (New Delhi Branch) & Heidelberg University, 1989, pp. 93-103 – repr. 1991, 1994; rev. ed. 1997, pp. 189-201.

— "Mathurā, a pattern for the history and development of the regional centres of krishnaite pilgrimage: commentaire de la contribution d'A. Entwistle, 'Mahātmya Sources on the Pilgrimage Circuit of

Mathurā'", in Bakker, Hans, ed., *The History of Sacred Places in India as reflected in Traditional Literature* (*Panels of the VIIth World Sanskrit Conference*, III), Leiden: E.J. Brill, 1990, pp. 29-31.

— "Les chants *garabī* de Pīr Shams", dans Mallison, Françoise, ed., *Littératures médiévales de l'Inde du Nord*, Paris: EFEO, 1991, pp. 115-38 – traduction anglaise en préparation par M. Waseem (New Delhi).

— ed., *Littératures médiévales de l'Inde du Nord, contributions de Charlotte Vaudeville et de ses élèves* (*Publications de l'EFEO*, 165), Paris: EFEO, 1991.

— "Lorsque Raṇachoḍarāya quitte Dwarka pour Dakor, ou comment Dvārakānātha prit la succession de Ḏaṇkanātha", dans Eck, D. & F. Mallison, eds., *Devotion Divine: Bhakti Traditions from the Regions of India. Studies in Honour of Charlotte Vaudeville*, Paris & Groningen, 1991, pp. 197-207.

— "Muslim Devotional Literature in Gujarati: Islam and Bhakti", in McGregor, R.S., ed., *Devotional Literature in South Asia. Current Research, 1985-1988*, Cambridge: Cambridge UP, 1992, pp. 89-100 – traduction en gujarati par Karamśī Pīrā, dans *Forbes Gujarātī Sabhā Traimāsika* 63:3 (juillet-septembre), 1998, pp. 149-158, sous le titre "Gujarātīmāṃ muslima bhaktimārgī sāhitya".

— "La secte ismaïlienne des Nizārī ou Satpanthī en Inde: Hétérodoxie hindoue ou musulmane?", dans Bouez, S., ed., *Ascèse et renoncement en Inde, ou la solitude bien ordonnée*, Paris: L'Harmattan, 1992, pp. 89-113.

— "A Study of Krishnaite Vallabhan Writings in Gujarat (16th-19th centuries)", in Wezler, A. & E. Hammerschmidt, eds., *Proceedings of the XXXIInd International Conference for Asian and North African Studies* (*Hamburg, 25th-30th August 1986*) (*Zeitschrift der Deutschen Morgenländischen Gesellschaft*, Supplementa IX), Stuttgart: Franz Steiner Verlag, 1992, pp. 516-7.

— "[Chronique: Inde] I: Vth International Conference on Devotional Literature in New Indo-Aryan Languages, II: Formation d'une équipe d'accueil à la section des Sciences historiques et philologiques de l'Ecole pratique des Hautes Etudes: Inde médiévale et moderne: textes et contextes", *Bulletin de l'Ecole Française d'Extrême-Orient* (Paris) 80:1, 1993, pp. 275-6, 287-8.

— "[compte rendu] 'The Eighty-Four Hymns of Hita Harivaṃśa' de R. Snell, London, 1991", *Journal of the Royal Asiatic Society* [3rd series] 3:2 (July), 1993, pp. 292-3.

— "Vallabhācārya's sampradāya and the Jagannātha Purī tīrtha", *Asmitā* (London: Gujarātī Sāhitya Akādami) 7, 1993, pp. 387-90.

— "[8 entries:] [1] Govardhanarāma (1855-1907) et la renaissance sanskrite dans les lettres gujarātī modernes; [2] Narasiṃha Mahetā (1414-1480?) et la Bhakti médiévale du Gujarat; [3] Narmada (1833-1886) et les pionniers de la littérature gujarātī moderne; [4] Premānanda (1640-1700?) et les récits gujarātī en forme d'ākhyāna; [5] Rāsa (les) et la littérature jaina en vieux-gujarātī; [6] Śāmaḷa (1695-1770) et le conte gujarātī; [7] Sureśa Jośī (1921-1986) et la révolution moderniste contemporaine au Gujarāt; [8] Umāśaṃkara Jośī (1911-[1988]) et le courant gandhien au Gujarāt", dans Didier, Béatrice, dir., *Dictionnaire Universel des Littératures*, Paris: Presses Universitaires de France, 1994, vol. II, pp. 1377-8, 2510-2, 2513-4, and vol. III, pp. 2664-5, 3107-8, 3380-1, 3661, 3957-8.

— "Early Kṛṣṇa Bhakti in Gujarat: The Evidence of Old Gujarati Texts Recently Brought to Light", in Entwistle, Alan A. & F. Mallison, eds., *Studies in South Asian Devotional Literature. Research Papers 1988-1991, presented at the Fifth Conference on Devotional Literature in New Indo-Aryan Languages, held at Paris - Ecole Française d'Extrême-Orient, 9-12 July 1991*, Paris & New Delhi: EFEO & Manohar, 1994, pp. 51-64 – traduction gujarati par H. Bhayani dans *Forbes Gujarati Sabha Traimasika* 60:2 (April-June) 1995, pp. 60-62, sous le titre "Madhyakālīna gujarātamāṃ kṛṣṇabhakti: hamaṇāṃ pragaṭa karayela jūnī gujarātī kṛtionon purāvo".

— "Le 'genre' hagiographique dans la bhakti médiévale de l'Inde occidentale", dans Balbir, Nalini, ed., *Genres Littéraires en Inde*, Paris: Presses de la Sorbonne Nouvelle, 1994, pp. 325-38.

— "Bombay as the Intellectual Capital of the Gujaratis in the Nineteenth Century", in Patel, Sujata & Alice Thorner, eds., *Bombay, Mosaic of Modern Culture*, Bombay: Oxford UP, 1995, pp. 76-87.

— "[Chronique: Inde] VIth International Conference on Early Literature in New Indo-Aryan Languages (University of Washington, July 7th-9th, 1994)", *Bulletin de l'Ecole Française d'Extrême-Orient* (Paris) 82, 1995, pp. 352-3.

— "Hagiography and Sects in the Medieval Vaiṣṇava *Bhakti* of Western India", in Vyas, R.T., ed., *Śilpasaṃvit, Consciousness Manifest. Studies in Jaina Art and Iconography and Allied Subjects in Honour of Dr. U.P. Shah*, Vadodara & Delhi: Oriental Institute & Abhinav Publications, 1995, pp. 217-27 – a shorter version is published in K.I. Koppedrayer (ed.), *Contact between Cultures. South Asia. Selected Papers from the 33rd ICANAS (Toronto, 19-25 août 1990)*, Queenstown, 1992, vol. 2, pp. 306-311.

— "Qui est un Vaiṣṇava, selon la poésie religieuse médiévale du Gujarat?", in Gurov, N.V. & Vasilkov Y.V., eds., *Sthāpakaśrāddham. Professor G.A. Zograph Commemorative Volume*, St. Petersburg: Russian Academy of Sciences - Institute of Oriental Studies, 1995, pp. 484-93.

— "[compte rendu] 'In the Absence of God, The Early Years of an Indian Sect. A Translation of Smṛtisthal with an Introduction' de A. Feldhaus et Sh.G. Tulpule, Honolulu, 1992", *Bulletin de l'Ecole Française d'Extrême-Orient* (Paris) 83, 1996, pp. 395sq.

— "[compte rendu] 'South Asian Archeology, 1993, Proceedings of the Twelfth International Conference of the European Association of South Asian Archeology, held in Helsinki University, 5-9 July 1993', édité par A. Parpola et P. Koskikallio, Helsinki, 1994", *Bibliothèque de l'Ecole des Chartes* 154, 1996, pp. 716.

— "Hymnologies vishnuite, jaina, parsi, tantrique et islamique en gujarati: mode de transmission et thèmes convergents", dans Champion, C., *Traditions orales dans le monde indien, études réunies* (*Puruṣārtha*, 18), Paris: Editions de l'Ecole des Hautes Etudes en Sciences Sociales, 1996, pp. 273-87.

— "Puṣṭimārgī Poetry in Gujarati: The Lord of Braj travelled to Gujarat twice", *Sambodhi* (Ahmedabad, L.D. Institute) XX, 1996, pp. 24-31.

— "[compte rendu] 'Praises to a Formless God, Nirguṇī Texts from North India' de David N. Lorenzen, Albany, 1996, et notices diverses sur des ouvrages concernant les études de littératures pre-modernes de l'Inde du Nord", *Bulletin de l'Ecole Française d'Extrême-Orient* (Paris) 84, 1997, pp. 442-7.

— "Rencontrer l'Absolu, ô Ami! Un hymne commun aux Hindous tantriques et aux Musulmans ismaéliens du Saurashtra (Gujarat)", dans Assayag, J. & G. Tarabout, *Altérité et identité. Islam et Christianisme en Inde, études réunies* (*Puruṣārtha*, 19), Paris: EHESS, 1997, pp. 265-76.

— "Le discours hagiographique dans les biographies du saint-poète gujarati Narasiṃha Mahetā", *Bulletin de l'Ecole Française d'Extrême-Orient* (Paris) 85, 1998, pp. 265-83.

— "[Edition d'un dossier] Cinq études pour un point de vue comparatif sur les littératures hagiographiques en Asie", *Bulletin de l'Ecole Française d'Extrême-Orient* (Paris) 85, 1998, pp. 257-384 – et Introduction, pp. 259-263.

— "A Somewhat revolutionary View of Society by a Disciple of Svāmī Nārāyaṇa: The *Satī Gītā* of Muktānanda (1823)", in Mistry, P.J. & Bharati Modi, eds., *Vidyopāsanā: Studies in Honour of Harivallabh*

C. Bhayani, Mumbai & Ahmedabad: Image Publications, 1999, pp. 125-33.

— "Contradictions and misunderstandings in the literary response to colonial culture in nineteenth century Gujarat", *South Asia Research* (New Delhi) 20:2, 2000, pp. 118-32.

— "*Sant-vāṇī* and Harijan, Mahāmārgī *Bhajan* and Ismaili *Ginān*: A New Appraisal of Popular Devotion in Saurashtra", Offredi, M., ed., *The Banyan Tree: Essays on Early Literature in New Indo-Aryan Languages*, New Delhi: Manohar, 2000, pp. 235-43.

— ed., *Constructions hagiographiques dans le monde indien: Entre mythe et histoire* (*Collection Bibliothèque de l'Ecole des Hautes Etudes. Sciences historiques et philologiques*, 338), Paris: Champion, 2001 – volume collectif de l'équipe "Inde médiévale et moderne: textes et contextes".

— "Resistant Ginãns and the Quest for an Ismaili and Islamic Identity among the Khojas", in Dalmia, V. & A. Malinar & M. Christof, eds., *Charisma and Canon: Essays on the Religious History of the Indian Subcontinent [in Honour of Professor H. von Stietencron]*, New Delhi: Oxford UP, 2001, pp. 360-75.

— "The definition of a vaiṣṇava according to medieval Gujarati devotional poetry", in Schokker, G., ed., *Bhakti in Current Research* (*1982-1985*), Lucknow & Delhi, [forthcoming].

— "Saints and Sacred Places in Saurashtra and Kutch: The Case of the Naklaṃki Cult and of the Jakhs", in [actes du colloque] *Sacred Biography and Sacred Places: Explorations in the Formation of Religious and Social Identity in Asia* (*McMaster and Toronto, Canada, 1-3 June 1998*), [forthcoming].

— "The 'True Vaiṣṇava': A Jaina Heritage in Gujarat", *Felicitation Volume for Professor H.C. Bhayani* (*Nirgrantha*, III), Ahmedabad, [forthcoming].

— "The *Delamī Ārādh* of Devāyat Paṇḍit: A Ritual Text of the Early Nizārī Ismailīs of Western India, still in use among the Tantric Mahāmārgī of Gujarat", [in preparation].

— "Histoire de la littérature gujarati", [in preparation].

Mallison, Françoise & Alan W. Entwistle, ed., *Studies in South Asian Devotional Literature. Research Papers 1988-1991, presented at the Fifth Conference on Devotional Literature in New Indo-Aryan Languages, held at Paris - Ecole Française d'Extrême Orient, 9-12 July 1991*, New Delhi & Paris: Manohar & EFEO, 1994.

Mallison, Françoise & Diana L. Eck, eds., *Devotion Divine: Bhakti traditions from the regions of India. Studies in honour of Charlotte*

Vaudeville, Groningen Oriental Studies, VIII, Groningen & Paris: Egbert Forsten & EFEO, 1991.

Mann, Gurinder Singh, "Teaching the Sikh Tradition: A Course at Columbia", in *Studying the Sikhs: Issues for North America*, Albany: SUNY Press, 1993.
— "Sikh Studies and the Sikh Educational Heritage", in *Studying the Sikhs: Issues for North America*, Albany: SUNY Press, 1993.
— *Studying the Sikhs: Issues for North America*. Hawley JS, co-ed., Albany: SUNY Press, 1993.
— "[ten entries]", in Smith, Jonathan Z. & al., eds., *The Harper Collins's Dictionary of Religion*, San Francisco: Harper, 1995.
— *The Goindval Pothis: The Earliest Extant Source of the Sikh Canon* (Harvard Oriental Series, 51), Cambridge, 1996.
— "Punjabi Proverbs", in Andrews, R. & al., eds., *The Columbia Worlds of Quotations*, New York: Columbia UP, 1996.
— "Guru Granth Sahib", in *Encarta Encyclopedia*, London: Websters International, 1997.
— "Guru Nanak", in *Encarta Encyclopedia*, London: Websters International, 1997.
— "Sikhs", in Levinson, D. & M. Ember, eds., *American Immigrant Culture*, New York: Simon and Schuster Macmillan, 1997.
— "Sikhism (and 32 related entries)", in *Merriam Webster's Encyclopedia of Religions*, Springfield (MA): Merriam Webster, 1999.
— "Canon Formation in the Sikh Tradition", in Shackle, Christopher, ed., *New Perspectives in Sikh Studies*, London: Curzon Press, 2000.
— *The Making of Sikh Scripture*, New York: Oxford UP, 2000.
— "Sikhism in the USA", in Coward, Harold, ed., *South Asian Religion in the Diaspora*, Albany: SUNY Press, 2000.
— "Sikhs in America", in Butler, Jon & Harry S. Stout, eds., *Religion in American Life*, New York: Oxford UP, 2000.

Manring, Rebecca, *Fabricating Tradition* – in preparation; a study of the biographical corpus of Advaitācārya and its position in and impact on Gauḍīya Vaiṣṇavism.
— "At Home in the World: The Lives of Sītādevī", *International Journal of Hindu Studies* 2:1, 1998.
— "The Gauḍīya Vaiṣṇava Philosophy and the Life of Advaitācārya", *Bulletin of the Ramakrishna Mission Institute of Culture* XLIX:9, 1998.

— "Advaita Prakāśa: Questions of authenticity in Vaiṣṇava hagiography", in Entwistle, Alan W. & Carol Salomon, eds., *Studies in Early Modern Indo-Aryan Language, Literature and Culture*, Delhi: Manohar, 1999.

— "Sukumar Sen o Vaiṣṇava Jīvanī Sāhityacarcā", *Baṅgīya Sāhitya Pariṣad Patrikā*, [forthcoming] – The Sukumar Sen (Barddhamān Sāhitya Sabhā) Manuscript Preservation Project. An as yet unnamed bilingual edited volume commemorating the birth centenary of Sukumar Sen.

— "Sītā Devī: An Early Vaiṣṇava Guru", in Prentiss-Pechilis, Karen, ed., *Guru / Ma*, New York: Oxford UP, [forthcoming].

Manring, Rebecca & Tony K. Stewart, "In the Name of Devotion: Acyutacaraṇa Caudhurī and the Hagiographies of Advaitācārya", *Journal of Vaiṣṇava Studies* 5:1, 1996, pp. 47-70.

Martin, Nancy M., "Homespun Threads of Dignity and Protest: Songs of Kabir in Rural Rajasthan", in Boehm-Tettelbach, Monika, ed., [2001].

— "Mīrābāī: Inscribed in Text, Embodied in Life", in Rosen, Steven, ed., *Vaiṣṇavī: Women and the Worship of Krishna*, Delhi: Motilal Banarsidass, 1996, pp. 7-46 – originally published in *Journal of Vaiṣṇava Studies* 3:4 (Fall), 1995, pp. 5-44; also published as "Mira Bai: Shastron mem Ullikhit, Jivan mem Rupayit" [Mangilal Nagda & Ashok Kumar Bhatnagar, trsl.], *Rangayan* 30:1 (Jan.-March), 1997, pp. 7-19.

— "Love and Longing in Devotional Hinduism", in Runzo, Joseph & Nancy M. Martin, eds., *The Meaning of Life in the World Religions*, Oxford: Oneworld Publications, 1999, pp. 201-19.

— "*Mīrā Janma Patrī* and Other Tales of Resistance and Appropriation", in Joshi, Rajendra & N.K. Singhi, eds., *Religion, Ritual, and Royalty*, Jaipur: Rawat Press, 1999, pp. 227-61.

— "Loving the Goddess in Hinduism", in Runzo, Joseph & Nancy M. Martin, eds., *Love, Sex and Gender in the World Religions*, Oxford: World Publications, 2000, pp. 89-111.

— "Mīrābāī in the Academy and the Politics of Identity", in Bose, Mandakranta, ed., *Faces of the Feminine from Ancient, Medieval and Modern India*, New York: Oxford UP, 2000, pp. 162-82.

— "Kabīr and Mīrābāī in Folk Traditions of Western Rajasthan: Meghwāl and Māṅganiyār Repertoires", in Offredi, Mariola, ed., *The Banyan Tree. Essays on Early Literature in New Indo-Aryan Languages*, Delhi: Manohar Press, 2000, pp. 391-418.

— "Hindi Devotional Literature", in Flood, Gavid, ed., *The Blackwell Companion to Hinduism*, [forthcoming].
— "North Indian Devotional Literature", in Flood, Gavin, ed., *The Blackwell Companion to Hinduism*, [forthcoming].
— "Mirabai", in Bryant, Edwin, ed., *Sources in the Krishna Tradition*, New York: Oxford UP, [forthcoming].
— *Mirabai: Woman Saint of India*, New York: Oxford UP, [forthcoming].

Martinetti, Piero with P. Caracchi, *La sapienza indiana*, Milano: Celuc Libri, 1981 – Corredata da un'antologia di testi indù e buddhisti a cura di P. Caracchi.

McLeod, W.H., "Guru Nanak and Kabir", in *Proceedings of the Punjab History Conference* (*1966 for 1965*), pp. 87-92.
— "Sikhs and the Turban", prepared for: the Justice Department GoC., court case John L. Grant et al. vs. the Attorney General et al. (Calgary, Jan.-Feb. 1994). Federal Court file no. T-499-91.
— "The Influence of Islam upon the Thought Of Guru Nanak", *Sikhism and Indian Society: Transactions of the Indian Institute of Advanced Study* IV, 1967, pp. 292-308 – slightly revised version reprinted in *History of Religions* VII:4 (May), 1968, pp. 302-316; repr. in *Exploring Sikhism*, New Delhi: Oxford UP, 2000, pp. 3-18.
— "Procedures in analysing the sources for the life of Guru Nanak", *Journal of Indian History* XLV:1 (April), 1967, pp. 207-27.
— "The Teachings of Guru Nanak", *The Sikh Review* XVI:172, 1967, pp. 9-14.
— *Guru Nanak and the Sikh Religion*, Oxford: the Clarendon Press, 1968 – 1st Indian (rev.) ed., Delhi: Oxford UP, 1976; 3rd impr. 1988, Oxford India Paperbacks 1996, 1998; repr. as a part of the omnibus volume *Sikhs and Sikhism*, New Delhi: Oxford UP, 2000.
— *The Sikhs of the Punjab. A text for use in secondary schools*, Auckland: Graphic Educational Publications, 1968 – 2nd ed., Auckland, New Zealand: Whitcombe & Tombs, 1970; Indian ed. Ludhiana: Lyall, 1969; UK ed. Newcastle-on-Tyne: Oriel Press, 1970.
— "The Life of Guru Nanak according to Bhai Gurdas", *The Punjab Past and Present* III:1-2, 1969, pp. 32-44 – translation with a brief introduction and notes of Bhai Gurdas's *Var* 1, stanzas 23-45, and *Var* 11, stanzas 13-14.

— "The Mahima Prakas Varatak: A History of the Ten Gurus", *The Punjab Past and Present* III:1-2, 1969, pp. 54-87 – translation with introduction and notes of the portion dealing with Guru Nanak.

— "The Miharban Janam-sakhi: An examination of the *gost* form with special reference to Pothi Hariji and Pothi Chaturbhuj of the Miharban Janam-sakhi", in *The Miharban Janam-sakhi*, Amritsar: Khalsa College, 1969, vol. II, pp. i-xii.

— "Sabad da sidhant: Guru Nanak ji te Kabir di tulana", in Singh, Pritam, ed., *Pahila Patasahi Sri Guru Nanak Dev ji*, Ludhiana: Panjabi Sahit Akademi, 1969, pp. 332-8 – in Panjabi; published first in *Alochana*, 1969.

— "Guru Nanak and the Impact of Modern Scientific Thought", *The Sikh Review* XVIII:169 (December-January), 1969, pp. 85-91.

— "Hakikat rah mukham Raje Sivanabh ki: An Account of the Way to the Abode of Raja Sivanabh", *Proceedings of the Punjab History Conference*, 4 (1969), 1970, pp. 96-105 – being an examination of a prose passage appended to many manuscript copies of the Adi Granth.

— "The Janam-sakhis as Sources of Punjab History", *Proceedings of the Punjab History Conference*, 4 (1969), 1970, pp. 109-21.

— "The Nanak of Faith and the Nanak of History", in Webster, J.C.B., ed., *History and Contemporary India*, Bombay: Asia Publishing House, 1971, pp. 46-56 – repr. in *Exploring Sikhism*, New Delhi: Oxford UP, 2000, pp. 37-46.

— "Sikhism", in Parrinder, Geoffrey, ed., *Man and his Gods: Encyclopedia of the World's Religions*, London: Hamlyn, 1971, pp. 210-21 – repr. in Parrinder, Geoffrey (ed.), *World Religions from Ancient History to the Present*, New York: Facts on File, 1983, pp. 250-261.

— "Sikhism", *Expository Times* 83:12 (September), 1972, pp. 356-9.

— "Inter-linear Inscriptions in Sri Lanka", *South Asia* 3:August, 1973, pp. 105-6.

— "The Kukas: A Millenarian Sect of the Punjab", in Wood, G.A. & P.S. O'Connor, eds., *W.P. Morrell: A Tribute*, Dunedin: University of Otago Press, 1973, pp. 85-103 – repr. in *The Punjab Past and Present* XIII:1 (April 1979), pp. 164-187; repr. in *Exploring Sikhism*, New Delhi: Oxford UP, 2000, pp. 189-215.

— "Pitfalls for the Writer of History", in *Proceedings of A Weekend School. Dunedin, 2-3 October 1971*, Dunedin: New Zealand Library Association - Otago Branch, 1973, pp. B1-17.

— "Ahluwalias and Ramgarhias: Two Sikh Castes", *South Asia* 4:October, 1974, pp. 78-90 – repr. in *Exploring Sikhism*, New Delhi: Oxford UP, 2000, pp. 216-234.

— "Ethical Standards in World Religions: The Sikhs", *Expository Times* 85:8, 1974, pp. 233-7 – repr. in *The Sikh Courier* 7:5 (Spring), 1975, pp. 4-9.

— *Guru Nanak de udesh.* Mohan Jit Singh, tr., Amritsar: Guru Nanak Dev University, 1974 – Punjabi translation of Part V of *Guru Nanak and the Sikh Religion.*

— "Nanak", in *Encyclopaedia Britannica*, 1974, pp. 821-2

— "The Significance of Baba Farid as a Symbol of Human Brotherhood", *The Journal of Religious Studies* V:1-2 (Spring-Autumn), 1974, pp. 225-37.

— "Colonel Steinbach and the Sikhs", *The Punab Past and Present* IX:2 (October), 1975, pp. 291-8.

— *The Evolution of the Sikh Community*, Delhi: Oxford UP, 1975 also Oxford: the Clarendon Press, 1976; Oxford India Paperbacks, 1996, 1998 (xi+127 pp.); reprinted as part of the omnibus volume *Sikhs and Sikhism*, New Delhi: Oxford UP, 2000.

— "Sikhism", in Basham, A.L., ed., *A Cultural History of India*, Oxford: the Clarendon Press, 1975, pp. 294-302 – repr. in Foy, Whitfield (ed.), *Man's Religious Quest*, London: Croom Helm in association with the Open University, 1978, pp. 287-297.

— *The Way of the Sikh*, Amersham (UK): Hulton Educational Publications, 1975 – for children 10-12 years; four reprints.

— "Mangal Singh of Otorohanga", *Art of Living* III:4 (April), 1976, pp. 9-10, 43 – repr. in *The Sikh Sansar* 6:1 (March) 1977, pp. 16-17.

— "Religious Tolerance in Sikh Scriptural Writings", in Talib, G.S., ed., *Guru Tegh Bahadur*, Patiala: Punjabi University, 1976, pp. 228-42.

— "Trade and Investment in sixteenth and seventeenth century Punjab: The Testimony of the Sikh Devotional Literature", in Singh, Harbans & N.G. Barrier, eds., *Essays in Honour of Doctor Ganda Singh*, Patiala: Punjabi University, 1976, pp. 81-91.

— "Punjabis in New Zealand", *NZASIAN* 4, 1977, pp. 13-21.

— "On the Word Panth: A Problem of Terminology and Definition", *Contributions to Indian Sociology* 12:2, 1979, pp. 287-95 – repr. in *Exploring Sikhism*, New Delhi: Oxford UP, 2000, pp. 139-148.

— "The Question of Semantics", in McMullen, Clarence O., ed., *Rituals and Sacraments in Indian Religions*, Delhi: ISPCK, 1979, pp. 9-15.

— "The Sikh Scriptures: Some Issues", in Juergensmeyer, Mark & N. Gerald Barrier, eds., *Sikh Studies: Comparative Perspectives on a Changing Tradition*, Berkeley: Berkeley Religious Studies Series, 1979, pp. 97-111.

— "The Sikhs of the South Pacific", in Juergensmeyer, Mark & N. Gerald Barrier, eds., *Sikh Studies: Comparative Perspectives on a Changing Tradition*, Berkeley: Berkeley Religious Studies Series, 1979, pp. 143-58.

— *The B40 Janam-sakhi*, Amritsar: Guru Nanak Dev University, 1980 – an English translation with introduction and annotations of the India Office Library Gurmukhi manuscript *Panj. B40*, a *janam-sakhi* of Guru Nanak, compiled in A.D. 1733 by Daya Ram Abrol.

— *Early Sikh Tradition. A Study of the Janam-sakhis*, Oxford: the Clarendon Press, 1980 – repr. as a part of the omnibus volume *Sikhs and Sikhism*, New Delhi: Oxford UP, 2000.

— "The Punjabi Community in New Zealand", in Tiwari, Kapil N., ed., *Indians in New Zealand*, Wellington: Price Milburn, 1980, pp. 113-21 – repr. as "The Sikhs and Sikhism in New Zealand", *The Panjab Past and Present* XVI-XVII (October 1982), pp. 407-416.

— "Kabir, Nanak, and the Early Sikh Panth", in Lorenzen, David N., ed., *Religious Change and Cultural Domination*, Mexico City: El Colegio de Mexico, 1981, pp. 173-91 – repr. in *Exploring Sikhism*, New Delhi: Oxford UP, 2000, pp. 19-36; Spanish edition: *Cambio religiso y dominacion cultural*, Mexico City: El Colegio de Mexico, 1982, pp. 191-209.

— "The Sikhs and the Maoris", *The Panjab Past and Present* XV:1 (April), 1981, pp. 232-3.

— "The Problem of the Panjabi Rahit-namas", in Mukherjee, S.N., ed., *India: History and Thought. Essays in Honour of A.L. Basham*, Calcutta: Subarnarekha, 1982, pp. 103-26 – repr. in *Exploring Sikhism*, New Delhi: Oxford UP, 2000, pp. 103-125.

— "Sikhism (40 entries)", in Hinnells, J., ed., *The Penguin Dictionary of Religions*, London: Allen Lane, 1983 – repr. in *The Facts on File Dictionary of Religions*, New York: Facts on File, 1984.

— *A List of Punjabi Immigrants in New Zealand 1890-1939*, Hamilton: Country Section of the Central Indian Association, 1984 – illustrated.

— *Textual Sources for the Study of Sikhism*, Manchester: Manchester UP, 1984 – also Chicago: University of Chicago Press, 1990.

— "The Khalsa Rahit: the Sikh Identity Defined", in Hayes, Victor C., ed., *Identity Issues and World Religions. Selected Proceedings of the Fifteenth Congress of the International Association for the History of*

Religions, Bedford Park (SA): The Australian Association for the Study of Religions at the South Australian College of Advanced Education, 1986, pp. 104-9 – repr. in *Exploring Sikhism*, New Delhi: Oxford UP, 2000, pp. 126-135.

— *Punjabis in New Zealand. A History of Punjabi Migration, 1890-1940*, Amritsar: Guru Nanak Dev University, 1986 – including illustrations and maps.

— *The Chaupa Singh Rahit-nama*, Dunedin: University of Otago Press, 1987 – the *rahit-nama* attributed to Chaupa Singh Chhibbar and the associated prose *rahit-nama* attributed to Nand Lal: Gurmukhi text and English translation, with introduction and notes.

— "The Development of the Sikh Panth", in Schomer, Karine & W.H. McLeod, eds., *The Sants: Studies in a Devotional Tradition of India*, Berkeley & Delhi: Berkeley Religious Studies Series & Motilal Banarsidass, 1987, pp. 229-49 – repr. in *Exploring Sikhism*, New Delhi: Oxford UP, 2000, pp. 49-69.

— "The Meaning of 'Sant' in Sikh Usage", in Schomer, Karine & W.H. McLeod, eds., *The Sants: Studies in a Devotional Tradition of India*, Berkeley: Berkeley Religious Studies Series, 1987, pp. 251-63 – repr. in *Exporing Sikhism*, New Delhi: Oxford UP, 2000, pp. 149-161.

— "The Sikhs: Crisis and Identity in a Religious Tradition", *Harvard Divinity Bulletin* XVII:2 (January-May), 1987, pp. 7-9.

— "Editor's Introduction", in O'Connell, Joseph & Milton Israel & Willard G. Oxtoby & W.H. McLeod & J.S. Grewal, eds., *Sikh History and Religion in the Twentieth Century*, Toronto: University of Toronto Centre for South Asian Studies, 1988, pp. 9-15.

— "History: 'An Academic Amusement'", in Maity, S.K. & Upendra Thakur & A.K. Narain, eds., *Studies in Orientology: Essays in Memory of Professor A.L. Basham*, Agra: Y.K. Publishers, 1988, pp. 90-4.

— "[several articles]", in Ainslie T. Embree, ed.-in-chief, *The Encyclopedia of Asian History*, New York & London: Asia Society of New York and Charles Scribner's Sons & Collier Macmillan, 1988 – articles on Sikhism: Nanak, Ranjit Singh, Akali Dal, Tara Singh, and Fateh Singh.

— "A Sikh Theology for Modern Times", in O'Connell, Joseph T. & Milton Israel & Willard G. Oxtoby & W.H. McLeod & J.S. Grewal, eds., *Sikh History and Religion in the Twentieth Century*, Toronto: University of Toronto Centre for South Asian Studies, 1988, pp. 32-43.

— "The First Forty Years of Sikh Migration: Problems and Some Possible Solutions", in Barrier, N.G. & V.A. Dusenbery, eds., *The Sikh Diaspora: Migration and Experiences beyond the Punjab*, Delhi & Columbia (Mo): Chanakya Publications & South Asia Publications, 1989, pp. 29-48 – repr. in *Studies in Sikhism and Comparative Religion* VIII:1 (April), 1989, pp. 130-141; and in *Exploring Sikhism*, New Delhi: Oxford UP, 2000, pp. 237-253.

— *The Sikhs: History, Religion, and Society*, New York: Columbia UP, 1989.

— *Who is a Sikh? The Problem of Sikh Identity*, Oxford: the Clarendon Press, 1989 – also: New Delhi: Oxford UP, 1989; repr. as a part of the omnibus volume *Sikhs and Sikhism*, New Delhi: Oxford UP, 2000.

— "The Role of Sikh Doctrine and Tradition in the Current Punjab Crisis", in Smith, Bardwell L., ed., *Religious Movements and Social Identity*, Delhi: Chanakya Publications, 1990, pp. 96-116 – also in *Boeings and Bullock-carts: Studies in Change and Continuity in Indian Civilization. Essays in Honour of K. Ishwaran*, vol. IV.

— "Teaching History to Undergraduates in India: A Trans-Indian View", in Singh, Amrik, ed., *On Being a Teacher*, New Delhi: Konark Publishers, 1990, pp. 190-204.

— "[23 articles on Sikhism]", in Hinnells, John R., ed., *Who's Who in the World Religions*, London: Macmillan, 1991.

— "The Contribution of the Singh Sabha Movement to the Interpretation of Sikh History and Religion", in Andrew, Maurice & Peter Matheson & Simon Rae, eds., *Religious Studies in Dialogue: Essays in Honour of Albert C. Moore*, Dunedin: Faculty of Theology - University of Otago, 1991, pp. 143-51 – repr. in *Exploring Sikhism*, New Delhi: Oxford UP, 2000, 91-99.

— *Popular Sikh Art. A selection of bazaar posters with accompanying text*, Delhi: Oxford UP, 1991 – illustrated.

— *Punjab to Aotearoa: Migration and Settlement of Punjabis in New Zealand, 1890-1990.* Bhullar SS, Hamilton: New Zealand Indian Association Country Section (Inc.), 1992 – illustrated.

— "The Sikh Struggle in the Eighteenth Century and Its Relevance for Today", *History of Religions* (University of Chicago) XXXI:4 (May), 1992, pp. 344-63 – repr. in *Exploring Sikhism*, New Delhi: Oxford UP, 2000, pp. 70-90.

— "[various articles]", in Singh, Harbans, ed.-in-chief, *The Encyclopaedia of Sikhism*, Patiala: Punjab University, 1992-1998 – articles: Adi Sakhian (vol. I, pp. 9-10), Angad Dev, Guru (pp. 146-149), B40 Janam-sakhi (pp. 232-233), Bala Janam sakhi (pp. 262-

265), Haumai (vol. II, pp. 265-267), Hukam (pp. 286-289), Janam-sakhi (pp. 337-340), Mani Singh Janam-sakhi (vol. III, pp. 41-42), Miharban Janam-sakhi (pp. 85-86), Puratan Janam-sakhi (pp. 410-413), Shabad (vol. IV, pp. 88-90).

— "The Study of Sikh Literature", in Hawley, John Stratton & Gurinder Singh Mann, eds., *Studying the Sikhs: Issues for North America*, Albany: State University of New York Press, 1993, pp. 47-68.

— "Cries of Outrage: History versus Tradition in the Study of the Sikh Community", *South Asia Research* 14:2 (Autumn), 1994, pp. 121-35 – repr. in *Exploring Sikhism*, New Delhi: Oxford UP, 2000, pp. 267-279.

— "The Hagiography of the Sikhs", in Callewaert, Winand M. & Rupert Snell, eds., *According to Tradition: Hagiographical Writing in India*, Wiesbaden: Harrassowitz Verlag, 1994, pp. 15-41.

— "Sikhism", *Collier's Encyclopedia*, New York: Collier, 1994, vol. 21, pp. 21-3.

— "Where It All Started", *The Sikh Review* 42:2 (Jan.), 1994, pp. 49-52.

— "[1] Sikh Hymns to the Divine Name; [2] The Order for Khalsa Initiation; [3] The Life of Guru Nanak", in Lopez, Donald S., ed., *Princeton Readings in Religions*, Princeton: Princeton UP, 1995, pp. 126-32, 321-5 and 449-461 – translations with introductions and commentary.

— "[63 entries on Sikhism]", in Hinnells, John R., ed., *A New Dictionary of Religions*, Oxford: Blackwell, 1995 – revised and expanded version of *The Penguin Dictionary of Religions*.

— *Historical Dictionary of Sikhism*, Lanham (Md.) & London: Scarecrow Press, 1995.

— "Adi Granth; Authoritative texts and their interpretation; Sikh; Guru, in Sikhism; Guru Gobind Singh; Khalsa; Dasam Granth; Janam-sakhis; Japji; Ks, the Five; Panjab; and Panth (related to Qaum)", in Smith, Jonathan, Z., ed. in association with the American Academy of Religion, *The Harper Collins Dictionary of Religion*, London: Harper Collins, 1996.

— "Gender and the Sikh Panth", in Singh, Pashaura & N. Gerald Barrier, eds., *The Transmission of the Sikh Heritage in the Diaspora*, New Delhi: Manohar, 1996, pp. 37-43.

— "Max Arthur Macauliffe", *British Association for the Study of Religions Bulletin* 78:June, 1996, pp. 6-12 – repr. in *Exploring Sikhism*, New Delhi: Oxford UP, 2000, pp. 257-263.

— "Phomen Singh", in *The Dictionary of New Zealand Biography*, Auckland: Auckland UP & Department of Internal Affairs, 1996, vol. 3, pp. 476.

— *Sikhism*, London: Penguin Books, 1997.

— *Gandhi and Indian Independence*. Webb R, Auckland: Macmillans, 1998.

— "Sikh Fundamentalism", *Journal of the American Oriental Society* 118:1 (Jan.-March), 1998, pp. 15-27 – repr. in *Exploring Sikhism*, New Delhi: Oxford UP, 2000, pp. 162-186.

— "Discord in the Sikh Panth", *Journal of the American Oriental Society* 119:3 (July-Sept.), 1999, pp. 381-9.

— "Sikhs and Muslims in the Punjab", in *Islam in History and Politics* (*South Asia* XXII, special issue), 1999, pp. 155-65.

— *Sikhs and Sikhism*, New Delhi: Oxford UP, 1999 – Omnibus volume containing reprints of *Guru Nanak and the Sikh Religion, Early Sikh Tradition, The Evolution of the Sikh Community*, and *Who is a Sikh?*, all originally published by the Clarendon Press, Oxford, and Oxford UP, New Delhi.

— "The Turban: Symbol of Sikh Identity", in Singh, Pashaura & N. Gerald Barrier, eds., *Sikh Identity: Continuity and Change*, New Delhi: Manohar, 1999, pp. 57-67.

— "What is History?", *New Zealand Legacy. Journal of the New Zealand Federation of Historical Societies* 11:2, 1999, pp. 16-22.

— *Exploring Sikhism: Aspects of Sikh Identity, Culture, and Thought. Collected Articles*, New Delhi: Oxford UP, 2000.

— "The Jap Sahib", in Mann, Gurinder Singh, ed., [forthcoming].

— "Methodology and Belief", [forthcoming] – prepared as a short paper (1400 words) for a Sikh conference, held in Birmingham, September 1998; to appear in the proceedings of the conference (possibly enlarged).

— "Researching the Rahit", in Singh, Pashaura, ed., [forthcoming].

— "Sikhism", in *Encyclopedia of Bioethics*, New York: Macmillan Publishing Company, [forthcoming].

— "Sikhs in Australia and New Zealand", in Mann, Gurinder Singh, ed., [forthcoming].

— "The Sikhs: Homeland, History, Religion, and the Impulse to Emigrate", [forthcoming].

— *Sikhs of the Khalsa: A History of the Khalsa Rahit*, [in the press].

McLeod, W.H. & Karine Schomer, eds., *The Sants: Studies in a Devotional Tradition of India* (*Berkeley Religious Studies Series*), Berkeley & Delhi: Motilal Banarsidass, 1987.

Mizokami, Tomio, "On Colloquial Styles of Hindi observed among students of Hindi at Delhi University", *Journal of Osaka University of Foreign Studies* 36, 1975.

— "Some Remarks on the Language Problems in urban North-India", *Japan Quarterly* (New Delhi) 2:3, 1976.

— "On Interrogative Expressions in Hindi and Bengali", *Asian & African Grammatical Studies* (Tokyo) 6, 1977.

— *Hindi* (*Asian and African Grammatical Manual*, no. 13a), Tokyo, 1980.

— "Ek Rickshawvale ki Kahani", *Jvalamukhi* (Tokyo) 2, 1981 – original short story in Hindi.

— *Panjabi* (*Asian and African Grammatical Manual*, no. 13e), Tokyo, 1981.

— "Chaurahe ke vich", *Jvalamukhi* (Tokyo) 3, 1982 – original short story in Hindi.

— *Introductory Panjabi*, Tokyo, 1983.

— "Japan men Hindi ka Prasar aur Prachar: Samasyaen aur Sambhavnaen", in *Vishva ke Manchitr par Hindi*, New Delhi, 1983.

— "Osaka men Grishmakalin Panjabi Gahan Pathyakram", *Jvalamukhi* (Tokyo) 4, 1983.

— *Panjabi Reader*, Tokyo, 1983.

— "Cultural Aspects of Multilingual Society", in Kondo, Osamu, ed., *Indo-Sekai*, Kyoto, 1984.

— "Friendship between Japan and India should be through the medium of mutual languages", *Japanese and Indian Culture* (Kobe), Special issue of 25th Anniversary of the Kansai Japan-India Cultural Society, 1984.

— "Vapasi", *Jvalamukhi* (Tokyo) 5, 1985 – original short story in Hindi.

— *Bengali Reader*, Tokyo, 1986.

— *Practical Panjabi Conversation*, Tokyo, 1986.

— "Japani se Hindi men Anuvad ki Samasyaen", in Tiwari, Bholanath, ed., *Videshi Bhashaon se Hindi men Anuvad ki Samasyaen*, New Delhi, 1987.

— *Language Contact in Panjab. A Sociolinguistic Study of the Migrants Language*, New Delhi: Bahri Publications, 1987.

— *Basic 1500 Panjabi Vocabularies*, Tokyo, 1988.

— *Grammatical Structure of Kashmiri* (*Study of Asian & African Grammar*, 17), Tokyo, 1988.

— *Bangla Sanlap*. Ray SP, co-auth., Tokyo, 1989.

— "Some Orthographical Problems in Panjabi", in *A Computer-assisted Study of South-Asian Languages. Annual Report*, vol. 1, Tokyo, 1989.
— "Word Order in Kashmiri", in *A Computer-assisted Study of South-Asian Languages. Annual Report*, vol. 2, Tokyo, 1991.
— "Panjabi & Lahnda", in Chino Eiichi, ed., *World Languages Dictionary*, Tokyo: Sanseido, 1992.
— *Ramanand Sagar*. Bakhshi G, co-ed., Osaka, 1992 – Ramayana with Japanese translation of the verses.
— ed., *Singing Japanese Songs in Hindi*. Bakhshi G, co-ed., Osaka, 1994 – translation of 101 popular Japanese songs into Hindi, including music scales.
— "On Urdu Vocabulary in T.V. Serial Ramayana", *Journal of Indian and Buddhist Studies* (Tokyo) 43:1, 1995.
— *Abhyas Pustika* [Workbook for Hindi], Osaka, 1999.
— "Historical spots in North-India", in Karashima Noboru & Teiji Sakata, eds., *Heritage of the World History: North India*, Tokyo: Yamakawa Shuppansha, 1999.
— "TV Serial *Ramayana* as a pedagogical tool", *Bulletin of Asia-Pacific Studies* (Osaka) IX, 1999.

O'Connell, Joseph T. & Milton Israel & Willard G. Oxtoby & W.H. McLeod & J.S. Grewal, eds., *Sikh History and Religion in the Twentieth Century*, Toronto: University of Toronto Centre for South Asian Studies, 1988.

Offredi, Mariola, "Il giornalismo hindi dalle origini al 1890 [Hindi Journalism from its Beginnings to 1890]", *Annali di Ca' Foscari* IX:3 (SO 1), 1970, pp. 131-214.
— trsl. & intr., *Premcand, Godan* (*Il dono della vacca*), Venezia-Dolo: ITE, 1970 – 2nd ed. (new introduction, translation and glossary), Milano: Cesviet, 1994, xxxii+364 pp.
— *I primi cento anni del giornalismo hindi* (*1826-1926*), Venezia-Dolo: ITE, 1971.
— "'Bharatendu' Harishchandra ironista e riformatore ['Bharatendu' Harishchandra as an Ironist and a Reformer]", *Annali dell'Istituto Orientale di Napoli* 32 (NS XXII), 1972, pp. 201-24.
— *La poesia di Ajñey*, Roma: Cesviet, 1972 – including a translation of Ajñey's poems.
— *Cand. Le gesta di Prithviraj. Parte 58 - La battaglia di Kannauj*, Roma: Cesviet, 1974.
— *Il romanzo hindi contemporaneo*, Roma: Cesviet, 1974.

— intr. & trsl., *Amnesty International, Le condizioni di detenzione nel Bengala Occidentale*, Milano: Cesviet, 1977.

— "Gli Anni Settanta nella stampa hindi: alla ricerca dell'identità nel mondo moderno [The Seventies in the Hindi Press: The Search for National Identity]", in Offredi, Mariola & C. Cossio & A. Simonelli, eds., *Contributi a uno studio sui rapporti fra Occidente e Terzo Mondo* [Contributions to a Study in the Relationship between Western Civilisation and the Third World], Milano: Cesviet, 1977, pp. 1-69.

— "Gajanan Madhav Muktibodh", in Offredi, Mariola & C. Cossio & S. Vannucchi, eds., *Tre tendenze della poesia hindi contemporanea* [Three Trends in Contemporary Hindi Poetry], Milano: Cesviet, 1980, pp. 9-147 – including a translation of *Andhere men* and other poems.

— trsl. & intr., *Rudr, Le onde della Ganga*, Milano: Cesviet, 1980 – including also a structural analysis and an essay on the history of Banaras.

— *Hindi patrkarita men athvan dashak*, New Delhi: Prasangik Prakashan, 1981 – Hindi translation by the author; published also in Italian as *Gli Anni Settanta nella stampa hindi...*, 1977.

— *L'acculturazione dei tribali del Bastar* (*India*), Milano: Cesviet, 1983.

— *I tessitori musulmani di Banaras e Mau* (*India*), Milano: Cesviet, 1984.

— "Fortuna letteraria nell'India moderna [(Virgil's) Literary Renown in Modern India]", in *Enciclopedia Virgiliana*, 1985, vol. II, pp. 941-3 – Virgil's influence on Michael Madhusudan Datt, 1824-1873.

— "'Dhumil': rivolta e rivoluzione [Dhumil's Poetry between Rebellion and Revolution]", in Offredi, Mariola & V. Mingiardi & D. Di Virgilio, eds., *Saggi sulla poesia hindi contemporanea* [Essays on Contemporary Hindi Poetry], Milano: Cesviet, 1986, pp. 219-401 – including a translation of the poem collection *Sansad se sarak tak*.

— "Kunvar Narayan; la maturazione di un poeta [Kunvar Narayan's Poetry in Progress]", in Offredi, Mariola & V. Mingiardi & D. Di Virgilio, eds., *Saggi sulla poesia hindi contemporanea* [Essays on Contemporary Hindi Poetry], Milano: Cesviet, 1986, pp. 7-117 – including a translation of the narrative poem *Atmjayi*, which is published also in book form as *Naciketa*, Napoli: Plural Edizioni, 1989.

— "The Impact of Development Policies on the Bastar District of Madhya Pradesh (1948-1978)", in Rothermund, D. & S.K. Saha, eds., *Regional Disparities in India*, New Delhi: Manohar, 1990, pp. 127-77.

— "The Importance of Literature and the Relevance of its Lay Themes in the Formation of Supraregional Languages", in Offredi, Mariola, ed., *Language versus Dialect*, New Delhi: Manohar, 1990, pp. 67-101.

— ed., *Language versus Dialect*, New Delhi: Manohar, 1990.

— *Lo yoga di Gorakh. Tre manoscritti inediti*, Milano: Cesviet, 1991 – including text and translation.

— "Arte moderna indiana [Modern Indian Art]", in *Enciclopedia Italiana*, 5th App. ed., 1992, pp. 649-53.

— ed., *Literature, Language and the Media in India*, New Delhi: Manohar, 1992.

— "The Search for National Identity as Reflected in the Hindi Press", in Offredi, Mariola, ed., *Literature, Language and the Media in India*, New Delhi: Manohar, 1992, pp. 221-67.

— "Poetry and Commitment. Change in post-1947 Hindi poetry as reflected in the works of Muktibodh (1917-1964) and Dhumil (1936-1975)", *Indian Literature* (New Delhi) 165:Jan.-Febr., 1995.

— "The Intellectual and Society in the Hindi Novel of the Fifties", *Archív Orientální* (Praha) 64:1, 1996, pp. 47-58.

— "The Muslim Weavers of Banaras and Mau (Uttar Pradesh) in the Seventies", in Bredi, D. & G. Scarcia, eds., *Ex libris Franco Coslovi*, Venezia: Poligrafo, 1996, pp. 303-36.

— "Man and Society in Contemporary Hindi Poetry", *Archív Orientální* (Praha) 65:1, 1997, pp. 84-120.

— "Mujhe to yahan har jagah zindagi mahsus hoti hai", *Uttar Pradesh* (Lakhnau) 26:1 (May), 1997, pp. 31-3, 36-7, 41-3.

— "Narrating the City: Bahti Ganga", in Dalmia, Vasudha & Theo Damsteegt, eds., *Narrative Strategies. Essays on South Asian Literature and Film*, Leiden: Research School CNWS, 1998, pp. 31-49.

— *La poesia di Vinod Kumar Shukl*, Milano: Cesviet, 1998 – including a translation of selected poems from the collection *Vah admi naya garam kot pahinkar cala gaya vicar ki tarah*, as well as the complete collection *Sab kuch hona baca rahega.*

— "Vinod Kumar Shukl ki kavita", *Samkalin Bhartiy Sahity* (New Delhi) 76:March-April, 1998, pp. 154-61.

— "The Concepts of Sound and Light in Gorakh Yoga through the Analysis of Three Nathpanthi Manuscripts of the Jodhpur Collection", in Singhvi, N.K. & Rajendra Joshi, eds., *Religion, Ritual and Royalty*, Jaipur: Rawat Publications, 1999, pp. 153-72.

— "The Hindi poet Vinod Kumar Shukl", *Archív Orientální* (Praha) 67:1, 1999, pp. 83-94.

— *Il poemetto Citrrekha di Malik Muhammad Jaysi*, Milano: Cesviet, 1999.
— "Some Concepts of Gorakh Yoga through the Analysis of Three Nathpanthi Manuscripts", in Entwistle, Alan & Carol Salomon & Heidi Pauwels & Michael Shapiro, eds., *Studies in Early Modern Indo-Aryan Languages, Literature and Culture*, New Delhi: Manohar, 1999, pp. 267-86.
— ed., *The Banyan Tree. Essays on Early Literature in New Indo-Aryan Languages*, 2 vols., New Delhi: Manohar, 2000.
— "Jaysi's Citrarekha", in Offredi, Mariola, ed., *The Banyan Tree. Essays on Early Literature in New Indo-Aryan Languages*, New Delhi: Manohar, 2000, pp. 83-94.
— "A Note on Marginality in Hindi Literature", *Hindi* (New Delhi) 1:April-June, 2000, pp. 116-32.
— "Kabir and the Nathpanth", in Boehm-Tettelbach, Monika, ed., *Proceedings of the International Symposium "The 600th Anniversary of Kabir's Birth", Heidelberg, 1999*, [forthcoming].

Pandey, S.M., *Lokamahākāvya Candainī*, Allahabad: Sāhitya Bhavan pvt. Ltd.
— "Mādhavānal Kāmakandalā Kathā", *Hindī Anuśilan* (Allahabad) 1, 1958.
— "Jāyasī kī Premasādhanā", *Hindustānī* (Allahabad) 10, 1959.
— "Manjhan kā Jīvan Vṛtta", *Tripathagā* (Lucknow) 3, 1959.
— "Manjhan ke Guru Shaikh Muhammad Ghaus", *Hindustānī* (Allahabad), 1959.
— "Satarahavīṃ Śatābdī Pūrva kā Asūfī Premākhā Sāhitya", *Hindustānī* (Allahabad) 20:4, 1959.
— "Sūfī Prem Darśan", *Hindustānī* (Allahabad) 21:1, 1960.
— "Fārasī ke Sūfī Premākhyān Hindustānī", *Hindustānī* (Allahabad) 20:2, 1961.
— "Padmāvat mê Nakhaśikh Varṇan", *Hindustānī* (Allahabad) 20:2, 1961.
— "Kabīr Granthāvalī. A review of P.N. Tivārī's edition", *Journal of the American Oriental Society* 84:3, 1964.
— *The Poems of Mīrābāī*, University of Chicago Press - South Asia Language and Area Center, 1964.
— "Contributions of Mīrābāī to the Bhakti Movement", *History of Religions* (Chicago) 5:1, 1965, pp. 54-73.
— "Candāyan mê Nakh Śikh", *Bhāratīya Sāhitya* (Agra) 11:1, 1966, pp. 143-64.

— "Mullā Dā'ud Kṛta Candāyan ke do Saṃskaraṇ", *Sammelan Patrikā* (Allahabad) 53, 1966, pp. 1-2.
— "Barāhmāsā kī Paramparā aur Padmavāt", *Sammelan Patrikā* (Allahabad) 47:1, 1967.
— "Madhumālatī ke Purva kā Sūfī Premākhyān Sāhitya", *Sammelan Patrikā* (Allahabad) 46:4, 1967.
— "Miragāvatī ke do Saṃskaraṇ", *Nāgarī Pracāriṇī Patrikā* (Vārāṇasī) 72:1-4, 1967, pp. 297-312.
— "Padmāvat ke Aitihāsik Īdhār kī Mimānsā", *Sammelan Patrikā* (Allahabad) 47:3, 1967.
— "Cilhavā/āsū aur Marohū Śabdoṃ ke Arthoṃ par Punarvicār", *Sammelan Patrikā* (Allahabad) 48:2, 1968.
— "Vinaycandra Sūri Kṛt Neminā th Catuṣpadikā", *Sammelan Patrikā* (Allahabad) 47:2, 1968, pp. 24-40.
— "Manhan kī Jīvanī par Nayā Prakāś", *Pariṣad Patrikā* (Patna) 9:3 (October), 1969.
— "The Hindī Oral Epic Candainī or *Lorikī*", *Orientalia Lovaniensia Periodica* 2, 1971, pp. 190-210.
— "Candāyan mê Bājir Mūrchā kā Prasaṅg", *Sammelan Patrikā* (Allahabad) 58:2-4, 1972, pp. 98-106.
— "Hindī aur Fārasī Sūfī Kāvyoṃ mê Til", *Nāgarī Pracāriṇī Patrikā* (Vārāṇasī) 1-4, 1972, pp. 155-74.
— "Khaṛībolī kā ek Pramākhyan Kissā Kāmrūp", *Sambhāvanā* (Kurukṣetra University) 1:1, 1972, pp. 18-33.
— "The Living Tradition of Mathura", *South Asian Review* 7:2, 1974, pp. 158-61.
— "Abduction of Sītā in the Rāmāyaṇa of Tulsīdāsa", *Orientalia Lovaniensia Periodica* 8, 1977, pp. 253-88.
— "Loka Mahākāvyõ kī Racanā Prakriyā", *Sammelan Patrikā* (Allahabad) 63:2, 1977, pp. 156-67.
— "Contributions of Maulānā Dā'ud to Hindī Sufi Literature", *Annali dell'Istituto Orientali di Napoli* 38:1, 1978, pp. 75-90.
— *The Hindī Oral Epic Lorikī*, Allahabad: Sāhitya Bhavan Ltd., 1979.
— *Lokamahākāvya Lorikī*, Allahabad: Sāhitya Bhavan pvt. Ltd., 1979.
— *Sūfī Kāvya Vimarśa*, Agra: Vinod Pustak Mandir, 1979.
— *Sūfī Mansūr Hallāj Kī Bānī*, Allahabad: Sāhitya Bhavan Ltd., 1979.
— "Some Problems in Studying Candāyan", in Callewaert, W.M., ed., *Early Hindi Devotional Literature in Current Research. Proceedings of the International Middle Hindi Bhakti Conference (April 1979)*, Leuven, 1980, pp. 127-40.
— "Mīrābāī, la poetessa kṛṣṇaita del sedicesimo secolo", *Annali dell'Istituto Orientale di Napoli* 41:2, 1981, pp. 119-39.

— *The Hindi Oral Epic Candainī*, Napels & Allahabad: Istituto Universitario Orientale & Sāhitya Bhavan, 1982.

— *Madhyayugīn Premākhyān*, 2nd ed., Allahabad: Lokabhāratī, 1982 – 1st ed., Allahabad: Mitra Prakāśan, 1961.

— "Love Symbolism in Candāyan", in Thiel-Horstmann, Monika, ed., *Bhakti in Current Research*, Berlin, 1983, pp. 269-93.

— *The Hindi Oral Epic Lorikāyan*, Naples & Allahabad: Istituto Universitario Orientale & Sāhitya, 1986.

— *Lokamahākāvya Lorikāyan*, Allahabad: Sāhitya Bhavan, 1986.

— "Problemi dell'insegnamento dell'hindī medievale", in Rossi, Adriano & Luigi Santa Maria & Antonia Soriente, eds., *Didattica del Lingue dell'Estremo Oriente: Metodologia ed Esperienze*, (*Series Minor, Dipartimento di Studi Asiatici*), Napoli: IUO, 1988.

— *Hindi aur Fārasī aur Sūfī Kāvya*, Allahabad: Sāhitya Bhavan, 1989.

— "Il Miragāvatī di Kutuban - Un Testo Sūfī in Hindi", *Annali dell'Istitute Orientale di Napoli* 50:3, 1990, pp. 295-319.

— "Maulānā Dā'ud racit Candāyan ke Malik Mubārak Kaun?", *Viśvabhāratī Patrikā* (Śāntiniketan, West Bengal) 31, 1990, pp. 66-72.

— *Lokamahākāvya Bhojpurī Lorikī*, Allahabad: Sāhitya Bhavan, 1991.

— "Kutuban's Miragāvatī: its content and interpretation", in McGregor, R.S., ed., *Devotional Literature in South Asia: Current Research, 1985-1988*, Cambridge UP, 1992, pp. 178-89.

— "The King and the Guru in Early Hindī Sūfī Poetry", *Orientalia Lovaniensia Periodica* 24, 1993.

— "Surasā, Siṃhikā and Lankā in Vālmīki and Other Rāmāyaṇas", *Indologica Taurinesia* 19/20, 1993, pp. 227-44.

— "Maulānā Dā'ud's Teacher Shaikh Zainuddīn", in Entwistle, Alan W. & Françoise Mallison, eds., *Studies in South Asian Devotional Literature*, Paris, 1994, pp. 285-92.

— *Bhojpurī Lorikī*, Naples & Allahabad: Istituto Universitario Orientale & Sāhitya Bhavan Ltd., 1995.

— "Kanhāvata, A Sūfī Text Attributed to Malik Muhammad Jāyasī", *Orientalia Lovaniensia Periodica* 26, 1995, pp. 187-98.

— "Santa and Asanta in the Rāmāyaṇa of Tulsīdāsa", in Pollet, G., ed., *Indian Epic Values. Rāmāyaṇa and its Impact*, Leuven, 1995, pp. 235-44.

— "Un poeta Sūfī Kṛṣṇaia", in *Un ricordo che non si spegne: Scritti di docenti e collaboratori dell'Istituto Universitario Orientale di Napoli in memoria di Alessandro Bausani*, Napoli, 1995, pp. 285-96.

— "Śabarī in Rāmacaritamānasa and Other Rāmāyaṇas", *Annali dell'Istituto Universitario Orientale* (Napoli) 56:4, 1996, pp. 497-506.

— "Il rapimento di Sītā nel Rāmāyana di Talasīdāsa", in *Persembhahan. Studi in onore di Luigi Santamaria*, Napoli: UIO, 1998, pp. 127-252.

— "Bārahmāsā in Candāyan and in Folktraditions", in Entwistle, Alan W. & Carol Salomon et al., eds., *Studies in Early Modern Indo-Aryan Languages, Literature and Culture*, New Delhi: Manohar, 1999, pp. 287-310.

— "Kyā Maulānā Dāūd Rudaulī ke the?", *Hindustānī* (Allahabad) 60:4, 1999, pp. 87-95.

— *The Poetic Influence on Bhakti*, Delhi: Aravali Books International, 1999.

— "*Nakh-śikh* in *Candāyan*", in Offredi, Mariola, ed., *The Banyan Tree. Essays on Early Literature in New Indo-Aryan Languages*, New Delhi: Manohar, 2000, pp. 27-59.

Pandey, S.M. & Norman Zide, *The Poems of Sūrdās. An Anthology with an Introduction and Translation*, University of Chicago Press - South Asia Language Center, 1963.

— "Songs of Vidyāpati", *Journal of the American Oriental Society* 85:1, 1965, pp. 197-204.

— "Sūrdās and Krishna Bhakti", in Singer, Milton, ed., *Krishna, Myth, Rites and Attitudes*, University of Honolulu: East West Center, 1966, pp. 172-99.

Pandey, S.M. & Simon Weightman, "The Semantic Fields of Dharma and Kartavya in Modern Hindi", in O'Flaherty, Wendy Donniger, ed., *Concept of Duty in South Asia*, London & New Delhi: SOAS & Vikas Publishing House Pvt. Ltd., 1978, pp. 217-27.

Pauwels, Heidi, "Harirām Vyās and the early Bhakti-milieu", in Mallison, F. & A. Entwistle, eds., *Studies in South Asian Devotional Literature. Research Papers 1988-1991, presented at the Fifth Conference on Devotional Literature in New Indo-Aryan Languages, held at Paris-Ecole Française d'Extrême Orient, 9-12 July 1991*, New Delhi & Paris: Manohar & EFEO, pp. 25-50.

— *The Rās-pañcādhyāyī and Mān kī śṛṅkhalā of Harirām Vyās: a critical edition, translation, and interpretation of the position of the goddess Rādhā* [Microfilm no. 95-04673], Ann Arbor University Microfilms, 1994 – Dissertation Abstracts International A. March 1996, vol. 55, issue 9a, p. 2838.

— "[review] R.S. McGregor, ed., The Oxford Hindi-English Dictionary, Oxford & Delhi: Oxford UP, 1993", *Journal of the Royal Asiatic Society* 5:3 (November), 1995, pp. 454-5.

— "The great Goddess and fulfilment in love: Rādhā seen through a sixteenth-century lens", *Bulletin of the School of Oriental and African Studies* 59:1 (February), 1996, pp. 29-43.

— *Kṛṣṇa's Round Dance Reconsidered: Harirām Vyās's Hindī Rās-pañcādhyāyī* (*London Studies on South Asia*, 12), London: Curzon Press, 1996.

— "[review] D.N. Lorenzen, Bhakti Religion in North India: Community Identity and Political Action, Albany: State University of New York Press, 1995", *Bulletin of the School of Oriental and African Studies* LIX:2, 1996, pp. 392-4.

— "[review] P. Mukta, Upholding the Common Life: The Community of Mirabai, (Gender Studies), Delhi: Oxford UP, 1994", *Bulletin of the School of Oriental and African Studies* LIX:2, 1996, pp. 394-5.

— "[review] W.S. Sax, ed., The Gods at Play: Līlā in South Asia, New York: Oxford UP, 1995", *Bulletin of the School of Oriental and African Studies* LIX:3, 1996, pp. 579-80.

— "[review] K. Pratap, The Goddess Lakṣmī: The divine consort in South Indian Vaiṣṇava tradition (Academy of Religion. Academy Series 95), Atlanta: Scholars Press, 1998", *Journal of the American Academy of Religion* 66:4 (Winter), 1998, pp. 955-8.

— "[review] R. Jeffery & P. Jeffery, Population, gender and politics: demographic change in rural North India, Cambridge: Cambridge UP, 1997", *International Journal of Hindu Studies* 2:1, 1998, pp. 139-41.

— "NIA poetry in performance: meter and oral formulae: as exemplified in the poetry of Harirām Vyās", in Entwistle, A. & al., eds., *Studies in Early Literature in New Indo-Aryan Languages. Proceedings of the Sixth International Conference on Early Literature in New Indo-Aryan Languages* (*Seattle, 1994*), Delhi: Manohar, 1999, pp. 311-38.

— "Different Voices, Different Songs: Early anthology versions of songs by Harirām Vyās", in Offredi, M., ed., *The Banyan Tree. Essays on Early Literature in New Indo-Aryan Languages*, Delhi: Manohar, 2000, vol. 2, pp. 469-512.

— "Three ways of falling in love: Tulsīdās's Phulvārī episode and the way it is portrayed in contemporary electronic media", in Bose, Mandakranta, ed., *A Varied Optic: Contemporary Studies in the Ramayana Culture. Research papers presented at the Conference on the Ramayana Culture held at the Institute of Asian Research,*

University of British Columbia, 20-21 February 1999, Vancouver: Institute of Asian Research (UBC), 2000, pp. 55-100.

— "Diptych in verse: Gender hybridity, language consciousness, and national identity in Nirālā's *Jāgo phir ek bār*", *Journal of the American Oriental Society* 121:3, [forthcoming].

— "Is love still stronger than *dharma*? What ever happened to Sītā's choice and the Gopīs's voice?", in Thomas, Lynn & Jacqueline Hirst, eds., *Dharma and Gender*, Richmond: Curzon Press, [forthcoming].

— "[review] V. Dalmia, The Nationalization of Hindu Traditions: Bhāratendu Hariścandra and Nineteenth-century Banaras, Delhi: Oxford UP, 1997", *International Journal of Hindu Studies*, [forthcoming].

— *In Praise of Holy Men: Hagiographical Poems by and about Harirām Vyās*, [forthcoming].

— "Paradise found, paradise lost: Harirām Vyās's love for Vrindāban and what hagiographers made of it", in Granoff, Phyllis, ed., *Sacred Biography and sacred space*, Toronto: University of Toronto Press, [forthcoming].

Pinch, William R., *Peasants and Monks in British India*, Berkeley: University of California Press, 1996.

— "Reinventing Ramanand: Caste and History in Gangetic India", *Modern Asian Studies* 30:3, 1996, pp. 549-72 – reissued with minor changes as "Remembering Ramanand: Caste and History in Gangetic India", *Journal of Vaiṣṇava Studies* 8:1 (Fall), 1999, pp. 35-57.

— "Soldier Monks and Militant Sadhus", in Ludden, David, ed., *Contesting the Nation: Religion, Community, and the Politics of Democracy in India*, Philadelphia: University of Pennsylvania, 1996, pp. 140-62 – this volume was published in India as *Making India Hindu: Community, Conflict, and the Politics of Democracy*, Delhi: Oxford UP, 1996.

— "Historicity, Hagiography, and Hierarchy in Gangetic India", in Radice, William, ed., *Swami Vivekananda and the Modernisation of Hinduism*, Delhi: Oxford UP, 1998, pp. 244-63.

— "Who was Himmat Bahadur Anupgiri Gosain? Ascetics, Rajputs, and the British in Bundelkhand, ca. 1800", *Indian Economic and Social History Review* 35:3 (November), 1998, pp. 293-335.

— "History, Devotion and the Search for Nabhadas of Galta", in Ali, Daud, ed., *Invoking the Past: The Uses of History in South Asia*, Delhi: Oxford UP, 1999, pp. 328-60.

— "Armed Ascetics and the Transition to British Rule in India", in Dewey, Clive, ed., *The Military Factor: Studies in the New Military History of South Asia*, [Oxford UP], [forthcoming].

Rinehart, Robin, "From *Sanātana Dharma* to Secularism: Hindu Identity in the Thought of Swami Rama Tirtha and the Swami Rama Tirtha Mision", *Religion* 26, 1996, pp. 237-47.

— "Interpretations of the Poetry of Bullhe Shah (1680-1758)", *International Journal of Panjab Studies* 3:1 (April), 1996, pp. 45-63.

— "Swami Rama Tirtha's 'Practical Vedanta': A Message without an Audience", *International Journal of Hindu Studies* 2:2 (August), 1998, pp. 185-221.

— "Hagiography", in Young, Serinity, ed., *Encyclopedia of Women and World Religion*, Macmillan, 1999, vol. 1, p. 389.

— *One Lifetime, Many Lives: The Experience of Modern Hindu Hagiography*, Scholars Press, 1999 – now available through Oxford UP.

— "The Portable Bullhe Shah: Biography, Categorization, and Authorship in the Study of Punjabi Sufi Poetry", *Numen* 46:1, 1999, pp. 53-87.

— "Hir/Ranjha", in Claus, Peter J. & Margaret A. Mills, eds., *South Asian Folklore: An Encyclopedia*, Garland Press, [forthcoming].

— "Waris Shah, Mullas, and the Mosque", in Ernst, Carl, ed., *Islam in Asia: In Practice*, Princeton UP, [forthcoming].

Rinehart, Robin & Tony K. Stewart, "The Anonymous Āgama Prakāśa: Preface to a Nineteenth Century Gujarati Polemic", in White, David G., ed., *Tantra in Practice*, Princeton UP, 2000, pp. 266-84.

Rosenstein, Lucy, "Sacetan Kahānī and Samāntar Kahānī - principal movements in the Hindi short story of the 1960s and 1970s", *South Asia Research* 13:2 (November), 1993, pp. 117-31.

— "Svāmī Haridās and *dhrupad*", *Journal of Vaiṣṇava Studies* 4:2 (Spring), 1996, pp. 149-56.

— *The Devotional Poetry of Svāmī Haridās: a study of early Braj Bhāṣā verse*, Groningen: Egbert Forsten, 1997.

— "The Rādhāvallabha and the Haridāsī *sampradāyas* - a comparison", *Journal of Vaiṣṇava Studies* 7:1 (Fall), 1998, pp. 5-18.

— "From Kṛṣṇa's mistress to the Mistress of Kṛṣṇa: the evolution of Rādhā in the Haridāsī's *sampradāya*", *Journal of Vaiṣṇava Studies* 8:2 (Spring), 2000, pp. 119-29.

— "'New Poetry' in Hindi: a quest for modernity", *South Asia Research* 20:1 (Spring), 2000, pp. 47-62.

Rousseva-Sokolova, Galina, "Jeu et poésie de la bhakti: aspects ludiques du *Sūrsāgar* de Sūrdās", *Revue de l'Histoire des Religions* CCXI:1 (Jan.-March), 1994, pp. 59-87.

— "Play – A New Perspective to Medieval Bhakti Poetry", in *Proceedings of the International Conference on Sanskrit and Related Studies* (*Cracow Indological Studies*, 1), Cracow: The Enigma Press, 1995, pp. 215-19.

— "The Tradition of *Varṣotsav-pad-saṅgrah*: A Different Perspective on Brajbhāṣā Devotional Poetry", in Offredi, Mariola, ed., *The Banyan Tree. Essays on Early Literature in New Indo-Aryan Languages*, New Delhi: Manohar, 2000, pp. 513-19.

— *Jeu et dévotion: Aspects ludiques de la bhakti krishnaïte au Braj* (coll. *Religions en perspective*), Genève: Labor et Fides, [forthcoming].

Sakata, Teiji, ed., *Indo, Nepaal, Suriranka no Mukashi-banashi*, Tokyo: Mikuni Shuppan, 1998 – Japanese translations, by eight scholars, from as many regions in South Asia.

— *Hindii-go Minwashuu*, Tokyo: Daigaku-shorin, 1999 – folktales told by the members of one family, in the original Hindi with Japanese translations.

— "Bhakti in Hindi Folktales", in Offredi, Mariola, ed., *The Banyan Tree: Essays on Early Literature in New Indo-Aryan Languages*, Delhi: Manohar, 2000, pp. 575-81.

— "Japanese Studies of Indian Languages and Literature - A Brief Survey Based on Japanese Translation of Indian Literary Works with Special Reference to the Period after the Second World War", in Nakane, Chie & Masao Naito, eds., *Towards Mutual Understanding: Fifty Years of Indo-Japanese Studies*, Tokyo, 2000, pp. 48-54.

Salomon, Carol, "A Contemporary Sahajiyā Interpretation of the Bilvamaṅgal-Cintāmaṇi Legend, as Sung by Sanātan Dās Bāul", in Park, Richard L., ed., *Patterns of Change in Modern Bengalī*, East Lansing: Asian Studies Center, 1979, pp. 97-110.

— "The Cosmogonic Riddles of Lalan Fakir", in Appadurai, Arjun & Frank J. Korom & Margaret Mills, eds., *Gender, Genre and Power in South Asian Expressive Traditions*, Philadelphia: University of Pennsylvania Press, 1991, pp. 267-304.

— "Baul Songs", in Lopez, David S. Jr., ed., *Religions of India in Practice*, Princeton: Princeton UP, 1995, pp. 187-208.

— "[review] Lālan Sā̃i: deś, kāl, evaṃ śilpa by Śaktināth Jhā", *Journal of the American Oriental Society* 118:1, 1998, pp. 128-32.

Sanford, A. Whitney, "Teaching the Teacher: The Sakhī's Role in Paramānand's *Māna* Poems", *Journal of Vaiṣṇava Studies* 1:4 (Summer), 1993.

— "An Evolution of Emphasis: A Comparative of the Story of 'Uddhava's Message' in the Bhramargīt in the Bhāgavata Purāṇa and the Bhramargīt of Nandadās", *Journal of Vaiṣṇava Studies* 1:4, 1994, pp. 113-40.

— "The Emotive Body: The Role and Function of the Body in the Ritual of Transformation of *Laukika* to *Alaukika* in Paramānand's *Padas* and the *Aṣṭayāma Līlā*", *Journal of the Faculty of Religious Studies* (McGill University) 25, 1997, pp. 101-21.

— "Real Men and Ideal Women: Gender Construction in the *Aṣṭayāma Līlā*", *Journal of Vaiṣṇava Studies* 5:4 (Fall), 1997.

— "The Gopīs as Role Models: Understanding Paramānand's Function as a Saint", in Entwistle, Alan W. & Michael C. Shapiro, eds., *Proceedings of the Sixth International Conference on Early Literature in New Indo-Aryan Languages, July 7-9, 1994*, New Delhi: Motilal Banarsidass, 1999, pp. 339-53.

— "Uneasy Partners: Balarāma as Embodiment of Wilderness", in Offredi, Mariola, ed., *The Banyan Tree. Essays on Early Literature in New Indo-Aryan Languages*, New Delhi: Manohar, 2000, pp. 363-87.

— "Complementary Pairings: Balarāma and Kṛṣṇa as Tropes", [forthcoming].

— "Negotiating for Śrīnāthajī, Daūjī and Jakheiyā: Narrative as Arbiter of Contested Sites in Braj", [forthcoming].

— "Painting Words Through Sound: Visions of Krishna in Paramānand's Sixteenth-Century Devotional Poetry", [forthcoming].

— *Seeing Through Hearing: Paramānand's Synaesthetic Approach to Krishna*, [forthcoming].

Shapiro, Michael C., "[review] Anvita Abbi, *Semantic Grammar of Hindi: A Study in Reduplication*", *Language* 58:2, 1982, pp. 487-8.

— "[review] Indira Yashwant Junghare, *Topics in Pali Historical Phonology*", *Journal of Asian Studies* 41:3, 1982, pp. 619-20.

— "[review] M.B. Emeneau, *Language and Linguistic Area*", *American Anthropologist* 83:3, 1982, pp. 647-9.

— "[review] Norihiko Uchida, *Studien zur Hindi-Vokalphonologie*", *Journal of the American Oriental Society* 102:3, 1982, pp. 552-3.

— "[review] Suniti Kumar Chatterji, *Selected Papers*, vol. 2, and *Select Writings*, vol. 1", *Journal of Asian Studies* 41:3, 1982, pp. 617-9.

— "Towards a history of the Hindi language", *South Asia Review* 6:3, 1982, pp. 148-59.

— "On Hindi Dictionaries and related matters", *Journal of the American Oriental Society* 103:4, 1983, pp. 749-54.

— "संयुक्त राज्य में हिन्दी भाषा और साहित्य का अध्ययन" [Research on Hindi Language and Literature in the United States]", संदर्भ भारती (Calcutta), January-March 1983 – also reprinted in *Proceedings of the Third International Hindi Conference*, New Delhi.

— "[review] Umberto Eco, *Semiotics and the Philosophy of Language*", *Studies in Second Language Learning*, October 1985, pp. 372-4.

— "The language of humour in Premchand's short stories", *Journal of South Asian Literature* 21:2, 1986, pp. 99-112.

— "On the semantics of Hindi *āge / ke āge*", *Studien zur Indologie und Iranistik* 11/12, 1986, pp. 233-143.

— "[review] Klaus Matzel, *Einführung in die singhalesische Sprache*", *Journal of the American Oriental Society* 106:4, 1986, pp. 885.

— "Hindi *lagnā*: a study in semantic change", *Journal of the American Oriental Society* 107:3, 1987, pp. 401-8.

— "Observations on the Core Language of the *Ādigranth*", *Berliner Indologische Studien* 3, 1987, pp. 181-4.

— "[review] Christopher Shackle, *An Introduction to the Sacred Language of the Sikhs*", *Journal of Asian Studies* 46:3, 1987, pp. 693-5.

— "[review] Winand M. Callewaert (ed.), *Early Hindi Devotional Literature in Current Research*, and Monika Thiel-Horstmann (ed.), *Bhakti in Current Research, 1979-1982*", *Journal of the American Oriental Society* 107:1, 1987, pp. 200-1.

— "[review] Konrad Meissner, *Mālushāhī and Rājulā: A Ballad from Kumāūn (India)*", *Journal of the American Oriental Society* 108:4, 1988, pp. 636-7.

— *A Primer of Modern Standard Hindi*, Delhi: Motilal Banarsidass, 1989.

— "Receuil d'Articles de Jules Bloch (1906-1955)", *Language* 65:2, 1989, pp. 421-2.

— "[review] Henry Yule and A.C. Burnell, *Hobson-Jobson: A Glossary of Colloquial Anglo-Indian Words and Phrases* (repr. ed.)", *Journal of the American Oriental Society* 109:3, 1989, pp. 474.

— "[review] Tej K. Bhatia, *A History of the Hindi Grammatical Tradition*", *Journal of Asian Studies* 48:3, 1989, pp. 644-5.

— "[review] Bh. Krishnamurti et al. (eds.), *South Asian Languages: Structure, Convergence and Diglossia*", *Journal of the American Oriental Society* 109:3, 1990, pp. 475-6.

— "[review] David Rubin, *After the Raj: British Novels of India Since 1947*", *South Asia in Review*, 1990, pp. 1-2.

— "[review] Richard K. Barz and Jeff Siegel, *Language Transplanted: The Development of Overseas Hindi*", *Journal of the American Oriental Society*, 1991.

— "[review] Christopher Shackle and Rupert Snell, *Hindi and Urdu since 1800: A Common Reader*", *Journal of the American Oriental Society* 112:1, 1992, pp. 157-8.

— "[review] Colin P. Masica, *The Indo-Aryan Languages*", *Language* 69:1, 1993, pp. 182-6.

— "[review] William Bright, *Language Variation in South Asia*", *Journal of the American Oriental Society* 113:1, 1993, pp. 151-2.

— "[review] R.S. McGregor (ed.), *The Oxford Hindi-English Dictionary*", *International Journal of Lexicography*, Winter 1995, pp. 351-6.

— "[review] Surendra K. Gambhir, *Spoken Hindi (Intonation, Accuracy, Usage)*", *Penn Language News*, 1995, pp. 8-9.

— "The theology of the locative case in *gurabāṇī*", in Lorenzen, D., ed., *Bhakti Religion in North India: Community Identity and Political Action*, Albany: SUNY Press, 1995.

— "[review] K.S. Singh and S. Monoharan, *Anthropological Survey of India: Languages and Scripts*", *Journal of the American Oriental Society* 116:2, 1996, pp. 354-5.

— "Hindi *to* as Discourse Marker", in Mistry, P.J. & Bharati Modi, eds., *Vidyopāsanā: Studies in Honour of Harivallabh C. Bhayani*, Mumbai & Ahmedabad: Image Publications, 1999, pp. 179-89.

— "[review] R. Breton, *Atlas of the Languages and Ethnic Communities of South Asia*", *Journal of the American Oriental Society* 119:3, 1999, pp. 495-6.

— "[review] Rajendra Singh and Rama Kant Agnihotri, *Hindi Morphology: A Word-based description*", *Lingua* 108, 1999, pp. 87-90.

— "[review] Robert D. King, *Nehru and the Language Politics of India*", *Language and Society* 28:4, 1999, pp. 624-8.

— "The Hindi Linguistic Tradition", in Auroux, Sylvain & al., eds., *Geschichte der Sprachwissenschaften*, Berlin: De Gruyter, 2000, vol. 1, pp. 178-81.

— "Hindi", in Cardona, George & Dhanesh K. Jain, eds., *Indo-Aryan Languages*, Richmond (Surrey, UK): Curzon, [forthcoming].

— "Hindi", in Garry, Jabe & Carl Rubino, eds., *Facts about the World's Major Languages*, H.W. Wilson Company, [forthcoming].

Shapiro, Michael C. & Harold F. Schiffman, *Language and Society in South Asia*, repr. ed., Publications in Language Sciences, Dordrecht: Foris Publications, 1983.

Shelke, Christopher, *Don Sakshatkari*, Poona, 1981 – comparative Spirituality of Saint Ignatius of Loyola and Sant Ramdas, Ph.D. Dissertation.

— "Sant Rāmdās āni St. Ignāti", *Ramdas 4th Century Publication*, Poona: Prasad, 1981.

— "Ramdasanche Guru", in *Itihas Sanshodhan Mandal*, Poona: Historical Research Association, 1982.

— "Sadguru and Holy Spirit", in McGregor, R.S., *Devotional Literature in South Asia. Current Research, 1985-1988*, Cambridge, 1988, pp. 153-62.

— *Cokhamela: Lobpreis des göttlichen Namens*, München: Kösel, 1991.

— "Dalit Theology: Emergence and Emergency", *Neue Zeitschrift für Missionswissenschaft* (Luzern), 1994, pp. 257-73.

— "The Idea of Sin in the Dasbodha", in *Studies in South Asian Devotional Literature. Research Papers 1988-1991*, Paris, 1994, pp. 175-91.

— "Cosmology and the Revelation of God", *Tenrikyo-Christian Dialogue*, Nara: Tenri UP, 1999, pp. 61-79.

Shima, Iwao, "Historical Development of Salvation Theories Found in Commentaries on the Bhagavadgītā: From Śaṅkara to Rāmānuja", *Journal of the Japanese Association for South Asian Studies* 4:October, 1992, pp. 1-14.

— "Deccan Bhakti and Untouchable: Cokhamela, A Sage of Untouchables", in Yamazaki, G. & T. Sato, eds., *Cast System and Untouchable* 1:October, Akashi Book Shop, 1994, pp. 225-44 – in Japanese.

— "Jñāneśvara's Interpretation of the Bhagavadgītā V-VI", in *Indian Thoughts and Buddhist Culture: Essays in Honor of Professor Junkichi Imanishi on His Sixtieth Birthday*, Tokyo: Shunjusha, 1996, pp. 29-42 – in Japanese.

— "A Japanese Translation of the Jñāneśvarī (Chapter 1)", *Maharastra* 5:July, 1999, pp. 43-72.

Shima, Iwao & C. Koiso, "Pilgrimage and Rituals for Viṭhobā", *Studies and Essays. Behavioral Sciences and Philosophy* 16:March, 1996, pp. 49-64 – in Japanese.

Shima, Iwao & H. Hikita, "A Japanese Translation of Five Commentaries on the Bhagavadgītā [1-3]", *Transactions of the Institute for Cultural Studies* (Aichigakuin University) 3-5, 1988, pp. 131-62, 53-80, 193-216.

— "A Japanese Translation of Five Commentaries on the Bhagavadgītā [4-5]", *Bulletin of the Faculty of Humanities of Aichigakuin University* 19-20, 1988, pp. 30-53, 161-76.

Singh, Bahadur, "The Bagaṛāvat. A Popular Heroic Narrative of Rajasthan", in Callewaert, W.M., ed., *Early Hindi Devotional Literature in Current Research. Proceedings of the International Middle Hindi Bhakti Conference (April 1979)*, Leuven, 1980, pp. 162-7.

— "The Episode of the Golden Shiva Image in the Bagaṛāvat", in Brückner, Heidrun & Lothar Lutze & Aditya Malik, eds., *Flags of Fame. Studies in South Asian Folk Culture*, New Delhi: Manohar Publications, 1993, pp. 411-21.

— "Kabīr: Recited and Sung Today in Rajasthan", in Offredi, Mariola, ed., *The Banyan Tree. Essays on Early Literature in New Indo-Aryan Languages*, New Delhi: Manohar, 2000, pp. 419-24.

— "Bemerkungen zum Verhältnis zur Natur bei den Viṣṇoī", in Wezler, A., ed., *Die indische Idee der Gewaltlosigkeit. zur Beziehung zwischen Mensch und Natur in Indien*, [forthcoming].

— "Problems of Authenticity in the Kabīr Texts Transmitted Orally in Rajasthan Today", in [Acta of the Conference "The 600th Anniversary of Kabir's Birth": 15-18 June 1999, Heidelberg], [forthcoming].

Singh, Pashaura, *The Guru Granth Sahib: Canon, Meaning and Authority*, New Delhi: Oxford UP, 2000.

Singh, Pashaura & N. Gerald Barrier, eds., *Sikh Identity: Continuity and Change*, New Delhi: Manohar Publishers & Distributors, 1999.

— eds., *The Transmission of the Sikh Heritage in the Diaspora*, New Delhi: Manohar Publishers & Distributors, 1996.

Smith, W.L., "The Jaiminibhārata and its Eastern Vernacular Versions", *Acta Orientalia* (Helsinki) 85, 1999, pp. 389-406.

— "On the Composition of Śaṅkaradeva's *Rukmiṇī haraṇa kāvya*", *Research Journal of the Sankaradeva Institute of Culture International* (Guwahati), 1999.

— "Shiva, Lord of the Plow", in Das, Rahul, ed., *Essays on Middle Bengali*, Calcutta: Firma K.L. Mukhopadhyaya, 1999, pp. 207-28.

— "Variants of the Lavakuśopakhyāna", in Josephson, Folke, ed., *Categorisation and Interpretation* (*Meijersbergs Arkiv för Svensk Ordforskning* series), Göteborg: Styrelsen för Meijerbergs Institut vid Göteborgs Universitet, 1999, pp. 107-23.

— *Dr W.L. Smith on Śaṅkaradeva.* P.Ch. Das (comp.), Guwahati (Assam): Oriental Institute for Sankaradeva Studies, 2000 – a collection of mostly previously published articles dealing with the works of the Assamese poet-saint Śaṅkaradeva.

— "Imagining the Life of Kabir", *Hindi: Language, Discourse, Writing* (New Delhi) 1, 2000.

— "Inventing Brajabuli", *Archív Orientální* (Prague) 68:3, 2000, pp. 387-98.

— *Patterns in North Indian Hagiography* (*Stockholm Studies in Indian Languages and Culture*, 3), Stockholm: University of Stockholm, 2000 – this is a study of hagiographical literatures in NIA languages, in which the dominant hagiographical motifs have been arranged in chronological order, relating the typical career of the North Indian saint in a sort of collective biography.

— "The Vaiṣṇava Parvan of the Assamese *Mahābhārata*", in Offredi, Mariola, ed., *The Banyan Tree: Essays on Early Literature in New Indo-Aryan Languages*, Venice & New Delhi: Manohar, 2000, pp. 343-50.

— *On Śaṅkaradeva.* P.Ch. Das (comp.), Guwahati (Assam): Institute for Sankaradeva Studies, 2001.

Stasik, Danuta, "Clash of Cultures - an Indian Immigrant in Great Britain", *Orientalia Varsoviensia* 1, 1987, pp. 81-90.

— "Work as an element of cultural contact in modern Hindi prose", *Acta Philologica* 20, 1991, pp. 205-14.

— "Environment as an element in contact of cultures", *Acta Universitatis Wratislaviensis. Classica Wratislaviensia* XVII / no. 1523, 1993, pp. 71-7.

— *Out of India: Image of the West in Hindi Literature*, New Delhi: Manohar Publishers, 1994.

— "The Divine Marriage: the Nuptials of Rām and Sītā as Seen by Tulsī", *Proceedings of the International Conference on Sanskrit and Related Studies* (*September 23-26, 1993*) (*Cracow Indological Studies*, 1), 1995, pp. 245-51.

— "On modern retellings of Rām-kathā in Hindi literature: Bhagvān Siṁh's novel *Apne-apne Rām*", *Berliner Indologische Studien* 11/12, 1998, pp. 259-68.

— "Text and Context: Two Versions of Tulsīdās's *Rām-lalā-nahachū*", in Entwistle, Alan & Carol Salomon & Heidi Pauwels & Michael Shapiro, eds., *Studies in Early Modern Indo-Aryan Languages, Literature and Culture*, Delhi: Manohar, 1999, pp. 379-91.

— *The Story of the Righteous King. The Rāmāyaṇa Tradition in Hindi Literature*, [forthcoming] – in Polish.

— "Tulsīdās and the Social Implications of His Vision of Rām and Sītā's Nuptials", [forthcoming].

Stasik, Danuta & T. Rutkowska, *Zarys historii literatury hindi*, Warsaw: Warsaw UP, 1992 – in Polish.

Steinbach, Henry, *The Punjab*, 2nd ed. (*Oxford in Asia Historical Reprints*), W.H. McLeod (intr.), Karachi: Oxford UP, 1976 – 1st ed. London, 1846.

Stewart, Tony K., "On Changing the Perception of Caitanya's Divinity", in O'Connell, Joseph T., ed., *Bengal Vaiṣṇavism, Orientalism, Society and the Arts* (*South Asia Occasional Paper*, 35), East Lansing (MI): Asian Studies Center - Michigan State University, 1985, pp. 37-45.

— "*Bhāva* and Divinity in the *Caitanya Bhāgavata*", *South Asia Research* 6:1 (May), 1986, pp. 53-60.

— "When Biographical Narratives Disagree: The Death of Kṛṣṇa Caitanya", *Numen* 38:2, 1991, pp. 231-60.

— "The Biographies of Śrī Caitanya and the Literature of the Gauḍīya Vaiṣṇavas", in Rosen, Steven J, ed., *Vaiṣṇavism: Contemporary Scholars Discuss the Gauḍīya Tradition*, New York: Folk Books, 1992, pp. 101-25 – with a forword by Edward C. Dimock, Jr.

— "One Text from Many: The *Caitanya caritāmṛta* as 'Classic' and 'Commentary'", in Callewaert, Winand M. & Rupert Snell, eds., *According to Tradition: Hagiographical Writing in India*, Wiesbaden: Otto Harrassowitz, 1994, pp. 317-56.

— "Encountering the Smallpox Goddess: The Auspicious Song of Śītalā", in Lopez, Donald S. Jr., ed., *The Religions of South Asia in Practice*, Princeton: Princeton UP, 1995, pp. 389-98.

— "The Exemplary Devotion of the 'Servant of Hari'", in Lopez, Donald S. Jr., ed., *The Religions of South Asia in Practice*, Princeton: Princeton UP, 1995, pp. 564-77.

— "The Goddess Ṣaṣṭhī Protects Children", in Lopez, Donald S. Jr., ed., *The Religions of South Asia in Practice*, Princeton: Princeton UP, 1995, pp. 352-66.

— "The Rescue of Two Drunkards", in Lopez, Donald S. Jr., The Religions of South Asia in Practice, Princeton: Princeton UP, 1995, pp. 375-88.

— "Satya Pīr: Muslim Holy Man and Hindu God", in Lopez, Donald S. Jr., The Religions of South Asia in Practice, Princeton: Princeton UP, 1995, pp. 578-97.

— "When Rāhu Devours the Moon: The Myth of the Birth of Kṛṣṇa Caitanya", *International Journal of Hindu Studies* 1:2 (August), 1997, pp. 1-44.

— ed., *The 'Caitanya Caritāmṛta' of Kṛṣṇadāsa Kavirāja* (*Harvard Oriental Series*, 56). Dimock ECJr, tr. & comm., Cambridge (MA): Harvard UP, 1999 – with an introduction by the translator and the editor; and including appendices, glossaries, bibliographies and indices.

— "Alternate Structures of Authority: Satya Pīr on the Frontiers of Bengal", in Gilmartin, David & Bruce B. Lawrence, eds., *Beyond Turk and Hindu: Rethinking Religious Identities in Islamicate South Asia*, Gainesville: University of Florida Press, 2000, pp. 21-54.

— "In Search of Equivalence: Conceiving Muslim-Hindu Encounter Through Translation Theory", *History of Religions* 40:3 (Winter), 2001, pp. 261-88.

— *Fabulous Females and Peerless Pirs: Mad Adventure in Old Bengali*, [forthcoming] – translations with introduction and notes.

— *The Final Word: How the Caitanya Caritāmṛta Created the Gauḍīya Vaiṣṇava Tradition*, [forthcoming].

— "In Search of Equivalence: Conceiving Muslim-Hindu Encounter through Translation Theory", in Eaton, Richard, ed., *Indian Islamic Traditions: 1000-1800*, Delhi: Oxford UP, [forthcoming].

— "Satya Pīr", in Mills, Margareth A. & Peter J. Claus, eds., *South Asian Folklore: An Encyclopedia*, London & New York: Routledge, [forthcoming].

— *Satya pīrer pāñca punthi: bikalpita kāhinīra aitihya.* Md.S.J. Miya (co-ed.): Sāhitya Patrikā, [forthcoming] – including *Tinlakṣyapīrer pāñcālī* by Anonymous [Harinārāyaṇa], *Trilakhya pīrera pāñcālī* by Harinārāyaṇa, *Galakāṭāphāsyarā pāla* by Rasamaya, *Satya pīrer pāñcālī* (Vallabha pāla) by Kṛṣṇśaṅkara, and *Satyanārāyaṇa kathā* (*Akṣoti pāla*) by Kavi Kāṇva – in Bengali.

— "Surprising Bedfellows: Vaiṣṇava and Shi'i Alliance in Kavi Āripha's 'Tale of Lālamon'", *International Journal of Hindu Studies*, [forthcoming] – Special Issue on Hinduism and Islam. Re-issued by New York: Lexington Press of Rowan and Littlefield, forthcoming.

Stewart, Tony K. & Carl W. Ernst, "Syncretism", in Mills, Margareth A. & Peter J. Claus, eds., *South Asian Folklore: An Encyclopedia*, London & New York: Routledge, [forthcoming].

Stewart, Tony K. & Chase Twitchell, *The Vaiṣṇava Poems of Rabindranath Tagore*, [forthcoming] – poems in translation with introduction, apparatus, and illustrations.

Stewart, Tony K. & Edward C. Dimock Jr., "Kṛttibāsa's Apophatic Critique of Rāma's Kingship", in Richman, Paula, ed., *Questioning Rāmāyaṇas*, New Delhi: Oxford UP, 2000, pp. 243-64.

Stewart, Tony K. & Hena Basu, "Bāṃlāya prakāśita vaiṣṇava sāmayika patrikā: ekṭi tathya nirdeśikā sūcī", *Baṅgīya Sāhitya Pariṣat Patrikā* 90:2, 1390, pp. 1-8 – an annotated reference guide to Vaiṣṇava journals in Bengali.

Stewart, Tony K. & Rebecca Manring, "In the Name of Devotion: Acyutacaraṇa Caudhurī and the Hagiographies of Advaitācārya", *Journal of Vaiṣṇava Studies* 5:1 (Winter), 1996, pp. 103-26 – special issue on Gauḍīya Vaiṣnavism, edited by Joseph T. O'Connell.

Stewart, Tony K. & Robin Rinehart, "The Anonymous *Āgama Prakāśa*: Preface to a 19th c. Gujarati Polemic", in White, David Gordon, ed., *Tantra in Practice*, Princeton: Princeton UP, 2000, pp. 266-85.

Thielemann, Selina, *The Darbhangā Tradition:dhrupada in the school of Pandit Vidur Mallik*, Varanasi: Indica Books, 1997.

— *Rāsalīlā. A Musical Study of Religious Drama in Vraja*, New Delhi: APH Publishing Corporation, 1998.

— *Sounds of the Sacred. Religious Music in India*, New Delhi: APH Publishing Corporation, 1998.

— *The Music of South Asia*, New Delhi: APH Publishing Corporation, 1999.

— *Musical Traditions of Vaiṣṇava Temples in Vraja. A Comparative Study of samāja and the dhrupad tradition of North Indian Classical Music*, New Delhi: ABC Oublishing House, 2000.

Vasishta, Om Parkash, comp., *Punjabi Shabd Jor Kosh*, Patiala: Punjabi University, 1968.

— *Chinh-Vigian ate Guru Nanak Bani*, Chandigarh: Punjab Prakashan, 1986.

— *Kosh-Vigian ate Punjabi Koshkari*, Chandigarh: Nancy Publishers, 1992.

Vasishta, Om Parkash & al., eds., *PSUTB English-Punjabi Dictionary*.

— *English-Punjabi Dictionary*, Patiala: Punjabi University, 1968.

— *Punjabi-Sanskrit Shabd Kosh*, Allahabad: Ganganatha Jha Kendriya Sanskrit Vidyapeetha, 1987.

Wulff, Donna M., "The Unitive Vision of Rabindranath Tagore", *Journal of Religious Studies* 3:1, 1971, pp. 99-120.

— "[review] The Classical Law of India, by Robert Lingat, translated from the French with additions by J. Duncan M. Derrett, Berkeley, 1973", *Religious Studies Review* 4:4 (October), 1978, pp. 305-6.

— "[review] Rachel van Meter Baumer and James Brandon, eds., Sanskrit Drama in Performance, Honolulu: University of Hawaii Press, 1981, and John Stratton Hawley, At Play with Krishna: Pilgrimage Dramas from Brindavan, Princeton: Princeton UP, 1981", *ASIA* :March-April, 1982.

— "A Sanskrit Portrait: Radha in the Plays of Rupa Gosvami", in Hawley, J.S. & D.M. Wulff, eds., *The Divine Consort: Radha and the Goddesses of India*, Berkeley: Berkeley Religious Studies Series, 1982.

— "On Practicing Religiously: Music as Sacred in India", in Irwin, Joyce, ed., *Sacred Sound: Music in Religious Thought and Practice* (*Journal of the American Academy of Religion.* Thematic Studies 50/1), Chico (CA): Scholars Press, 1983, pp. 149-72.

— *Drama as a Mode of Religious Realization: The Vidagdhamadhava of Rupa Gosvami* (*American Academy of Religion Academy Series*, 43), Chico (California): Scholars Press, 1984.

— "Images and Roles of Women in Bengali Vaisnava *Padavali kirtan*", in Haddad, Yvonne Yazbeck & Ellison Banks Findly, eds., *Women, Religion and Social Change*, Albany: State University of New York Press, 1985, pp. 217-45 – also publ. in O'Connell, Joseph T., ed., *Bengal Vaisnavism, Orientalism, Society and the Arts*, East Lansing: Asian Studies Center - Michigan State University, 1985, pp. 11-28.

— "Radha", in Eliade, Mircea et al., ed., *The Encyclopedia of Religion*, The Free Press, 1987, vol. 12, pp. 195-7.

— "Religion in a New Mode: Aesthetics and Supreme Realization in Medieval India", *Journal of the American Academy of Religion* LIV:4 (Winter), 1987, pp. 673-88.

— "Sarasvati", in Eliade, Mircea et al., ed., *The Encyclopedia of Religion*, The Free Press, 1987, vol. 13, pp. 71-2.

— "Medieval Bengali Devotional Poetry", *Bulletin* (Center for the Study of World Religions, Harvard University) 14:1 (Winter), 1988.

— "Internal Interpretation: The *akhar* Lines in Performances of *padavali kirtan*", in Koppedrayer, K.I., ed., *Contacts Between*

Cultures: South Asia, Queenston (Ontario): The Edwin Mellen Press, 1992, vol. 2, pp. 317-24.

— "The Play of Emotion: *Lilakirtan* in Bengal", in Sax, William S., ed., *God's Play: Lila in South Asia*, New York: Oxford UP, 1995, pp. 99-114.

— "Radha: Consort and Conqueror of Krishna", in Hawley, J.S. & D.M. Wulff, eds., *Devi: Goddesses of India*, Berkeley: University of California Press, 1996.

— "[review] Guy L. Beck, Sonic Theology: Hinduism and Sacred Sound, Columbia: University of South Carolina Press, 1993", *Journal of Asian Studies* 55:2 (May), 1996, pp. 485-6.

— "Hindu Nationalism: An Oxymoron", *The Brown Journal of World Affairs* IV:2 (Summer/Fall), 1997, pp. 163-76.

— "Radha's Audacity in *kirtan* Performances and Women's Status in Greater Bengal", in King, Karen L., ed., *Women and Goddess Traditions: Studies from Asia, the Ancient Mediterranean, and Contemporary Goddess Thealogy* (*Studies in Antiquity and Christianity*), Minneapolis (Minn.): Fortress Press, 1997.

— "Rupa's Radha: Passionate, Worshipful, Strong-willed, Divine", *Journal of Vaisnava Studies* 8:2 (Spring), 2000, pp. 73-94.

— "Radha", in Young, Serinity, ed., *Encyclopedia of Women in World Religions*, Macmillan, [forthcoming].

— "Troublesome Stories, Tendentious Interpretations", in Wulff, Donna M., ed., *Radha: Divine Consort, Audacious Mistress*, [forthcoming].

— "The Theology of a Lovers' Quarrel: Classical and Contemporary Interpretations of Krishna's Humiliation", in Offredi, Mariola, ed., *The Banyan Tree: Essays on Early Literature in New Indo-Aryan Languages*, New Delhi: Manohar, 2000, pp. 167-84.

Wulff, Donna M. & John Stratton Hawley, eds., *The Divine Consort: Radha and the Goddesses of India*, Berkeley: Berkeley Religious Studies Series, 1982 – paperback ed.: Beacon Press, 1986.

— eds., *Devi: Goddesses of India*, Berkeley: University of California Press, 1996.

Yajnik, Hasu, *Anuragkatha. Vedic stories of Urvashi-Pururava, Yama-Yami, Sanskrit-Prakrit Love Stories of Udayan Vasvadatta etc.*, Ahmedabad: Gurjar Grantharatna Karyalay.

— *Bansari Vadan*, Ahmedabad: Gurjar Grantharatna Karyalay.

— "Gujarati Lok-Git Madhil Ramakatha", in Vani, K.S., ed., *Lok-Sahitya va Lokparampara*, Devpur: Marathi Pragat Adhyayana Sanstha – in Marathi.

— *Gujarati Lok-Gito Jivancakra-rachana* (*life cycle*), Gandhinagar: Gujarati Sahitya Akademi – Gujarati folk songs.

— *Gujarati Lok-Gito Ma Kathagit*, Gandhinagar: Gujarat Sahitya Akademi – Gujarati folk songs: narratives.

— *Gujarati Lok-Gito Ma Krsnacarit*, Gandhinagar: Gujarat Sahitya Akademi – Gujarati Folk Songs.

— *Gujarati Lok-Gito Ma Ramakatha & Pandavcarit*, Gandhinagar: Gujarati Sahitya Akademi – Gujarati folk songs.

— *Gujarati Lok-Gito Ma Rtucakra-rachana*, Gandhinagar: Gujarat Sahitya Akademi – Gujarati folk songs: Season cycle.

— *Gujarati Lok-Sahitya*, Gandhinagar: Gujarati Sahitya Akademi – collected articles studying the six collections edited by the same author, on Indian classical music and instrument-playing.

— *Kam-Katha. Part I-II: stories from Sanskrit, Prakrit and Gujarati*, Ahmedabad: Gurjar Grantharatna Karyalay.

— *Karmonium Vadan*, Ahmedabad: Gurjar Grantharatna Karyalay.

— *Lok-Sahitya Manka ni Lok-Kathao*, Gandhinagar: Gujarat Sahitya Akademi – Gujarati folk tales.

— *Madhyakalin Katha Sahitya. A Collection of Papers on Sanskrit-Prakrit-Old Gujarati Narratives*, Ahmedabad: Gurjar Grantharatna Karyalay.

— *Madyakalin Gujarati Prem-Katha*, Ahmedabad: Gurjar Grantharatna Karyalay – Ph.D. study on Gujarati Love-stories.

— "The Oral Tradition of Ramakatha in Gujarati Folk-Songs", in Entwistle, Alan et al., ed., *Early Modern Indo-Aryan Languages, Literature and Culture*, New Delhi: Manohar Publ.

— *Pharsi-Katha: Persian Stories from Shahnama*, Ahmedabad: Gurjar Grantharatna Karyalay.

— *Shamal. Monograph on Gujarati Narrative Poet*, Ahmedabad: Gurjar Grantharatna Karyalay.

— *Shashtriya Raga Darshan*, Ahmedabad: Gurjar Grantharatna Karyalay.

— *Tibet Ni Tantra-Sadhana*, Ahmedabad: Gurjar Grantharatna Karyalay – Secret Lore of Tibet, Kashmir and Bengal.

— *Violin-Vadan*, Ahmedabad: Gurjar Grantharatna Karyalay.

— *Vishva Sahitya Ma Varta-Toonki Varta*, Ahmedabad: Gurjar Grantharatna Karyalay – a critical study and survey of the main twenty areas of World Literature and Modern Stories.

— "Gujarati Lok-Gito Men Ramakatha", *Rangayatana* (Udaipur, Rajasthan) Dec. 1999 – in Hindi.

— "The Saraju Songs: A Living Tradition within the Devī-worship Ritual of the Vaiśya Sutār and Sorathiā and Bhopā Rabārī of

Saurashtra", in Offredi, Mariola, ed., *The Banyan Tree. Essays on Early Literature in New Indo-Aryan Languages*, New Delhi: Manohar, 2000, pp. 223-34.

Yajnik, Hasu & H.C. Bhayani, not. & ed., *Gokul Ma Tahukya Mor*, Gandhinagar: Gujarat Sahitya Akademi – muscial notations of Pad Bhajan.

— not. & ed., *Harivenvaya Chhe Re Ho Vann Ma*, Gandhinagar: Gujarat Sahitya Akademi – musical notations of Pad Bhajan.

— "Krsna in Gujarati Folk-Song Tradition", in Eck & Mallison, eds., *Devotion Divine: Bhakti Traditions from the Regions of India. Studies in Honour of Charlotte Vaudeville*, Paris: EFEO.

— not. & ed., *Zina Zaramar Varse Meh*, Gandhinagar: Gujarat Sahitya Akademi – musical notations of Pad Bhajan.

Zelliot, Eleanor, "The Medieval Bhakti Movement in History - An Essay on the Literature in English", in Smith, Bardwell L., ed., *Hinduism - New Essays in the History of Religions*, Leiden: E.J. Brill, 1976, pp. 143-68 – Numen Series; reprinted in 1982.

— "Chokhamela and Eknath: Two Bhakti Modes of Legitimacy for Modern Change", *Journal of Asian and African Studies* XV:1-2 (January-April), 1980, pp. 136-56 – reprinted in Jayant Lele (ed.), *Tradition and Modernity in Bhakti Movements*, Leiden: E.J. Brill, 1981; as well as in Aloka Parasher-Sen (ed.), *Subordinate and Marginal Groups in Early India up to 1500 A.D.*, Oxford UP, [forthcoming].

— "A Medieval Encounter between Hindu and Muslim: Eknath's Drama-poem *Hindu-turk samvad*", in Clothey, Fred, ed., *Images of Man: Religion and Historical Process in South Asia*, Madras: New Era, 1982, pp. 171-95.

— "The World of Gundam Raul", in Feldhaus, Anne, *The Deeds of God in Ṛddhipur*, New York: Oxford UP, 1984, pp. 30-6.

— "Eknath's Barude: the *Sant* as link between Cultures", in Schomer, Karine & W.H. McLeod, eds., *The Sants: Studies in a Devotional Tradition of India*, Berkeley & Delhi: Religious Studies Series & Motilal Banarsidass, 1987, pp. 91-109.

— "Four Radical Saints of Maharashtra", in Israel, Milton & N.K. Wagle, eds., *Religion and Society in Maharashtra* (*South Asian Papers*, 1), Centre for South Asian Studies - University of Toronto, 1987, pp. 131-44.

— "Introduction", in Engblom, Philip, trsl., *Palkhi by D.B. Mokashi*, Albany: New York State University Press, 1987, pp. 31-58 – repr. Hyderabad: Orient Longman, 1990.

— "Cokhamela: Piety and Protest", in Lorenzen, David, ed., *Bhakti Religion in North India: Community, Identity and Political Action*, Albany: State University of New York Press, 1995, pp. 212-20.

— "The Religious Imagination of Maharashtrian Women Bhaktas", in Paranjpe, Shrikant & Raja Dixit & C.R. Das, eds., *Western India: History, Society and Culture* (*Dr. Arvind Deshpande Felicitation Volume*), Kolhapur: Itihas Shikshak Mahamandal, 1997, pp. 91-108.

— "The Householder Saints of Maharashtra", in Entwistle, Alan W. & Carol Salomon et al., eds., *Studies in Early Modern Indo-Aryan Languages, Literature and Culture*, Delhi: Motilal Banarsidass, 1999, pp. 417-26 – paper delivered at the Sixth International Conference of Early Literature in New Indo-Aryan Languages, University of Washington, 1994.

— "Women in the Homes of the Saints", in Glushkova, Irina & Rajendra Vora, eds., *Home, Family and Kinship in Maharashtra*, New Delhi: Oxford UP, 1999, pp. 89-100.

— "Sant Sahitya and Dalit Movements", in Kosambi, Meera, ed., *Intersections: Socio-Cultural Trends in Maharashtra*, Hyderabad: Orient Longman, 2000, pp. 187-93.

— "The Untouchable Women Saint-Poets of Maharashtra", in Offredi, Mariola, ed., *The Banyan Tree. Essays on Early Literature in New Indo-Aryan Languages*, New Delhi: Manohar, 2000, pp. 273-82.

— "Women Saints in Medieval Maharashtra", in Bose, Madrakanta, ed., *Faces of the Feminine in Ancient, Medieval, and Modern India*, New York: Oxford UP, 2000, pp. 192-200.

— "Ovi [and] Tamasha", in Claus, Peter J., ed., *South Asian Folklore: An Encyclopedia*, Garland Publishing Company, [forthcoming].

— "Untouchable Saint-Poets: Tamil, Marathi, Hindi", in Aktor, Mikail, ed., Curzon Press, [forthcoming].

Zelliot, Eleanor & Anne Feldhaus, "Marathi Religions", in Eliade, Mircea, ed., *Encyclopedia of Religion*, New York: Macmillan, 1986, pp. 190-4.

INDEX*

* As far as possible the diacritical signs of the entries have been respected.